James Nogalski
Literary Precursors to the Book of the Twelve

Beihefte zur Zeitschrift für die alttestamentliche Wissenschaft

Herausgegeben von
Otto Kaiser

Band 217

Walter de Gruyter · Berlin · New York
1993

James Nogalski

Literary Precursors
to the Book of the Twelve

Walter de Gruyter · Berlin · New York
1993

∞ Printed on acid-free paper which falls
within the guidelines of the ANSI to ensure
permanence and durability

Library of Congress Cataloging-in-Publication Data

Nogalski, James.
  Literary precursors to the Book of the Twelve / James Nogalski.
      p.   cm. — (Beihefte zur Zeitschrift für die alttestamentliche
Wissenschaft, ISSN 0934-2575 ; Bd. 217)
  Part of thesis (Th. D.) — Universität Zurich.
  Includes bibliographical references and index.
  ISBN 3-11-013702-X (alk. paper) : DM 138,00 ($ 92.00 U.S. : est.)
  1. Bible. O. T. Minor Prophets—Criticism, interpretation, etc.
I. Title. II. Series: Beihefte zur Zeitschrift für die
alttestamentliche Wissenschaft ; 217.
  BS410.Z5   vol. 217
  [BS1560]
  224′ .9066 — dc20   93-32171
                                                                                          CIP

Die Deutsche Bibliothek — Cataloging in Publication Data

Nogalski, James:
Literary precursors to the book of the twelve / James Nogalski.
— Berlin ; New York : de Gruyter, 1993
  (Beihefte zur Zeitschrift für die alttestamentliche Wissenschaft ; Bd.
  217)
  Zugl.: Zürich, Univ., Diss., 1991
  ISBN 3-11-013702-X
NE: Zeitschrift für die alttestamentliche Wissenschaft / Beihefte

ISSN 0934-2575

Preface

Gratitude, like the pilgrimage which has led to this work, knows no boundaries. Formative years in the United States spent under the instruction of professors such as Dr. Karen Joines, Dr. J.J. Owens, and Dr. Page Kelley, provided me not only with the basic tools for further study, but inspired me to pursue these goals. My time in Switzerland has allowed me to benefit from the tutelage of Dr. Hans-Harald Mallau, whose time and interest went beyond the requirements demanded of him. His enthusiasm and energy were exceeded only by the technical competence he brought to our discussions of my masters thesis. Special thanks go to Dr. Odil Hannes Steck whose encouragement and insights helped bring this work to fruition. His direction, and particularly his observations concerning methodological clarity, have had a profound impact upon the final work. My thanks extend also to Dr. Hermann Spieckermann for his comments and suggestions. Additionally, the willingness of these two gentlemen to read this work in my native language rather than their own speaks not only for their scholastic expertise, but also reflects the openness which they have extended to me from the beginning of our relationships.

Many colleagues and friends, to whom I am sincerely grateful, have been supportive of this endeavor in ways which are too numerous to list in detail. Three in particular deserve mention for their willingness, in various stages of this work, to listen to my latest thoughts or to sit patiently while I talked through the latest problems. In this regard, my thanks go to Dr. Mark Edward Biddle, Dr. Kandy Queen-Sutherland, and Ole Lundegaard.

My sincere appreciation also extends to Dr. Otto Kaiser for accepting this work into the *BZAW* series in two volumes. His suggestions for editorial alterations helped to reshape the original dissertation for division into two meaningfully divided volumes.

If gratitude knows no boundaries, then it knows no end for the friendship, patience, discussion, and sacrifice, provided by my wife Melanie. Her constant presence, her interaction and interest in my work, and the delay of her own career goals during these years have not only enabled me to complete this project, but to remain sane in the process.

Table of Contents

Introduction ....

1. Further Evidence for the Unity of the Book of the Twelve
2. Brief History of the Study of the Book of the Twelve
3. Methodological Considerations

The Catchword Phenomenon

1. Hosea 14:10 and Joel 1:1
2. Joel 4:21 and Amos 1:1-2:16
3. Amos 9:13 and Obad 1-10
4. Obad 21 and Mic 1:1
5. Mic 7:8-14:20 and Jonah 1:1-2
6. Jonah 2:2-10 and Mic 1:1-7
7. Mic 7:8-20 and Nah 1:1-8
8. Nah 3:1-19 and Hab 1:1-17
9. Hab 3:1-19 and Zeph 1:1-18
10. Zeph 3:16-20 and Hag 1:1-4
11. Hag 2:20-23 and Zech 1:1-17
12. Zech 8:9-23 and Mal 1:1-4(?)
13. Summation

Hos 1:2-9, 2:1

1. The Macrostructure of Hosea and the Role of 1a-2:3(1)
2. Literary Analysis of Hos 1:1-2:9 and 2:1-3
3. The Literary Horizon of Hos 2:4-4:19
4. Outward in Hosea
5. Onward in Joel

Amos 9:1-15

1. The Macrostructure of Amos
2. The Literary Unity in Amos 1:1-2:16
3. The Structure of Amos 9:1-15
4. The Function of the Units in Amos 9:1-15

Table of Contents

Preface v

Introduction
1. Ancient Evidence for the Unity of the Book of the Twelve . 2
2. Explanations of the Unity of the Book of the Twelve 3
3. Methodological Considerations 12

The Catchword Phenomenon
1. Hos 14:5-10 and Joel 1:1-12 21
2. Joel 4:1-21 and Amos 1:1-2:16 24
3. Amos 9:1-15 and Obad 1-10 27
4. Obad 15-21 and Mic 1:1-7 31
5. Obad 11-14,15b and Jonah 1:1-8 33
6. Jonah 2:2-10 and Mic 1:1-7 35
7. Mic 7:8-20 and Nah 1:1-8 37
8. Nah 3:1-19 and Hab 1:1-17 40
9. Hab 3:1-19 and Zeph 1:1-18 45
10. Zeph 3:18-20 and Hag 1:1-4 49
11. Hag 2:20-23 and Zech 1:1-11 51
12. Zech 8:9-23 and Mal 1:1-14 53
13. General Summation 56

Hos 14:2-10
1. The Macrostructure of Hosea and the Role of 14:2-10 58
2. Literary Analysis of Hos 14:2-9 and 14:10 65
3. The Literary Horizon of Hos 14:2-9,10 69
    3.1 Backward in Hosea 70
    3.2. Forward to Joel 72

Amos
1. The Macrostructure of Amos 74
2. The Literary Units in Amos 1:1-2:16 82
3. The Structure of Amos 9:1-15 97
4. The Function of the Units in Amos 9:7-15 99

4.1. The Function of 9:7-10: Interpretation of Final
Vision 99
4.2. The Function of 9:11-15: Restoration, Domination,
and Abundance 104
4.3. The Growth of Amos 9:11-15 110

Micah

1. The Macrostructure of Micah and Its Implications for
Dating 123
2. The Literary Units in Mic 1:1-9 126
   2.1. Mic 1:1 127
   2.2. Mic 1:2-9 129
3. Mic 1:1-9: Redactional Introduction Within a Larger
Corpus 137
4. The Extent of the Deuteronomistic Micah Corpus 141
5. Determination of the Units in Mic 7:8-20 144
6. The Unity of Mic 7:14-20 154
7. Tradition-Historical Observations Effecting Mic 7 155
   7.1. Allusions to Isa 9-12 and the Hezekiah Tradition ... 155
   7.2. The Role of Bashan and Gilead 158
   7.3. The Use of lmrk as "Thicket" within Anti-Assyrian
   Polemic 159
   7.4. The "Rod" of YHWH 164
8. The Relationship of Mic 7:11,12,13 166
9. The Unity of 7:8-10,11-13,14-20 168

Zephaniah

1. The Macrostructure of Zephaniah 171
2. The Date of Zephaniah 178
3. The Units in Zeph 1:1-2:3 181
   3.1. Zeph 1:1 181
   3.2. Zeph 1:2-3 187
   3.3. Zeph 1:4-13 189
   3.4. Zeph 1:14-18 191
   3.5. Zeph 2:1-3 192
4. Two Judgments in Zephaniah 1:2-2:3 193
5. The Function of the Habakkuk - Zephaniah Connection ... 198
6. The Literary Units and Context of Zeph 3:18-20 201
7. The Literary Horizon of Zeph 3:18-20 204
   7.1. Identity of the Groups 204

7.2. Backward to Micah 209
7.3. Forward to Haggai 212

Haggai
1. The Macrostructure of Hag 1:1-11 216
2. The Literary Units in Hag 1:1-11 217
3. The Literary Horizon of Hag 1:1-11 219
4. The Literary Units in Hag 2:10-23 221
5. Literary Additions in Hag 2:15-19,20-23 226
6. The Character of Redactional Work on Hag 2:15-19,20-23 . 234

Zechariah 1-8
1. The Macrostructure of Zech 1-8 238
2. Literary Observations on Zech 1:1-6 240
3. Zech 1:7-17: The First Vision 248
4. Zech 1 and the Book of the Twelve 256
5. Zech 8:9-23 in Its Context 257
6. Literary Observations on Zech 8:9-23 263

Summary and Reflections
1. Editorial Expansion for the Book of the Twelve 276
2. Pre-existing Multi-volume Corpora 278
3. Concluding Remarks 281

Works Cited 283

Alphabetical Index of Biblical and Extra-Biblical Citations 292

Appendix of Allusions and Citations 301

Introduction

Long-standing traditions in ancient Jewish and Christian sources provide incontrovertible evidence that the twelve Minor Prophets were transmitted on a single scroll and considered as a single book. This acknowledgement poses questions about the origin, purpose, and nature of this unity. Who has unified different books in one volume? When, where, why, and how? These questions have received little attention in Old Testament research. Some introductions to the Old Testament evade these questions by not mentioning the unity, or by generalizing their comments.[1] Others repeat older observations and opinions without concern for a methodological approach to the problem. It is particularly rare to find a reference to the question if and how this unification affected the shape and content of the original writings.

Several monographs and essays dedicated to the combination of the twelve prophets reveal a wide range of alternative interests and presuppositions, but they exhibit little care for the techniques employed in the combination of the prophetic writings and their possible consequences for the individual books.[2] It is this question for which this study will attempt to provide a systematic approach and a reasonable answer. An understanding of the problem necessitates treating several issues: the reasons for considering the Book of the Twelve as one corpus; a rehearsal of previously attempted explanations postulating how these twelve prophetic writings were combined on one scroll; and a procedural overview of this investigation.

---

[1] For example, George Anderson, *A Critical Introduction to the Old Testament* (London: Gerald Duckworth, 1959), 141; Otto Eissfeldt, *The Old Testament: An Introduction* (New York: Harper and Row, 1965), 383-384; Georg Fohrer and Ernst Sellin, *Introduction to the Old Testament* (Nashville: Abingdon, 1968), 363. Brevard Childs, *Introduction to the Old Testament as Scripture* (Philadelphia: Fortress, 1979), has no discussion of the issue.

[2] These works are discussed beginning on page 3.

1. Ancient Evidence for the Unity of the Book of the Twelve

Several early references indicate the writings of the twelve prophets were considered as one book. The earliest explicit reference appears in Jesus Ben Sirach 49:10 (c. 200 B.C.), which mentions the twelve prophets in the context of other prophets including Isaiah (48:20), Jeremiah (49:6), and Ezekiel (49:8).[3] Both 4 Ezra 14 and Josephus treat the Book of the Twelve as a single book because of the number of the Old Testament books they count.[4] Archeological data from Qumran reinforces evidence that the unity of the Book of the Twelve was already established.[5]

The evidence from the Septuagint is complicated, and only one aspect is mentioned here. Septuagint textual traditions display several orders of the writings in the Book of the Twelve, but only two have substantial attestation.[6] Despite the different orders of these writings, it is very significant that these twelve always occur together.[7] Additionally, solid evidence suggests that the alternate Septuagint order depends upon MT.[8]

---

[3] Sir 49:10 says, "May the bones of the twelve prophets revive from where they lay, for they comforted the people of Jacob, and delivered them with confident hope."

[4] 4 Ezra 14 recounts Ezra's 'inspired' recitation of ninety-four books. Among these were the previously destroyed twenty-four canonical books, including the Book of the Twelve. Josephus ("Against Apion" I.40.) considers twenty-two books canonical. There is some uncertainty to their identity, but the thirteen prophetic works he mentions must count the Book of the Twelve as one book.

[5] Frank Moore Cross, *The Ancient Library of Qumran and Modern Biblical Studies*, (Garden City, New York: Doubleday, 1958), 34. Compare also Dale Schneider, *The Unity of the Book of the Twelve* (Yale University Dissertation, 1979), 220-21. According to Cross, Cave 4 has yielded eight partial manuscripts of the Book of the Twelve. Several contain more than one writing, and all these confirm the Masoretic order, though none contains a copy of the entire corpus. Recently, in an oral presentation at the SBL meeting in New Orleans, November, 1990, Eric Meyers cited second hand evidence which stated that one manuscript, 4Q12a, contains a copy of the Book of the Twelve in which Jonah appears as the last writing, but until publication of the manuscript allows some outside verification, it is doubtful that this single manuscript points to an earlier order of the Book of the Twelve.

[6] A complete list of the orders attested may be found in H.B. Swete, *An Introduction to the Old Testament in Greek* (Cambridge: University Press, 1914), 201-214. The first order follows the MT order, while the second changes the first six writings (Hosea, Amos, Micah, Joel, Obadiah, Jonah).

[7] This consistency is significant in light of the different orders of the other prophetic books which both precede and follow the twelve as a group.

[8] Schneider, *The Unity of the Book of the Twelve*, 223-226. Schneider notes that the alternate order can be explained by the fact that the Septuagint simply brings the older

Hence, despite a different order, the Septuagint also confirms that the Book of the Twelve formed a single corpus.

In the Babylonian Talmud, Baba Batra 13b-15a contains two references that further confirm the unity of the Book of the Twelve. First, this passage provides instructions for copying Biblical books. These instructions state four lines should appear between the canonical books, but an exception is made for the Book of the Twelve which requires only three lines (13b). Second, this passage refers to the order in which the biblical books occur, and it cites the Twelve collectively (14b), as one book not twelve. In addition to the early Jewish literature, Jerome confirms the unity of the Book of the Twelve explicitly. He states, "unum librum esse duodecim prophetarum."[9]

The evidence gleaned from the Hellenistic and Roman periods conclusively demonstrates that the Book of the Twelve was considered a single book. None of these ancient sources, however, provides any direct, reliable evidence concerning the origin of this unity.[10]

2. Explanations of the Unity of the Book of the Twelve

At least since Jerome, explanations for the unity of the Book of the Twelve have included chronological factors as well as the size of the corpus.[11] Those writings having dates in their superscriptions appear in chronological order. Modern scholarship, however, has cast considerable doubt upon the reliability of the dates, and has corrected the erroneous assumption that the undated prophecies come from the time of the last

---

writings (Hosea-Amos-Micah) to the front of the corpus. The remaining writings still appear in their Masoretic order.

[9] "Incipit Prologus Duodecim Prophetarum," *Biblica Sacra Vulgata*, vol. 2 (Stuttgart: Würtembergische Bibelanstalt, 1969), 1374.

[10] Sir 49:10 characterizes the Book of the Twelve as one of hope, but this characterization provides no clues for the question of the motivation behind the combination of the writings. 4 Ezra 14 and Baba Batra 15a do provide legendary remarks, but they offer no real help. See below, footnote number 13.

[11] "Incipit prologus duodecim prophetarum," *Biblica Sacra Vulgata*, vol. 2, 1374. Jerome notes the chronological character of the Book of the Twelve by stating that the undated writings are to be read as prophesying during the time of the last king mentioned. "In quibus autem tempus non praefertur in titulo, sub illis eos regibus prophetasse sub quibus et hii qui ante eos habent titulos prophetaverunt."

date mentioned.[12] Modern scholars have been slow, however, to correct the assumption that the order of the Book of the Twelve should be attributed to the false chronology of an early scribe.[13] This scribe supposedly placed these smaller writings together to keep them from getting lost.[14] The size of the individual writings allows them all to be copied onto one scroll, but their preservation does not necessitate that they must be.[15] Doubtless, chronology and size played a role in the shaping of the Book of the Twelve, but they are not absolutely determinative for the order of the writings.

Several attempts have been made to trace the growth of the Book of the Twelve by analyses of the superscriptions. Ewald proposes a three-stage process of collection based upon his study of the titular elements.[16] He dates the first stage in the seventh century and maintains it contained Joel, Amos, Hosea, Micah, Nahum, and Zephaniah.[17] Ewald's second stage consists of the post-exilic addition of Obadiah, Jonah, Habakkuk, Haggai, and Zechariah 1-8, and the reordering of the corpus. The third stage, in the latter years of Nehemiah, added Zechariah 9-14 and Malachi. Steuernagel determines seven stages, relying on the formal characteristics

---

[12] For examples, see Theodor Lescow, "Redaktionsgeschichtliche Analyse von Micah 1-5," *ZAW* 84 (1972), 61-64; Hans Walter Wolff, *BK* 14/1 (Neukirchen: Neukirchener Verlag, 1961), 1-5; Schneider, *The Unity of the Book of the Twelve*, 162-191.

[13] For examples, see Eissfeldt, *Introduction*, 383; Fohrer, *Introduction*, 363. 4 Ezra and the Talmud offer hints of tradition as to who was responsible for the origin of the Book of the Twelve. Ezra is said to have been inspired to recite all the lost canonical books, including the Book of the Twelve (4 Ezra 14). The background of this tradition is impossible to trace. Baba Batra 15a says "the men of the great assembly" wrote Ezekiel, the twelve minor prophets, Daniel and the scroll of Esther." This reference is perhaps of some import, however, it is neither possible to determine the meaning of "wrote" in this context, nor to determine the origin of the tradition.

[14] Augustine's reference (*De Civitate Dei*, 18:29) to the Book of the Twelve Prophets "qui propterea dicuntur minores" changed the emphasis from the unity of the corpus to the size of the writings.

[15] Even today, scholars continue to believe that the alternate LXX order derives from a scribal decision to order the books of the first half of the corpus according to their length. This explanation ignores the fact that Obadiah, the shortest book in the Old Testament, precedes Jonah. Most proponents of this theory also do not even ask the question why size would be determinative for the first five, but not the last seven.

[16] Heinrich Ewald, *Die Propheten des Alten Bundes erklärt* (Göttingen: Vandenhoeck & Ruprecht, ²1868), 74-82.

[17] Schneider, *The Unity of the Book of the Twelve*, 7, mistakenly lists Jonah instead of Joel.

of the superscriptions.[18] The first, during Josiah's reign, contained Hosea, Micah, and Zephaniah. The second stage added Amos during the exile. The third stage added Haggai and Zechariah around 500. The fourth added an original form of Nahum before 300. The fifth added Habakkuk and chapter one of Nahum around 300. The sixth stage added Zechariah 9-14 shortly afterward. The seventh stage added Joel, Obadiah, and Jonah in the third century.

These widely disparate views exemplify the problems inherent in an attempt to determine the growth of the Book of the Twelve by the superscriptions. Many similar headings introduce works and portions of works vastly different in content. For example, Ewald's strictly formal perspective concluded Joel entered the collection with Hosea, while Steuernagel maintains Joel was incorporated several centuries later.

The early part of this century saw attempts to explain the character of the Book of the Twelve as a result of extensive redactional activity. Budde proposed that a systematic program of redaction in the 4th century B.C. sought to eliminate all non-divine material in the Book of the Twelve, including narrative material and first person prophetic accounts.[19] Budde anticipates a major problem with his theory by indicating three passages where redactors failed to eliminate "human" material.[20] However, these exceptions are by no means exhaustive, a fact that helps account for the lack of serious attention this article received.[21]

Another attempt at a redactional explanation was the work of R.E. Wolfe.[22] He suggested a history of redactional strata which could be isolated into thirteen distinct groups.[23] These strata led him to postulate

---

[18] Carl Steuernagel, *Lehrbuch der Einleitung in das Alten Testament* (Tübingen: Mohr, 1912), 669-672.

[19] Karl Budde, "Eine folgenschwere Redaktion des Zwölfprophetenbuchs," *ZAW* 39 (1921), 218-229.

[20] Hos 1 and 3; Amos 7:1-7; and Mic 2:6-11.

[21] Examples of other "human" exceptions include the entire writing of Jonah, which Budde maintains post-dates this redaction; the report style of Haggai, and the night visions of Zech 1:7-6:8 in the prophetic first person which Budde does not mention.

[22] R.E. Wolfe, "The Editing of the Book of the Twelve." *ZAW* 53 (1935): 90-129. Based upon his unpublished dissertation *The Editing of the Book of the Twelve*, (Harvard, 1933 [not available to the author]).

[23] A chronological listing of these strata is provided here for convenience. 1. The Judaistic Editor of Hosea (c. 650) 2. The Anti-High Place Editor (621-586) 3. The Late Exilic Editor (540-500) 4. The Anti-Neighbor Editor (500-450) 5. The Messianist (520-445) 6. The Nationalistic School of Editors (360-300) 7. The Day of Jahwe Editor (325) 8. The Eschatologists (310-300) 9. The Doxologist (early post-exilic period) 10.

the growth of the corpus in groups of two, six, nine, and twelve.[24] Many problems exist with his proposed reconstruction, not the least of which is the inconsistency with which he applies his methodology.[25] Additionally, Wolfe assumes that all the "hymns" were added simultaneously as the work of one editor despite their differences in theology, and the dates he gives for the constituent parts of the redactional strata have not withstood critical scrutiny.

The attempts to explain the character of the Book of the Twelve as due to redactional processes failed to receive acceptance. The proposals of both Budde and Wolfe reinforced the premise that common redactional work effected the shape of the Twelve. Simultaneously, they cast doubt upon the possibility of determining the extent of that editorial work.

Two articles and a dissertation accentuate the importance of catchwords as a principle for the collection of the writings in the Book of the Twelve. Delitzsch mentions catchwords found in the first nine writings.[26] Nearly a century later, Cassuto briefly notes catchword connections which he maintains account for the order of the writings.[27] These scholars were not the first to notice common language among the prophets. Their significance rests in tying these common words to the

---

The Anti-Idol Polemist (300-275) 11. The Psalm Editor (275-250) 12. The Early Scribes (250-225) 13. Later Scribal Schools (200-175).

[24] The two were Hosea and Amos; Micah, Zephaniah, Nahum, and Habakkuk; were added to make six; Joel, Jonah, and Obadiah were added to make nine; Haggai, Zechariah, and Malachi were added to complete the collection of individual writings.

[25] For example, Wolfe's dating of the Doxologist in the early post-exilic period cannot explain why all the passages added by this redactor are found in Amos at a point when it was, according to Wolfe, part of the book of the six. This runs directly counter to Wolfe's own contention the editors "did not work upon individual prophetic writings as such but occupied themselves in revising the books of the two, six, nine, or twelve" ("The Editing of the Book of the Twelve," *ZAW* 53 [1935]: 126).

[26] Franz Delitzsch, "Wann weissagte Obadja?," *ZLThK* 12 [1851]: 92-93. Delitzsch refers to passages which have a certain "Gleichartigkeit des Inhalts" (p. 92), and cites the common agricultural language between Hosea 14 and Joel 1; Joel 4:16 and Amos 1:2; Amos 9:12 and Obadiah (particularly verse 19); the reference to messenger sent among the nations in Obadiah 1 as a reason Jonah is placed after Obadiah; the description of god's attribute in Jonah 4:2, Mic 7:18; Nah 1:2-4; the *Massa* headings of Nahum and Habakkuk; and common language in Hab 2:20 and Zeph 1:7.

[27] Umberto Cassuto, "The Sequence and Arrangement of the Biblical Sections" (1947), *Biblical and Oriental Studies*, vol. 1 (Jerusalem: Magnes Press, 1973), 5-6. Cassuto cites only the verbal connection בוא, in Hosea 14 and Joel 2; the doublet in Joel 4:16 and Amos 1:2; the reference to Edom in Amos 9:12 and Obadiah; and the common language of Hab 2:20 and Zeph 1:7.

ordering of the Book of the Twelve.[28] Other scholars have adopted the idea that catchwords explain the order of certain writings where chronology does not appear determinative.[29]

These articles were very influential to the dissertation of Schneider.[30] Schneider uses these and other "parallels" to postulate a four stage "gradual accretion of prophetic traditions" in which "the prophets themselves explicitly worked as custodians and interpreters of earlier prophecies."[31] The first stage consists of Hosea, Amos, and Micah; the second stage of Nahum, Habakkuk, and Zephaniah; the third stage of Joel, Obadiah, and Jonah; and the final stage of Haggai, Zechariah, and Malachi. Schneider utilizes a synchronic approach to these parallels. He argues that the prophets authored their own works and collected the works of earlier prophets influential to them.[32]   Schneider campaigns against multidimensional understandings of redactional activity which "outdo one another in complexity."[33] He refuses to take seriously the growth of the texts over several generations.

Thus, the works of Delitzsch, Cassuto, and Schneider demonstrate catchwords are present in the Book of the Twelve which impact the order of individual writings. However, these works assume *apriori* that the shape of the writings was unaffected by these catchwords. A corrective to such a supposition will be offered in this work.

Lee takes a "canonical" approach to the question of the unity of the Book of the Twelve, and presents summaries of research on various passages of hope in the Book of the Twelve.[34] Lee's work, however, is difficult to evaluate. On the one hand, he maintains that post-exilic redactional activity on the Book of the Twelve "heightens" the sense of hope. On the other hand, he claims most of the optimistic passages

---

[28] For example, Isaac Abravanel (*Rabbi Isaaci Abrabanelis Commentarius in Hoseam cuius praemissum prooemium in duodecim prophetas Minores*, Lugduni in Balaris, 1688, orig. 1506) noted several connections, but did not tie them to the order of the Book of the Twelve.

[29] Carl Friedrich Keil, *The Twelve Minor Prophets*, vol. 1 (Grand Rapids: Eerdmans, 1949, orig. 1866), 2-4; Curt Kuhl, *Die Entstehung des Alten Testaments* (Bern: Francke, 1953), 217-218. H.W. Wolff, *BK* 14, no. 2 (Neukirchen: Neukirchener Verlag, 1977), 1-2; Rudolph, *KAT* 13, no. 4 (Gütersloh: Gütersloher Verlagshaus, 1976), 297-298.

[30] Schneider, *The Unity of the Book of the Twelve*.

[31] Schneider, *The Unity of the Book of the Twelve*, 18.

[32] Schneider, *The Unity of the Book of the Twelve*, 154-162.

[33] Schneider, *The Unity of the Book of the Twelve*, 31.

[34] Andrew Lee, *The Canonical Unity of the Scroll of the Minor Prophets*. (Dissertation: Baylor University, 1985).

typically considered as redactional additions are in actuality primary to their respective works.[35] Lee works on the presupposition that the Book of the Twelve is a "collection" compiled under the direction of Nehemiah. He maintains that the individual writings affect the understanding of the other writings, but he does not portray a programmatic shaping of the corpus as a whole.[36] Lee allows for redactional activity upon the larger corpus, but his chief concerns center upon presenting the history of research for particular passages which large contingents of scholarship have argued represent later additions to the individual writings. Lee's work does not advance any new argument about the *origin* of the Book of the Twelve, and he does not significantly relate his discussions of the passages to the question of the growth of the Book of the Twelve beyond purely thematic criteria.[37]

Blenkinsopp and Weimar respectively point toward additions to the writings in the Book of the Twelve which tend toward the eschatological, and the existence of "*Querverbindungen*" which argue for more than merely the collection of independent writings.[38] Blenkinsopp notes several of the writings have received substantial additions with an eschatological character. Blenkinsopp is not unique in noticing these additions, but he describes them

---

[35] Lee, *Canonical Unity*, 217.

[36] Lee, *Canonical Unity*, 225-226.

[37] Methodologically, Lee follows Childs. He introduces the individual writings, and then discusses the passages which scholarship of the last century has labeled secondary. In the chapters on the individual writings, Lee does not go much beyond this presentation to interpret the texts against one another, or to synthesize how the different emphases relate to one another — even within the same writing. In addition, Lee operates with an assumption (sometimes made explicit), that the additions to the writings (when he does not harmonize the problem passages) are somehow more authoritative the earlier that one can date them. For example, when speaking of Obad 19-21 (90), Lee states, "There is no overwhelming reason why the appendix of vv. 19-21 should not be dated as early as possible..." In the end, Lee presupposes that the individual writings were simply collected into the Book of the Twelve, but that their canonical position allows their *interpretation* as though they were written by the same author for the same purpose. Lee states this position in his conclusion (220): "When the books of the XII are conjoined, the interpretation of one is influenced by the other. The judgments in Nahum against Nineveh cannot escape being read as an indictment against whichever nation happens to be the enemy at the time, whether it be Babylonia or some future foe."

[38] Joseph Blenkinsopp, *Prophecy and Canon* (Notre Dame: Notre Dame Press, 1977), 106-108; and Peter Weimar, "Obadja. Eine redaktionskritische Analyse," *BN* 27 (1985): 94-99.

as a common characteristic in the literary history of the Book of the Twelve.[39]

Weimar considers the question of the growth of the Book of the Twelve from the perspective of Obadiah. He argues that Obadiah must be viewed in light of several redactional levels across the Book of the Twelve which point to a common history. Weimar mentions one progressive level of redaction on the prophetic collection which produced literary "*Querverbindungen*" through the aid of "*Stichwortentsprechungen*." He suggests that at this level the "collection" took the shape of a "book."[40] The brevity of his remarks does not indicate an exact definition of what Weimar terms "*Stichwortentsprechungen*," but he presumably refers to the "parallels" cited by Schneider.[41] The remarks of both Blenkinsopp and Weimar offer a point of departure for the interests of this study. They raise the possibility anew that the final form of the individual writings has been affected by their transmission and/or incorporation into the Book of the Twelve.

Finally, recent works by Bosshard and House deserve brief introduction, since the arguments of both, particularly the former, will be brought into the dialogue throughout this work. In a recent article Bosshard makes significant observations which impact upon a discussion of the unity of the Book of the Twelve.[42] Bosshard documents a strong correlation of themes and vocabulary appearing in parallel locations between Isaiah and the Book of the Twelve. This phenomenon exhibits substantial continuity, failing only with Jonah and Malachi. Bosshard argues further that several of the passages containing the parallels (Joel 1:15; 2:1-11; Obad 5f,15ff; Zeph 2:13-15; 3:14-18) demonstrate signs of redactional shaping in which the passages from the Book of the Twelve deliberately take up the vocabulary and motifs of the Isaiah passages. Finally, Bosshard makes an effort to relate the Isaiah-related parallels in

---

[39] Joseph Blenkinsopp, *Prophecy and Canon*, 108, lists several of these additions, including Amos 9:11-15, Obad 16-21, Zeph 3:9-20.

[40] Peter Weimar, "Obadja." *BN* 27 (1985): 98. Weimar argues that the starting point of the corpus was a deuteronomistic collection (including Hosea, Amos, Jonah, Micah, and Zephaniah), based on superscriptions and content. To this collection was added Obadiah, Nahum, and Habakkuk toward the end of the exile. He suggests that Haggai, Zechariah 1-8, and Malachi possibly entered the corpus at the progressive redactional level of the book, while Joel and Zechariah 9-14 were added later.

[41] Weimar shows familiarity with Schneider's work, but does not indicate that he means something beyond the parallels described therein.

[42] Erich Bosshard, "Beobachtungen zum Zwölfprophetenbuch," *BN* 40 (1987): 30-62.

the Book of the Twelve to redactional emphases in Isaiah. Bosshard's observations are difficult to evaluate. On the one hand, the sheer number of the words he notes, together with the consistency of the phenomenon are quite impressive, and deserve attention. On the other hand, the presentation of these words should by no means imply that these are the only passages in the Book of the Twelve and Isaiah which share common images and vocabulary. Some passages in the Book of the Twelve rely heavily on other Isaiah passages, but do not relate specifically to the parallel positions cited by Bosshard.[43] Bosshard also admits that some parallels are not strong enough to determine intentionality clearly.[44] Bosshard makes no claim to finality in his article, and in fact he demonstrates that he continues to wrestle with these questions by later expanding his views concerning Malachi.[45] Nevertheless, Bosshard provides enough evidence to argue plausibly that the same circles transmitted Isaiah and the Book of the Twelve during a significant period which affected the shape of the latter corpus. His views on individual passages will be brought into the dialogue in the appropriate places.

House approaches the question of the unity of the Book of the Twelve by drawing from American formalism.[46] In the heart of his work, he discusses the genre, structure, plot, characters, and point of view of the Book of the Twelve. House defines the *genre* of the Book of the Twelve as "written prophecy," which inherently contains a tri-partite thematic concern (sin, punishment, salvation).[47] House's isolation of a three-fold repetition of themes within "written prophecy" leads him to postulate that these thematic elements provide the outline for the tri-partite *structure* of

---

[43] For examples, see discussions of the relationship of Mic 7:8ff with Isa 10, and Nah 2:1 with Isa 52:7.

[44] For example, Bosshard, *BN* 40 (1987): 35f, admits that the parallels between Proto-Zechariah and Isaiah are not very strong.

[45] Erich Bosshard and Reinhard Gregor Kratz, "Maleachi im Zwölfprophetenbuch," *BN* 52 (1990): 27-46. In his earlier article, Bosshard does not treat Malachi in detail since Malachi exhibits no Isaiah parallels. In the later article with Kratz, Bosshard argues that an early form of Malachi formed the redactional continuation of Proto-Zechariah. Fuller discussion of these views will appear in the treatment of Mal 1:1ff in my subsequent volume.

[46] Paul R. House, *The Unity of the Twelve*, Bible and Literature Series 27 (Sheffield: Almond Press, 1990).

[47] House, *The Unity of the Twelve*, 61f, defines "written prophecy" as literature which uses either prose or poetry as its medium; whose content declares "an urgent message of sin, judgment, and restoration in a unified and unique way;" and which uses "first or third person narration for specific purposes."

the Twelve.[48]   House finds "definite patterns in the positioning of the minor prophets."[49]   These patterns manifest themselves in a structure which runs across the Twelve, and which documents the sin of Israel and the nations (Hosea through Micah), the punishment of that sin (Nahum through Zephaniah), and restoration (Haggai through Malachi).   House sees the *plot* of the Twelve as comedic within the confines of the structure he has already described.[50]   House also devotes chapters to the characters (YHWH, prophet, the nations, and Israel — which House subdivides into rebel and remnant), and to the point of view (discussion of the "narrator," audience, implied author, and type of narration) of the Twelve.

House's work raises methodological questions about what constitutes the "unity" of the Twelve.   House refuses to postulate on who placed these texts together, or upon the growth of the individual writings, preferring instead to look at the writings synchronically.   The categories he uses to describe the unity are so broad (and sometimes questionable) that one gets the distinct impression that they could be imposed upon any combination of prophetic writings.[51]   House offers no solid *criteria* for arguing that one

---

[48]   House, *The Unity of the Twelve*, 71, states: "Since the major thematic aspects of the minor prophets and their neighbors are ... the sin of the covenant people, the purging of that sin, and the reclamation of the sinners, it is best to envision a tri-partite structure of the Twelve."   This circular logic creates severe problems, not only methodologically, but by attempting to force the Twelve into these rather broad structural categories.

[49]   House, *The Unity of the Twelve*, 68.

[50]   House, *The Unity of the Twelve*, 111-115, does not use the term "comedic" in the sense of "funny," but in the more classic literary sense as a contrast to tragedy.   Whereas in tragedy the fortunes of a superior character change from good to bad, a comedic plot triumphs a seemingly inferior character, in spite of apparently insurmountable opposition.   This emphasis upon the comedic leads House to see the plot of the Twelve in terms of a downward trek (Hosea through Micah) containing an "introduction" (Hosea, Joel), and a complication (Amos through Micah).   This complication leads to the crisis point of the Twelve (Nahum and Habakkuk), which in turn draws the reader to the climax and falling action (Zephaniah).   House sees the three remaining works (Haggai through Malachi) as manifestations of the restorative resolution of the plot.

[51]   House, *The Unity of the Twelve*, 68, anticipates this problem to a certain degree when he acknowledges questions regarding the literary character of the unity of the Book of the Twelve, but his suggestion that the unity of the Twelve may be assumed via comparisons to other "complicated" literary works such as *The Canterbury Tales*, *Gulliver's Travels*, or *Don Quixote* is hardly convincing.   He diagrams and discusses these literary aspects in terms which are entirely too broad to describe adequately the great variety of literature found therein.   For example, he groups Hosea through Micah as the punishment section of the Twelve, virtually ignoring the many passages of

must view these writings as a literary unity.[52] Rather, House presumes a loose literary unity.

The modern literary analysis of House's work represents the latest in a long line of theories of the Book of the Twelve. The discussion above reveals a wide range of approaches, presuppositions, and conclusions regarding the question of the Book of the Twelve. To enter this discussion purposefully, some consideration of methodological questions requires attention.

3. Methodological Considerations

Two phenomena motivate this study. First, long-standing traditions reaching back into antiquity treat the writings of the Book of the Twelve as a single unit. These traditions clearly indicate that these writings were not only transmitted on a *single scroll*, they were also counted as a *single book*. These traditions and subsequent attempts to explain their ramifications

---

salvation present in those books (e.g. Hos 11:8-12; 14:1-9; Amos 9:11-15; Joel 3:1-5 [MT]; Obad 17-21; Mic 4-5, 7:8-20). In addition, he labels Haggai through Malachi as the restoration section of the Twelve. However, Haggai never realizes restoration (only the beginning of the temple reconstruction). Similarly, Malachi is much more realistically characterized as a dialogue about cultic abuse than a treatise of restoration. House also portrays the characters of the Book of the Twelve in the broadest possible categories. He does not even distinguish between the attitudes toward the Northern kingdom and the Southern kingdom, or between characterizations of Samaria and Jerusalem, choosing instead to relegate them all to the rubric "Israel."

[52] This observation points to perhaps the most serious critique against House. House's work arises from his perception of the literary character of the unity the Twelve. Despite his insistence that the Twelve is a *literary* unity, House rejects redactional analyses. House cites an oft-repeated axiom among conservative scholars that "the final form of the Twelve ... is in question here. This final text represents the *only* redactional level we possess for sure." (226) While this axiom can perhaps be applied with some logic to certain Biblical material, it cannot be used in the context of a discussion of the literary unity of the Book of the Twelve, because this corpus contains twelve individual writings, each one with a *final form* which claims its own literary integrity. At the very least one has to reckon with *the* final form of Twelve different books. House struggles to present the Twelve as a literary unity while vacillating between an image of a single author of this unity and the authors of the individual writings. A classic example appears when on the same page (237) House refers to the "book's implied author" (referring to the Twelve) and the "writers" of Hosea-Zephaniah. This vacillation raises strong doubts about the clarity and/or appropriateness of his view of 'authorship' and 'unity.'

have already been noted.[53] The second phenomenon motivating this work, the use of catchwords to unite two writings, has not received adequate treatment to date. Already, discussion of scholarly theories on the unity of the Book of the Twelve, demonstrates a developing awareness that catchwords played a role in the *positioning* of some of the writings of the Book of the Twelve.[54] In his discussion of possible explanations for the order of the writings of the Book of the Twelve, House states, "Catchwords certainly exist in the Twelve, but one would be hard pressed to find enough catchwords to unite all the books."[55] An easy dismissal such as this statement is no longer possible, however, when one recognizes that the Book of the Twelve manifests a very consistent catchword phenomenon between the writings. The extent of this phenomenon in the Book of the Twelve will be documented in the following chapter, but several summary remarks are in order because of the methodological implications they carry.

The seams between the writings in the Book of the Twelve *do indeed* manifest a remarkably consistent phenomenon. The end of one writing contains several words and phrases that reappear in the beginning units of the adjacent writing. Considering the ancient traditions treating the Book of the Twelve as a single work, the extent and significance of these common words requires investigation. This phenomenon appears in most writings in the Book of the Twelve. Only two passages do not exhibit this phenomenon, but even this inconsistency illuminates other phenomenon. Jonah 4 exhibits no strong catchword links with Mic 1:1ff, but the hymn in Jon 2:3ff (long argued as secondary by a large contingent of scholars) does share common words with Mic 1:1ff. In addition, if one removes Jonah from consideration, then an even stronger catchword connection appears between the concluding verses of Obadiah and the opening verses of Micah. Thus the inconsistency in Jonah raises the question whether the psalm entered Jonah in relationship to its incorporation into the Book of the Twelve, and simultaneously suggests the possibility that the entire book was inserted into a previously existing context between Obadiah and Micah. Zech 14:1ff represents the second inconsistency in the catchword phenomenon. Yet while there is no catchword phenomenon relating Zech 14:1ff with Malachi, there is a very strong connection between Zech 8:9ff and Mal 1:1ff. The appearance of common words between these passages represents a potentially significant aspect to the phenomenon since, for over

---

[53] See above discussion of the ancient traditions, page 2ff.

[54] See above discussion of Delitzsch, Cassuto, and Schneider, page 6.

[55] House, *The Unity of the Twelve*, 66.

a century, a large segment of scholars has contended that Zech 1-8, most frequently called Proto-Zechariah, existed as a separate corpus before the addition of Zech 9-14 (Deutero- and Trito-Zechariah). Thus, as with Jonah, the lack of catchwords illuminates another phenomenon which raises the possibility that a pre-existing catchword relationship was obscured through the insertion of material into an existing context.

Documenting the existence of this phenomenon presents a comparatively easy task in comparison to its interpretation. Naturally, the methodology one utilizes influences the results of any given work. House opts to work with a synchronic descriptive methodology in an attempt to demonstrate the Book of the Twelve exhibits a literary character. Lee allows for accretions to the individual writings, but assumes those portions which were added entered the corpus as part of the transmission of the individual books. Schneider works with a model of prophets who transmit their own works and the works of their predecessors. Despite this view of prophets as transmitters of prophetic tradition, he refuses to consider redactional approaches because they "seek to outdo one another in complexity."[56] The present work deliberately seeks to incorporate redactional questions, not in an attempt to derive a complex theory of the growth of the texts, but in the conviction that the catchword phenomenon itself demands that these questions be asked. The preponderance of shared words in the seams between the writings in the Book of the Twelve leads to the suspicion that this repetition cannot be accidental. However, suspicion alone does not offer evidence which can be evaluated and refined or discarded. If the words do relate in some manner to the question of the unity of the Book of the Twelve, then the question of the editing of the individual writings cannot be ignored.

The first question which one must answer is how to approach the texts themselves in attempting to evaluate the relationships of these words to one another. The majority of scholars treating the question of the unity of the Book of the Twelve assume that only the final form of a given writing was incorporated into the larger corpus.[57] The catchword phenomenon will not allow this assumption. Too many catchwords appear in contexts which have long been argued as additions to the prophetic writings in which they appear. On the other hand, one may not go to the other extreme and assume that every occurrence of common words reflects the hand of a

---

[56] Schneider, *The Unity of the Book of the Twelve*, 31.
[57] A few exceptions, such as Wolfe, Blenkinsopp, Weimar, and Bosshard have been noted above.

redactor working on the Book of the Twelve. Many of these words can be attributed to material already contained in one of the writings. Sometimes the catchwords can be explained as components of a pre-existing block of material specifically incorporated into a writing to further the interests of the Book of the Twelve.[58]

These observations require that each *connection* be treated separately to see if it illuminates the question of the unity of the Book of the Twelve. One cannot presume that the techniques used in one writing will apply in the next. This separate treatment requires evaluation of the individual passages from several perspectives simultaneously: 1) from the perspective of the integrity of the words in their immediate context;[59] 2) from the perspective of the transmission of the individual writing in which the words appear;[60] 3) from the perspective of the function within the Book of the Twelve;[61] 4) from the perspective of the theological/literary relationships to other parts of the Old Testament.[62] Evaluation of these various perspectives helps to guard against too quickly deciding one portion of the text or another should be classified as a redactional implantation. Simultaneously, these considerations allow one to begin to categorize the texts to provide insights into the hermeneutical interests and/or the historical suppositions behind a given, phrase, sentence, or passage.

In any given connection, one must therefore evaluate the various possibilities to attempt to determine whether the presence of these words in neighboring writings should be attributed to "accident," to a "collection principle," or to a "redaction principle." Assigning two passages to a

---

[58] Examples of the latter include the semi-acrostic poem in Nah 1:2ff, the theophanic hymn in Hab 3:1ff, the song of Jonah in Jonah 2:3ff, and above all the use of Jer 49:14-16,9 in Obad 1-5.

[59] These words appear in different relationships to their immediate contexts. They can appear as short phrases not integrally related to the context, causing some scholars simply to delete them as "glosses" (for example, see the discussions of Nah 3:15; Hag 2:19); the words can be firmly entrenched in their contexts; or the words can appear as part of a single verse or sentence which has been inserted (Hab 3:17) into the context.

[60] For example, Nah 3:18f has long been noted as contextually peculiar, but further investigation reveals that it functioned as part of the redactional frame of a previous edition of the writing, meaning that the words in these verses were not composed for their location in the Book of the Twelve.

[61] This perspective concentrates upon the relationship to the neighboring writing, but it cannot limit itself to only the neighboring work. Compare the discussion of Zeph 3:20, which serves as a bridge to Haggai, but which is also cognizant of its position in the Book of the Twelve in doing so.

[62] See the use Jer 49:14-16,9 in Obad 1-5 and the taking up of Isa 9-12 in Mic 7:8ff.

collection principle would imply that two completed passages were placed next to one another, presumably because of the words they shared. By contrast, assigning a passage or portions of a passage to the work of a redactor implies the intentional growth of the text. Naturally, one must also delineate which of the two parts draws from the other, or conceivably if both received additions at the hand of the redactor.

This approach to the Book of the Twelve represents a different tactic than these texts traditionally receive. Nevertheless, this approach by no means reflects a fringe interest of Old Testament studies. The last fifteen years have seen a renewed interest in the final form of the text, as scholars attempt to explain how the Biblical writings were compiled and composed. Various quarters of the discipline have approached these questions from different perspectives. Structuralism, canonical criticism, rhetorical criticism, and "new literary criticism" have all attempted to explain the "final form" of the texts. Correspondingly, redaction studies have received renewed interest, particularly in Europe, but they manifest a change of focus from earlier redactional studies, which assumed that the earliest recoverable form of the text was the most "authoritative." As a result, older redactional work peeled back the layers of the text in an attempt to find the ever elusive original form of a prophetic saying. Recent redactional studies attempt to do the opposite. They attempt to peel back the literary layers of a given text in order to put it back together, assuming this process provides insights into the thoughts and the situations of those responsible for the present state of the writings.

Another recent development in Old Testament studies affecting this study concerns the way redactors worked. There is a developing awareness that these redactors increasingly presented their own message, particularly in prophetic literature, by drawing from those works available to them. This use of other Old Testament material takes many forms. The method is called by various names, inner-biblical exegesis, inter-textuality, *Schriftprophetie*, etc., but the phenomenon plays a significant role in recent studies.[63] This technique will play an important part in the following study as well. The presence of catchwords represents an objective

---

[63] Compare for example the detailed work of Michael Fishbane, *Biblical Interpretation in Ancient Israel* (Oxford: Clarendon Press, 1985); and the methodological introductions in Siegfried Bergler, *Joel als Schriftinterpret*. Beiträge zur Erforschung des Alten Testaments und des antiken Judentums 16 (Frankfurt: Peter Lang, 1988); and Helmut Utzschneider, *Künder oder Schreiber? Eine These zum Problem der »Schriftprophetie« auf Grund von Maleachi 1,6-2:9*. Beiträge zur Erforschung des Alten Testaments und des Antiken Judentums 19 (Frankfurt: Peter Lang,1989).

phenomenon, but interpreting it requires a broader perspective than merely documenting its presence. Catchwords offer a springboard into the editorial work of the Book of the Twelve. One cannot, however, concentrate upon these words myopically and exclude other editorial factors.

Technical questions regarding the presentation of this work deserve mention. The evidence for intentional shaping of these prophetic writings on the basis of catchwords is not equally distributed. Some passages allow one to postulate redactional activity with a higher degree of certainty, because they provide *relatively* objective criteria for determining redactional activity on the text. Passages such as Obad 1-5 and Nah 1:2ff fall into this category.[64] Other passages require one to choose between several options based on less objective criteria. These criteria require a certain "feel" for the interests of the larger corpus.[65] Observations on some of these passages result in conclusions which will undoubtedly create controversy, but these conclusions are nevertheless supportable and meaningful.[66] Complicating the picture still further, many of the observations interact with conclusions reached in previous chapters, in chapters which have yet to be discussed, or in passages which will be treated in a subsequent volume.[67] Finally, for reasons of size, the completion of a detailed examination of these passages could not readily be completed in a single volume without excising significant background discussions on the individual writings.

For this reason, discussion of the relevant passages required an artificial division into meaningful categories. The process of exegetical evaluation indicated that entry into the Book of the Twelve affected the

---

[64] Obad 1-5 has an almost exact parallel in Jer 49:14-16,9 with which it can be compared on the basis of Amos 9:1ff. Nah 1:2ff contains a semi-acrostic poem whose acrostic pattern has been interrupted through deliberate redactional changes, some of which are directly related to the Book of the Twelve.

[65] So, for example, the incorporation of the theophanic hymn in Hab 3:1ff. While the insertion of Hab 3:17 presents relatively solid criteria that categorize it as an insertion, the incorporation of the body of the hymn requires balancing several criteria which do not all point in the same direction.

[66] So particularly, the discussion of the composition of Joel. It will be argued in the subsequent volume that while the composition of Joel (with the consensus) does not support the supposition of a long redaction history, several factors argue that Joel was composed and/or compiled specifically for the Book of the Twelve: its own particular compositional technique, its awareness of Hosea and Amos, and the frequent insertion of material in other writings which draw upon Joel paradigmatically.

[67] Catchwords appearing in Joel, Obadiah, Jonah, Nahum, Habakkuk, Zech 9-14, and Malachi will be treated in my forthcoming volume, *Redactional Processes in the Book of the Twelve*, BZAW (Berlin: De Gruyter).

literary forms of some of the writings more significantly than others. A second volume will therefore concentrate upon those writings whose final forms appear more substantively affected by incorporation into the Book of the Twelve. This current volume investigates those writings whose final forms typically involve less extensive redactional shaping which can be linked literarily to the compilation of the Book of the Twelve.[68] The author postulates that *part* of the explanation for this distinction requires that one deal with two multi-volume collections whose common transmission predated the compilation of the Book of the Twelve. These two pre-existing corpora (literary precursors) postulated in this volume are the Deuteronomistic corpus (Hosea, Amos, Micah, Zephaniah) and the Haggai-Zechariah corpus (Haggai, Zech 1-8). *Preliminary* evidence for the existence of these corpora will be presented in the discussions of the relevant passages.[69]

Discussion of the passages relevant to the catchword phenomenon must include several elements: 1) an overview of the scholarly discussion of the transmission history of the individual writings; 2) evidence that the writings had a (common) literary history, often protracted, which preceded their incorporation into the Book of the Twelve; 3) discussion of the individual cases where evidence indicates an intentional addition to the text tied explicitly to the literary interests of the *Book of the Twelve*.

The work will proceed by documenting the long overlooked presence of catchwords, a task which requires fresh translations and textual comparisons with the LXX, Vulgate, and Syriac versions. Following documentation of the catchwords, the beginning and end of the six writings

---

[68] Zephaniah represents a partial exception since the evidence suggests that it was expanded significantly for its position in the Book of the Twelve, even though it already exhibits concerns linking it redactionally to the Deuteronomistic corpus.

[69] The primary task of this volume seeks to interpret the implications of the catchword phenomenon for the Book of the Twelve. Postulation of a common transmission for the Deuteronomistic corpus remains tentative. Furthering this theory will require further investigation at some later date in order to bring more definitive arguments which take account of other passages within these writings more fully than can be done in this context. While the question of the common transmission remains tentative for these writings, evidence indicating they existed in literary form prior to their incorporation into the Book of the Twelve remains strong. By contrast, theories concerning a common transmission of Haggai and Zech 1-8 have been forcefully argued by others. No evidence in the current investigation counters those arguments. Rather, the existence of this volume actually clarifies certain tensions.

will be evaluated from several perspectives.[70] Each chapter will observe the larger context by discussing the macrostructure of the individual writings.   This discussion will also dialogue with recent (or dominant) scholarly theories concerning the redaction history of each writing as a springboard to treating the individual passages.   Each chapter will then investigate the immediate context of the opening and concluding passages to determine their literary units and sub-units.   Significant factors influencing questions of the unity and/or the development of the passage will be noted.   Finally, each section will include an assessment of how the literary units of the passage relate to the catchwords.

---

[70] Because it is not directly involved with the catchword connections, the beginning of Hosea will not be treated separately.

The Catchword Phenomenon

Fresh translations of relevent passages reveal that the seams between the writings of the Book of the Twelve exhibit a remarkably consistent phenomenon which has received little scholarly attention. Throughout the Book of the Twelve, the end of one writing contains significant words which reappear in opening sections of the next writing.[1] Because of the nature of translating from one language to another, modern and ancient translations of the Book of the Twelve do not illuminate the full extent of the words and phrases shared between these writings. This chapter, therefore, will make a substantial effort to provide literal translations of these passages, in the conviction that these literal translations provide the best means for accentuating the common words between the respective passages. Admittedly, such translation techniques face the danger of sounding rather wooden at times, but for this task, that risk must be accepted. The accompanying text notes serve two functions. First, they will serve the traditional function, offering text-critical rationale for necessary decisions where inconsistencies in the versions and scholarly debate require comment. Second, these text notes will pay careful attention to the presence of the catchwords within these passages in order to verify their presence in the text, and to ascertain whether the versions demonstrate any awareness of these words as literary connectors. For convenience, the results of this comparison will be summarized briefly for each section following the text notes.

---

[1]   Jonah 4:1ff and Zech 14:1ff are exceptions, but even these exceptions point out other phenomena, which bear strikingly upon the question of the growth of the Book of the Twelve. While Jonah 4:1ff contains no significant repetition of words, the hymn in 2:3ff — long argued as a secondary addition to the writing by a large contingent of scholars — does exhibit this catchword phenomenon. This hymn (Jon 2:3ff) will be translated here with Mic 1:1ff. Zech 14:1ff, the conclusion of Deutero-Zechariah, likewise contains no real evidence of catchwords, but Zech 8:9ff, the conclusion of Proto-Zechariah, shares numerous words and phrases with Mal 1:1ff. Therefore, Zech 8:9ff will likewise be translated in this context.

1. Hos 14:5-10 and Joel 1:1-12

1.1. Translation of Hos 14:5-10 and Joel 1:1-12

Divine Promise (14:5-9) and Wisdom Motto (14:10)

5.   I will heal their apostasy.[a]
    I will love them voluntarily,[b]
    For my anger is returned from him.[c]

6.   I will be like dew to Israel.
    He will blossom like the lily,
    And he will set his roots[a] like Lebanon.[b]

7.   His young sprouts will go,
    And his splendor will be like the olive tree,
    And the fragrance (belonging) to him (will be) like Lebanon.

8.   [a]The *inhabitants* will return[a] in his shade.[b]
    They will[c] grow[d] *grain*.[e]
    They will flourish like the *vine*;
    His renown (will be) like the *wine* of Lebanon.

9.   Ephraim, what are idols to me[a] any longer?
    I answer,[b] and I will consider him.[c]
    I am like a luxuriant cypress.
    From me has your fruit been found.

10.   Who is wise that he can discern *these*[a] things;
    And[b] discerning that he knows them?
    For the ways of YHWH are right,
    And the righteous will walk in them,
    But transgressors will stumble in them.

Summons to Mourning

1.   The word of YHWH which came to Joel son of Pethuel.[a]

2.   Hear *this* elders. Give ear, all the *inhabitants* of the land.
    Has *this*[a] happened in your days or[b] in the days of your fathers?

3.   Relate about it to your sons, and your sons to their sons, and their sons to the next generation.

4.   The left-over of the gnawing locust, the swarming locust has eaten. And the left-over of the swarming locust, the creeping locust has eaten.
    And the left-over of the creeping locust, the stripping locust has eaten.

5.   Awake drunkards[a] and weep,
    And wail all the drinkers of *wine*,
    Because of the new wine[b] cut off[c] from your mouth.

6.   For a nation has gone up to my land, mighty and without number.
    Its teeth are the teeth of a lion.
    It has the fangs of a lion.

7.   He made my *vine* for destruction,

And my fig tree for splintering.
And stripping it, he stripped it and cast it away.
Its branches become white.[a]

8.   Lament[a] like the virgin[b] girded with sackcloth because of the Baal[c] of her
          youth.

9.   The cereal offering and the drink offering have been cut off from the house of
          YHWH.
          The priests, the ministers of YHWH, mourn.[a]

10.   [a]The field is destroyed.
          The land mourns, for the *grain* is destroyed.
          The new wine is dried up.
          The fresh oil is languished.

11.   Be ashamed[a] plowmen.
          Wail, vinedressers, over the wheat and over the barley,
          Because the harvest of the field has perished.

12.   The *vine* has withered.[a]
          The fig-tree has languished.
          The pomegranate, the palm-tree, and the apple-tree —
          All the trees of the field have withered,
          For rejoicing has withered from the sons of men.

1.2. Textual Notes for Hos 14:5-10 and Joel 1:1-12

Hos 14:5: a-מְשׁוּבָתָם. "Their apostasy" is incorrectly understood by G from the root ישׁב,
and translated as "dwellings" (κατοικίας). G does this also in 11:7. b-נְדָבָה. G translates
as ὁμολώς, the Syriac as "their vows," and V as "spontanee." c-מִמֶּנּוּ. G harmonizes "from
him" as plural (ἀπ αὐτῶν).

Hos 14:6: a-יַךְ from נכה, is here used in the sense of striking or putting down roots. G
translates βαλεῖ, causing *BHS* to suggest the roots נטה or ירה. However, 1Sam 2:14 has
נכה used in the similar sense of "thrusting." b-Lebanon here refers to the cedars of
Lebanon. *BHS* proposes "poplar" (לִבְנֶה) on the basis of 4:13. However, the recurrences
of "Lebanon" in this unit (14:7,8) and attestation in the versions support its presence here.
(Cf. Also Ps 29:5; 104:16).

Hos 14:8: a-aG inserts καί, and uses καθοῦνται instead of inhabitant, thus reading "they
shall return and dwell in his shade." Syriac translates "return" as "build" (contra *BHS*). In
the MT inhabitants is the subject of יָשֻׁבוּ and *status constructus* with "his shade" (*GK* §89,
§130a). The sense of this translation comes close to the similar phrase, "return in peace,"
in Gen 28:21 and 1 Kgs 22:17. b-בְּצִלּוֹ. *BHS* and others propose reading בְּצִלְי on form
critical grounds that this is a YHWH speech. Such a conjecture has no textual support and
disregards the use of the third person singular in these verses. c-G inserts the conjunction
καί; and an extra verb (μεθυσθήσονται). d-יְחַיּוּ. The difficulty of this verb in the piel used
with grain has been overstated and need not be emended, contra Coote ("Hosea 14:8: 'They
Who Are Filled With Grain Shall Live.'" *JBL* 93 [1974]: 161-173) and others. The piel
imperfect is used elsewhere both with an inanimate object and with a causative nuance (cf
esp. Neh 3:34; 1Chr 11:8). It is also used with cattle (Isa 7:21). e-דָגָן, "grain" (also Joel

1:10); גֶּפֶן, "vine" (also Joel 1:7,12); and יַיִן, "wine" (and Joel 1:5) are attested in all the versions.

Hos 14:9: **a-**מַה־לִּי. G reads מַה־לוֹ to avoid the implication that YHWH once had something to do with idols. The Syriac inserts וַיֹּאמֶר, changing the speaker, but attests to מַה־לִּי, making it likely that both have noticed the difficulty of מַה־לִּי. **b-**עֲנִיתִי. G assumes the root ענה, to be bowed down, afflicted and not to answer. **c-**וַאֲשׁוּרֶנּוּ. G translates κατισχύσω, to overcome.

Hos 14:10: **a-**וְיָבֵן. The ו following a question introduces the consecutive clause (*GK* §166). **b-**אֵלֶּה. The plural pronoun is attested in the versions.

Joel 1:1: **a-**פְּתוּאֵל. G has βαθουηλ (cf. Gen 22:22f; 24:15; Josh 19:4; 1Chr 4:30), instead of the otherwise unknown Pethuel.

Joel 1:2: **a-**זֹאת. Wolff translates as כָזֹאת, "like this," citing 1Sam 4:7; Isa 66:8; Jer 2:10 as support. However, all of these references have the preposition כ attached. Syriac inserts אֵיךְ, understanding "like this" with what follows. G translates with the plural (once with the enclytic), while V translates "hoc" only once here, but adds "hoc" in 1:3. **b-**וְאִם. The use of וְאִם is uncommon in a disjunctive question, and presupposes a negative answer (*GK* §150g. Cf. Gen 17:17; Job 21:4).

Joel 1:5: **a-**G inserts ἐξ οἴνου αὐτῶν. **b-**עַל־עָסִיס. G has read as referring to "drinkers of wine" and translates it εἰς μέθην. **c-**G inserts a new subject for נִכְרַת, inserting εὐφροσύνη καὶ χαρά, taking the reference from Joel 1:16 as a more appropriate reason for lamentation.

Joel 1:7: **a-**G supposes nation as the subject of הִלְבִּינוּ.

Joel 1:8: **a-**אֱלִי. Hapaxlegomenon from the root אלה, to lament. G reads the consonants twice and translates θρήνησον πρός με. **b-**בְּתוּלָה. G translates this as "for the bride" (ὑπὲρ νύμφην) and not as "like the virgin." "Bride" is used elsewhere for בתולה (see Jer 2:32). The use of ὑπὲρ with the accusative denotes the comparitive "more than," but does not presuppose another text. The use of the definite object is explained in a discussion of the literary horizon of Joel. **c-**The translation Baal instead of the more frequent "husband" is explained under the literary discussion of Joel 1:8.

Joel 1:9: **a-**אָבְלוּ. G translates as imperative reading אִבְלוּ, but an imperative is here out of place and not attested in MT. See literary discussion.

Joel 1:10: **a-**G inserts ὅτι to conform to 1:10b.

Joel 1:11: **a-**הֹבִישׁוּ. G understands the root יבשׁ instead of בושׁ. The imperative pointing of MT is here preferred.

Joel 1:12: **a-**וּבָשׁוּ. G understands the root בושׁ recognizing the word play from verse 11.

1.3. Conclusions

Several textual observations above have direct bearing on the *Stichwort* connections between Hosea and Joel. The words themselves are fully attested in the versions. In spite of this attestation, there is no concern to translate the *Stichwörter* identically.[2] On the other hand certain words have been added which strengthen the connection.[3] This paradox leads to the conclusion that the *Stichwort* connection between Hosea and Joel was not noticed or not important to the translators of the versions.

2. Joel 4:1-21 and Amos 1:1-2:16

2.1. Translation of Joel 4:4-8,14-21 and Amos 1:1-2,6-12

Judgment on the Nations and Eschatological Promise of Salvation

4.   And moreover what are you to me *Tyre*,[a] and Sidon, and all the [b]*regions of
          Philistia?*[b]
        Is it a recompense you are repaying against me,
        [c]Or which you are rendering against me?[c]
        Swiftly, speedily I will return your recompense on your head.
5.   Since you took my silver and my gold,
        And my precious treasures you brought to your temples,
6.   And the sons of Judah and the sons of Jerusalem you sold to the sons of the
                Greeks in order to remove them from their borders.
7.   Behold I am arousing them from the place from which you sold them,
        And I will return your recompense on your head.
8.   And I will sell your sons and your daughters into the hand of the sons of Judah,
        And they will sell them to the Sabeans, to a distant nation,
        For YHWH has spoken.
        ...
14.   Multitudes, mulitudes in the valley of verdict,
        For the day of YHWH draws near.
15.   The sun and the moon grow dark,
        And the stars withdraw their brightness.
16.   And [a]*YHWH roars from Zion,*
        And from Jerusalem he utters his voice[a]
        And the heavens and earth shake.
        And YHWH is a refuge to his people,
        And a stronghold for the sons of Israel.
17.   And you will know that I am YHWH your god,
        The one abiding in *Zion* - my holy mountain.
        And *Jerusalem* is holy,

---

2   Compare the different words for יֹשֵׁבִי in Hos 14:8 and Joel 1:2 in both G and V.
3   In Joel 1:3 "hoc" has been inserted by V where it does not occur in MT, and in Joel
        1:2 G translates the singular pronoun as plural.

And strangers will not pass over[a] her any more.

18.   And it will be on that day:
[a]The mountains will drip new wine,
And the hills[a] flow with milk,
And all the channels[b] of Judah will flow (with) water,
And a spring will go forth from the house of YHWH
And it will water the wady of Shittim.

19.   Egypt will become a desolation,
And *Edom* will become a wilderness of desolation
From the violence (done) to[a] the sons of Judah,
When they poured out innocent blood in their land.

20.   But Judah will be inhabited forever,
And *Jerusalem* for generation to generation.

21.   [a]And I will empty out their blood that I have not emptied out[a].
For YHWH dwells in *Zion*.

Zion Motto and Oracles Against the Nations

1.   The words of Amos, who[a] was among the shepherds[b] from Tekoa, which[c] he saw
concerning Israel[d] in the days of Uzziah, king of Judah, and in the days of
Jeroboam, son of Joash king of Israel, two years before the earthquake.

2.   And he said
'YHWH roars from Zion
And from Jerusalem he utters his voice,
And the pastures of the shepherds mourn
And the head of Carmel withers.'

...

6.   Thus says YHWH,
For three transgressions of *Gaza* and for four I will not turn it back,
Because of [a]their exiling a whole population[a] to deliver up to *Edom*.

7.   Thus I will send fire on the walls of *Gaza*,
And it will consume her citadels.

8.   And I will cut off the inhabitants from *Ashdod*,
And the one holding the scepter from *Ashkelon*,
And I will turn my hand against *Ekron*,
And the remnant of the *Philistines* will perish,
Says Adonai YHWH.

9.   Thus says YHWH,
For three transgressions of *Tyre* and for four I will not turn it back,
Because of their delivering up a whole population to *Edom*,
And they did not remember the covenant of their brothers.

10.   Thus I will send fire on the walls of *Tyre*,
And it will devour her citadels.

11.   Thus says YHWH,
For three transgressions of *Edom* and for four I will not turn it back,
Because of his pursuing his brother with the sword,
And he destroyed his allies.

And his anger tore continually,
And he kept his fury forever.
12.   I will send fire on Teman,
       And it will devour the citadels of Bozrah.

2.2. Textual Notes on Joel 4:4-8,14-21 and Amos 1:1-2,6-12

Joel 4:4: **a**-Tyre, and the remaining country names are attested in the versions. **b-b**The regions of Philistia, gives difficulty to the translators, but is present in the text. G changes to Galilee and V to Palestine. According to Josh 13:2f, this term means precisely those regions appearing in Amos 1:6-8. **c-c**This second half of the ה ... ואם question is a continuation of the first in synonymous parallelism with the object גמול assumed from the first half. See GK §150h, and literary discussion below.
Joel 4:16: **a-a**Doublet missing in Sinaiticus, but attested elsewhere.
Joel 4:17: **a**-G reads διελεύσονται, meaning "dispersed" or "broken up."
Joel 4:18: **a**-Doublet to Amos 9:13b. **b**-אֲפִיקֵי are the rivulets followed by brooks (*BDB*, 67).
Joel 4:19: **a-a**Intends violence done to the sons of Judah, not by them.
Joel 4:21: **a-a**וְנִקֵּיתִי דָמָם לֹא־נִקֵּיתִי. The piel נָקָה, to leave unpunished, is inconsistent with the context. It is often argued that G assumes different roots, נקם, "to avenge," for the first verb (ἐκδικήσω), but נקה with MT for the second (ἀθωώσω). V translates both from the same root נקם, "to avenge." In spite of problems, MT is preferred. G has problems translating the verb נקה when it is used twice: Exod 34:7; Num 14:18; Jer 30:11; Nah 1:3. In addition, G elsewhere translates נקה with ἐκδικήσω (Zech 5:3 [twice]). Other suggested translations: 1) The word derives from an Akkadian root meaning to "sacrifice, offer a libation"; 2) Emending the text; 3) The word is used here in the sense of "to empty" (cf Isa 3:26; see *ThWAT*, 592; Rudolph, *KAT* 13/2, 78); 4) The opening phrase is translated as a question ("shall I leave their blood unpunished?") followed by a denial ("I will not"). The first option would not fit the context, and the second option lacks textual support. The latter two options are textually possible and a decision must be made on literary grounds. Based on the literary discussion below, option #3 has been chosen here.
Amos 1:1: **a**-The first אשר refers to Amos, though G assumes "words" (οἳ ἐγένοντο). **b**-בְּנֹקְדִים. G reads as a place (νακκαριμ) reading ר for ד. Aquila, Symachus, and Theodotion confirm MT. **c**-The second אֲשֶׁר refers to דִבְרֵי. Other examples of חזה with דָּבָר in Mic 1:1 and Isa 2:1. **d**-G reads "Jerusalem" to correlate with 1:2.
Amos 1:6: **a-a**Literally "their exiling a complete exile."
Amos 1:11: **a**-רַחֲמָיו. For the covenantal background of this term, see Fishbane, *JBL* 91 (1972): 391-393; and Coote, *JBL* 90 (1971): 206-208.

2.3. Conclusions

The text of Joel 4:4-8,14-21 and Amos 1:1-2,6-12 confirms the presence of the *Stichwörter* in the versions, with the exception that Joel 4:16 is missing in one manuscript of G. In addition, G reads "Jerusalem" rather than "Israel" in Amos 1:1. It is possible that this deviation reflects the awareness of the *Stichwörter* connection to Joel, but it is more probable that G changed Amos 1:1 on the basis of 1:2. Another indication of the lack of awareness of the *Stichwörter* is the difficulty which both G and V have in translating "regions of Philistia."

3. Amos 9:1-15 and Obad 1-10

3.1. Translation of Amos 9:1-15 and Obad 1-10

Inescapability from YHWH and Eschatological Promise of Salvation

1. I saw Adonai standing upon the altar, and he said,
   Smite the capitals so that the threshholds shake.
   And break them on the heads of all of them,
   And those remaining[a] I will slay with the sword.
   The one fleeing will not flee to them[b],
   And the fugitive will not slip away to them.
2. *Though*[a] they dig into Sheol,
       from there my hand shall take them.
   And *though* they ascend to heaven,
       [b]*from there I will bring them down.*[b]
3. And *though* they hide on the summit of Carmel,
       from there I will *search*[a] and take them.
   And *though* they hide from before my eyes on the floor of the sea,
       from there I will command the serpent and it will bite them.
4. And *though* they go into captivity before their enemies,
       from there I will command the sword that it will slay them.
   And I have set my eyes upon them for evil and not for good.
5. And Adonai YHWH Sebaoth,
   The one touching the earth so that it melts,
   And all its inhabitants mourn,
   And all of it will rise up like the Nile,
   And it will subside like the Nile of Egypt;
6. The one building his stairs in the heavens,
   And (who) has founded his vaulted dome over the earth,
   The one calling out to the waters of the sea,
   And (who) will pour them out upon the face of the earth,
   YHWH is his name.
7. Are you not like the sons of Ethiopia to me, sons of Israel?
   Utterance of YHWH.
   Have I not brought Israel up from the land of Egypt,
       and the Philistines from Caphtor, and Aram from Kir?

8.   Behold the eyes of Adonai YHWH are upon this sinful kingdom,
       And I will destroy it from the face of the ground;
       Except that I will not utterly destroy the House of Jacob,
       Utterance of YHWH.

9.   For behold I am commanding;
       I will shake the house of Israel among all the nations,
              just as if it were shaken in a sieve,
       And[a] not a pebble will fall (to) the earth.

10.   All the sinners of my people will die by the sword —
              Those saying the evil will not draw near or confront us.

11.   *On that day*[a] I will raise up the [b]fallen booth[b] of David.
       And I will wall up their breaches[c],
       And I will raise his ruins[d],
       And I will build it like in the days of old,

12.   In order that they will possess[a] the remnant of *Edom*[b] and all the *nations*[c] over
              whom my name was called.
       Utterance of YHWH who is doing this.

13.   Behold the days are coming — utterance of YHWH —
       When the plowman[a] will draw near to the reaper[b],
              and the one treading grapes to the one sowing seed,
       And the *mountains*[c] will drip new wine,
       And all the hills will undulate.

14.   And I will restore the captivity of my people Israel,
       And they will build the ruined cities, and they will dwell (in them)[a],
       And plant vineyards and drink their wine,
       And make gardens and eat their fruit.

15.   And I will plant them upon their soil,
       And they will not be rooted up any longer from upon the soil which I gave to
       them,
       Says YHWH your God.[a]

Judgment on Edom

1.   The vision of Obadiah:
       Thus says Adonai YHWH concerning[a] *Edom*:
       We have heard[b] a report from YHWH,
       And a messenger[c] has been sent[d] among the *nations*.
       Rise up. Let us rise up against her[e] for battle.

2.   Behold I have made you small among the *nations*,
       You are greatly despised.

3.   Your insolent heart has deceived you,
       The one dwelling in the hiding places of the cliffs, the height of his dwelling[a],
       Saying in his heart[b]: "Who can bring me down to earth?"

4.   Though you build as high as the eagle,
       And *though* your nest [a]is placed among the *stars*,[a]
              from there I will bring you down — utterance of YHWH.

5.   If thieves came to you, or destroyers by night —

How you would be ruined —
Would they not take their sufficiency?
Or if grape gatherers came to you, would they not leave gleanings?

6. How Esau will be *sought out*[a].
His treasures will be sought out.

7. All the men of your covenant send you to the border.
The men of your peace[a] deceive you.
They overpower you.
Your bread[b] they make as a trap under you.
There is no understanding in him.

8. Surely[a] *on that day* — utterance of YHWH —
I will destroy the wise men from *Edom* and understanding from the *mountain* of Esau?

9. Your strong men will be terrified, Teman, in order that everyone will be cut off from the mountain of Esau because of the slaughter.[a]

10. Because of the violence[a] done to your brother Jacob you will be covered with shame, and you will be cut off forever.

3.2. Textual Notes for Amos 9:1-15 and Obad 1-10

Amos 9:1: **a**-וְאַחֲרִיתָם. Literally "their afterpart" refers to those who survive the breaking of the capitals on their head, thus synonymous with survivor. **b**-לָהֶם. The twice used phrase "to them" is often understood as reflexive and left untranslated, but it should correctly be understood as a reference to the the capitals and threshold which have been destroyed. Compare similar constructions: 2 Sam 18:17; 19:9.

Amos 9:2: **a**-The repetition of the אִם ... מִשָּׁם clauses are attested with only minor variations in Amos 9:2-4 and Obad 4 in both G and V. **b-b**This phrase appears here and Obad 4 in both G and V.

Amos 9:3: **a**-אֲחַפֵּשׂ. This verb is used here and Obad 6, and is attested in G (ἐξερευνάω) and by V (scrutor).

Amos 9:10: **a**-The waw is sometimes incorrectly translated adversatively, but such a translation misunderstands the sieve metaphor. See literary discussion.

Amos 9:11: **a**-בַּיּוֹם הַהוּא. G translates here ἐν τῇ ἡμέρᾳ ἐκείνῃ but changes word order in Obad 8 (ἐν ἐκείνῃ τῇ ἡμέρᾳ). V has "in die illo" here and the more specific "in die illa" in Obad 8 (see Karl Ernst Georges, *Ausführliches lateinisch-deutsches Handwörterbuch*, vol 1 [Basel: Benno Schwabe, [9]1951], col. 2142-2143). These insignificant differences indicate lack of awareness of the *Stichwort* connections. **b-b**סֻכַּת. MT pointing presumes a singular noun, but the context presents a confusing array of suffixes. The versions offer no help text-critically, since G, S, and V harmonize MT suffixes in the second half of the verse (see text notes 'c'and 'd'). See literary discussion, below. **c**-פִּרְצֵיהֶן. G uses 3fs suffix to harmonize, while MT has 3fp, intending סכת as plural. S has 3mp; V has neuter singular. The three different suffixes make MT the *lectio difficilior*. **d**-וַהֲרִסֹתָיו. G harmonizes with 3fs suffix; MT has 3ms; V reads as a verb; S has 3mp.

Amos 9:12: **a**-יִירְשׁוּ. G translates ἐκζητήσωσιν supposing יִדְרְשׁוּ. **b**-אֱדוֹם. G translates τῶν ἀνθρώπων supposing אָדָם. This eliminates the *Stichwort* connection to "Edom" in Obad 1. V confirms MT, but is also unaware of *Stichwort*, translating "idumae" here (indicating the people of Edom) and "Edom" in Obadiah. c-הַגּוֹיִם. G uses ἔθνη here and Obad 2. V uses "nationes" here but "genitibus" in Obad 2.

Amos 9:13: a-חוֹרֵשׁ. G (ἀλοητὸς), supposing דָּיִשׁ (that which is threshed) represents a deliberate change (perhaps on the basis of Lev 26:5). b-בַּקֹּצֵר. G (τρύγητου) supposes בָּצִיר which is the "vintage" and not the person reaping the grain. This represents a deliberate change, (cf. also Lev 26:5). c-הֶהָרִים. G and V use the same word here and in Obad 9. d-תִּתְמוֹגַגְנָה. The use of מוג in the hithpael refers to the the image of the vines blowing in the wind, hence "undulations" (Paul Joüon, "Notes de Lexicographie Hebraique," *Bib* 7 [1926]: 167).

Amos 9:14: a-The phrase "in them" is assumed to complete the thought.

Amos 9:15: a-אֱלֹהֶיךָ. G omits the suffix and adds παντοκράτωρ (supposing צְבָאוֹת). G also adds צְבָאוֹת to MT in 5:8 and 9:6.

Obad 1: a-לֶאֱדוֹם. The לְ (here "concerning") is unique to prophetic superscriptions, but coincides with the *Vorlage* in Jer 49:7. b-שְׁמַעְנוּ. G follows the 1cs of Jer 49:14, but follows MT with the 1cp in Obad 1b. c-צִיר. G translates "message," (περιοχήν) and not "messenger." In G, the accusative parallels ἀκοήν. d-חשֻׁלַּח. G reads שָׁלַח as active, supposing YHWH as the subject. e-עָלֶיהָ. Only here is "Edom" feminine in Obadiah. Other feminine occurrences of Edom are Jer 49:14,17; Ezek 25:13; 32:29; 35:15; Mal 1:4.

Obad 3: a-שִׁבְתּוֹ. G harmonizes the change to the 3ms suffix, but V confirms MT. b-בִּלְבּוֹ. See note 3a.

Obad 4: a-aMissing in Jer 49:16 where nest (קִנֶּךָ) is the object of תַגְבִּיהַ. G and V support MT.

Obad 6: a-נֶחְפְּשׂוּ. G reads נֶחְפַּשׂ. MT assumes Esau as collective.

Obad 7: a-אַנְשֵׁי שְׁלֹמֶךָ. This is the subject of both הִשִּׁיאוּךָ and יָכְלוּ. b-לַחְמְךָ. G has omitted "your bread," but the presence of ἀρτόν in Aquila and Theodotion confirms MT. Many commentators suggest adding a י and repointing to make לֹחֲמֵיךָ (those eating your bread) parallel to the "men of your peace". Davies (*VT* 27 [1977]: 484-487) points out that elsewhere the verbal form לחם with a suffix requires the suffix as direct object, which is impossible here. His own suggestion of dittography is unconvincing. The solution offered here understands MT "your bread" as a parallel expression to "your covenant" and "your peace". Since the sealing a covenant could involve the ceremonial sharing of bread (cf Josh 9:11-14), this parallelism is understandable, and is preferred to emendation.

Obad 8: a-הֲלוֹא is here used emphatically meaning "surely."

Obad 9: a-מִקָּטֶל. The מ here has a causative force (cf. GK §119z). G understands with מֵחֲמַס in v. 10, but this ordering misses the parallelism of the two verses.

Obad 10: a-מֵחֲמַס. G, V, and Syriac versions have copulatives reading מִקָּטֶל from verse nine as part of this sentence.

3.3. Conclusions

The *Stichwort* connections are not known or not a concern to the translators of G and V. G translates בַּיּוֹם הַהוּא using different word orders and changes "Edom" to "mankind." V uses different forms of "dies," different words for "nation," and different understandings for Edom. Slight variations in the "if ... from there" clauses likewise indicate the translators made no special effort to accentuate or to mask the *Stichwort* connections.

4. Obad 15-21 and Mic 1:1-7

4.1. Translation of Obad 15-21 and Mic 1:1-7

Supremacy of Zion

15. For the day of YHWH is near to all nations.
    Just as you have done it will be done to you.
    Your dealing will return on your head.
16. Just as you drank[a] on my holy *mountain*,[b]
    All the nations will drink continually.[c]
    They will drink and swallow[d],
    And become as though they had not been.
17. But on the *mountain* of Zion there will be fugitives,
    And it will be holy,
    And the house of *Jacob* will possess their possessions.[b]
18. And the house of *Jacob* will be a *fire*[a],
    And the house of Joseph a flame,
    And the house of Esau for stubble
    And they will burn among them and devour them,
    And there will not be a survivor to the house of Esau,
        for YHWH has spoken.
19. And the Negev will possess[a] the *mountain* of Esau,
    And the Shephelah the Philistines,
    And they will possess the *field*[b] of Ephraim and the *field of Samaria*[c]
    And Benjamin (will possess) Gilead.
20. And the exiles of this rampart[a] belonging to the sons of Israel,
        who (are among)[b] the Canaanites to Zarephath,
    And the exiles of Jerusalem who are in Sepharad —
    They will possess the cities of the Negev.
21. And the deliverers[a] will go up on the *mountain* of Zion to judge the *mountain* of Esau,
    And the kingdom will belong to YHWH.

Reason for Punishment

1. The word of YHWH which came to Micah of Moresheth, in the days of Jotham, Ahaz, Hezekiah, kings of of Judah, which he saw concerning *Samaria* and Jerusalem.
2. Listen, peoples, all of them;
   Attend, earth and everything in it;

> Let Adonai YHWH be against you as a witness,
> Adonai from his holy temple.
3. For behold YHWH going forth from his place,
   and he has descended and tread on the high places of the earth.
4. The *mountains* melt beneath him,
   And the lowlands burst open like wax before the *fire*,
   Like water pouring down the slope.
5. For the rebellion of *Jacob* is all of this,
   And for the sins of the house of Israel.
   What is the rebellion of *Jacob*? Is it not *Samaria*?
   And what are the high places of Judah? Is it not Jerusalem?
6. And I will make *Samaria* into a heap of ruins of the *field*,
   Into a planting place for a vineyard.
   And I will hurl down her stones to the valley,
   And her foundations I will make bare.
7. And all her idols will be destroyed,
   And all her earnings will be burned in the *fire*,
   And all her images I will make a desolation,
   Because she has gathered the earnings of a harlot,
   And to the earnings of a harlot they will return.

4.2. Textual Notes for Obad 15a,16-21

Obad 16: **a**-שְׁתִיתֶם. G and V use singular to harmonize with 15b. **b**-הַר. G uses ὄρος and V uses "monte" in every instance in these two passages. Also G adds ὄρος in Obad 19. **c**-תָּמִיד. G frequently translates οἶνον (wine) presuming תִּירוֹשׁ (Hos 2:10,24; 7:14; 9:2; Mic 6:15; Joel 1:10; 2:19,24; Hag 1:11; Zech 9:17). Many mss read סָבִיב on the basis of Jer 25:15. **d**-וְלָעוּ. Hapaxlegomenon which G incorrectly translates καταβήσονται while several mss have ἀναβήσονται supposing וְעָלוּ.

Obad 17: **a**-בֵּית יַעֲקוֹב. The collective here uses a plural verb contra V. 18 Where "house of Jacob" takes the singular, because the verb הָיָה requires agreement between "house of Jacob" and "fire" which is never used in the plural. "House of Jacob" is attested in G and V. **b**-מוֹרָשֵׁיהֶם. MT reads "their possessions." G, V, and T understand the "ones possessing them" (מוֹרִשֵׁיהֶם). MT is followed here on the basis of Ezek 35:10.

Obad 18: **a**-אֵשׁ. G uses πῦρ here and Mic 1:4,7. V uses "ignis."

Obad 19: **a**-יִרְשׁוּ. The subject is Negev and Shephelah. The syntax parallels "and Benjamin (shall possess) Gilead." **b**-שְׂדֵה. G reads ὄρος, as parallel with "mountain of Esau" in this verse. **c**-"Field of Samaria" is attested in G and V.

Obad 20: **a**-הַחֵל הַזֶּה. Literally, "this fortress," is often assumed to have no clear antecedent. Duhm ("Anmerkungen zu dem Zwölfpropheten III," *ZAW* 31 [1911]: 178) suggests emending to חֵלָח זֶה, where the exiled Israelites were taken north of Nineveh (2 Kgs 17:6; 18:11). G read MT הַחֵל as "this power" (ἡ ἀρχὴ αὕτη), and V as "this army" (exercitus huius), both assuming חַיִל. MT followed here, see literary discussion. **b**-MT needs a verb to be comprehensible. היה is here assumed with preposition בְּ. See literary discussion.

Obad 21: **a**-מֹשִׁעִים. G reads מְשַׁעִים (ἄνδρες σεσωσμένοι). Symmachus supports the MT (σώζοντες).

For text analysis of **Mic 1:1-7** see below, beginning page 35.

4.3. Conclusions

A study of the text of this unit indicates the *Stichwörter* connection was present between these two writings. However, there appears to be no deliberate concern to preserve a known phenomenon on the part of the translators, hence the addition of "mountain" for "field" in Obad 19 by G.

5. Obad 11-14,15b and Jonah 1:1-8

5.1. Translation of Obad 11-14,15b and Jonah 1:1-8

Crimes of Edom

11. On the day of your standing far off,
     On the day of the strangers taking captive his wealth,
     When foreigners entered his gate,[a] and they [b]*cast lots*[b] for Jerusalem,
     Moreover, you were like one of them.
12. And you should not[a] look on the day of your brother, on the day of his misfortune.
     And you should not rejoice concerning the sons of Judah on the day of their destruction.
     You should not make your mouth great on the day of his distress.
13. You should not enter the gate[a] of my people on the day of their calamity,[b]
     And moreover, you will not look on *his evil*[c] on the day of his calamity.
     And you will not send away[d] his wealth on the day of his calamity.
14. And you should not stand in the fork of the road to cut down his fugitives;
     And you should not imprison his survivors on the day of distress.
15b Even as you have done it will be done to you.
     Your dealing will return on your head.

The flight of Jonah

1. And the word of YHWH came to Jonah, son of Amittai saying:
2. "Arise, go to Nineveh the great city and proclaim unto her that *their evil*[a] has come up before me.
3. And Jonah rose to flee toward Tarshish from before YHWH, and he went down to Joppa and found a ship going to Tarshish, and he paid his fare, and he descended in it to go with them toward Tarshish from before YHWH.
4. And YHWH hurled a great wind to the sea and there was a great storm on the sea and the ship was about to be broken up.

5.   Then the sailors became afraid and every man cried to his god, and they threw the
      cargo which was in the ship into the sea to lighten it from them. But Jonah had gone
      below into the hold of the ship and lain down and fallen asleep.

6.   And the chief of the sailors approached him and said to him "why are you sleeping?
      Arise, call out to your god. Perhaps the Elohim will give a thought to us and we will
      not perish".

7.   And each man said to his neighbor, "Come, let us *cast lots* in order that we may know
      on whose account[a] *this evil* has struck us." And they *cast lots* and the *lot fell* on Jonah.

8.   And they said to him, [a]"Tell us please on whose account *this evil* has come to us?[a]
      What is your occupation? And where do you come from? What is your country? And
      what people are you?"

5.2. Textual Notes for Obad 11-14, 15b and Jonah 1:1-8

Obad 11: a-שְׁעָרָו. The Qere plural of MT is incorrect. G has plural here, but elsewhere
inconsistently uses plural (Amos 5:10,12,15) or singular (Zeph 1:10; Zech 14:10). V has
plural in 11 (portas) and singular in 13 (portam). Q confirms MT. b-bG translates
κλήρους and a form of βάλλω, and V translates "sortes" with "mittere" here and in Jonah
1:7, not distinguishing between the verbs in Obadiah (ידד) and Jonah (נפל).

Obad 12: a-The negative command using the jussive (cf. GK §109e).

Obad 13: a-בְּשַׁעַר. Singular here has no Qere. b-אֵידָם. G translates πόνων αὐτῶν
presupposing אוֹנוֹ. אֵיד is here used three times with different translations by G, indicating
deliberate change. V translates the last two the same. c-בְּרָע תוֹ. G translates עוֹ
συναγωγὴν αὐτῶν presupposing בַּעֲדָתָם, meaning the *Stichwort* is missing. V confirms
MT (in malis eius) but repoints as plural בְּרָע תוֹ, a form unattested. d-תִשְׁלַחְנָה. The 2fp
suffix is foreign to Obadiah. G, T (תִשְׁלַח יָדְךָ), and V use 2ms. Carl Keller (*CAT* 11b,
258) and others have suggested נָה is a form of the particle נָא, but such a spelling is
elsewhere unknown. The variant is here accepted.

Jonah 1:2: a-רָעָתָם. G adds κραυγὴ, "cry," and harmonizes the 3mp suffix to 3fs.

Jonah 1:7: a-בְּשֶׁלְמִי. "On whose account" is composed of four elements; the preposition בְּ;
the שֶׁ for אֲשֶׁר; the preposition לְ; and the interrogative מִי. The full spelling is found in
1:8.

Jonah 1:8: a-aThis question is unnecessary, having been decided by the casting of the lots
in 1:7. The phrase is missing in several Hebrew and Greek mss. The question of whether
it is missing because it was deleted as unnecessary, or whether it was added to certain mss.,
perhaps as a marginal note to explain the unusual form בְּשֶׁלְמִי (Wolff, *BK* 14/3, 83), is
difficult. The Greek mss. from which it is missing (B-S-V) go back to a common source
(Ziegler, *Septuaginta* [Göttingen: Vandenhoeck und Ruprecht, [2]1967], 39), making it more
likely that the phrase was deleted as redundant from these than that it could have been
incorporated into so many others. This, with its presence in V, means that this phrase,
although unnecessaary, was part of the *Vorlage*. See literary discussion.

5.3. Conclusions

The Septuagint was either unaware or unconcerned with the *Stichwörter* in these passages. It omits the reference to "wickedness" in Obad 11, but translates the phrase "to cast lots" with the same verb in spite of the two different verbs used in MT. V follows MT in all the *Stichwörter*, and likewise translates the same verb for "cast" in Obad and Jonah. The question in Jonah 1:8 with the *Stichwort* "evil" is missing in several manuscripts, apparently deleted as unnecessary.

6. Jonah 2:2-10 and Mic 1:1-7

6.1. Translation of Jonah 2:2-10 and Mic 1:1-7

Hymn of Thanksgiving

2. And Jonah prayed to YHWH his god, from the belly of the fish.
3. And he said:
    I called out from my distress to YHWH and he answered me.
    From the depth of Sheol I cried for help.
    You heard my voice.
4. And you cast me into the deep[a] in the heart of the seas and a river round about me.
    All your breakers and your waves passed over me.
5. And I said,
    I have been driven out from before your sight,
    However, I will again look to *your holy temple*.[a]
6. *Water*[a] encompassed me to the point of life,[b]
    The deep surrounded me, weeds wrapped around my head.
7. To the [a]base of the *mountains*[ab] *I descended*.[c]
    The *earth*,[d] its bars were around me forever.
    But you caused my life to ascend from the pit, YHWH my god.
8. In the fainting away of my life, I remembered YHWH,
    And my prayer went to you, to *your holy temple*.
9. The ones keeping the vain *idols*[a] forsake their faithfulness.
10. But I will sacrifice to you with a voice of thanksgiving,
    That which I have vowed I will pay.
    Salvation is from YHWH.

Reason for Punishment

1. The word of YHWH which came to Micah of Moresheth, in the days of Jotham, Ahaz, Hezekiah, kings of Judah, which he saw concerning Samaria and Jerusalem.
2. Listen,[a] peoples all of them[b].

Attend, *earth* and everything in it.[c]
That Adonai YHWH be against you as a witness,
Adonai from *his holy temple*.

3. For behold YHWH going forth from his place,
    And he has *descended* and tread[a] on the high places of the *earth*.
4. The *mountains* melt[a] beneath him,
    And the lowlands burst open like wax before the fire,
    like *water* pouring down the slope.
5. For the rebellion of Jacob is all of this,
    And for the sins of the house of Israel.
    What[a] is the rebellion of Jacob? Is it not Samaria?
    And what are the high places[b] of Judah? Is it not Jerusalem?
6. And I will make Samaria into a heap of ruins[a] of the field,
    Into a planting place for a vineyard.
    And I will hurl down her stones to the valley,
    And her foundations I will make bare.
7. And all her *idols* will be destroyed,
    And all her earnings of harlotry will be burned in the fire,
    And all her images I will make a desolation,
    Because she has gathered[a] from the earnings of a harlot,
    And to the earnings of a harlot they will return.

6.2. Textual Notes for Jonah 2:2-10 and Mic 1:1-7

Jonah 2:4: **a-**מְצוּלָה. The "depth" is a secondary explanation of "in the heart of the seas" which interrupts the rhythm and lacks the expected preposition בְּ.

Jonah 2:5: **a-**הֵיכַל קָדְשֶׁךָ. G translates הֵיכַל as ναός here but in Mic 1:2 uses οἶκος. V uses "templum" for both.

Jonah 2:6: **a-**מַיִם. G uses ὕδος here and in Mic 1:4. V uses "aqua" in both. **b-**עַד נֶפֶשׁ. "Unto the soul" connotes a threat to life.

Jonah 2:7: **a-**לְקִצְבֵי הָרִים. G understands with 2:6. **b-**הָרִים. G translates "mountain" with ὄρος here and in Mic 1:4. V uses "mons" in both. **c-**יָרַדְתִּי. G uses καταβαίνω here and in Mic 1:3. V uses "descendere" for both. **d-**הָאָרֶץ. G uses γῆ here and in Mic 1:2,3. V uses "terra" in all three.

Jonah 2:9: **a-**הַבְלֵי שָׁוְא. Synonymous with "idols" (פְּסִילִים) in Mic 1:7. G uses μάταια καὶ ψευδῆ here and γλυπτὰ in Mic 1:7. V uses "vanitates frustra" in Jonah 2:9 and "sculptilia" in Mic 1:7.

Mic 1:2: **a-**G inserts λόγους to refer to 1:1. V supports MT. **b-**כֻּלָּם. Here means "all together" (*GK* §135r). **c-**מְלֹאָהּ. Vollers' suggestion ("Das Dodekapropheton der Alexandriner," *ZAW* 4 [1884]:2) that G read this as מְלָאִים ignores the fact that G translates ἐν αὐτῇ corresponding to מְלֹאָהּ.

Mic 1:3: **a-**וְדָרַךְ. Missing in 1QpMi. Lescow ("Redaktionsgeschichtliche Analyse von Micha 1-5," *ZAW* 84 [1972]: 54) argues וְדָרַךְ was added on the basis of Deut 33:29 and Amos 4:13.

Mic 1:4: **a-**נָמַסּוּ. G translates σαλευθήσεται (to be shaken) which apparently reads נָמוֹטוּ or נָמוֹגוּ. The lacuna in Q calls for four letters, supporting MT.

Mic 1:5: a-מִי. 1QpMi reads מה but G supports MT as the lectio difficilior. b-בָּמוֹת. G has
ἁμαρτία and adds οἴκου to standardize the references.
Mic 1:6: a-לְעִי. G has ὀπωραφυλάκιον meaning "gardener's hut," but another text cannot
be reconstructed.
Mic 1:7: a-קִבְּצָה. Syriac and V suppose קִבָּצוּ. G confirms MT.

6.3. Conclusions

An analysis of the textual evidence above, with regard to the
Stichwörter between Jonah and Micah, indicates the translators were
unaware or unconcerned with the presence of connecting links between the
writings. One reaches this conclusion from the use of different words for
"temple" by G (Jonah 2:5,8 and Mic 1:2). The Vulgate uses the same word
for all the *Stichwörter* in both writings, with only minor syntactical changes.
It is also unlikely that the Vulgate translators were aware of the *Stichwörter*
connections because they did not make an effort to translate the
synonymous phrases in Jonah 2:9 and Mic 1:7 in a manner more readily
showing the correlation.

7. Mic 7:8-20 and Nah 1:1-8

7.1. Translation of Mic 7:8-20 and Nah 1:1-8

Salvation from the Enemy

8.   Do not rejoice over me *my enemy*.[a]
        Though I have fallen, I will rise.
        Though I will dwell in *darkness*, YHWH is a light to me.
9.   I will bear the raging of YHWH, because I have sinned against him,
        Until he pleads my case and does my judgment,
        He will lead me forth to light.
        I will see his righteousness.
10.   And *my enemy* will see and shame will cover her,
        The one saying to me, "Where is YHWH your god?"
        My eyes will look on her.
        Then she will be a trampling, like mud in the streets.
11.   [a]A *day* for building your walls is that *day*.
        The boundary becomes distant that *day*.[a]
12.   And he will come to you[a] from Assyria and the cities[b] of Egypt,
            and from Egypt and to the *river*[c]

and ^dfrom *sea* to *sea* and from ***mountain*** to ***mountain***.^d

13. And the *land*^a will become a desolation because of its ***inhabitants***^b on account of the fruit of their deeds.

14. Shepherd your people with your staff,
The flock of your possession,
The one dwelling alone, a forest in the midst of ***Carmel***.^a
Let ***Bashan***^a and Gilead feed like the *days* of old,

15. Like the *days* of your going out from the *land*^a of Egypt.
I will show him^b extraordinary things.

16. The nations will see and be ashamed of all their strength.
They will place hand on mouth.
Their ears will be silent.

17. They will lick the *dust*^a like the snake.
Like the serpents of the ***earth*** they will come trembling out of their fortresses.
To YHWH our god they will come dreading,
And they will fear before you.

18. Who is a god like you, bearing iniquity and ***passing over***^a the transgression to the remnant of his possession?
He does not strengthen^b his ***anger***^c forever,
For he delights in mercy.

19. He will return^a his compassion on us.
He will subdue our iniquity.
And you will cast^b all their sins^c into the depths of the sea.

20. You will give truth to Jacob, mercy to Abraham,
Which you swore to our fathers from *days* before.

Judgment against Nineveh

1. The oracle of Nineveh.
The book of the vision of Nahum, the Elkoshite.

2. A God jealous and avenging is YHWH.
YHWH is avenging^a and lord of rage.
YHWH is avenging to his adversaries and waiting for his ***enemies***.

3. YHWH is slow of ***anger*** but great of strength
And YHWH will not leave unpunished.
In the whirlwind and in the storm is his way,
And the clouds are the *dust* of his feet.

4. The one rebuking the *sea*,^a he dries it up,
And all the ***rivers*** he causes to dry up.
Bashan and ***Carmel*** grow weak,^b
And the sprout of Lebanon grows weak.

5. ***Mountains*** quake before him,
And the hills melt,
And the *land* is lifted up before him,
And the world and all the ***inhabitants*** in it.

6. Who will stand before^a his indignation?
And who will rise with the burning of his ***anger***?

His wrath is poured out like fire,
And rocks are broken down before him.
7.   YHWH is good, a refuge[a] in the *day* of trouble.
The one who knows him seeks refuge in him.
8.   [a]And in the flood he is *passing over*.[a]
He will make a complete end of his high places
And *his enemies* he will pursue in *darkness*.

7.2. Textual Notes for Mic 7:8-20 and Nah 1:1-8

Mic 7:8: **a-אֹיַבְתִּי**. G translates ἐχθρά and the appropriate pronoun in Mic 7:8, 10; Nah 1:2,8, and V uses "inimicus."

Mic 7:11: **a-a**The use of the "that day" three times strains the syntax. This reading changes only the word order, following the suggestion of G which does not bind the third יוֹם הוּא syntactically to verse 12. The syntactical division into one nominal sentence (יוֹם הַהוּא יוֹם לִבְנוֹת גְּדֵרָיִךְ) paralleled by a verbal sentence (יִרְחַק־חֹק יוֹם הוּא) not only reads smoother, it solves two minor grammatical problems. First, this reading explains the presence of the article ה in the second "that day" phrase (הַהוּא). The article accents the second use of "that day". Second, by reading the third "that day" with 7:11, and not with 7:12, the *waw* with וְעָדֶיךָ in 7:12 functions normally as the introduction of a new sentence. One is not forced to postulate an unlikely grammatical formulation (so Wolff, *BK* 14/4, 188, text note 11c) or to omit or ignore the conjunction (so Willi-Plein, 107; Allen, 391).

Mic 7:12: **a-וְעָדֶיךָ**. MT incorrectly points 2ms suffix when 2fs is expected from 7:11. **b-וְעָרֵי**. Some commentators suggest reading ד instead of ר to smoothe the syntax, but G (πόλεις) confirms MT. **c-נָהָר**. G uses ποταμοῦ here and Nah 1:4. V uses "flumen" here and Nah 1:4. **d-וְיָם מִיָּם וְהַר הָהָר**. G translates ὕδατος καὶ θορύβου (day of water and clamor). G has read MT, but incorrectly read יָם as day; מַיִם as water; and וְהַר הָהָר as תְּרוּעָה. The latter involves liberty with MT. Many mss do translate with θάλασσα and ὄρος; and V uses "mare" and "mons," confirming MT.

Mic 7:13: **a-אֶרֶץ**. G uses γη and V uses "terra" in Mic 7:13,15,17 and Nah 1:5. **b-יֹשְׁבֶיהָ**. G uses κατοικέω here and Nah 1:5.

Mic 7:14: **a**-Carmel and Bashan appear in G and V here and Nah 1:4.

Mic 7:15: **a-אֶרֶץ**. G shortens "land of Egypt" to Egypt. **b-אַרְאֶנּוּ**. "I will show him," assumes YHWH as new speaker, and utilizes 3ms referent of the suffix, apparently with עַם (7:14) as the antecedent. G changes to 2mp, but V (ostendam ei mirabilia) confirms MT. For the suffix see also Ps 50:23 in hiphil, and Num 23:9; 24:17; Jer 23:24; Gen 45:28 in Qal.

Mic 7:17: **a-עָפָר**. Synonymous with אָבָק in Nah 1:3. G uses χοῦν here and κονιορτός in Nah 1:3, while V uses "pulvis" in both.

Mic 7:18: **a-עֹבֵר**. G translates ὑπερβαίνω here and πορείας in Nah 1:8. V uses "transis" here and "practereunte" in Nah 1:8. **b-לָעַד**. G (εἰς μαρτύριον) assumes לְעֵד. **c-אַפּוֹ**. G translates ὀργή here and Nah 1:6, and G translates זַעְמוֹ with ὀργή. But in Nah 1:3 G translates אֶרֶךְ אַפַּיִם idiomatically as μακρόθυμος (patient). V uses "furorem" here, but "patiens" in Nah 1:3 and "in ira furoris" in Nah 1:6.

Mic 7:19: **a-שׁוּב** here means "again" (*GK* §120g). **b-תַּשְׁלִיךְ**. G, V, Syriac, and T harmonize with 3ms. The address change in 7:20, to the second person address to god, and the future translation used by G, argue for 2ms. **c-חַטֹּאותָם**. *BHS* suggests reading חַטֹּאתֵנוּ on the basis of G,V, and Syriac. Graphically, the confusion of נו and ם is possible, but the ם stands out in the context so dramatically that it must be considered the *lectio difficilior*, and it is thus more likely that G, V and Syriac harmonize as "our sins."

Nah 1:2: **a-**נְקֶם יְהֹוָה. Missing in G through haplography.
Nah 1:4: **a-**יָם. G translates θάλασσα,and V uses "mare." **b-**אֻמְלָל. The presence of אֻמְלָל breaks the acrostic, leading to the argument that דָּלְלוּ was original. However, G never translates דלל with ὀλιγοῦν, but does use ὀλιγοῦν with אֻמְלָל (Joel 1:10,12). The second verb, ἐξέλιπεν, does not necessarily imply another text, since it can be used for אמל (cf. Isa 38:14). V likewise uses two different words ("infirmatus" and "elanguit") but this likely relates to the two different subjects. Some (e.g. Christensen, *Transformations of the War Oracle*, 168f) have suggested the verb was originally דאב, but it is difficult to perceive how these consonants could have been confused with אמלל, and it could not easily explain the reading in G.
Nah 1:5: **a-**הָרִים. G uses ὄρος and V uses "mons." Compare 7:12d.
Nah 1:6: **a-**לִפְנֵי. Breaks the acrostic. Compare literary discussion.
Nah 1:7: **a-**לְמָעוֹז. G has τοῖς ὑπομενουσιω αὐτὸν (the ones waiting for him) reading לְמִקְנָיו. V translates "confortans," confirming MT.
Nah 1:8: **a-a**Must be read with the preceding line to complete the acrostic, creating literary problems (see below).

7.3. Conclusions

The translators of G and V were not aware of the *Stichwort* connections. They translate the same Hebrew words differently (7:12d,18a,18c). Further analysis in these passages reveals no systematic attempt to hide the *Stichwort* connections (compare common translations for "anger" added by G: 7:18c).

8. Nah 3:1-19 and Hab 1:1-17

8.1. Translation of Nah 3:1-19 and Hab 1:1-17

Nineveh's Imminent Destruction

1.   Woe to the bloody city,
       All of it is full of lying and plunder.
       The prey will not depart.
2.   The sound of the whip and the sound of the shaking of the wheel,
       And the *horse*[a] dashing and the chariot skipping about,
3.   *Horsemen*[a] ascending,

And the flame of the sword and the lightning of the spear,
And a multitude of *slain*[b] and the corpses are numerous,
There is no end to the dead bodies,
And they will stumble over the dead bodies

4. Because of the multitude of the harlotry of the harlot,
The pleasant one of favor, the mistress of sorcery,
The one selling *nations*[a] by her harlotry and clans by her sorcery.

5. Behold I am against you says YHWH Sebaoth.
I will uncover your skirt over your face,
And I will show *nations* your private part and kingdoms your dishonor

6. And I will throw filth on you,
And I will treat you as a fool,
And I will make you like a spectacle.

7. And it will be that each one who *sees*[a] you will retreat from you, and will say,
"Nineveh is devastated, who will lament for her?"
From where shall I seek comforters for you?

8. Are you better than Thebes,
The one dwelling by the streams, water surrounding her,
Whose *fortress*[a] was the sea, from the *sea*[b] was her wall?

9. Cush was her *might*, and Egypt, and there was no end,
Put and Lubim were her[a] assistance.

10. Indeed, she went to exile in *captivity*,[a]
Indeed, her children were dashed in pieces at the head of every street,
And they cast lots over her honorable men,
And her great men were bound with fetters

11. Indeed, you will become drunk.
You will become hidden,
Indeed, you will seek refuge from the enemy.

12. All your *fortifications*[a] are fig trees [b]with first-fruits.[b]
If they are shaken, then they fall into the mouth of the *devourer*.[c]

13. Behold your *people* are women in your midst.
The gates of your land are opened wide to your enemies.
Fire consumes your gate bars.

14. Draw for yourself water for the siege.
Strengthen[a] your *fortifications*.
Go into the mud and trample in the clay,
Take hold of the brick mold.

15. There fire will *devour* you.
The sword will cut you down.
It will *devour* you like the creeping locust.
Make yourself numerous like the creeping locust.
Make yourself numerous like the swarming locust.

16. You have multiplied your traders more than the stars of the heavens.
The creeping locust strips off and then will *fly*[a] away.

17. Your guardsmen are like the swarming locust
And your marshals like *hordes*[a] of grasshoppers,
The ones encamping on your walls on a cold day,

The sun rises and he flees,
And his *dreadful*[b] *place*[c] is not known.

18.   *King*[a] of Assyria, your *shepherds*[b] grow drowsy.
Your nobles are lying down.
Your *people* are *scattered*[c] upon the mountains,
And there is not one who gathers together.

19.   There is no relief for your breakdown,
Your wound is diseased.
All those hearing report of you clap hands about you,
For upon whom has your *evil*[a] not *continually*[b] passed over?

Delay of Punishment of the Wicked

1.   The oracle which Habakkuk the prophet saw.

2.   How long YHWH will I call for help and you will not hear?
I cry out 'violence' to you but you do not deliver.

3.   Why do you make me *see* iniquity and regard trouble?
And destruction and violence are before me.
And there is strife,[a] and contention raises up.

4.   Therefore the law grows numb,
And justice does not go forth forever,
For the wicked surround the righteous.
Therefore justice comes out perverted.

5.   Look among the *nations*.[a]
Observe, marvel, be astonished,[b]
Because a work is working[c] in your days —
That you would not believe if you were told.

6.   For behold I am about to raise the Chaldeans,[a]
That bitter and hasty *nation*,
The one going to the expanses of the earth to seize dwelling *places* which do not belong to him.

7.   He is *dreadful* and feared.
From himself goes forth his justice and his uprising.

8.   His *horses* are swifter[b] than leopards,
And keener than wolves in the evening.[b]
His horsemen[c] *gallop*, and *his horsemen* come from afar.
He will *fly* like the eagle to *devour* swiftly.

9.   All of them[a] come for violence.
The *horde*[b] of their faces moves forward.
He collects *captives* like sand.

10.   He mocks[a] at *kings*, and *rulers* are a laughing matter to him.
He laughs at every *fortress*,
He heaps up dust and then captures it.

11.   Then he will sweep through like the wind and pass on,
But he will become guilty,[a]
He whose *strength* is his god.

12.   Truly you are from everlasting YHWH, my god, my holy one.

We will not die.

You, YHWH, have set him to judge.

You have decreed him a rock to correct.

13. Too pure of eyes to *see evil*,[a] and you are not able to look on trouble.

Why do you look on the ones dealing treacherously,

Become silent when the wicked swallows one more righteous than he?

14. And have you made man like the fish of the *sea*,

Like creeping things with no ruler over him?

15. All of them he brings up with a hook,

And he drags him away in his net,

And then he gathers him with his fishing net.

Therefore he will rejoice and be glad.

16. Therefore he will sacrifice to his net,

And he will burn insense to his fishing net,

Because in these his portion grows robust,

And his food becomes fat.

17. Will he therefore empty his net,

Indeed, *continually* to *slay nations* without sparing?

8.2. Textual Notes for Nah 3:1-19 and Hab 1:1-17

Nah 3:2: **a-**וסוס. G uses ἵππος here and in Hab 1:8. V uses "equus" in both places.

Nah 3:3: **a-**פָּרָשׁ. G has ἱππέως here and Hab 1:8. However, the two occurrences of פרשׁ in Hab 1:8 have been simplified to one in G. V uses "gladii" in Nah 3:3 and "equites" twice in Hab 1:8. **b-**חָלָל. G uses τραυματιῶν here and αποκτέννειν for the synonym, הרג, in Hab 1:17. V uses "interfectio" in both.

Nah 3:4: **a-**גּוֹיִם. G and V confirm the presence of nation here, Nah 3:13,18, and Hab 1:6,17, although slightly different words appear in some instances. V lacks reference to nations in Nah 3:5, and G reads MT in Hab 1:5 differently (see text note 1:5a).

Nah 3:7: **a-**אַיִךְ ר. The presence of ראה in various forms is attested by G and V both here and in Hab 1:3, although both use synonymns to reflect the sytactical variation of the passages.

Nah 3:8: **a-**חֵיל. G (ἀρψη = dominion) and V (Divitiae = riches) have difficulty associating "fortress" with the sea in this verse, but the parallelism and the metaphor argue for the priority of MT. This word is thus synonymous with the use of "fortifications" in 3:12 (see text note 3:12a). **b-**מַיִם. Following G, the versions translate the consonants as "water," which makes sense, but does not do full justice to the extended metaphor. See literary discussion.

Nah 3:9: **a-**Here read with G and Syriac. MT has your (2fs), but the 2fs would have to refer to Nineveh in this passage, not to Thebes, and there is no historical verification for Assyria having received such assistance. Also, such a reading would run counter to the tenor of the passage, which is speaking of the might of Thebes.

Nah 3:10: **a-**בַּשְּׁבִי. While "captivity" here captures the meaning, "captive" fits the context in Hab 1:9. Accordingly G uses two different words built from the same root (αἰχμάλωτος, αἰχμαλωσία), whereas V uses only "captivitatem."

Nah 3:12: **a-**מִבְצָרַיִךְ. G uses ὀχύρωμα here, 3:14, and Hab 1:10. V uses "munitiones" in all three places. **b-b**In light of Hos 9:10, where G uses σκοπός (watcher) for "first fruit," there is no need to change MT as Elliger (in BHS) suggests. **c-**אֹוכֵל. The root אכל is confirmed in G and V here, 3:15 (twice), and Hab 1:8.

Nah 3:14: **a-**חַזְקִי. The verb here has a nominal synonymn (כֹּחַ) in Hab 1:11, confirmed by all versions, though they use different words.

Nah 3:16: **a-**וַיָּעֹף. G and V use varying forms of "fly" here and in Hab 1:8 on the basis of the animal flying, but nevertheless confirm the verb's presence in both verses.

Nah 3:17: **a-**כָּאַרְבֶּה. Locust hordes are intended, making this word a thematic synonym with מְנַמַת in Hab 1:9. G uses ἀττέλοβος here and ἄνθεστηκότος in Hab 1:9. V uses "lucustae" here and "urens" in Hab 1:9. **b-**אַיֵּם in MT, but read אַיֵּם as in Hab 1:7. MT is highly unlikely: "its (ms) place where they (mpl) are." V agrees with MT, but it translates all the singular references in the verse as plural. G (οὐαὶ αὐτοῖς) confirms the MT consonants, but reads the interjection אִי with a 3mp suffix, hence "woe to them." This also does not fit the context well. The syntactical and linguistic problem is solved with the suggested change to the adjective אָיֹם (dreadful), modifying "his place." **c-**מְקֹומֹו. "His place" refers to the place where the locust can be found and in this regard is synonymous with the "dwelling places" (מִשְׁכָּנֹות) in Hab 1:6.

Nah 3:18: **a-**מֶלֶךְ. G uses βασιλεύς here and Hab 1:10. V uses "rex" in both. **b-**רֹעֶיךָ. Shepherds as leaders are synonymous with the "rulers" which parallels kings in Hab 1:10. **c-**נַפֹּשׁוּ. The niphal of פוש is used here, while the qal in Hab 1:8 has another root meaning. G uses ἀπῆρεν here and ἐξιππάσονται in Hab 1:8. V likewise translates with different words; "latitavit" (to be concealed) here and "diffundentur" in Hab 1:8.

Nah 3:19: **a-**רָעָתְךָ. G has κακία here and πονηρά in Hab 1:13. V has "malitia" here and "malum" in Hab 1:13. **b-**תָּמִיד. G and V confirm the presence of "continually" here and in Hab 1:17, using the same words in both places.

Hab 1:3: **a-**מָדֹון. G translates κριτής (judge) reading דִּין with a preposition.

Hab 1:5: **a-**בַגֹּויִם. G has καταφρονταί (the ones despising) which reads בֹּגְדִים. The פשר for this verse in 1QpHab *possibly* confirms G as a variant Hebrew *Vorlage*, although the actual text is missing — leaving the question open. See further possibilities in the literary discussion. A scribal error is the likeliest explanation for the two readings. **b-**G inserts ἀφανίσθητε (disappear). **c-**פֹּעַל. G adds ἐγώ,interpreting by context.

Hab 1:6: **a-**הַכַּשְׂדִּים. G translates μαχητάς (warrior) assuming גִּבֹּרִים. This deliberate change generalizes the enemy, on its understanding of 1:8 (see 1:8b; cf. also Amos 9:12).

Hab 1:8: **a-**וּקַלּוּ. 1QpHab has קֹול, regarded as scribal error. **b-**עֶרֶב. G translates the consonants as the "Arabians". **c-**פָּרָשָׁיו. The verbal form in 1QpHab, וּפָרְשׁוּ, is unconfirmed by the versions. G omits one appearance of פָּרָשׁ and translates οἱ ἱππεῖς (calvary). V and Syriac confirm MT.

Hab 1:9: **a-**כֹּל ה. G has συντέλεια incorrectly reading the MT consonants as a noun. **b-**מְגַמַּת. Hapaxlegomenon from the root גמם "to collect". G and V have trouble translating and add ἀνθεστηκότας and "urens" respectively.

Hab 1:10: **a-**יִתְקַלָּס. 1QpHab (יקלס) does not affect the meaning.

Hab 1:11: **a-**וְאָשֵׁם. 1QpHab (וישם) presumes שׂים or שׂמם as root.

Hab 1:13: **a-**רָע. 1QpHab has ברע, adding the preposition.

8.3. Conclusions

The evaluation of the textual evidence indicates the translators of the versions were not aware of a *Stichwort* connection between Nahum and Habakkuk. G uses the same word for "horsemen" (Nah 3:3; Hab 1:8), but V uses different words. Both G and V use the same word for "fortification" (Nah 3:12,14; Hab 1:10), and translate the homonym פוש with different words (Nah 3:18; Hab 1:8). G uses different words for "evil" (Nah 3:19; Hab 1:13), and V uses "malitia" (Nah 3:19) and "malum" (Hab 1:13). The Qumran literature confirms the appearance of the *Stichwörter* in Habakkuk with the exception of "nations" in 1:5. In addition, a number of common words and synonyms appear in these two passages which are not accented in any of the versions (see for example 3:3b; 3:10a; 3:12c).

9. Hab 3:1-19 and Zeph 1:1-18

9.1. Translation of Hab 3:1-19 and Zeph 1:1-18

YHWH Goes to Battle

1. The prayer of Habakkuk the prophet according to Shigionoth.[a]
2. YHWH, I have heard your report.
   I fear your work.
   In the midst of the years, revive it.
   In the midst of the years, make (it) known.
   When raging, remember to have compassion.
3. God will come from Teman.
   And the holy one from Mount Paran.   Selah.
   His splendor will cover the heavens,
   And his praise will fill the *earth*.[a]
4. And the brightness will be like light (with) rays from his own hand.
   And there is the hiding place of his strength.
5. Pestilence goes before him.
   And plague goes forth at his feet.
6. He stood and measured[a] the *earth*.
   He looked and startled the nations.
   The eternal mountains were shattered;
   The *hills*[c] of perpetuity collapsed.
   The ways of perpetuity belong to him.
7. I saw the tents of Cushan[a] [b]under distress.[b]
   The curtains of the *land* of Midian trembled.

8. Was YHWH[a] angry with the rivers,
    Or was your anger with the rivers,[b]
    Or your *fury*[c] with the *sea*,[d]
    That you rode on your horses, your chariots of salvation?

9. [a]The nakedness of your bow was made bare.
    The curses of the rods were spoken.[a]   Selah.
    You cleaved the *earth* with rivers.

10. The mountains saw you; they quaked.
    The flood of water passed over.
    The deep uttered its *voice*.[a]
    The sun[b] lifted its hands high.

11. The moon stood in its abode.
    They went to the light of your arrows,
    To the gleaming and flashing of your spear.

12. In indignation you march the *earth*.
    In anger you tread the nations.

13. You went forth for the salvation of your people,
    For the salvation of your anointed.
    You wounded the head of the house of *evil*,[a]
    Making the base bare to the neck.   Selah.

14. With his rod you pierced the head of his warriors.[a]
    They stormed along[b] to scatter me.[c]
    Their exultation was thus to devour the oppressed in secret.

15. You tread your horses on the *sea* — a heap of great waters.

16. I heard and my inward parts trembled.
    At the *sound*[a] my lips quivered.
    Decay came into my bones,
    And beneath me I tremble when I wait for the *day of trouble*,[a]
    For the people rising up who will attack us.

17. Though the fig tree will not bloom,
    And no produce will be on the vine,
    (Though) the yield of the olive has failed,
    And the fields do not produce food,
    (Though) the flock is divided from the field,
    And there is no *cattle*[a] in the stalls,

18. Still I will exult in YHWH.
    I will rejoice in the god of my salvation.

19. YHWH Adonai is my strength,
    And he places my feet like the hinds,
    And he makes me tread on my high places.
    To the choir director on my stringed instruments.

The Day of YHWH

1. The word of YHWH which came to Zephaniah, the son of Cushi, the son of
    Gedeliah, the son of Amariah, son of Hezekiah, in the days of Josiah, son of Amon,
    king of Judah.

2. I will utterly destroy everything from the face of the *land*—utterance of YHWH.

3. I will destroy man and *cattle*;

  I will destroy the birds of heaven and the fish of the *sea*, ^aand the stumbling-blocks with the ones doing *evil*.^a

  And I will cut off man from upon the face of the *land*—utterance of YHWH.

4. And I will stretch out my hand against Judah and against all the inhabitants of Jerusalem,

  And I will cut off the remnant of Baal from this place, the name of the idol-priests with the priests,

5. And those bowing down upon the rooftop to the host of heaven,

  And those bowing down, swearing to YHWH, while swearing by their king^a

6. And those turning away from YHWH, and who do not ^aseek YHWH and do not seek^a him.

7. Be quiet before Adonai YHWH, for the day of YHWH draws near,

  For YHWH has prepared a sacrifice;

  He has consecrated his holy ones.

8. And it will be on the day of the YHWH's sacrifice

  That I will punish the princes and the sons of the king and all those putting on a foreign garment.

9. And I will punish all who are leaping upon the threshhold on that day, those filling the house of their God with violence and deceipt.

10. And there will be on that day—utterance of YHWH—the *sound* of a cry from the gate of the fish, a wail from the second quarter, and a great shattering from the *hills*.

11. The inhabitants of the mortar will wail.

  All the people of Canaan will be destroyed.

  All those laden with silver will be cut off.

12. And it will be at that time I will search Jerusalem with lamps,

  And I will punish the men thickening upon their lees, those saying in their hearts, YHWH will neither do good nor evil.

13. And their wealth will become plunder, and their houses desolation.

  And they will build houses, but not inhabit.

  And they will plant vineyards, but not drink their wine.

14. Near is the great day of YHWH, near and very quickly speeding.

  The sound of the day of YHWH is ^abitter, the one crying there is a warrior.^a

15. That day is a day of *fury*, a *day of trouble* and constraint,

  A day of destruction and desolation,

  A day of darkness and gloom,

  A day of clouds and dark clouds.

16. A day of the horn and the battle cry against the fortified cities, and against the high corners.

17. And I will cause violence to man,

  And they will walk like the blind for they sinned to YHWH.

  And their blood will be poured out like dust, and their bowels^a like dung.

18. Neither their silver nor their gold will be able to deliver them on the day of the *fury* of YHWH.

And in the fire of his jealousy all the *earth* will be devoured for he will make an end,
indeed a terrible one, to all the inhabitants of the *earth*.

9.2. Textual Notes for Hab 3:1-19 and Zeph 1:1-18

Hab 3:3: **a**-הָאָרֶץ. Appears here and Hab 3:6,7,9,12 and Zeph 1:18. The synonym הָאֲדָמַה
appears in Zeph 1:2,3. G uses γῆ in every case for both words, V uses "terra."
Hab 3:6: **a**-וַיְמֹדֶד. "He measured" does not parallel "startled" in the second half of the
verse. G and T perhaps read יָמוּג "to shake." MT here accepted. **b**-גִּבְעֹת. Used here and
Zeph 1:10. G uses βοθνοί. V uses the plural of "collis."
Hab 3:7: **a**-כוּשָׁן. Hapaxlegomenon which G translates Αἰθιόπων (= כוּש). **b**-bG has ἀντὶ
κόπων, but elsewhere translates κόπος for אָוֶן (Job 5:6; Mic 2:1; Hab 1:3, 3:7; Zech 10:2).
Hab 3:8: **a**-יְהוָה. G incorrectly reads as second person address to harmonize with the rest
of the verse. **b**-bם אִם בַּנְּהָרִים. This phrase is missing in several manuscripts, apparently
through haplography. **c**-כֶּ עֶבְרָתֶךָ appears here and Zeph 1:15,18. G uses ὁρμημά here and
ὀργῆς in Zeph 1:15,18. V uses "indignatio" here and "irae" in Zeph 1:15,18. **d**-ם-בַּ appears
here and 3:15 and Zeph 1:3. G uses θάλασσα and V uses "mare" for each occurrence.
Hab 3:9: **a**-aMT is obscure. The versions offer no help. See the literary discussion which
follows.
Hab 3:10: **a**-קֹול. "Sound" is confirmed in the versions. **b**-שֶׁמֶשׁ. Syntactically tied to 3:10,
but MT places it with 3:11.
Hab 3:13: **a**-רָשָׁע appears here, and in Zeph 1:3 as plural participle (compare note Zeph
1:3a).
Hab 3:14: **a**-פְּרָזָו. So LXX, V and T. MT is a hapax legomenon from an uncertain root.
Summary of possible related derivatives in Koehler-Baumgartner ([3]1983), 908. **b**-יִסְעֲרוּ.
Read as יִסְעֲרוּ. **c**-לַהֲפִיצֵנִי. "To scatter me." The change to the first person here is
continued in 3:16-19.
Hab 3:16: **a**-לְיֹום צָרָה. Appears here and in Zeph 1:15. G uses θλίψεως in both passages
and V uses "tribulationis" in both.
Hab 3:17: **a**-בָּקָר. Appears here and the synonym בְּהֵמָה is used in Zeph 1:3. G uses βόες
here and κτήνη in Zeph 1:3. V uses "armentum" here and "pecus" in Zeph 1:3, but
translates צ אן as "de ovili pecus" in Hab 3:17.

Zeph 1:3: **a**-aMissing in G, but present in several mss. (Symmachus. W.36.48. L [some]), and
in Theodotion, perhaps to correct it according to the MT. It is present in V and Syriac.
MT is accepted.
Zeph 1:5: **a**-So MT. Lucian has "Milkom," reading the same consonants. The context
condemns the syncretism of the worshippers. While this would appear to make Milkom the
more likely reading, several (e.g. Kapelrud, Rudolph, Robertson) have advanced theories
that "their king" means Baal, which would also fit the context (see 1:4).
Zeph 1:6: **a**-Translated literally, but the separate roots בקש and דרש are synonyms.
Zeph 1:14: **a**-aG and Syriac read מַר צָרְהֵשָׁם גִּבּוֹר (Gerleman, p.20).
Zeph 1:17: **a**-ם-וּלְחֻמָם. "Their bowels." G uses σάρκας. Syriac understands as "flesh." V
and T understand as "corpse."

9.3. Conclusions

The textual investigation offers one feature to distinguish it from others within the Book of the Twelve. Specifically, many of the Greek manuscripts omit the phrase "and the ruins along with the ones doing evil" (Zeph 1:3). However, multiple attestations of this phrase in the Syriac, the Vulgate, and several Greek mss confirm MT. The remainder of the *Stichwörter* are present in the versions, although there is again no concern to translate common words identically (cf. 3:6b, 3:17a.).

10. Zeph 3:18-20 and Hag 1:1-4

10.1 Translation of Zeph 3:18-20 and Hag 1:1-6

Divine Promise of Salvation

18. The ones suffering[a] [b]without appointed feast[b] I will gather from you.[c]
    They were[d] a burden[e] upon her, a reproach.[f]
19. Behold what I am about to do[a] to all your oppressors,[b] *at that time*.[c]
    And I will deliver the lame, and I will gather the outcast.
    And I will make them into a praise,
    And their shame[d] into renown in all the earth.
20. *At that time*[a] I will *bring*[b] you,
    And *at the time* of my gathering you,
    Then I will give you renown and praise among all the *peoples*[c] of the earth in my
       returning your fortunes[d] before your eyes — says YHWH.

Rebuilding the Temple

1. In the second year of Darius the king,
   on the first day of the sixth month,
   the word of YHWH came by the hand of Haggai the prophet[a]
   to Zerubbabel the son of Shealtiel, governor[b] of Judah,
   and to Joshua the son of Jehozadak, the high priest, saying:
2. Thus says YHWH Sebaoth, saying:
   This people says *the time* has not yet[a] come,[b] *the time* to build the house of YHWH.
3. And then the word of YHWH came by the hand of Haggai the prophet saying,
4. Is it *time* for you yourselves to rest in your boarded houses[a] and this house be desolate?
5. But now, thus says YHWH Sebaoth, place your ways to your heart.
6. You have sown much, but it *brought* little:
   (there is) to eat, but not to satisfy;

to drink, but not to become drunk;
to clothe, but not to warm one's self;
and the wage earner is earning into a pouch which is pierced.

10.2. Textual Notes to Zeph 3:18-20 and Hag 1:1-6

Zeph 3:18: **a-**נוּגֵי. Omitted by G and Syriac. **b-b**מִמּוֹעֵד. G and Syriac insert "day" and read with verse 17. The translation here understands the מ as "without" (see GK §119w). **c-**מִמֵּךְ. G translates συντετριμμένους, reading מֵכֶם. Syriac follows MT. Here the athnach is moved forward one word so that מִמֵּךְ is read with אַסְפְתִי. **d-**הָיוּ. G reads הוֹי and translates οὐαί. The shifting of the athnach provides a good sentence, albeit with a certain literary tension, see discussion below. **e-**מַשְׂאֵת. G reads מִי נָשָׂא and translates τίς ἔλαβεν as a question. **f-**עָלֶיהָ. The third feminine singular suffix is out of context, but fully attested. The suggestion of Rudolph (*KAT* 13/3, 294), following Sellin, that ה be read as the article is rejected on grounds of version attestation and because the following word, חֶרְפָּה, is never used elsewhere with the article.

Zeph 3:19: **a-**עֹשֶׂה. Used in the absolute state with direct object (GK §116f). **b-**מְעַנַּיִךְ. G translates ἔνεκεν σοῦ reading אֶת־כָּל־מְעַנַּיִךְ instead of MT. **c-**בָּעֵת הַהִיא. G translates this phrase ἐν τῷ καιρῷ ἐκείνῳ here and in 3:20, but without the pronoun in 3:20, following MT. V likewise uses "tempore" for all of these without the pronoun for the second phrase. For the use this phrase in Haggai, see Hag 1:2b. **d-**בָּשְׁתָּם. G reads as a verb with verse 20. בָּשְׁתָּם is here translated as a second object, parallel to the 3mp suffix in שמתים.

Zeph 3:20: **a-**G adds ὅταν καλῶς ὑμῖν αὐνήσω. **b-**אָבִיא. The use of בוא in hiphil appears here and in Hag 1:6. **c-**עֵמְ. The presence of עם is attested in all versions here and in Haggai. **d-**שְׁבוּתֵיכֶם. For plural ending on a singular noun, see GK §91l.

Hag 1:1: **a-**G adds λέγων εἰπὸν to correlate with 2:1-2. **b-**פֶּחָה. G deliberately changes to φυλῆς, as if reading מִשְׁפָּחַת (cf. 1:14; 2:2,21 in G).

Hag 1:2: **a-**לֹא. Here means "not yet" (Gen 2:5, 29:7; Ps 139:16; Job 22:16). **b-**בֹא. G has οὐχ ἥκει ὁ καιρὸς τοῦ οἰκοδομῆσαι with only one occurrence of "time." Hitzig (*Die zwölf kleinen Propheten* [Leipzig: Hirzel, [4]1881], 324) proposed that G read עֵת בָּא, assuming the short form of עַתָּה. However, Steck ("Zu Hag 1:2-11," *ZAW* 83 [1971]: 361f, note 21) observes this creates even more problems: The short form עֵת is difficult since the longer form is used in Hag 1:5; 2:3,4,15; the use of עַתָּה would be as unnecessary as the use of עֵת; and the parallel syntactical structure of 1:4 argues against the presence here of the entire phrase עֵת בָּא. Steck opts for dittography between the ת and the א. The appearance of this phrase among the *Stichwörter* raises the question of whether it is to be seen in light of text-critical or redaction-critical questions. See literary discussion below. The pointing of G (בָּא) is here accepted over against MT. This raises no problems of gender; compare Ezek 7:7,12, where the feminine עת is used with the masculine בָּא.

Hag 1:4: **a-**בְּבָתֵּיכֶם. Several mss, Syriac, and V are missing the כ in the suffix, reading בְּבָתִים.

10.3. Conclusions

The textual investigation shows again that by the time of the translations there was no longer a concern for *Stichwörter* between writings. The grammatically awkward phrase "the time has not come", in Hag 1:2, raises the question as to whether the phrase is the result of a scribal error, or the result of redactional activity.

11. Hag 2:20-23 and Zech 1:1-11

11.1. Translation of Hag 2:20-23 and Zech 1:1-11

Promised Overthrow of the Nations

20.   And the word of YHWH came to Haggai a second time on the twenty-fourth of the month saying,
21.   Speak to Zerubbabel,[a] governor of Judah saying, I about to cause the heavens and the *earth*[b] to quake.
22.   I will overturn the thrones[a] of the kingdoms. I will exterminate the strength of the kingdoms of the nations. I will overturn the chariot and *its riders*,[b] and the *horses*[c] and *their riders* will go down *each man*[d] by the sword of his brother.
23.   In that day—utterance of YHWH Sebaoth—I will take you Zerubbabel son of Shealtiel, *my servant*[a]—utterance of YHWH. I will make you like the signet for I have chosen you—utterance of YHWH Sebaoth.

Admonition to Learn from the Mistakes of the Past

1.   In the eighth month,[a] in the second year of Darius the word of YHWH came to Zechariah the prophet, son of Berechiah, son of Iddo[b] saying,
2.   YHWH was very angry[a] with your fathers.
3.   And you say to them, thus says YHWH Sebaoth, return to me—utterance of YHWH Sebaoth—and I will return to you says YHWH Sebaoth.
4.   Do not be like your fathers to whom the former prophets called saying, thus says YHWH Sebaoth, please turn from your evil ways and from your evil deeds, but they did not listen and they did not attend to me—utterance of YHWH.
5.   Your fathers, where are they? And will the prophets live forever?
6.   Indeed, my word and my statutes,[a] which I commanded[b] to *my servants* the prophets, did they not overtake your fathers? And they returned and said just as YHWH Sebaoth proposed to do to us for our ways and our deeds, thus he did with us.
7.   On the twenty-fourth day of the eleventh month—[a]it is the month of Shebat[a]—in the second year of Darius, the word of YHWH came to Zechariah the prophet, the son of Berechiah, son of Iddo saying,

8.   I saw (in) the night and behold a *man*, a *rider* on a red *horse* and he was standing among myrtle trees[a] in the valley,[b] and behind him were red,[c] sorrel, and white *horses*.

9.   And I said what is this Adonai? And the messenger who was speaking with me said to me, I will show you what these are.

10.   And the *man* who was standing among the myrtles answered, and he said, these are the ones who YHWH has sent to travel the *earth*.

11.   And they answered the messenger of YHWH standing among the myrtles, and said, we have traveled the *earth* and behold all the *earth* is resting and undisturbed.

11.2. Textual Notes on Hag 2:20-23 and Zech 1:1-11

Hag 2:21: **a**-G adds "the son of Shealtiel" to harmonize with 1:1,12; 2:12. **b**-אֶרֶץ. G adds καὶ τὴν θάλασσαν καὶ τὴν ξηράν to harmonize with 2:6b. G uses γῆν here and Zech 1:10, 11 [twice], and V uses "terra" in all four places.

Hag 2:22: **a**-כִּסֵּא. The singular followed by the genitive expresses the plural (GK §124r). **b**-וְרֹכְבֶיהָ. G uses ἀναβάτης twice here and Zech 1:8. V uses "ascensus" here and "ascendens" in Zech 1:6. **c**-סוּסִים. G uses ἵππος here and Zech 1:8 [twice]. V uses "equus" in these instances. **d**-אִישׁ. Used in Haggai in the sense of "everyone," while in Zech 1:8,10 it refers to an individual. G uses ἕκαστος in Haggai, and ἀνήρ in Zech 1:8, denoting the semantic distinctions of the word. V uses "vir" for both.

Hag 2:23: **a**-עַבְדִּי. G uses δοῦλος here and Zech 1:6. V uses "ascensus" here and "serve" in Zech 1:6.

Zech 1:1: **a**-בַּחוֹדֶשׁ. Syriac understands this as the "first of the month." **b**-בֶּן־עִדּוֹ. Refers to Berechiah, but compare Ezra 5:1; and 6:14 which list Zechariah only as the descendant of Iddo.

Zech 1:2: **a**-קָצַף. Strengthens the verb, see also Zech 1:15.

Zech 1:6: **a**-וְחֻקַּי. G inserts δέχεσθη, assuming קְחוּ. **b**-G inserts "in my spirit" to harmonize with 7:12.

Zech 1:7: **a-a**The explanatory phrase here is likely a gloss.

Zech 1:8: **a**-G inserts ὀρέων. **b**-בַּמְּצֻלָה. MT has a defective pointing for "in the deep" (בַּמְצוּלָה), but "the deep" is only used in reference to great distress (Ps 69:3) or more frequently to depths of the sea (Ps 88:7). Here, the consonants presumably represent a locality around Jerusalem, hence a hollow, or small valley (cf G). **c**-קשָׂרֹ. G translates correctly as ψαροί (speckled).

11.3. Conclusions

Again, the investigation of the text shows that the translators of the different versions were not concerned with the *Stichwörter* connection between these two writings. This lack of concern is seen in the different translations for אִישׁ in G, according to the semantic of the word, and the related translations for רכב by V.

12. Zech 8:9-23 and Mal 1:1-14

12.1. Translation of Zech 8:9-23 and Mal 1:1-14

Promise of Blessing

9.   Thus says YHWH Sebaoth,
      Let *your hands*[a] be strong in these days, you who are hearing these words from the
            mouth of the prophets, who (spoke) on the day the house of YHWH Sebaoth
            was founded, in order that the temple might be built.

10.   For before those days there was no wage for man,[a]
      And a wage for cattle there was not.
      And to the one going out and coming in there was not peace from the adversary.
      And I sent away all mankind, each man with his neighbor.

11.   But now I am not like the former days to the remnant of this *people*[a] — utterance of
            YHWH Sebaoth.

12.   For a seed[a] (there is) peace.
      The vine gives its *fruit*[b],
      And the land gives its produce,
      And the heavens give their dew.
      And I have caused the remnant of this *people* to inherit all these.

13.   And it will be that even as you were a *curse*[a] *among the nations*[b] — house of Judah
            and house of Israel — so I will deliver you, and you will be a blessing.
      You should not fear.
      Let *your hands* be strong.

14.   For thus says YHWH Sebaoth,
      Just as I proposed to do *evil* to you when your *fathers*[a] provoked me — says YHWH
            Sebaoth — and I did not relent.

15.   So, I have *returned*;[a] I propose in these days to do good to Jerusalem and to the
            house of Judah.
      You should not fear.

16.   These are the things[a] you should do.
      Speak truth, each man to his neighbor.
      Judge truth[b] and a judgment of peace in your *gates*[c].

17.   And each of you should not consider in your hearts the *evil*[a] of his neighbor,
      And you should not *love*[b] an oath of falsehood,
      For these (are) what *I hate*[c] — utterance of YHWH.

18.   And the word of YHWH Sebaoth came to me saying,

19.   Thus says YHWH Sebaoth,
      The fast of the fourth, the fast of the fifth, the fast of the seventh, and the fast of the
            tenth will become for the house of Judah exultation, and joy, and good
            festivals,
      So *love* truth and peace.

20.   Thus says YHWH Sebaoth,

Yet will the *peoples* come, and the inhabitants of many cities.

21.   And the inhabitants of one[a] will go to another saying, "let us go now to *entreat the face*[b] of YHWH, and to seek[c] YHWH Sebaoth."
Moreover, I will go.

22.   And many *peoples* and mighty *nations* will come to seek YHWH Sebaoth in Jerusalem and to *entreat the face* of YHWH.

23.   Thus says YHWH Sebaoth,
In those days when ten men from all the tongues of the *nations* grasp, and they grasp the garment of a Jewish man saying, let us go with you for we have heard Elohim is with you.

YHWH Demands Respect

1.   An oracle. The word of YHWH to Israel by the *hand* of Malachi.[a]

2.   I *loved* you said YHWH.
But how have you *loved* us?
Was not Esau a brother to Jacob — utterance of YHWH — but I loved Jacob,

3.   And Esau *I hated*.
And I made his mountain a desolation and his possession to the jackals[a] of the wilderness.

4.   Though Edom will say,[a]
"We are beaten down, but we will *return* and build the ruins."
Thus says YHWH Sebaoth,
They may build, but I will tear down,
And they will call them a territory of wickedness and the *people* who are an indignation of YHWH forever.

5.   And your eyes will see it,
And you will say, "Great is YHWH beyond[a] the territory of Israel."

6.   A son will honor a *father* and a servant his lord,
But if I am a *father*, where is my honor?
If I am a lord,[a] where is my respect? — Says YHWH Sebaoth to you, the priests despising my name.
But you say, how have we despised your name?

7.   By presenting defiled bread upon my altar.
But you say, "How have we defiled you?"[a]
In your saying, "The table of YHWH, it is despised."

8.   And when you present the blind for sacrifice, is it not *evil*?
And when you present the lame and the sick, is it not *evil*?
Would you approach to your governor?
Would he be pleased with you or lift[a] up your *face*?
Says YHWH Sebaoth?

9.   But now, will you *entreat the face* of God, that he will show kindness to us?
This is from *your hand*.
Will he lift up your *faces*, says YHWH Sebaoth?

10.   Would[a] that one among you will shut the *gates* and not kindle my altar in vain.
There is not pleasure with you for me, says YHWH Sebaoth, and I will not accept offerings from *your hand*.

11. For from the rising of the sun to its setting, great is my name *among the nations*,
     And in every place incense[a] is offered to my name, and an offering that is pure for
          great is my name *among the nations*,
     Says YHWH Sebaoth,
12. But you are profaning it, with your saying the table of Adonai is defiled, and *its
     fruit*[a], its food is despised.
13. But you say behold, weariness, and you sniffed it,[a] says YHWH Sebaoth,
     And you bring plunder and the lame and the sick, and then bring the offering.
     Should I receive it from *your hand*, says YHWH?
14. And *cursed* is the swindler,[a] when there is a male[b] in his flock,
     And the one vowing when sacrificing a blemished animal to Adonai,
     For I am a great king, says YHWH Sebaoth,
     And my name is feared *among the nations*.

12.2. Textual Notes to Zech 8:9-23 and Mal 1:1-14

Zech 8:9: **a-יְדֵיכֶם**. "Hands" is attested in G by χεῖρες and V by "manus" and Mal 1:10,13.
Zech 8:10: **a-G** inserts εἰς ὄνησιν (for profit, advantage).
Zech 8:11: **a-הָעָם**. G uses λαός and V uses "populi" in in 8:12,20,22 and Mal 1:4.
Zech 8:12: **a-זֶרַע**. G smoothes the phrase זֶרַע הַשָּׁלוֹם כִּי, and translates δείξω εἰρήνην (I
will show peace). MT is attested in S and V. **b-פִּרְיָה**. G translates "fruit" with καρπός and
V as "fructum." The synonym in Mal 1:12 is problematic in G and V. See text note Mal
1:12a.
Zech 8:13: **a-קְלָלָה**. "Curse" is here translated with κατάρα by G and with ἐπὶ κατάρπατος
in Mal 1:14. V translates "maledictio" and "maledictus" respectively. **b-גּוֹיִם**. "Nations" is
translated uniformly in G and V here; 8:22,23; Mal 1:11 (twice),14.
Zech 8:14: **a-אָב**. G and V translate "father" consistently here and Mal 1:6.
Zech 8:15: **a-שַׁבְתִּי**. The root שׁוב used here with the sense of "again" and perhaps also in
Mal 1:4. Its presence is attested in the versions.
Zech 8:16: **a-הַדְּבָרִים**. Literally MT means words. **b-אֱמֶת**. G eliminates to smooth the
translation, but MT attested in several mss (B, S, V, etc.). **c-שַׁעַר**. The synonyms are
attested here and Mal 1:10.
Zech 8:17: **a-רָעַת**. G translates the noun with κακίαν here and the adjective with κακόν
in Mal 1:8 (twice). V uses "malum" in all three locations. **b-אהב**. Translated here and
Mal 1:3 with ἀγαπάω in G, and "odio" in V.
Zech 8:21: **a-אַחַת**. Refers to city. G has "five cities" (πέντα πόλεις) but affords no
suitable reconstruction. Riessler (*Die kleinen Propheten oder das Zwölfprophetenbuch.*)
suggests G read הֶעָרִים following יֹשְׁבֵי with the article understood as "five." This
explanation accounts for G, but does not explain MT. **b-פְנֵי אֶת לְחַלּוֹת**. Occurs here, 8:22
and in Mal 1:9 (with imperative and different name for God). G translates the verb
δεηθῆναι here, but ἐξιλάσκεσθαι in Zech 8:22 and Mal 1:9 . V uses the same verb, but
different words for face here and 8:22 ("faciem") compared to Mal 1:9 ("vultum"). The
phrase only appears in the Book of the Twelve elsewhere in Zech 7:2. **c-G** inserts τὸ
πρόσωπον κυρίου after בקשׁ here and 8:22.

Mal 1:1: a-מַלְאָכִי. G translates as a title, not a name (ἐν χειρὶ ἀγγέλον αὐτου), and inserts the admonition θήσθε δή ἐπί τάς καρδίας ὑμῶν.

Mal 1:3: a-לְתַנּוֹת. G translates δόματα (dwelling) possibly tying it to the Arabic *tana'a*.

Mal 1:4: a-אָמְרָה. Here understood as 3fs. See note to Obadiah 1e.

Mal 1:5: a-מֵעַל. Understood as "over," not "beyond" (GK §119c).

Mal 1:6: a-Several mss insert φοβηθήσεται to parallel 1·6b.

Mal 1:7: a-גֵאַלְנוּךְ. G has ἠλισγήσαμεν αὐτούς with the pronoun referring to bread. The lectio difficilior is MT, which also corresponds to the 2ms reference to God in 1:6b.

Mal 1:8: a-הֵיּשָׂא. G translates this as 1cs to fit the context.

Mal 1:10: a-מִי. Here used to show desire (GK §151a).

Mal 1:11: a-מֻקְטָר. The participle translated substantivally.

Mal 1:12: a-נִיבוֹ. Understood as "fruit" (*BDB*, 626). The difficulty of the image causes G and V to translate "the things on it (the table); and Syriac and T to omit it altogether. The word appears elsewhere only in Isa 57:14.

Mal 1:13: a-אוֹתוֹ. The scribal emendation has אוֹתִי.

Mal 1:14: a-נוֹכֵל. "Swindler" is incorrectly translated from יכל by G, and omitted in Syriac. b-זָכָר. The proposal in *BHS* to read זכר (male) as זכה (pure) is rejected on the basis of full attestation of MT.

12.3. Conclusions

A summary of the textual evidence reveals that the process of joining these two writings through *Stichwörter* was no longer a factor by the time of their translations. G and V translate similar words and phrases differently from MT (see notes Zech 8:13a,21b and Mal 1:12a), but do not systematically attempt to hide these common occurrences.

13. General Summation

The preceding investigation allows both positive and negative conclusions. Positively, the evaluation of the catchwords in the various versions demonstrates conclusively that the common words were part of the transmitted text at the time of the earliest translations.[4] Negatively, the

---

[4] This observation should surprise no one, but it does help to distinguish the character of the Book of the Twelve from other writings whose translation into Greek predated the conclusion of the productive growth of the *Vorlage*. For example, the LXX of Jeremiah represents an earlier version of that prophetic writing. The version exhibited by the MT continued to develop, resulting in two versions of Jeremiah, examples of both of which have been found in Qumran.

preceding investigation discloses strong evidence that the translators exhibit no cognizance of these words as a unifying technique in the compilation of the Book of the Twelve.[5] This last statement should not be understood as a refutation of the possibility that these catchwords served a unifying function in the compilation of the Book of the Twelve. Logically, one may make only limited deductions from this evidence, namely, that the use of catchwords to create a reading "logic" between the individual writings was not a decisive factor in the wording of the translations. One may further speculate reasonably that the translators were *unaware* of these catchword connections, and thus made no effort to accentuate them. The implications from these observations indicate that knowledge of any connecting function these words played in the formation of the Book of the Twelve was limited to a specific chronological period and/or a particular geographical location.

---

[5] At least once in almost every seam, the translators utilized different words when translating the same Hebrew word from two different writings. These variations of words does not appear as a deliberate attempt to conceal the existence of the common words because it does not occur with enough regularity. One may generally explain the changes contextually, based upon the translator's syntactical and conceptual understanding of the individual writing.

Hos 14:2-10

1. The Macrostructure of Hosea and the Role of 14:2-10

The majority of commentators recognize a structure in the book of Hosea which distinguishes the transmission of chapters 1-3 from 4-14.[1] The first three chapters exhibit a clearly definable alternation between passages of judgment and salvation (1:2-9 with 2:1-3; 2:4-15 with 2:16-25; and 3:1-4 with 3:5). A clear ordering principle is more difficult to discern in chapters 4-14. Most scholars treat chapters 4-11 and 12-14 as major thematic blocks, if not separate transmission blocks.[2] Most argue as well that the chronology of the material in chapters 4-14 plays some role in its organization and structure.[3] Hos 4-14 also exhibits movement from accusation to threat to salvation, although in much longer blocks than in

---

[1] An exception is Gale Yee, *Composition and Tradition in the Book of Hosea: A Redaction-Critical Approach.* SBL Dissertation Series 102. (Atlanta: Scholars Press, 1987). She maintains the *final* redactor of the Hosea book was responsible for the composition of chapters 3, 11, and 14. Chapter 3 was composed as a means of creating a narrative frame around the poetic (mostly Hoseanic) material of chapter 2. She thus recognizes the standard divisions of the book as 1-3; 4-11; 12-14, but considers the chapters at the end of each of those sections to come from one and the same hand. More will be said about Yee's work in the discussion, below page 62.

[2] A partial yet significant selection is provided of those arguing for such a division: Wolff, *BK* 14/1, XXIIIff; Rudolph, *KAT* 13/1, 26; Jeremias, *ATD* 24/1, 18f; Mays *Hosea*, 15f. Weiser, *ATD* 24, 3; Jacob, *CAT* 12f. A dissenting opinion is offered by Edwin M. Good, "The Composition of Hosea," *Svensk Exegetisk Arsbok* 31 (1966): 21-63. Good sees a series of oral complexes combined literarily by means of various "modes of compilation" (54) such as compilation in a series, compilation by ring or bracket, compilation by a chiastic or envelope technique. In his scheme, Good concludes that complexes 9:1-10:15 and 11:1-14:1 were joined together after which they were attached to the complex 5:8-8:14. A later step brought together the united complex of 5:5-14:1 with 14:2-9, followed by the attachment of 4:4-5:7. 4:1-3 was composed as a general heading to the complex of 4:4-14:9. A pre-existent collection (chapters 1-3) was added to the front on the basis of the harlotry themes in 1-3 and 4:4-5:7.

[3] See especially Wolff, *BK* 14/1, XXV, Jeremias, *ATD* 24/1, 18, and Rudolph, *KAT* 13/1, 26, who although less confident of the extent of chronology as an ordering principle than the other two, nevertheless admits it has played a role in Hosea.

chapters 1-3.[4] The present discussion attempts to elucidate the role played by chapter 14: the definition and characterization of its units, its relationship to the immediate context, and its relationship to the structure of the entire book.

Hos 14:2 begins a new unit which extends to 14:9. The previous unit, ending in 14:1, deals thematically with judgment and addresses Israel directly. By contrast, 14:2-9 thematically concerns salvation, and involves YHWH and the prophet as speakers.[5] At the other end of this unit, the summary character of Hos 14:10 traditionally leads exegetes to associate the verse with post-exilic wisdom schools. A strong consensus exists that the verse has the entire book in its scope.[6] Theories of the origin of Hos 14:2-9 typically place it into one of four categories: 1) genuine Hoseanic material,[7] 2) a composition from Hosea's disciples at a time not long after the prophet lived,[8] 3) a post-exilic composition of salvation,[9] and 4) an exilic redactional composition.[10] A brief discussion of these options will help to clarify its function within Hosea.

The view most often discarded regards Hos 14:2-9 as a post-exilic composition by an individual or group believing that a prophetic book must end with a passage of hope. Proponents of this view have normally been those of the old literary critical school, and their presuppositions have been challenged regarding this passage.[11] Their arguments that the same

---

[4] The salvation passages come in 11:1-11 and in 14:2-9. Wolff, *BK* 14/1, XXVI; see also Rudolph, *KAT* 13/1, 26; Mays, *Hosea*, 15f.

[5] Hos 14:2-4 present a prophetic address to the people, whereas 14:5-9 reflect divine speech about Israel.

[6] Further discussion of this consensus and recent challenges regarding the wisdom provenance of 14:10 are mentioned below, page 68.

[7] In addition to most conservative scholars, see Wolff, *BK* 14/1, XXVf (although he admits a certain reworking for liturgical purposes); Rudolph, *KAT* 13/1, 249f; Mays, *Hosea*, 16.

[8] Jörg Jeremias, *Der Prophet Hosea. Übersetzt und erklärt*, *ATD* 24/1 (Göttingen: Vandenhoeck & Ruprecht, 1983), 170.

[9] Marti, *HAT* 105; Duhm, "Anmerkungen zu den zwölf Propheten übersetzt und erklärt," *ZAW* 31 (1911): 42; Nowack, 79 (although less certain than Duhm and Marti).

[10] Gale A. Yee, *Composition and Tradition in the Book of Hosea: A Redaction-Critical Approach*, (Atlanta: Scholars Press, 1987), 131-142. See also the summary of her conclusions, 305-13.

[11] Duhm, "Anmerkungen zu den zwölf Propheten II," *ZAW* 31 (1911): 42; Marti, *HAT*, 105; and Nowack, 79, are the most often cited examples. It is of some interest that the likes of Ronald E. Clements, "Patterns in the Prophetic Canon," in *Canon and Authority: Essays in Old Testament Religion and Theology*, 42-55 (Philadelphia: Fortress, 1977), 48, says there is little opposition to the claim that *Amos 9:13-15* and *Hos 14:2-9*

prophet could not speak words of judgment and of hope have long been refuted for Hosea.[12] Others argue Hos 14:2-9 reflects genuine Hoseanic material. They cite the appropriateness of the passage to the reign of the Assyrian king Shalmanezer V (726-722), shortly before the destruction of Samaria, which excludes exilic origin of the passage. Although this date is perhaps too early, it helps to indicate that 14:2-9 contains primarily pre-exilic material.[13]

The most common view argues that Hos 14:2-9 reflects the words of Hosea, with posssible minor additions.[14]   Proponents often go to considerable length to place the passage in Hosea's time, or they proceed from the argument that no compelling evidence refutes Hoseanic authorship.[15]   However, recent studies have demonstrated a marked theological distinction in chapter 14, compared to other portions of more genuine material.[16] These works share several motifs which advance the understanding of Hos 14:2-9 within the book, although none offers an entirely satisfactory model.

Jeremias offers the best point of departure for an understanding of the role played by 14:2-9.[17] He notes the relatedness of this chapter to other chapters in the book (2 and 11), and argues for understanding 14:2-9 as a composition from Hosea's disciples following the destruction of Samaria. Jeremias claims the passage uses both Hoseanic vocabulary (14:5,9) and vocabulary more related to Isaiah (14:4) to create an extended call to repentance. The value of Jeremias' work lies in his observation of the inner movement of 14:2-9. Most commentators understand 14:5-9 as

---

"derive from the sixth century or later." While this statement is true of the Amos passage, it cannot in be said of Hos 14:2-9, for this passage is much more debated. See also Johannes Lindblom, *Prophecy in Ancient Israel*, (Oxford: Blackwell, 1962), 283.

[12] See, for example, Eissfeldt, *Introduction*, 387.

[13] Wolff, *BK* 14/1, XXV, 303; Rudolph, *KAT* 13/1, 250; Mays, *Hosea*, 185.

[14] In addition to Wolff, Rudolph, and Mays cited above, one could place in this category: Ina Willi-Plein, *Vorformen der Schriftexegese innerhalb des Alten Testaments. Untersuchungen zum literarischen Werden der auf Amos, Hosea und Micha zurückgehenden Bücher im hebräischen Zwölfprophetenbuch.* BZAW 123 (Berlin: DeGruyter, 1971), 232f; Artur Weiser, ATD 24. [3]1974, 86.

[15] Wolff, *BK* 14/1, 234; Weiser, *ATD* 24, 86.

[16] See especially Jörg Jeremias, "Zur Eschatologie des Hoseabuches," in *Die Botschaft und die Boten. Festschrift für H.W. Wolff* (Neukirchen: Neukirchener Verlag, 1981), 217-34. Yee, *Composition and Tradition*, 131-142, also recognizes this distinction, although her association of this passage with the same hand as chapters three and eleven remains problematic. See below, page 62.

[17] Jeremias, *ATD* 24/1, 169-174.

the divine response to the confession of 14:4, but Jeremias convincingly demonstrates that the entire passage should be seen as an *invitation* to repentance. His reasons are four-fold. 1) The material in 14:5-9 does not directly address Israel, but uses the third person, and is therefore not an *Erhörungszusage* for a potential confession. 2) Hos 14:5 does not suppose a change on the part of Israel, but speaks of the healing of Israel's apostasy. 3) The situation in the concluding verse presupposes a situation *prior* to the pronouncement of a presumed confession as seen in the content of 14:9a. 4) The 2ms address to Israel in 14:9b and 14:2 essentially creates a frame for the unit, and corresponds to the use of the same stylistic form at the beginning and end of units elsewhere in Hos (4:11-14; 5:3f; 10:1-8). Hos 14:5-9 offers the reason for the invitation. It is not a promise of God if Israel repents. It reflects the salvific desire of YHWH which, for the first time, allows the repentance called for in 14:2-4.

Two further works present differing views regarding the role played by 14:2-9 in the formation of the book. Good sees the unit as an oral complex which was joined to other complexes well along the collection process using a ring compositional method.[18]   He cites several places where he maintains 14:2-9 demonstrates a distinct intention to reverse the picture of chapter 13.[19]   Good does not, however, claim that 14:2ff limits its scope only to 13:1ff, but claims the chapter exhibits connections to other parts of Hos 4-14 as well.[20]   Good's own list of connective passages goes well beyond the bounds of his theory of attachment to a 5:8-14:1 complex. Observations by Jeremias and others who have noted connections to Hos

---

[18]   Good, "The Composition of Hosea," 61.

[19]   Good, "The Composition of Hosea," 60-61. He cites some rather enigmatic parallels, however, to prove this point. He finds "connections" between the two chapters between אמרו אליו in 14:3 and several words in 13:1ff: כדבר (13:1), להם הם אמרים (13:2), אשר אמרת (13:10). Good claims 14:3 is the exact opposite of all three of these citations from the previous chapter. Good presents stronger evidence of a relationship, however, when he also cites the following reversals of the picture in chapter 13: 14:4c-d with 13:2b-d; 14:5c with 13:11a; 14:6a with 13:3b; 14:6-8 with 13:15b-e; 14:8b with 13:14a-d; 14:9a with 13:2c; and 14:9b with 13:7b. While some of his examples are methodologically suspect, he presents enough evidence to demonstrate that 14:2-9 presupposes the existence and reverses the picture of chapter 13.

[20]   Good, "The Composition of Hosea," 33. This material is in the form of repeated themes from other parts of the book, namely "stumbling" (14:2b; cf 4:5; 5:5), "the rejection of harlotry" (14:4, cf especially 8:3-6; 13:2), "healing" (14:5, cf 5:13; 6:1; 7:1), and the plant metaphors in 14:6-8 which recall those in chapters 9-10.

2:3ff, argue strongly against a reconstructed growth based solely on Good's argumentation.[21]

Yee attempts a redactional approach to the book of Hosea, but intentionally inverts the normal methodological order, deliberately working backward based on her conviction "that with the book of Hosea it (redaction criticism) should be the *first analytical step* (her emphasis) in understanding the book's formation."[22] Yee goes on to say:

> As such, our investigation will treat the literary composition of the final redactor first. Whereas previous studies view the book's formation as an aggregate of smaller units with layers of redaction accretions, we choose to see the final redacted state as the work of an author, the final redactor who used *literary* traditions attributed to Hosea.[23]

Yee correctly argues that the final form of the text needs to be taken seriously, and that many of the long noted inconsistencies can plausibly be explained by assuming different literary traditions. Yee places too much emphasis on a final redactor, however, when she argues that the entire structure of a book like Hosea, can be attributed to a single redactor. The problem with Yee's approach begins with the assumption that one final redactor is responsible for the entire "redacted state" of the work. This assumption not only flies in the face of most modern Hoseanic scholarship, it offers little methodological control to determine what criteria should be used to distinguish said "final redactor" from the very "literary traditions attributed to Hosea" which she cites.[24] In addition, a single final redactor

---

[21] Note particularly Good's citation ("The Composition of Hosea," 33) of the stumbling motif in Hos 4:5.

[22] Yee, *Composition and Tradition*, 47.

[23] Yee, *Composition and Tradition*, 48, emphasis mine.

[24] Yee, *Composition and Tradition*, 49, names two criteria for isolating the final redactional layer, but they are sufficiently vague so as to inspire little confidence in their usefulness. The first is "the presence of *aporiae* or difficulties in the text. The second criterion is the *structure*. To her credit, Yee acknowledges the need to evaluate the many *aporiae* in Hosea from the perspective of the entire book, compiling and evaluating the observations on the text. However, most of the categories she proposes to classify these tensions are rather formal. Authors from different centuries could have used word plays, or older material could be moved to a new location. To determine if there is any similarity or rationale (redactional or stylistic) in these tensions, one must incorporate more than a compilation of stylistic techniques and thematic similarities. In addition, it is not precisely clear, how this methodological description differs from standard methodological steps against which she claims to be campaigning. The description she presents starts from an awareness of the whole, observes the smaller units, and moves outward. The major difference lies in her *assumptions* regarding the book's structure, which she incorporates into a

theory has real difficulties adequately explaining the extent of other layers of material in Hosea, whose presence even Yee recognizes.[25] Yee concludes that this final redactor composed the superscription (1:1) and the subscription (14:10), three compositional blocks at the end of major thematic sections, and various verses scattered throughout the book.[26] She graphically demonstrates the redactional material and the thematic motifs of the book in the following manner:[27]

---

methodological foundation regarding the responsibility of the final redactor for the overall shape of the whole. Throughout the remainder of this present work it should become clear that a great deal of redactional work post-dated the work of those who had given structural shape to a given work.

[25] Yee herself finds no less than four "stages of redaction" (see her conclusions, *Composition and Tradition*, 305-313) which include Hoseanic material (labeled H), a collector (C) perhaps from the time of Hezekiah whose hand is only visible in parts of chapters 1 and 2, a first redactor (R1) who was a Judean, influenced by Deuteronomistic thought, and the final redactor (R2) who also had a Deuteronomistic orientation, but from the perspective of the exile. This final redactor worked primarily with paronomasia including antanaclasis (the use of the same word with a different meaning), double entendres, metaphony (a similar sounding root with different meanings), parasonancy, consonantal transposition, assonance, epanastrophe, and alliteration. (309) This final redactor is also responsible for structural changes to conform to the motifs he was creating. See her diagram reproduced here.

[26] The problems of an exilic dating for major compositional pieces, have already been mentioned above. The interest here is to concentrate on certain methodological questions and the conclusions Yee draws for her understanding of the structure of the book. Most significantly, Yee does not offer significant explanation as to how the same hand could have composed such radically different pieces as 3:1-5; 11:1-11; and 14:2-10. The latter two bear much more similarity to one another than chapter three, but it still seems unlikely that they derive *en toto* from the same hand. Despite the question of the origin of the compositional blocks, Yee's assignation of the (two) later redactional stages to Deuteronomistic circles has considerable merit.

[27] Yee, *Composition and Tradition*, 310. What is not clear from this chart is the extent of other material in the book which Yee attributes to R2, but does not include in this chart. A list of passages which Yee assigns to the final redactor include: 1:1,5,6b-7; 2:1-3,8-9,10b,15b-18aa,19-20,22b-25; 3:1-5; 4:3,6a,7-12a,12bb,14,16b,17b; 5:2b,4,13b; 5:15-6:3,5;6:11b-7:1*;7:4,10,12a*,12b,15*,16;8:4b-5a,6*-7,13-14;9:2-4,6,8-9,14,17;10:9-10,12, 13b-14; 11:1-11; 12:1b,5-7,10-12,14; 13:1-11,14; 14:2-10.

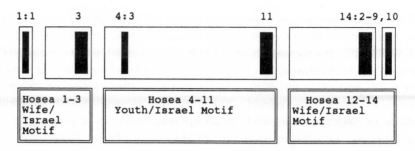

The thematic consistency in her chart is highly problematic. A thorough critique is not possible, but some observations upon her claims regarding Hos 14:2-9 are necessary.

Yee contends, following Feuillet, that 14:2-9 subtly reverts to the marriage motifs of 1-3.[28] Two flaws detract from the argumentation of both Feuillet and Yee. First, their case rests in large part upon an emended text, which has no support in the versions. They unqualifyingly accept the frequently suggested emendation of MT בצלו (his shade) to בצלי (my shade), an emendation already rejected above as both unnecessary and unattested.[29] Second, the contention that 14:2-9 utilizes marriage imagery appears inappropriate since this passage, unlike chapter two, depicts *both Israel and YHWH as masculine*, making speculation that the passage intends marriage imagery highly tenuous.

In summary, several recurring themes may be extracted from the discussion above, which will help explain the character and scope of Hos 14:2-9. First, this passage is appropriate to the macrostructure of the book.

---

[28] Yee, *Composition and Tradition*, 138-140. Yee's conclusions are based in large part on the article by A. Feuillet, "'S'asseoir à l'Ombre' de l'epoux (Os. 14:8a et Cant. 2:3)." *RB* 78 (1971): 391-405. Feuillet argues that the phrase "to sit in my shade" in Hos 14:8a actually refers to Israel sitting in the shade of YHWH, and is essentially associated with the marriage metaphor in Hos 2. He also claims the perspective of chapters 2, 11, and 14 all present a dialogue of love.

[29] See text note 14:8b,c. Strangely, this emendation runs counter to Yee's stated aim to avoid emendation, if possible, and to emend only on the basis of version attestation if necessary (*Composition and Tradition*, 131). In light of this statement, her rationale for emending 14:8a appears particularly strained since she emends, not on textual grounds, but on the basis of metaphony and style (*Composition and Tradition*, 347, note 17). Other evidence cited by Feuillet and Yee includes vocabulary similarities to Cant 2:2f, but they fail to demonstrate whether Hos 14:2ff draws upon these traditions or the other way around. In light of the late date of Canticles as a book, with a strong contingent of scholars dating its formation in the third century, this question represents no small oversight. Cf. Eissfeldt, *Introduction*, 490; Kaiser, *Introduction*, 365f.

The word of salvation and hope at the end of 12-14 is expected considering the oscillation of these themes in both 1-3 and the positive message of 11:1-11, which ends the thematic block of Hos 4-11. Second, while the material is itself not from Hosea, it is not so young (on the whole) that one could claim it is post-exilic, although recent work (Yee) does suggest the passage originates in the exilic period. Third, the use of meaningful theological motifs and word associations from all the major sections of Hosea argues 14:2-9 possesses a *literary* awareness of Hos 1-3, 4-11, and 12-14.

2. Literary Analysis of Hos 14:2-9 and 14:10

The following describes the complicated literary structure of the divine promise in Hos 14:2-9 (An Extended Call to Repentance), and the concluding motto in 14:10:[30]

2-4 Prophetic Call to Repentance

2	Call to Israel to return to YHWH (2ms)
3a	Further call (to people) (2mp)
3b-4	Suggested prayer for the people (1cp)

5-9 Divine Promise of Weal with Botanical Imagery

5a	Decision of YHWH to heal apostasy of people (3mp)
5b	Removal of YHWH's anger from Israel (3ms)
6aa	YHWH's promise to be like dew to Israel (3ms)
6ab-7, 8b	Metaphorical description of dew's effects on Israel (3ms)
8a	Parenthetical statement about the inhabitants' (3mp) return to Israel (3ms)
9a	Rhetorical question of YHWH to Ephraim (2ms)
9ba	YHWH answers question (3ms)
9bb	Statement of YHWH to Ephraim (2ms)

10 Concluding Motto

10a	Double rhetorical question
10b	Three-fold statement about the ways of YHWH

Formally, these verses contain three distinct units: the prophetic call to repentance in 14:2-4, the divine promise in 14:5-9 and the concluding motto

---

[30] All of Hos 14:2-10 is distinguished in character from its context by the positive manner in which Israel is portrayed. Such swings from the negative to the positive appear elsewhere in Hosea (2:16-25; 6:1-3; 11:8-11). See also above discussion on the delineation of units.

in 14:10. The first two of these units are joined together to create an extended, composite call to repentance, as has already been noted by Jeremias.[31] Hos 14:2-4 is a prophetic call to repentance, in which the prophet addresses Israel about YHWH. The use of cultic language, and the relationship of these verses, especially 3-4, to other passages (e.g. Isa 30:16; Deut 17:16) support the arguments of post-Hoseanic composition.[32] In addition, the mention of Assyria in these verses presupposes the destruction of Samaria, after which time it would be painfully obvious to all that Assyria was no political redeemer.

Hos 14:5-9 comprises a YHWH speech which should be interpreted with the prophetic call to repentance in 14:2-4, although 14:5 contains no hint of the anti-Assyrian polemic of 14:2-4, a fact which points toward independent origin. This speech utilizes several elements, whose distinctive markers appear in the references to Israel.[33] Hos 14:5 functions as the two level introduction of 14:5-9. Hos 14:5b announces YHWH's salvific decision consistent with the bulk of the material in 14:6-8, while 14:5a (together the כי in 14:5b) introduces the divine speech and joins the verse to 14:2-4. Verses 6-7,8b speak in metaphorical language about Israel. YHWH is still the speaker by context, but the style changes from 5a.[34] Hos 14:9 ends the metaphorical description of Israel, and reverts to the 1cs speech of YHWH as in 14:5, effectively framing the YHWH speech.[35] In

---

[31] See discussion of structure above, page 60. Jeremias does not, however, clearly distinguish between the background of the prophetic (14:2-4) and the divine (14:5-9) speakers in the two portions, although he provides the basis for doing so (170f). He notes that 14:2-4 presupposes the culmination of the destruction of Samaria announced in 13:15 as well as other portions of Hosea. This literary awareness implies a literary awareness not inherently present in 14:5-9.

[32] In addition to Jeremias, see Ina Willi-Plein, *Vorformen der Schriftexegese innerhalb des Alten Testaments. Untersuchungen zum literarischen Werden der auf Amos, Hosea und Micha zurückgehenden Bücher im hebräischen Zwölfprophetenbuch.* BZAW 123 (Berlin: DeGruyter, 1971), 231.

[33] In 14:5a the reference to Israel uses the third person plural; 14:5b-8 utilizes the third person singular; while 14:9 refers to "Ephraim" in both the second and third person singular.

[34] The change of style is evident from the lack of divine first person, the 3ms description of Israel, and the changes of imagery to botanical and agricultural metaphors describing the future health of Israel as a result of the decision of YHWH in verse 14:5.

[35] Hos 14:9 is not consistent with regard to the referent. Hos 14:9a addresses Ephraim rhetorically, while in 14:9b Ephraim is spoken about in the third person as in the preceding verses (14:5-8), and addressed in the second person singular. Wolff, *BK* 14/1, 212, distinguishes between Ephraim, used in a more limited geographical sense, and Israel, which refers to the people of YHWH. This verse is consistent with those places

addition, the variation of the 2ms and 3ms references in 14:9 indicates its compositional character. The verse not only frames the YHWH speech of 14:5-9, but, by inclusio, picks up the perspective of 14:2, and fashions several word plays which connect it to 14:4,5 as well. It is thus aware of a context extending across the prophetic and divine speeches.[36]

The plural subject of the verbs (וישבו, יחיו, ויפרחו‎) literarily isolates Hos 14:8a from the singular references in 14:6-7,8b.[37] This sentence creates confusion to those seeking to understand Israel (plural) as the subject of ישבו‎.[38] Instead, Hos 14:8a should be seen as a *parenthetical statement* whose subject is inhabitants, not Israel. Similarly, the reference to "his shade" is not to be understood as the shade of YHWH, but rather the shade of Israel. While many emend MT to read בצלו‎ as בצלי‎, such a reading ignores the change from a singular to plural subject, and has no textual support.[39] In addition the syntax of 14:8a interrupts the sentence structure of 14:7,8b as can be demonstrated:

14:7 ——————

ילכו ינקותיו
ויהי כזית הודו
וריח לו כלבנון>

14:8 ——————

ישבו ישבי בצלו
יחיו דגן
ויפרחו כגפן
זכרו כיין לבנון>

---

in Hosea which mention Ephraim after referring to Israel (cf. 13:12).

[36] Jeremias, *ATD* 14/1, 169, notes the inclusio to 14:2, see above discussion. Note also the word plays between 14:9 and 14:4,5: Ephraim (אפרים‎) in 14:9 and "I will heal" (ארפה‎) in 14:5, as well as "I will save him" (ואשורנו‎) in 14:9 and "Assyria will not save us" (אשור ל א יושיענו‎) in 14:4.

[37] The only exception to the use of the singular is ילכו‎ in 14:7, however, the subject there is integrally related to the image of Israel as a tree in which "*his* roots" is specifically the subject of ילכו‎. This metaphorical consistency is clearly distinguishable from 14:8 where "inhabitants" has no such intrinsic connection to the tree metaphor.

[38] For example, see Wolff, *BK* 14/1, 301 (note 8a) and Rudolph, *KAT* 13/1, 248 (note 8a), who give priority to the reading of LXX; and James Mays, *Hosea* (London: SCM, 1969), 189, who assumes LXX with no explanation.

[39] The assumption that shade must refer to the protection of YHWH purely on form-critical grounds is questionable, in light of the alternative explanation offered here. This form-critical assumption demands unwarranted emendation, even if such emendation appears slight. See text note 14:8b. Commentators emending this text are numerous: Mays, *Hosea*, 184; Wolff, *BK* 14/1, 301; Weiser, *ATD* 25/1, 85; Jacob *CAT* 11a, 95; Yee, 136; Feuillet, 394; Rudolph, *KAT* 13/1, 247f. By contrast only a handful have accepted MT here, such as: Robinson, *HAT* 14, 52; Keil, 166.

When 14:8a is removed, the text consistently references Israel as subject, leaving one with the conclusion that 14:8a is secondary. Further, the imagery is such that 14:8a could not have been added prior to the composition of 14:6f. Hos 14:8a presupposes the picture of Israel as a fruitful tree present in these verses (hence "his shade"), but adds the image of Israel as a geo-political entity to which the inhabitants may return.[40] The theme of the return of the inhabitants denotes a post-exilic perspective, contrary to the remainder of the passage.

Hos 14:10 has been added as a conclusion to the Book. Its summary function and the third person references to YHWH separate this verse from the preceding unit so dramatically that 14:10 receives almost universal treatment as a motto for the end of the writing. The long held view that the verse exhibits a wisdom background has justifiably been called into question in recent literature. These works accent the affinity of 14:10 to Deuteronomistic redactional work and motifs within the book, and they demonstrate the folly of treating this verse as a sign of transmission circles which differ substantially from the remainder of the writing.[41]

In summary, the prophetic call to repentance in 14:2-4 and the composition of promised weal (14:5-9) should be read as part of the same exhortation. The YHWH speeches in 14:5,9 which frame the metaphorical descriptions in 14:6-7,8b, are intended as divine exhortations calling for

---

[40] For the geo-political use of the term shade in reference to the political protection of one nation for another, see Isa 30:2f (Egypt); Ezek 17:23 (Israel); and Ezek 31:16f (Assyria).

[41] For further information on the background of 14:10, see Wolff, *BK* 14/1, 310-311; Rudolph, *KAT* 13/1, 253; Mays, *Hosea*, 190; Jeremias, *Hosea*, 174. While none doubt its function as conclusion to the entire book, the provenance of the verse has recently been called into question. Yee, *Tradition and Composition*, 140f, and C.L. Seow, "Hosea 14:10 and the Foolish People Motif," *CBQ* 44 (1982): 212-224, both admit the verse has summary elements, but deny the language requires a specific wisdom tradent for the transmission of the book. Yee (140f) considers 14:10 the composition of R2 because 1) that redactor has a fondness for framing units; 2) the language more nearly approaches Deuteronomistic and Deuteronomic material elsewhere (esp. Deut 4:6; Jer 9:11); 3) the verse takes up other redactional passages from the same author (2:8f); 4) the stumbling theme takes up 14:2 as inclusio. Seow argues Hos 4-14 exhibits a "foolish people" motif, and while the passages he cites (4:7; 4:10b-12a; 4:14; 7:11a; 8:7; 9:7; 12:2; 13:3; and 14:10) are not all of the same value in trying to isolate this so-called motif, he does present a plausible case. In his conclusion, Seow mentions some other passages which, although he does not discuss them in detail, offer more evidence of the interrelatedness of the summary verse with content in the remainder of the book. He cites the references to the stumbling of the foolish people (4:5; 5:5; 14:2) and their sinning against YHWH (7:13) and his law (8:1).

Israel's repentance. In spite of the compositional nature of 14:2-9, Hos 14:8a is noticeably distinguished as a later insertion on syntactical, stylistic, situational, and theological grounds. Hos 14:10 serves as an ending to Hosea, whose composition likely stems from Deuteronomistic circles, and it may have been penned as a transition from Hosea to Amos.

3. The Literary Horizon of Hos 14:2-9,10

It should already be clear that the literary horizon of the majority of the material in Hos 14:2ff may best be as explained inner-Hoseanic, as noted in recent works.[42] The existence of a literary insertion in 14:8a, which brings an entirely different perspective to the text, and which contains the majority of the catchwords to Joel, raises questions, however, best answered with the assumption of a wider literary horizon. This wider horizon encompasses not only Hosea (significantly parts of chapter two), but also a connection to Joel, and the utilization of themes recurring at significant positions in the Book of the Twelve.

The catchwords noted between Hos 14:5-10 and Joel 1:1-14 are "inhabitants" (Hos 14:8, Joel 1:2), "grain" (Hos 14:8, Joel 1:10), "vine" (Hos 14:8, Joel 1:7,12), "wine" (Hos 14:8, Joel 1:5), and the pronoun אלה (Hos 14:10) with its singular counterpart זאת (Joel 1:2 [twice]). Three of the five *Stichwörter* in the Hosea - Joel connection appear in 14:8a, whose presence has been isolated above as distinct from the majority of Hos 14:2-9,10. The remaining catchwords appear in verses already present at the point of connection between Hosea and Joel. In the metaphorical material of 14:8b, "wine" appears as a symbol of renown in the reference to the wine of Lebanon, and clearly belongs to the earlier material (see literary discussion above, page 66f). While 14:10 is separate from the remainder of the unit, its field of vision nevertheless centers on the book of Hosea, indicating its inclusion in the Hosea corpus predated Hosea's placement adjacent to Joel.[43] One must concentrate upon the addition of 14:8a as

---

[42] While there is certainly no agreement on an exact description of the date, and along with that the question of authorship, many have shown the manner in which 14:2-10 takes up themes in a meaningful manner from the remainder of the book, making it possible to argue the majority of chapter 14 was intended as a theological conclusion to the book. See above discussion on Hosea's macrostructure.

[43] Association of the verse with a Deuteronomistic tradent (see above, page 68), raises the possibility that this verse was composed originally as a transition from Hosea to Amos. Support for this suggestion, while not definitive, points in that direction. Hos

a meaningful connecting device backward to portions of Hos 2, forward to Joel, and in light of the recurrence of similar images and motifs in the Book of the Twelve.

3.1 Backward in Hosea

The catchwords grain, vine, and inhabitants in Hos 14:8a appear elsewhere in Hosea, but their repetition in 14:8 intentionally incorporates certain motifs from Hosea as an intermediary step to the message of Joel.[44] A look at the situation presumed by 14:8a and the literary connections to Hosea and Joel demonstrates a high degree of interplay between the books in which 14:8a plays a significant role.

When one asks what situation is presumed in Hos 14:8a an interesting picture develops. The first phrase presupposes a deportation of the inhabitants. It is self-evident that the promise of a return of the inhabitants is only meaningful if they have been already taken away. This elementary observation instantly raises a question. Which deportation does 14:8a presume, that which followed the destruction of Samaria or Jerusalem? The immediate context would initially appear to argue that the destruction of Samaria is intended. The announced destruction of Samaria at the end of chapter 13 and the surrounding material citing Israel (as the Northern Kingdom) make this option possible. An isolated reading of Hos 14 would have no reason to suspect otherwise. However, there is good reason to suggest that an isolated reading of Hos 14 was not the intention of the author of 14:8a, and that its composition must have occurred at a time which presupposes the fall of Jerusalem.[45]

14:10 predicts judgment on "those sinning," which would serve as a suitable introduction to the refrain of the oracles in Amos "for three sins and for four ..." (Amos 1:3,6,9, 11,13; 2:1,4,6). The use of צדק could point forward to Amos as well (2:6; 5:2,7,24; 6:12). See more detailed discussion of the Deuteronomistic corpus in the discussion of Amos, Micah, and Zephaniah.

[44] "Inhabitants" appears in Hosea only in 14:8 and 4:1, where YHWH brings suit against the "inhabitants of the land." The plural pronoun "these" is used in Hosea only in 14:10. "Wine" occurs ten times in Hosea. This includes both יין (Hos 4:11; 7:5; 9:4; 14:8) and the synonym תירוש (2:10,11,24; 7:14; 4:11; 9:2). "Vine" occurs three times in Hosea (2:14; 10:1; 14:8). "Grain" occurs ten times in the Book of the Twelve, and nine of those ten occurrences are found in Hosea and the first two chapters of Joel (Hos 2:10,11,24; 7:14; 9:1; 14:8; Joel 1:10,17; 2:19).

[45] This argument must necessarily presuppose the interplay with Joel, whose post-exilic date (be it 6th or 4th century) is rarely disputed any longer. See discussion below on the date of Joel at the end of the discussion of Joel 4:1-21.

Three of the catchwords of 14:8 appear in an interrelated context in chapter two (grain, new wine [תִּירוֹשׁ], and vines).[46] In essence these elements in chapter two function as the hermeneutical key for understanding how they are to be understood in the remainder of the book. These elements appear in divine speeches within an anti-idolatry polemic. YHWH accuses his wife/Israel of taking these and other agricultural elements which he provided (2:10f), and using them in the worship of Baal (2:10,15), which in turn instigates his punitive action, the removal of the elements themselves (2:11). This pictorial presentation of false worship and ensuing punishment is elaborated or reiterated in other passages (4:11; 7:14; 9:1f), and at least in part functions as an introduction to those passages which are to come. However, chapter two contains a later section in which a divine salvific promise offers future restoration of these elements following the return of the wife/Israel to YHWH (2:23f).[47]

The promised future restoration of the agricultural elements appears again in 14:8a, summarized in the promise that the inhabitants will again grow grain. The motifs of false worship (14:4,9) and repentance (14:2f) are already present in the chapter, but the promise of the return of fruitful agricultural elements is not present.[48] This final element appears in Hosea only in 2:23f and in 14:8a.

Hos 2:23ff comprises part of a larger eschatological section (הַהוּא בַּיּוֹם in 2:18,20,23) which takes up motifs from chapter two in summary fashion, and which shares images and phrases from significant portions of the Book of the Twelve.[49] The close connection between Hos 14:8, Hos 2:18ff and Joel 1-2, suggest the possibility that a single literary layer incorporated the two passages.

---

[46] See Hos 2:10f,14f,23f.

[47] The nature of this promise is frequently recognized by exegetes as betraying a perspective which presupposes the surrounding text of 1-3, and post-dates the time of Hosea. A date shortly after the siege of Jerusalem in 701 is most often mentioned, but even this date is probably too early. See Rudolph, *KAT* 13/1, 25f,78; Jeremias, *ATD* 24/1, 38; Weiser, *ATD* 24, 13; Jacob, *CAT* 11a, 31. Wolff, *BK* 14/1, 58, has difficulty in maintaining the genuineness of the passage while acknowledging the tensions of the sayings.

[48] This statement recognizes a distinction between the comparative material in which Israel is associated with healthy fruit bearing plants, and the literal promise of renewed agricultural fortune of the kind promised in 2:23f and 14:8a.

[49] Compare discussions of Joel, Zephaniah, Micah, Hag, Zech 8, all of which reflect backwards upon the imagery of Hos 2, albeit sometimes through Joel.

3.2. Forward to Joel

Much could be written about the manner in which Hos 14:8 has Joel in its literary scope, but only a few general comments on the character of this interplay will be offered here.[50]   The purpose of 14:8 in its relationship to Joel appears to be two-fold and paradoxical: 1) Hos 14:8 seeks to reiterate a hope for a time of productivity which has both agricultural (they will grow grain) and demographic (they will blossom like the vine) implications of well being. 2) Hos 14:8 serves to extrapolate this hope further into the future than would be understood in an isolated reading of Hosea. While the first objective of 14:8 should be clear and straightforward, the second deserves some explanation.

The entire tenor of 14:2-9 is one of promise. YHWH has a salvific plan for Israel whose realization requires Israel's acceptance of that plan, in the form of true repentance. The ending of Hosea leaves the reader with the impression of certainty that the events will occur, and a feeling of the nearness of their fulfillment. Hos 14:8 heightens the salvific picture, while simultaneously preparing the reader for the sudden reversal of those images. Hosea promises the revival of grain, but Joel dramatically portrays the devastated state of the grain (1:10,17). One assumes the reference to the vine means a healthy vine in 14:8, but Joel 1:7 dashes those hopes by picturing YHWH's vine as the wasted remains left over from a marauding nation. In short, while Joel deliberately juxtaposes the healthy images in Hos 14 with his own picture of reality, Hos 14:8 heightens this juxtaposition noticeably by its anticipatory use of grain and vine in elements of promise.

Formally, the addition of Hos 14:8a functions similarly to the end of other "pre-exilic" sections of the Book of the Twelve in that it adds a promise of restoration to the promise of well-being.[51] Hos 14:8a formally parallels the restoration promises in Joel 4:18-21; Amos 9:11,14f; Obad 17ff; and Zeph 3:18ff. Not only is it necessary that Israel will again be fruitful,

---

[50]   Such a discussion is necessary for methodological clarity, as a reminder that Hos 14:8a points both forward and backward, but it is simultaneously premature in that it anticipates the discussion of the redactional nature and function of Joel in a subsequent volume of this work.

[51]   The use of the term "pre-exilic section of the Book of the Twelve" in this context refers *not to the time of composition*, but to their placement and *function* in the literary movement of the Book of the Twelve. Hosea through Zephaniah function as a compendium of YHWH's prophetic message leading up to and including the exile. Haggai through Malachi, on the other hand presume a post-exilic situation, not only on the basis of their composition, but on the basis of their message as well.

but from the perspective of the Book of the Twelve, the promise of restoration must be reiterated continually to verify YHWH's intention when the exiles return (beginning with Haggai).

Turning briefly to the question of authorship, it is conceivable that Hos 14:8a was added as part of the Deuteronomistic corpus (Hos/Amos/Mic/Zeph), since that corpus received salvific redactions of its own.[52] One cannot entirely eliminate the possibility that 14:8a entered with the Deuteronomistic corpus, not the larger corpus now known as the Book of the Twelve, pending a more detailed analysis than this work allows. This scenario would treat Hos 14:8a as a literary addition to Hos 14:2-9, which would already have been available to Joel. This suggestion might help account for extensive compositional work on the part of Joel, but tentative observations argue against the assignation of Hos 14:8a to the Deuteronomistic corpus. One of the identifying marks of the Deuteronomistic corpus is the very clear differentiation between the fate of Israel and Judah. Israel's fate is destruction, and even in salvific layers, Israel tends to be subsumed under a Jerusalem-centered restoration of the Davidic monarchy (Amos 9:11,14; Mic 4:1ff; 5:2), and does not lose the negative judgments of earlier layers (cf Mic 1:2-7; 6:16). Hos 14:8a is not consistent with this tendency, since the verse promises the inhabitants will live in the shade of Israel. By contrast, by Joel's time Israel was a more inclusive term that would not have presented these difficulties.

---

[52] See discussions of Amos, Micah and Zephaniah for further reflections on the shape of this Deuteronomistic corpus.

Amos

1. The Macrostructure of Amos

The final form of the Book of Amos has been the subject of several investigations in recent Old Testament studies. Although these investigations create no absolute consensus concerning the extent and date of individual units, it has become increasingly accepted that any discussion of Amos must come to terms with both the tradition complexes and the redaction history of the book. Chapters 1-2 constitute a stylized series of oracles against the nations which culminate in the denunciation of the Northern kingdom. Scholars typically characterize chapters 3-6 as a collection of prophetic sayings. Amos 7:1-9:6 comprises the so-called vision cycle, and 9:7-10,11-15 present problematic passages which are often only vaguely categorized as the (hopeful) ending of the book. One notes quickly, however, that although each of these larger complexes has a certain character, they each have more than one layer of material present in them.

This investigation will treat the structure and composition of the initial (1:1-2:16) and final complexes (9:1-6,7ff) of Amos in more detail, in light of their involvement with the catchword connections to the neighboring works, but first, several observations require mention regarding the character and growth of Amos 3-6 and 7:1-9:6. Amos 3-6 divides into five smaller blocks on the basis of the unifying introductions used to open each unit.[1] The first three subsections open with the phrase, "Hear this word ..." in slightly varying forms (3:1; 4:1; 5:1),[2] while the marker "alas" (הוי in 5:18;

---

[1] The organization function of these passages requires more attention than it receives in most commentaries. Rudolph, *KAT* 13/2, 100f, notes briefly the organizational function of 3:1; 4:1; 5:1. Mays, *Amos*, 13,55,103 presents a typical view when he treats Amos 3-6 as a block, but makes no specific reference to the effect created by the different elements in 3:1; 4:1; 5:1; 5:18; 6:1. These introductions create the impression that impending judgment draws closer. Three times the command is given to "hear," followed by two lament introductions which strongly color the remaining oracles with the conviction that the words have not been heeded.

[2] The first and third application of the phrase manifest identical constructions in that both display the plural imperative (שמעו) followed by the "this word" with the direct object marker (את־הדבר הזה) and an אשר clause. The middle unit lacks the object marker and the אשר clause. All three contain vocative constructions, although with

6:1) begins the last two. The introductions serve to order and separate the collection of oracles which follow them. Thematically, these oracles center around the judgment of the Northern Kingdom, but they do demonstrate some interest in Jerusalem as well.[3]

The vision cycle (7:1-9:6) contains more than vision reports. The five visions (7:1-3,4-6,7-9; 8:1-3; 9:1-4) certainly fashion the core of the unit, but these visions neither stem from the same redactional level, nor do they represent the only *Gattung* within the larger complex. These chapters also contain a narrative account of the confrontation between Amos and Amaziah in 7:10-17, and individual speeches in 8:4-14. The constituent elements are arranged so that they comment upon and expand the message of the visions, based upon other portions of the book. The position of these various elements plays a redactional role, with the visions providing the frame for an escalation of tension in the movement of the entire section. This escalation becomes particularly evident when one compares the responses to the various visions.[4] Despite this escalation within the visions, substantial scholarly opinion argues that the fifth and final vision represents a later immitation of the other visions.[5] The redactional role of this vision will become clearer in the following discussion.

In the first two visions, the prophet petitions YHWH not to complete the destruction of Israel (7:2,5), and YHWH responds by changing his mind (7:3,6). The third vision provokes no prophetic petition from Amos, but in its current form leads instead to the narrative of the Amaziah confrontation (7:10-17). In the context of the vision cycle, Amaziah represents the response of Israel proper to the preaching of Amos (cf 7:17). As such, the

---

variations. The first and third again bear more similarity, exhibiting combinations of Israel (Sons of Israel, House of Israel), while the middle introduction addresses the "cows of Bashan" on the mountain of Samaria and appears more integrally bound to the oracle which follows.

[3] Note that Amos 6:1 incorporates Jerusalemites as well as the Northern Kingdom, beginning with a warning to heed the same message: "Woe to those who are at ease in Zion, and to those who feel secure in the mountain of Samaria."

[4] See Hartmut Gese, "Komposition bei Amos," *VT.S* 32 Congress Volume (1980): 75-85, particularly 83-85, where he notes the climactic literary escalation accomplished by the fifth vision.

[5] Scholars note the final vision differs significantly in its introductory formula, style, language, and content, although not all assign the vision to a different author. For more thorough summaries of the differences, see discussions in Willi-Plein, *Vorformen*, 48, and particularly Günter Bartczek, *Prophetie und Vermittlung. Zur literarischen Analyse und theologischen Interpretation der Visionsberichte des Amos*, Europäische Hochschulschriften Series 23, vol. 120 (Bern: Peter Lang, 1980), 71-90.

redactor who placed this account here portrays the people's rejection of YHWH's overtures. The fourth vision continues the escalation immediately with the famous vision of the "end".[6] This vision also contains no prophetic petition, but climaxes with YHWH's pronouncement that he will no longer spare Israel. This fourth vision report invokes an extended portrayal of the results of YHWH's judgment. The portrayal of these results begins with a summary of YHWH's accusation against the people (8:4-6), and continues with oracles concerning the theme of the day(s) of YHWH's destruction of Israel (8:7-14). The final vision report (9:1-4) takes this elevation one step further, portraying the prophet as a mere spectator who observes YHWH give the command to destroy Israel, and leave no survivors.

As stated earlier, not all of the material in these larger tradition blocks derives from the same layer of redaction. Considerable evidence suggests Amos was edited at several points in its long history. Numerous models of this redaction history have been proposed. Wolff, Coote, Rudolph, Schmitt, Kellermann, Weimar, Watts and Soggin all offer various schema, occasionally interacting with one another, to postulate the growth of the book.[7] A complete analysis of the scholarly debate is not possible here, but some general comments are necessary.[8]

Amos attests to its growth beginning with the superscription in 1:1. The superscription contains dating elements, typically attributed to

---

[6] The vision utilizes a word play on the Hebrew word for summer fruit (קיץ) and "end" (קץ), and announces complete judgment upon Israel.

[7] Wolff, *BK* 14/2, 129-138; Rudolph, *KAT* 13/2, 100-103; Robert B. Coote, *Amos among the prophets: Composition and Theology* (Philadelphia: Fortress, 1981), 1-10; Werner H. Schmidt, "Die deuteronomistische Redaktion des Amosbuches. Zu den theologischen Unterschieden zwischen dem Prophetenwort und seinem Sammler," *ZAW* 77 (1965): 168-193; Ulrich Kellermann, "Der Amosschluss als Stimme deuteronomischer Heilshoffnung." *EvTh* (1969): 169-183; J. Alberto Soggin, *The Prophet Amos* (London: SCM, 1987), 16-18; John D.W. Watts, "The Origin of the Book of Amos." *Expository Times* 66 (1954/55): 109-112; Peter Weimar, "Der Schluss des Amos-Buches. Ein Beitrag zur Redaktionsgeschichte des Amos-Buches." *BN* 16 (1981): 60-100.

[8] A complete analysis would necessitate a discussion of the methodology and results of these various authors. For example, Coote deliberately seeks to oversimplify the growth of the book into three movements, whereas Wolff finds six different redactional stages and Weimar isolates five layers, based upon his study of Amos 9, which he relates to the remainder of the writing. Rudolph operates with an idea of the unification of collections of "genuine" Amos material which receives a number of secondary glosses and additions in the course of transmission.

Deuteronomistic redaction of prophetic writings.[9] In addition, some argue that the remaining information derives from the combination of two distinct collections: the words and the visions of Amos, representing 1-2/3-6 and 7:1-9:6 respectively.[10] Although most scholars acknowledge multiple layers in 1:1, they debate the original form of the superscription.[11] They almost universally treat the phrase "the words of Amos" and the phrase "two years before the earthquake" as parts of the earliest superscription. Two אשר clauses complicate Amos 1:1. The first clause ("who was among the shepherds from Tekoa") relates to Amos, and the second ("which he saw") refers back to "words".[12] This second clause, and the synchronization in the royal date formula, are normally considered later elements.[13] The remaining material causes consternation for attempted reconstructions.[14]

---

[9] Note especially the synchronization of the reigns of both Northern and Southern kings. See further Werner H. Schmidt, *ZAW* 77 (1965): 170; J.D.W. Watts, "The Origin of the Book of Amos," *ET* 66 (1954/55): 109; Wolff, *BK* 14/2, 150f; Gene M. Tucker, "Prophetic Superscriptions and the Growth of a Canon," in *Canon and Authority: Essays in Old Testament Religion and Theology*, George W. Coats and Burke O. Long, eds. (Philadelphia: Fortress Press, 1977, 56-70), 62.

[10] Note above all Watts' article, "The Origin of the Book of Amos," *ET* 66 (1954/55): 109-112, in which he argues that the two elements of the words and the vision exhibit the essential characteristics of chapters 1-6 and 7-9. For alternative views on the use of חזה with דבר, see Rudolph, *KAT* 13/2, 112, who relates the verb חזה to Amos 7:12.

[11] A recent commentator who apparently goes against the grain is Douglas Stuart, *Hosea-Jonah*, Word Biblical Commentary 31 (Waco, Texas: Word Books, 1987), 296-299. Stuart does not explicitly state that the superscription was written by a single author, but he strongly implies this idea by drawing parallels from other superscriptions to counteract those arguments normally offered in support of multiple levels.

[12] Charles D. Isbel, "A Note on Amos 1:1." *JNES* 36 (1977): 213-214, picks up on the long noted fact that LXX understands the first אשר clause as a reference to "words" and not to Amos. Isbel considers LXX as the proper understanding of the phrase, and interprets the first clause as a statement about the transmission of the corpus. While he correctly demonstrates that MT can grammatically be read in such a manner (GK §146), his attempt to make the case that this was the intended meaning lacks convincing power. Isbel translates MT as "The sayings of Amos which were (current) among the shepherds from Tekoa." He argues this statement is further evidence for a wisdom background. However, the prominence given to sheep herders as tradition carriers for a prophetic corpus would be unique.

[13] Weiser, *ATD* 24, 113; Mays, *Amos*, 18f, and Amsler, *CAT* 11a, 167, consider the second clause original and the first secondary, but Watts, *ET*, 109, Wolff, *BK* 14/2, 146f, and Rudolph, *KAT* 13/2, 111f, correctly note the close correlation of this phrase with the material in chapters 7-9.

[14] The following represents a sample of views on the form of the original superscription. Wolff *BK* 14/2 146f: "The words of Amos ... from Tekoa ... two years before the

In spite of the uncertainty of the form of the original superscription, a general consensus agrees that its conflation joined at least two separate collections of Amos material.

Confusion as to the definition and extent of the "Deuteronomistic" redaction(s) further complicates an entirely lucid depiction of the redaction history of Amos. Some authors believe the Deuteronomistic additions limit themselves essentially to the first six chapters, while other commentators argue that Deuteronomistic work extends into chapters 7-9 as well, even though they differ on precisely which passages reflect Deuteronomistic redaction.[15] Kellermann even argues that substantial portions of the ending to Amos (9:9*,11-12,14-15) reflect Deuteronomistic elements of hope from the exilic period.[16]

Recently Bosshard notes a phenomenon which throws light on the function of Amos 7:1-9:6 as it relates to chapters 1-6.[17] He observes a

---

earthquake"; Rudolph, *KAT* 13/2, 109-115: "The words of Amos ... from Tekoa ... concerning Israel ... two years before the earthquake." (introduced 1:3-2:16); Watts, *ET* 66 (109-112) "The words of Amos." (introduced 1-6); Soggin, *Amos*, 24-27: "The words of Amos ... from Tekoa"; Weiser, *ATD*, 113f; Mays, *Amos*, 18-20; Amsler, *CAT* 11a 167: "The words of Amos ... of Tekoa which he saw concerning Israel ... two years before the earthquake." One author goes so far as to postulate a preliterary stage of the collection and finds five different levels of work within the confines of 1:1. See Hans F. Fuhs, "Amos 1:1. Erwägungen zur Tradition und Redaktion des Amosbuches," in: *Bausteine biblischer Theologie. Festgabe für G. Johannes Botterweck zum 60. Gegurtstag dargebracht von seinen Schülern*. Bonner Biblische Beiträge 50. 271-289. Köln-Bonn: Peter Hanstein Verlag, 1977.

[15] See especially Watts, *ET* 66 (1954/55): 112, who limits Deuteronomistic work to chapters 1-6. The work of Werner Schmidt, *ZAW* 77 (1965): 168-193, agrees in large part with the observations of Watts. One notable exception, however, relates to Schmidt's attribution of substantial portions of Amos 1:1 to the Deuteronomistic redaction. This Deuteronomistic material in 1:1 corresponds, however, to the very material which most authors would say is dependent upon the biographical material gleaned from 7:10-17, meaning that at the very least these redactors had access to the material in 7-9 in some form. Wolff, *BK* 14/2, 137, raises the possibility that one passage (8:11f) is conceivably attributed to the Deuteronomistic redaction, but he hesitates to state this with certainty. However, this lack of Deuteronomistic work in Amos 7-9 is countered by the fact that for Wolff, other redactions, whose traces appear in both 7-9 and 1-6, precede the Deuteronomistic redaction. Rudolph, *KAT* 13/2, 102, recognizes only a few later glosses, and does not ascribe these to a systematic Deuteronomistic redaction of Amos. One interesting question which remains unanswered is why so little Deuteronomistic material appears in Amos 7-9.

[16] Ulrich Kellermann, *EvTh* (1969): 169-183.

[17] Bosshard, *BN* 40 (1987): 33.

series of inclusios that fashion Amos 1:1-9:6. He sketches his observations as follows:

```
┌──────── 1:1      Earthquake
│ ┌────── 1:2      אבל. ראש הכרמל
│ │ ┌──── 2:14     מלט. נוס
│ │ │ ┌── 4:6ff    cf. לחם (4:6); ונעו and מים (4:8); בחור (4:10)
│ │ │ │ ┌ 5:1ff    קינה
│ │ │ │ │ 5:18ff   cf. יום (5:18,20); חשך (5:18,20); אור (5:18,20)
│ │ │ │ │ 6:8      יעקב. גאון. נשבע
│ │ │ │ │
│ │ │ │ └ 8:7      יעקב. בגאון. נשבע
│ │ │ └── 8:9      אור, חשך, יום
│ │ │     8:10     קינה
│ │ └──── 8:11ff   cf. לחם and ונעו (8:11); מים (8:12);
│ │                  and בחור (8:13)
│ └────── 9:1      מלט. נוס
│ ┌────── 9:3      ראש הכרמל
└─┴────── 9:5      Earthquake, אבל
```

Bosshard's observations demonstrate that while the oracles against the nations (1:3-2:16) were present, only the end of the oracle against Israel participates in the inclusios. In addition, the first four visions and the narrative account in 7:10-17 are present, but not accented by the inclusios, implying this material was present but treated as a block.

Kratz takes Bosshard's initial observations and expands them in an attempt to explain the redactional intentions of 8:3-14 and 9:1-6.[18] He suggests a double schema, likely due to separate redactional layers, in which the first stage, containing 8:3ff*, comments upon passages in chapters 3-7, while the second stage broadens the horizon to the entire Amos corpus to that point (reaching to 9:6). Kratz schematicizes his observations as follows:[19]

Stage 1

```
┌──── 3f*/5:1-17
│ ┌── 5:18ff (1st woe)
│ └─  6:1ff  (2nd woe)
│ ┌─  6:9f  and visions in 7f*
│ │
│ └─  8:3
└─┴── 8:9,10 (1st and 2nd woe)
      8:13ff
```

---

[18] The following briefly summarizes a colloquium presentation by Dr. Reinhold Gregor Kratz on Feb 16, 1989 at the University of Zürich. Unfortunately, these observations are to date unpublished.

[19] The double line on the right of stage 2 was not part of Kratz's presentation, but represents an additional observation that Amos 1:1 is normally recognized as dependent upon the narrative material in 7:10-17. The significance of this observation is discussed below, page 80.

Σταγε υ

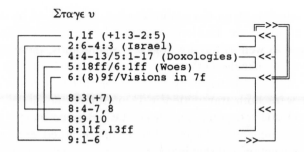

```
        ┌────── 1,1f (+1:3-2:5)              ┐ <<┐┌=>>┐
        │┌───── 2:6-4:3 (Israel)             ┘  ││   │
        ││┌──── 4:4-13/5:1-17 (Doxologies)─┐ <<-││   │
        │││┌─── 5:18ff/6:1ff (Woes)         │    ││   │
        ││││┌── 6:(8)9f/Visions in 7f      ─┘ <<=┘┘   │
        │││││                                         │
        ││││└── 8:3(+7)                               │
        │││└─── 8:4-7,8                          <<-  │
        ││└──── 8:9,10                                │
        │└───── 8:11f,13ff                       ─┐   │
        └────── 9:1-6                            ->>─┘
```

If the suspicions of Kratz are correct that two levels of material are present in chapter 8, these observations would indicate that 3-6/7-8* existed as a collection prior to the fifth vision and prior to the presence of the oracles against the nations.[20]

Combined, the observations of Kratz and Bosshard help to visualize a version of Amos which had its own complicated literary structure and history, but which extended only as far as 9:6.[21] The suggestion by Rudolph that the "original" version of the superscription only introduced the material as far as 2:16, thus becomes very plausible.[22] Indeed, the union of two collections (1-2 and 3-8*) is best explained as occurring with Kratz's stage two. One additional observation (noted in the schematization with double lines) buttresses their arguments by noting that not only is 9:1-6 aware of 1:1f, but scholars normally accept 1:1 as dependent upon 7:10-17 for much of the biographical information about Amos. The dependency of 1:1, in its present form, upon 7:10ff could not have been accomplished prior to the inclusion of the vision cycle with the oracles against the nations, a process which appears only to have been accomplished with stage two.

The increasing acceptance of the early to middle exilic period for a Deuteronomistic redaction of certain pre-exilic prophetic writings offers significant help in dating stage two.[23] The observations noted above allow a tentative date in this period for the version of Amos which extended to

---

[20] The oracles against the nations therefore presumably existed as an independent collection which later joined the collection of 3-8.

[21] These results coincide with much of the scientific work done on Amos in the past century which has noted that beginning with 9:7 the character of the book changes. See discussion below on 9:7-10,11-15.

[22] Rudolph, *KAT* 13/2, 100. See discussion of Rudolph's view about the original superscription, above note 14.

[23] Schmidt, *ZAW* 77 (1965): 169-173; Wolff, *BK* 14/1, 1f; *BK* 14/2, 138; 14/4, 2f; Mays, *Amos*, 18; Jörg Jeremias, "Die Deutung der Gerichtsworte Michas in der Exilszeit," *ZAW* 83 (1971, 330-354): 352f; and others. Contra Rudolph, *KAT* 13/2, 112.

9:6, since this date describes a corpus which includes all of the material normally ascribed as Deuteronomistic (excluding the arguments of Kellermann), as well as the doxologies. Significantly, these observations also indicate the likelihood that the unification of 1-2 with 3-8 took place in Deuteronomistic circles, or else — but less likely — that the separate collections were both transmitted in Deuteronomistic circles.[24] Thus, a "Deuteronomistic redaction" should not be described merely in terms of occasional unconnected glosses. The evidence noted here points to a substantial collection and shaping on the part of redactors from this school, who incorporated their message at both ends of Amos based upon pre-

---

[24] This model requires a certain flexibility in the form of a willingness to ascribe more of this material to "Deuteronomistic" influence than has heretofore been supposed. Yet this flexibility is not unwarranted since both 1-2 and 3-8 contain "Deuteronomistic" passages. Schmidt, *ZAW* 77 (1965): 169, for example, does not include the doxologies (4:13; 5:8f; 9:5f) in his list of Deuteronomistic material. He does not, however, say whether he believes their origin pre- or post-dates the Deuteronomistic editor. It is conceivable that their redactional placement was accomplished at this time, although the inclusios in Amos 9:5f raise serious questions regarding earlier assumptions that the doxologies were part of a single hymn. Most recent work indicates that these passages also stem from the exilic or post-exilic period. See James L. Crenshaw, *The Doxologies of Amos: A Form-Critical Study in the History of the Text of Amos* (Vanderbilt University, 1964), 174; Jörg Jeremias, *Theophanie. Die Geschichte einer alttestamentlichen Gattung* (Neukirchen: Neukirchner Verlag, 1965), 161; Werner Berg, *Die sogenannten Hymnenfragmente im Amosbuch* (Bern: Lang, 1974), 322-326; Fabrizio Foresti, "I brani participiali di Amos: 4:13; 5:8s; 9:5s," *Biblica* 62 (1981, 169-184), 176f; Soggin, *Amos*, 79. These arguments rely essentially upon parallels of the participial use of ברא for creator in 4:13, elsewhere only used in Deutero- and Trito-Isaiah (40:28; 42:5; 43:15; 45:7,18; 57:19; 65:17; 65:18). An Alternative view is held by Cullen I.K. Story, "Amos — Prophet of Praise." *VT* 30 (1980): 67-80. He maintains the structural involvement of all three hymns with their context makes it more likely that they go back to the time of Amos. Similar arguments are used by Rudolph, *KAT* 13/2,183. Wolff, *BK* 14/2, 256, considers 4:6-13 (including the first "doxology") as a liturgy based upon Josiah's destruction of the sanctuary at Bethel. Wolff subsequently argues for a similar provenance for the remaining doxologies, and dates his anti-Bethel editor in the time of Josiah. His observations may have some bearing upon a date for stage 1 above, but he stretches his point too far when he relates 9:1-6 to the anti-Bethel editor. Bethel plays no explicit role beyond Amos 7:13, whereas immediately prior to Amos 9:1ff, the text explicitly cites the "guilt of Samaria" prior to the final vision of destruction of the altar. Prudence demands this context take priority, particularly in light the redactional function of chapter eight and of the significance of Samaria in the Deuteronomistic corpus. See discussion of Mic 1:2ff, detailing the use of destruction of Samaria as a paradigm of warning to Jerusalem.

existing cycles.[25]   At any rate, the observations of Kratz and Bosshard, combined with other works on the Deuteronomistic redaction of Amos, become important for this study, because they allow the assumption that by the middle exilic period the book of Amos existed in a form which extended from Amos 1:1-9:6.

The remainder of Amos 9:7-10,11-15 will be treated later in this chapter. The major thrust of these verses display no interest in shaping the entire book of Amos, since they assume the fixed order of 1:1-9:6. Amos 9:7-10 comments upon a limited portion of the pre-existing book, and 9:11-15 introduces a salvific message missing from the remainder of the book.

2. The Literary Units in Amos 1:1-2:16

Three units comprise Amos 1:1-2:16: 1:1; 1:2; 1:3-2:16. The problem of the multi-layered superscription in **Amos 1:1** has been addressed above.[26] The relationship of this verse with its surrounding context as well as a more thorough discussion of the similarity of the Deuteronomistic form of Amos 1:1 to other prophetic superscriptions deserve discussion.

Amos 1:2 presupposes Amos 1:1 in some form. This statement is mandated by the form ויאמר ("and he said") opening Amos 1:2, which must refer to Amos as the antecedent since YHWH is mentioned in the third person hymnic style. It is not likely that ויאמר was the introduction to 1:3-2:16 since the messenger formula beginning 1:3 makes 1:2 redundant as an introduction to 1:3ff. It is thus possible to deduce that ויאמר belongs with 1:2. The question as to which level of the superscription is assumed is more complicated. It is possible that the phrase ויאמר (and 1:2 with it) could have been attached to the superscription at an early stage. Since the early form of 1:1 contained no verb, the use of אמר would not be out of place. On the other hand, with the addition of so many secondary clauses in 1:1, it is also possible that its use as a marker to refer back to Amos was thus necessary for clarity. In weighing the possibilities, it would appear

---

[25] It is important to note that these redactors assimilated much of their own material through the immitation of pre-existing material. Both the Deuteronomistic additions to the oracles against the nations and the fifth vision of Amos (9:1-4) utilized the form of the dominant element in their respective cycles, with 1:9f,11f; 2:4f being formulated very similarly to the earlier oracles in 1-2, and 9:1-4 imitating the formulations of 7:1-3,4-7; 8:1-3. See the fuller treatment of additions to the oracles against the nations and Amos 9:1-4 in the literary discussions of the respective passages.

[26] See above, page 76.

more likely that ויאמר in 1:1 is related to a layer of 1:1 which did not contain the royal synchronizations or the אשר clauses. The phrase would make sense following "The words of Amos from Tekoa two years before the earthquake", whereas if it was added later for clarification, it would seem more likely that someone would have also added the subject again.

The hymnic style of Amos 1:2 is at odds with early Amos material, and the verse has long been cited as a redactional motto for the book.[27] As noted above the combined form of 1:1-9:6 utilized the motto for the beginning of its version of Amos, but this observation does not determine at what point 1:2 entered the corpus.[28]   One may safely deduce a Jerusalemite origin for 1:2 since the verse describes Zion/Jerusalem as the place from which YHWH's voice proceeds in judgment against Carmel and the surrounding region. Is it possible to narrow the provenance of this motto further? Wolff argues 1:2 relates best to a cultic redaction of the Amos book, probably from around the time of Josiah, which encompasses most of the current form of Amos, while others do not acknowledge a clear link to the Bethel tradition.[29]   What Wolff does not point out, however,

---

[27] While almost all scholars treat Amos 1:2 as the motto for the book, some see Amos as the author of 1:2 or at least the one responsible for using older material. They argue that only its position serves a redactional purpose. So Rudolph, *KAT* 13/2, 116-118; and Ina Willi-Plein, *Vorformen der Schriftexegese innerhalb des Alten Testaments. Untersuchungen zum literarischen Werden der auf Amos, Hosea und Micha zurück-gehenden Bücher im hebräischen Zwölfprophetenbuch*, BZAW 123 (Berlin: DeGruyter, 1971) 15. Others more convincingly argue that 1:2 derives from a Jerusalem setting much later than Amos' time. So, e.g. Wolff, *BK* 14/2, 155f; Mays, *Amos*, 21.

[28] A definitive decision on this question would require a more thorough-going analysis of the redaction history of Amos than possible in this context. In the interest of space, and because of the nature of the catchwords, it is necessary to begin with the relatively safe arguments that 9:6 concluded the book of Amos at a significant point in its history. In addition to the observations of Kratz and Bosshard, see the discussion by Coote, *Amos Among the Prophets*, 47f, who (consciously simplifying) refers to Amos 1:1-9:6 as the B-stage of Amos responsible for fixing the order of the majority of the book. Plausibly, this motto could actually have been the introduction for the collection of 3-8, which was, together with 1:1, placed at the beginning of the two collections when they were combined. The difficulty in deciding the point of incorporation rises in part from the fact that it is not inconceivable that someone incorporated the verse earlier, as an introduction to the oracles against the nations prior to their combination with 3-8, particularly in light of the earthquake imagery at the conclusion of those oracles.

[29] Wolff, *BK* 14/2, 151f. So also Coote, *Amos Among the Nations*, 52. See the critique on the basis of the tradition background in Rudolph, *KAT* 13/2, 115-117; and another view that the verse comes nearer the later inclusion of the pro-Jerusalem motif of Amos 9:11f, Mays, *Amos*, 21. Because of the *inclusio* to 9:6, Mays' view suggests a

is that explicit evidence for this anti-Bethel tradition only appears in 3-7.[30]
The *unqualified acceptance* of Jerusalem as the place from which YHWH
proceeds in judgment would be very difficult to comprehend after
Jerusalem's own destruction,[31] but would fit well during the reign of Josiah
when religious fervor, coupled with political potential, raised the possibility
of a Jerusalem centered expansion.[32] Weighing all of the evidence, the
thesis regarding the Josianic reign as the time period for a redaction of
Amos, carries considerable weight, but this corpus probably did not include
Amos 1-2.

Scholars often relate the accretions of Amos 1:1 to a Deuteronomistic
redaction of several prophetic works.[33] Most commonly listed as the
recipients of this redactional superscriptive work are the books of Isaiah,
Jeremiah, Hosea, Amos, Micah, and Zephaniah. As noted in the
introduction, several scholars already cite the superscriptions of Hosea,
Amos, Micah, and perhaps Zephaniah as evidence of an incipient form of
the Book of the Twelve. This suggestion contains merit, but to date little
work has attempted to determine if these writings actually fashioned a
literary corpus, and if so, to what extent these works were edited. Were
they merely given common headings, or were certain theological motifs

---

redactional layer too far along in Amos' redaction history.

[30] Bethel appears in Amos 3:14; 4:4; 5:5f; 7:10,13. If Amos 1:2 is therefore related to an
anti-Bethel movement, it would seem more probable that 1:2 originally introduced 3-8*
(or roughly) stage one using Kratz's terminology.

[31] The exile so drastically changed the perception of Zion, that one would be hard pressed
to explain Amos 1:2 in light of its function as motto for the book to that point. Amos
1:2 depicts a theophany in which YHWH proceeds *from Jerusalem* northwards, but not
against a non-Israelite enemy. There is no hint of the guilt of Jerusalem so prevalent
in the early exilic literature (cf Lamentations), and no hint of the desolation in
Jerusalem so predominant in the late exilic and early post-exilic literature (cf Isaiah 50-
54; Hag 1). Finally, an exilic or early post-exilic date could not readily account for the
fact that the judgment depicted in 1:2 is directed against the head of Carmel. Enemies
were easy to find during this time (Babylon, Edom, Tyre, etc), and a tradition directed
exclusively against the North would make little sense.

[32] One may safely deduce that political tensions created during this period, whether or not
Josiah actually took over Northern territories. The centralization policies and ideals
of Josiah doubtless fueled these tensions. See summaries of the political overtones of
Josiah's reforms in Miller-Hayes, *A History of Ancient Israel and Judah*, 397-401;
Soggin, *A History of Israel*, 240-47; Guuneweg, *Geschichte Israels*, 120-122.

[33] See discussion above, page 77.

introduced and developed in this corpus as well? Were other works already included which did not contain this stereotypical heading?[34]

In all likelihood those pre-exilic works in the Book of the Twelve which experienced this redactional shaping in their superscriptions were configured at the same time and on the same scroll. Those who have made this suggestion in the past have done so on the basis of purely formal characteristics shared by Hosea, Amos, Micah, and Zephaniah.[35] None of these commentators, however, note that the similarity of these superscriptions goes beyond the sharing of these common components. The names and order of these kings provides a pattern which gives the impression of a deliberate effort to fashion a single corpus from these works. The order of the kings mentioned appears as follows:

Hosea	Amos	Micah	Zephaniah
Uzziah	—— Uzziah		
Jotham		—— Jotham	
Ahaz		—— Ahaz	
Hezekiah		—— Hezekiah	—— (Hezekiah)
Jeroboam	—— Jeroboam		
			Josiah

Several observations deserve attention. First, this order is not strictly chronological, but priority is given to the kings of Judah. Hos 1:1 mentions four Southern kings followed by a single Northern king, who was only contemporary with the first king mentioned. The approximate dates of the kings are:[36] Uzziah (786-746),[37] Jeroboam II (786-746), Jotham (756-

---

[34] Only a tentative answer to this question may be suggested currently, based on observations made in the remainder of this volume and the forthcoming volume.

[35] These formal elements are in themselves enough to convince one of a common circle, but not necessarily a common corpus. See a summary of the relationships of various superscriptions by Gene M. Tucker, "Prophetic Superscriptions and the Growth of a Canon," in Canon and Authority: Essays in Old Testament Religion and Theology, George W. Coats and Burke O. Long, eds. (Philadelphia: Fortress Press, 1977, 56-70), 62ff. Only Hosea, Amos, Micah, and Zephaniah are here included because they are the only ones of the Book of the Twelve which bear the synchronistic dating of the kings of Judah and/or Israel. Joel and Jonah contain similar elements, but other indications place the date of these works as post-exilic. See the discussion of their dates elsewhere in this work.

[36] Dates taken from Gunneweg, Geschichte Israels, 193-197.

[37] This dating supposes the redactional note of 2 Kgs 14:21 which adds an earlier coronation to the history than would be presumed from 2 Kgs 15:1, a passage which dates Uzziah's reign as beginning only in the 27th year of Jeroboam. See Gunneweg,

741),[38] Ahaz (742-725), Hezekiah (725-696), Josiah (639-608). This Southern priority leads to a second, related, point. The five kings of Hos 1:1 reappear in Amos and Micah. Amos 1:1 mentions both Uzziah and Jeroboam, again giving priority to the Southern king in spite of the Northern orientation of Amos. Hos 1:1 carries the dating at least 20 years beyond the death of Jeroboam, but makes no attempt to correlate this additional time with the reign of Northern kings.[39] This extension of Southern kings corresponds exactly to Micah's listing of only these three kings, yet Micah demonstrates no attempt at a Northern correlation, in spite of the fact that Northern kings still reigned during the reigns of Jotham, Ahaz, and Hezekiah.[40] Third, the superscription in Hosea precedes Amos, and functions as the dominant frame to Micah despite the fact that most generally consider Amos to be the oldest of the writing prophets. Fourth, Zeph 1:1 traces the prophet's genealogy (not Josiah's) back to Hezekiah by means of a son whose existence is otherwise unattested.[41] This citation of Hezekiah connects the superscription of Zephaniah with Micah despite the passing of more than sixty years between the time periods mentioned. All of these observations taken together lead to the conclusion that this series of kings is no accidental formulation.

If the selection and ordering of the kings in these four superscriptions represents a deliberate pattern, the purpose of such a schema naturally raises questions. One quickly notes that Hosea, Amos, and Micah summarize a period of Judean/Israelite history which culminates in Hezekiah, whereas Zephaniah begins with a reference to Hezekiah, from the perspective of Josiah's reign. This connection draws specific attention to Hezekiah (the connecting element) and to Josiah (the final element). Leaving the formal realm, one asks what would motivate someone to

---

Geschichte Israels, 111.

[38] Jotham was co-regent for roughly 10 years before becoming king.

[39] The same phenomenon may be noted in Isa 1:1, which lists the same five kings as Hosea, in the same order, adding more weight to the argument of a common tradent for the Isaiah corpus and the Book of the Twelve from at least the time of the exile.

[40] The following Northern kings are thus omitted: Zechariah (746), Shallum (746), Menahem (746-734), Pekahiah (736-734), Pekah (734-732), and Hosea (732-723).

[41] This statement is not designed to cast aspersions upon the historicity of the ancestry, since the Old Testament rarely mentions all of a king's children. It does, however, stress the likelihood that the reference to Hezekiah was no accident since no other prophet has his ancestry so extensively documented. For discussion of other explanations, see the discussion of Zeph 1:1 in the chapter on the Habakkuk/Zephaniah connection.

correlate these two kings, presumably from an exilic Deuteronomistic perspective (assuming the theory of a Deuteronomistic redaction is correct)? 2 Kings provides the basis for correlating these two kings. It presents both Hezekiah and Josiah as the two reforming monarchs whose reforms staved off the destruction of Jerusalem.[42] Hezekiah's reforms create the backdrop with which the historian contrasts the fate of Samaria to that of Jerusalem (cf 2 Kgs 18:9-12 with 18:13ff, and parallels). In spite of the reforms, the accounts make clear that Jerusalem's reprieve was only temporary and would not prevent its destruction at the hands of Babylon (cf 2 Kgs 20:12-19 for Hezekiah; and 2 Kgs 23:26f for Josiah).

Many of these themes recur in redactional passages in the Book of the Twelve's four Deuteronomistic works. A complete delineation of the extent of this redaction would exceed the scope of this work centering on the seams of the Twelve, but recognition of the existence of these motifs throws light on the role of several passages related to the broader discussion. The Book of the Twelve opens with the citation of the need for cultic reform. Hos 1:2 accuses the land of harlotry in forsaking YHWH. Hos 2 expands this theme (in more than one level of material) with specific reference to Baal worship. These images of harlotry/idolatry recur consistently throughout Hosea and in redactional passages in Amos and Micah.[43]

---

[42] Compare the extended accounts of the two reforms in 2 Kgs 18:1-12 (Hezekiah), and chapter 22f (Josiah). Hezekiah's reforms are credited with affording him the power of expanding Judean territory (18:7), and with the deliverance of Jerusalem from the hands of Senacherib (2 Kgs 18-20). Hezekiah's prominent reputation continued to grow even after the recording of the Deuteronomistic history. Compare, for example, the inclusion of 2 Kgs 18-20 into the Isaiah corpus, and the additional positive material presented by the Chronicler (2 Chr 29:3-36; 30:1-27; 31:2-21; 32:2-8). Josiah similarly reforms religious practice by destroying the idols in Jerusalem and beyond (particularly Bethel). See 2 Kings 23. The parallels between these two reforming kings are even more pronounced in the Chronicles material, which deliberately patterns the two reigns after one another. Note especially the renewal of the passover by both kings in 2 Chron 30:1-27 (Hezekiah) and in 35:1-17 (Josiah). Whether intentionally or not, note the similar titles for the synoptic paragraphs offered for these kings (§§148-160; 163-166), in James D. Newsome, *A Synoptic Harmony of Samuel, Kings, and Chronicles: With Related Passages from Psalms, Isaiah, Jeremiah, and Ezra* (Grand Rapids: Baker, 1986), 12f. Even later Jesus ben Sirach accents both Hezekiah and Josiah (skipping directly from one to the other), as the only two positive kings in addition to David.

[43] Within those writings which experienced a Deuteronomistic redaction one may note the following: Hos 1:2; 2:4,6,7; 3:3; 4:10,12,14,18; 5:3; 9:1; Amos 7:17; Mic 1:7. Not surprisingly, the dominance of this material in Hosea is explained because it was so involved in the Hosea tradition from a very early stage. The motif appears in both Amos and Micah in passages which have experienced Deuteronomistic shaping. The

Their presence marks an effort to warn Judah that it is treading the same path to destruction as Israel.[44] Bethel and Samaria receive considerable attention as provocateurs of god's anger.[45]

An early version of Zephaniah culminates this Deuteronomistic corpus with the contention that the judgment is at hand. Jerusalem did not heed YHWH's word, resulting in the punishment of "Judah", "the inhabitants of Jerusalem", the "remnant of Baal", and "the idolatrous priests".[46] In addition, this earlier version of Zephaniah, prior to the post-exilic promise of 3:8*-20, concludes with a stinging denunciation of Jerusalem. This denunciation terminates Zephaniah's oracles against the nations in a manner reminiscent of the Amos oracles which culminate in a pronouncement of judgment against Israel.

In summary, the final form of Amos 1:1 is associated with a Deuteronomistic redaction of at least four of the prophetic works in the Book of the Twelve, which specifically sought to explain the destruction of Jerusalem based upon a theological conviction of its own guilt. This corpus was not originally compiled to offer hope, but to explain the destruction in the context of YHWH's continued warnings to Judah and Jerusalem. This redactional work has only been roughly sketched here. Enough evidence has been noted to indicate these elements (some redactional, and some part

---

harlotry motif is used in Hosea, Amos, and Micah in relationship to the North. This application helps explain why Zephaniah does not have these images, although Zephaniah uses similar motifs of cultic abuse and syncrestistic practices in references to Jerusalem. Harlotry as an image appears also in Joel 4:3 and Nah 3:4. Joel 4:3 is a considerably later composition (coming from the late Persian period), and it does not use the imagery as a synonym for idolatry. Nah 3:4 draws on similar imagery when it accuses Nineveh of harlotry, understanding this "harlotry" along with "sorcery" as the reason for its destruction, but other considerations of the transmission of that writing do not place it within the realm of the Deuteronomistic corpus containing Hosea, Amos, Micah, and Zephaniah.

[44] Compare secondary passages in Hos 4:15; 6:11; 8:14; and 12:1,3, Amos 2:4f; and particularly the redaction of Mic 1:2-7,9 (discussed in a separate chapter).

[45] Bethel is cited in Hos 10:15; 12:5; Amos 3:14; 4:4; 5:5f; 7:10,13. Samaria is condemned in Hos 8:5; 10:7; 14:1; Amos 3:9,12; 4:1; 6:1; 8:6,14. Significantly, Mic 1:1,5 uses the destruction of Samaria as a paradigm for warning Judah and Jerusalem to change before it is too late. This is the last time in the Book of the Twelve that Samaria is mentioned. See discussion below on the Obadiah-Micah connection.

[46] Zeph 1:4. The last two titles are especially significant when read in light of Hosea. See the discussion of Zeph 1:1ff, below. The phrase "remnant of Baal" corresponds to the frequent anti-Baal polemic of Hosea and Amos, while the reference to the idolatrous priests occurs only in Hos 10:5 (and perhaps 4:4), Zeph 1:4, and the story of the Josianic reforms in 2 Kgs 23:5.

of earlier material placed in key locations) appear in their present locations by design. More will be said in the appropriate places concerning later expansion of these passages. A complete investigation of this Deuteronomistic transmission is not possible here, but its existence goes a long way toward explaining the current shape of the Book of the Twelve.

The oracles against the nations in **1:3-2:16** constitute first major literary block in Amos. In their present form, they comprise a series of eight highly stylized oracles culminating in the oracle against Israel itself. As noted above, these oracles do not all stem from the same redactional layer. Scholars have long noted that certain form-critical distinctions indicate the oracles against Tyre (1:9f), Edom (1:11f), and Judah (2:4f) reflect the concerns of the exilic period. In spite of a recent backlash against these arguments which claims they over-emphasize minute distinctions, the arguments in favor of the insertion of these three oracles still appear stronger than the arguments for the original unity of the collection.[47] A summary of the arguments for both sides is presented here.

---

[47] The following authors argue for the *unity* of the entire collection. Several argue on the basis of reconstructed historical events during and prior to the time of Amos: M. Haran, "Observations on the Historical Background of Amos 1:2-2:6," *Israel Exploration Journal* 18 (1968): 201-212; Simon Cohen, "The Political Background of the Words of Amos," *Hebrew Union College Annual* 36 (1965): 153-160; Keith N. Schoville, "A Note on the Oracles of Amos against Gaza, Tyre, and Edom," *VT.S* 26 (1974): (55-63), 56. Reventlow argues for unity on the basis of a reconstructed ritual: Henning Graf Reventlow, *Das Amt des Propheten bei Amos* (Göttingen: Vandenhoeck & Ruprecht, 1962), 58ff. Others argue the unity on the basis of structural patterns: Shalom Paul, "Amos 1:3-2:3: A Concatenous Literary Pattern," *JBL* 90 (1971): 397-403; and by the same author "A Literary Reinvestigation of the Authenticity of the Oracles Against the Nations in Amos," In *De la Tôrah au Messie. Études d'exégèse et d'Herméneutique Bibliques Offertes à Henri CAZELLES pour se 25 années d'Enseignement á l'Institut Catholique de Paris (Octobre 1979)*, Maurice Carrez, et al, eds. (Paris: Desclée, 1981), 189-205; Albert Condamin, "Amos 1:2-3:8. Authenticité et structure poétique," *Recherches de Science Religieuse* 20 (1930): 298-311. Some merely reject the ideas based on the minutiae of the arguments and their own apparent presuppositions: Stuart, *Word 31*, 309. The majority of scholars argue that at least some of the oracles have been *added or edited later* to reflect the events of other generations while still imitating the style of Amos. Christensen (following Wright) argues only the Judah oracle is secondary: Duane L. Christensen, "The Prosodic Structure of Amos 1-2," *HTR* 67 (1974): (427-436), 428; and by the same author *Transformations of the War Oracle in Old Testament Prophecy: Studies in the Oracles Against the Nations*, Harvard Dissertations in Religion 3 (Missoula, Montana: Scholars Press, 1975), 59. Rudolph, *KAT* 13/2, 120, believes only the Edom oracle was added later in its entirety, while the Judah oracle had a single line added. The following consider all three oracles as later

Three rationales dominate the arguments of those considering the oracles against the nations as an unchanged unity: the geographical, the historical, and the structural. Those claiming that geography necessitates the inclusion of all the oracles in their current order cite a pattern in the naming of entities which moves about the compass points in a patterned manner. Contra this geographical argument, one must note two important aspects which are not often addressed. First, the underlying assumption of the geographical argument rests upon a highly questionable tenet that only a prophet would have the ingenuity to place these oracles in a meaningful order.[48] Second, the geographical "pattern" is not as strong as they claim. They cite a "general" direction for this pattern (NE-SW-NW-SE-S-Israel). A major problem lies in the oracles they label "southeast". Does the order of these countries (Edom, Ammon, Moab) really indicate any geographical concern? Edom, the southern most of the three is mentioned first, followed by Ammon, the northern most, and finally Moab which lies in the middle. This vacillation complicates a "pattern" unnecessarily if it were intentional.

A second objection to the geographical argument is even more significant. The geographical pattern is improved tremendously if the oracles against Tyre, Edom, and Judah are removed.[49]

---

additions: Julius Wellhausen, *Die kleinen Propheten übersetzt, mit Noten* (Berlin: Reimer, 1892), 69-71; Wilhelm Nowack, *Die kleinen Propheten übersetzt, und erklärt*, 3rd ed. (Göttingen: Vandenhoeck & Ruprecht, 1922), 113f; Werner H. Schmidt, "Die deuteronomistische Redaktion des Amosbuches," *ZAW* 77 (1965): 174f; Hartmut Gese, "Komposition bei Amos," *VT.S* 32 (1980): 86ff; Wolff, *BK* 14/2, 137f; Ina Willi-Plein, *Vorformen der Schriftexegese innerhalb des Alten Testaments*, BZAW 123 (Berlin: Walter de Gruyter, 1971), 16f; Ludwig Markert, *Struktur und Bezeichnung des Scheltworts*, BZAW 140 (Berlin: Walter de Gruyter, 1977), 55-61,67-71; Soggin, *Amos*, 37-40; Amsler, *CAT* 11a, 170f; Weiser, *ATD* 24, 119f; Mays, *Amos*, 33-36, 40-42. Karl Marti, *Das Dodekapropheton*, HCAT 13, 152, and others claim the oracle against the Philistines was also secondary, but this view has long been abandoned.

[48] Recent scholarship clearly establishes the existence of Old Testament redactional work which demonstrates the skill and ingenuity of those who were responsible for preserving and adapting the Biblical materials. For this reason, the image must be abandoned which envisions a redactor as simply a copyist who occasionally inserts an arbitrary (or meaningless) statement. For a detailed treatment of various aspects of the reworking of older traditions, see Michael Fishbane, *Biblical Interpretation in Ancient Israel* (Oxford: Clarendon Press, 1985).

[49] In this chart, the numbers to the right of the southeast group denote their geographical position from north to south in relation to one another.

Current			Previous		
Damascus	NE		Damascus	NE	
Philistia	SW		Philistia	SW	
Tyre	NW		Ammon	SE	1
Edom	S(E)	3	Moab	SE	2
Ammon	SE	1	Israel	NW	
Moab	SE	2			
Judah	S				
Israel	N				

Without the three questionable oracles the pattern still alternates compass points, but on the fourth and decisive change of direction, where one would expect a northwest direction, this geographical pattern remains consistent by condemning Israel. In addition, one may more readily speak of a "southeast" group since Ammon and Moab appear in a north-south order consistent with the movement of the complex to that point. If the geographical argument should be used at all, one must concede that it argues more consistently for the growth of the corpus. The argument that a geographical pattern was disturbed by the addition of the oracles against Tyre, Edom, and Judah carries more weight than the assumption of a geographical pattern for an inherently unified corpus.

The second argument brought on behalf of the unity of 1:3-2:16 is the historical argument. Proponents of this argument claim that events during Amos' lifetime (or before) precipitated threats against these nations. Against using this argument, it must be noted that one runs into difficulty by attempting to isolate specific events for any of the oracles, but particularly those against Tyre, Edom, and Judah. One is hard pressed to find corroborating evidence for suspecting a deep seated hostility toward these nations (especially Tyre and Judah) during Amos' time. Often those suggesting specific events reach back 100 years before Amos to find events which would have precipitated a particular oracle.[50] Others postulate the reference stems from some event as yet unknown to us. By contrast, other Old Testament traditions afford ample evidence of oracles against Tyre and Edom which are exilic or later.[51] The Babylonian destruction of Jerusalem and its aftermath furnishes an event which could explain the animosity against Edom, and the necessity of a word against Tyre, while the theological tendency of the Deuteronomistic editors to remind Judah and Jerusalem of their guilt provides suitable parallels during the exilic

---

[50] For examples, see Schoville, *VT.S* 26 (1974): 58f,61f; Hammershaimb, *Amos*, 33.

[51] See Mays, *Amos*, 34,36.

period.[52] As with the geographical argument, the historical argument better serves those treating the three oracles as a later insertion than those arguing for the unity of the entire complex.

The third argument cited by those who claim an inherent unity in the oracles against the nations in Amos 1:3-2:16 is the structural argument. The use of structural arguments in Amos studies dictates comment.

Excursus: The Use of Structural Arguments in Amos.

Few modern scholars deny the validity of the structure of a passage as *a tool* for understanding its movement and intention. Structure aids the understanding of both small and large units of Old Testament material. However, as with any Old Testament exegetical tool, structuralism *used by itself* provides little of value for a determination of the "original" form of extended passages, since a redactor as well as an "author" could be responsible for an existing structure. Given the likelihood that prophetic books began with the collection and *ordering* of oracles and sayings of a particular prophet, one must acknowledge that already this process (not performed by the prophet as a rule) demonstrates the extensive ingenuity required by those responsible for assembling prophetic books. In Amos studies in particular, one notes a substantial number of scholars who fall into the trap of overemphasizing structure to the exclusion of other vital tools. The result is a flat exegesis which detracts from the message of a given passage, and which falls prone to *two major pitfalls* of structuralist studies: 1) the assumption that structure occurs only on a single "inspired" level; and 2) the temptation to permit the quest for structural patterns to override the intention of the text itself. A single case in point will demonstrate both problems. Condamin describes a structural unity, which he argues includes not only the oracles against the nations, but a unity which begins with Amos 1:2, and which continues all the way to 3:8.[53] Condamin describes this "unity" as four larger sections, each with its own introduction followed by two strophes, diagrammed as follows:[54]

---

[52] See Wolff's discussion, *BK* 14/2, 137, of this tendency on the part of Deuteronomistic redactors.

[53] Condamin, *Recherches de Science Religieuse* 20 (1930): 298-311. One may apply similar critiques to more recent works attempting to fashion a structural unity for the entire book of Amos. See especially: Claude Coulot, "Propositions pour une structuration du livre d'Amos au niveau rédactionnel," *Revue des Sciences Religieuses* 51 (1977): 169-186; and William A. Smalley, "Recursion Patterns and the Sectioning of Amos," *The Bible Translator* 30 (1979): 118-127; Shalom Paul, "Amos 1:3-2:3: A Concatenous Literary Pattern," *JBL* 90 (1971): 397-403.

[54] Condamin, *Recherches de Science Religieuse* 20 (1930): 306.

1:2 Prelude
1:3-5 Against Damascus   1:6-8 Against the Philistines

1:9-12 Against the brotherhood of Israel
1:13-15 Against Ammon   2:1-3 Against Moab

2:4-5 Against Judah
2:6-8 Against Israel   2:9-12 YHWH's good deeds for Israel

2:13-16 Threat of Punishment
3:1-4 Effect without cause?   3:5-8 Cause without Effect?

On the surface, the impressive symmetry of Condamin's structure strikes a pleasant chord, but one must object to the implications and methodology of this structure, by asking what this structure proves about the unity of Amos 1:2-3:8. First, one must ask how Condamin derives his sections. The units he defines create serious problems. For example: Why does Judah deserve an accented place by itself as introduction, whereas he relegates the message to Israel to subsidiary levels? Would this emphasis not run counter to the situation of Amos, who preached to the Northern kingdom? Would an emphasis upon Judah not also ignore the intent of the extended oracles which culminate in judgment against Israel, not Judah? Second, what role does the prelude play in this structure? Condamin argues the verse forms an *inclusio* to 3:8 on the basis of the verb שאג, but demonstrates no clear relationship between this introduction and the two following units. He may have a point about the inclusio, but not as he defines the structure. Third, should 1:9-12 really be considered one unit? Condamin isolates the oracles against Tyre and Edom into a single unit on the basis of the catchword "brother," but this catchword hardly distinguishes these oracles in light of the overriding refrain, "for three transgressions and for four ..." which dominates the beginning of each of these oracles. In determining the structure of a passage, one must begin with the natural divisions of the text as determined by the literary markers, such as introductory elements, closing formulas, peculiar stylistic formulations, etc.

Leaving aside the problematic units and titles, one notes Condamin claims four sections structure the "unity." However, if one eliminates those sections considered "secondary" by scholars (1:2,9-12; 2:4-5: in boldface) another schema emerges whose symmetry is equally impressive but more consistent with the message of the text.

1:3-5 Against Damascus   1:6-8 Against the Philistines
1:13-15 Against Ammon   2:1-3 Against Moab

2:6-8 Against Israel

2:9-12 YHWH's good deeds for Israel   2:13-16 Threat of Punishment
3:1-4 Effect without cause?   3:5-8 Cause without Effect?

This second schema utilizes Condamin's own problematic titles, but points out that the insertion of three oracles and the motto for the book appears to have disturbed

> a more logical structure. In short, Condamin provides an example that falls prey to both major temptations of structuralism. He implants a system upon the text which is not consistent with the message of the text, and the very structure he imposes argues more strongly for the growth of the text than it does for the unity.

When one evaluates most structural treatments of Amos in light of the two temptations of structuralism, one observes that those who use this tool, especially for the oracles against the nations, largely fail to *exclude* the possibility that any "pattern" they note does not result from the growth of 1:3-2:16.[55] In addition, these authors often impose questionable units upon the text.

The three leading arguments for the original unity of 1:3-2:16 thus exhibit serious methodological flaws which limit their ability to convince. When investigated closely, these arguments function better as arguments against the unity they seek to defend. What then are the arguments used by those arguing that the oracles against Tyre, Edom, and Judah are insertions? The proponents utilize form-critical, stylistic, and theological observations. Wolff offers a classic summary of these arguments.[56]

Four of the speeches (1:3-5,6-8,13-15,2:1-3) in the oracles against the nations are formed completely alike and demonstrate *five common elements*: 1) An introductory messenger speech formula; 2) A general announcement of sin with a statement on the certainty of punishment; 3) A more explicit and particular pronouncement of the reason for guilt; 4) The particular announcement of the execution of punishment; 5) A closing messenger speech formula. Wolff next summarizes the formal characteristics which *differentiate* the Tyre (1:9-10), Edom (1:11-12), and Judah (2:4-5) strophes from the remainder. Only elements #1 and #2 appear consistently. Element #3 begins with עַל (as those above) but the infinitive portion is shortened, and then the entire element is expanded through one (1:9) or several 1:11; 2:4) verbal sentences. Element #4 is radically shortened, whereas element #5 is entirely absent from these three speeches.

---

[55] Condamin again represents no isolated example: Two articles by Shalom Paul, "Amos 1:3-2:3: A Concatenous Literary Pattern," *JBL* 90 (1971): 397-403; and "A Literary Reinvestigation of the Authenticity of the Oracles Against the Nations in Amos," in *De la Tôrah au Messie*, 189-205, argue for a literary connection ordering of the oracles based upon catchwords in the successive order. Paul admits that no catchword exists between the Edom and Moab oracles, but he does not note that if the Tyre and Edom oracles are removed, the catchword principle is present in all four remaining oracles.

[56] Wolff, *BK* 14/2, 164-171.

These formal observations are important because they separate the oracles into two groups, each of which offer consistent characteristics. These arguments may be supplemented by the tradition-critical arguments that other Tyre and Edom oracles seldom precede the exile, and that the Judah oracle betrays strong Deuteronomistic motifs and language. Additionally, all three oracles contain a more religious orientation than the others.[57]

Questions about the events which precipitated the inclusion of Tyre, Edom, and Judah into the oracles against the nations depend heavily upon whether one accepts them as later additions. The evidence noted above permits the assumption of their insertion during the exilic period.[58] Beginning with the Judah oracle, the Deuteronomistic language makes it clear that this oracle is a theological explanation for the destruction of Judah and Jerusalem. The oracle against Edom makes reference to the aftermath of the destruction of Jerusalem when Edom participated in offenses against YHWH's people. The oracle against Tyre accuses that city of two crimes which create certain problems for dating. The first (delivering up an entire population to Edom) merely copies the indictment from the previous oracle against Gaza. The second accuses Tyre of *forgetting* the covenant of brothers. No specific reference to a "covenant of brothers" exists between Israel and/or Judah and Tyre.[59] The reference to a brother in the context of a covenant normally indicates a political alliance.[60] Three situations might indicate an alliance with Tyre: the

---

[57] See Schmidt, "Die deuteronomistische Redaktion des Amosbuches," *ZAW* 77 (1965): 174-178.

[58] Those assuming the early date have considerable difficulty pinpointing situations to which these oracles are addressed. Normally, the Tyre oracle is said to refer to the treaty between Hiram of Tyre and Solomon (1 Kgs 5:26). They maintain evidence of a pro-Phoenician policy with reference to an alliance can also be found in the time of Ahab, when he married Jezebel the daughter of the king of Sidon (1 Kgs 16:31). See Richard S. Cripps, *A Critical and Exegetical Commentary on the Book of Amos* (London: SPCK, 1955), 126-129. The oracle concerning Edom is most often associated, by those arguing it comes from Amos, with the rebellion in the time of Joram (2 Kgs 8:20-22). But even Rudolph, who holds this oracle as genuine, admits real difficulty in making this correlation. The description of an aggressive Edom in Amos 1:11 ("He pursued his brother with the sword") would not readily coincide with the picture in 2 Kgs 8 in which Joram crossed into Edomite territory. In addition, said events would have pre-dated the time of Amos by nearly a century. See Rudolph, *KAT* 13/2, 134.

[59] The closest reference is found in the relationship between Hiram and Solomon who are referred to as brothers (1 Kgs 9:10-14) and who seal a covenant (1 Kgs 5:26).

[60] See John Priest, "The Covenant of Brothers," *JBL* 84 (1965): (400-406), 400f.

relationship of Hiram and Solomon, the pro-Phoenician policy of Ahab, and an anti-Babylonian coalition in the time of Zedekiah.[61] The first two pre-date Amos by a century or more, and both appear to have been broken by the pro-Assyrian policy of Jehu, not by Tyre.[62] The pro-Phoenician alliance with Ahab may or may not have included Tyre since Jezebel was from Sidon. The third possibility deserves consideration. It is based upon the tradition of the anti-Babylonian coalition depicted in Jeremiah 27-28. Edom, Moab, Ammon, Tyre and Sidon attended a meeting in Jerusalem to pursue an anti-Babylonian confederation. Unfortunately the Jeremiah account does not relate the results of this meeting, so it is not possible to know with certainty if they formalized an alliance. Such an alliance would go far, however, in accounting for the enigmatic phrase "covenant of brothers." In this context, one would presume that to forget the covenant would imply that Tyre offered no aid following the Babylonian attack. The fact that Tyre itself was besieged by Babylon would make Amos 1:9f explanatory in nature, clarifying the punishment upon Tyre from an exilic perspective in much the same manner as the Judah oracle in 2:4f seeks to explain the destruction of Judah. The remaining participants of the Jerusalem conference had either already been addressed by Amos (Ammon, Moab), were in no position to offer assistance to Jerusalem at the time of destruction (Sidon), or simultaneously received an oracle for even more dastardly crimes than forgetting the covenant (Edom).[63] Of some importance for the current investigation is the suggestion that the oracle against Tyre in Amos is based upon Joel 4:4ff.[64] Against this claim, one must note that the balance of the evidence weighs heavily against this

---

[61]   While most would accept the historicity of this meeting, Carroll suggests the meeting is a later redactional device depicting Jeremiah as a prophet to the nations. See Robert P. Carroll, *Jeremiah: A Commentary*, Old Testament Library (London: SCM, 1986), 529ff. Carroll considers it impossible that Zedekiah (appointed by the Babylonians) would have rebelled against them at such an early stage. In light of the fact that Zedekiah did revolt against Babylon (2 Kgs 24:20; 2 Chr 36:13; Jer 52:3) this argumentation lacks force.

[62]   So Schoville, *V.T.S* 26 (1974): 63. Schoville postulates from this observation that Gaza, Tyre, and Edom would have rebelled against the policies of Jehu, and it is for this reaction which Amos condemns these countries. Such speculation is, however, unwarranted given the lack of evidence.

[63]   Admittedly, this suggestion contains some speculation, but no more than other explanations of this enigmatic phrase. This phrase creates difficulty to both sides attempting to isolate historical rationale. See for example, Wolff, *BK* 14/2, 193f.

[64]   See especially Haran, "Observations on the Historical Background of Amos 1:2-2:6," *Israel Exploration Journal* 18 (1968): 201.

possibility. Other evidence indicates Joel 4:4-8 comes from the late Persian period, well after the exile. The similarity of the Tyre, Edom, and Judah oracles make it unlikely that the Tyre oracle would have entered apart from the other two, and they both have clear exilic concerns.

In summary, the common argument that the oracles against Tyre, Edom, and Judah were added to Amos 1:3-2:16 during the exilic period is a sound argument.   These oracles share form-critical, stylistic, and theological characteristics. Considerable evidence argues that the Edom and Judah oracles derive from events around the time of the destruction of Jerusalem. The possibility remains open that the Tyre oracle could also be explained from this same historical perspective. Counter-arguments against the insertion of the three questionable oracles have been suggested in recent years, but these geographical, historical, and structural arguments actually offer more evidence of the growth of the collection than they do for the unity.

Despite clear indications of the growth of Amos 1:3-2:16, one may safely presume this growth pre-dated the composition of Joel 4:1-21 based on the investigation of that passage.[65]   This observation allows the conclusion that the Amos oracles existed in their entirety, and served as a model from which the author of Joel 4:1-21 drew.

3. The Structure of Amos 9:1-15

Previous discussion of the macrostructure demonstrated that a version of Amos existed (probably during the exile) which ended with Amos 9:6.[66] This version incorporated smaller "collections" of Amos into a book. *Inclusions* to other portions of the book, in both the fifth vision (9:1-4), and the doxology (9:5f), characterize the ending of that corpus as one which had a strong interest in condemning the former Northern kingdom. The remainder of Amos 9 functions differently, and introduces other theological interests.

The text markers in chapter nine reveal several clear units, but the relationship of those units is not immediately clear. Amos 9:1 begins the

---

[65] Joel 4:1-21 will be treated in volume 2 of this work (forthcoming), tentatively subtitled *Redactional Processes in the Book of the Twelve*.

[66] See previous discussion of the macrostructure and its redactional implications, beginning page 74.

final vision with the change of speaker to the prophetic "I" in the context of a vision. This vision continues until the change of style in 9:5 introduces the final doxology. A third unit begins with the rhetorical question in 9:7, although the extent of this unit is initially confusing because 9:8 begins with הנה, and 9:9 with כי־הנה, both of which may function as text markers. In their present contexts, however, these markers do not introduce independent units. A clear break appears again in 9:11 with the ביום ההוא marker, introducing the theme of Davidic restoration, and again in 9:13 with the marker הנה ימים באים, which introduces eschatological images of agricultural plenty.

In addition to the markers at the beginning of the units, the appearance of the phrase נאם יהוה requires some explanation. It appears four times in the chapter (9:7,8,12,13). Only in 9:12 does this phrase appear at the end of a unit, but there its formulation is very much at odds with its immediate context.[67] In the remaining cases it functions as an accentuation of an opening statement. In 9:7 and 9:8b נאם יהוה introduces the argument and counter-argument of two opinions regarding the interpretation of the final vision. In 9:13, נאם יהוה also functions as an accentuation of the opening statement, but this unit appears to be formed as an immitation of 8:11 since this verse also contains the phrase "behold the days are coming — utterance of YHWH."[68] In Amos 9, נאם יהוה thus functions differently from other Amos passages utilizing this formulaic expression at the end of a unit.[69]

In summary, Amos 9 contains five units (9:1-4,5-6,7-10,11-12,13-15) as it now stands. Stylistic changes delineate the first three of these units by clear transitions from a vision (9:1-4) to a hymn (9:5f) to a discussion (9:7-10). The last two units are introduced with יום formulas (9:11f, 13-15), and their interrelationship with the context demands closer inspection.

---

[67] See discussion below, page 105.

[68] See discussion below, page 108.

[69] See Amos 2:16; 3:10,15; 4:3,5,6,8,9,10,11. This fact alone is not evidence for a separate redactional layer in light of other passages which likewise use נאם יהוה in rhetorical questions (2:11) or as accentuation devices in the midst of an assertion (6:8,14; 8:3) or in opening formulae (8:9,11).

4. The Function of the Units in Amos 9:7-15

4.1. The Function of 9:7-10: Interpretation of Final Vision

A discussion of the relationship of the units inside Amos 9 must begin with the recognition that Amos 9:1-6 formed the ending of the book at a significant point in its redactional history. This ending, presuming Wolff is correct, most likely relates to an early to middle exilic Deuteronomistic corpus which theologically justified Jerusalem's destruction.[70] It represents a highly negative and pessimistic view that God's judgment entailed total destruction. It is easy to imagine that such a negative polemic would invariably cause difficulties of interpretation, and the controversial nature of 9:1-6 may be detected in the discussion it generated. A literary summary of this discussion is preserved in 9:7-10. The meaning and origin of these verses cause considerable debate because they contain at least two different reactions to Amos 9:1-6.[71] There is, however, universal consensus that the verses must be understood in the context of Amos 9:1ff. The microstructure of the passage indicates that this polarity is intentional. These verses represent two distinct opinions, whose theses are marked with the phrase נאם יהוה.

Thesis 1:	Thesis 2:
Israel, you are like other nations	But I will not totally destroy the house of Jacob
Utterance of YHWH	Utterance of YHWH
Example 1:	Example 2:
Exodus was not unique	Sieve metaphor
Result 1:	Result 2:
I will destroy the sinful kingdom	I will destroy the sinners among my people

---

[70] See discussion of the macrostructure of the book of Amos above, 74.

[71] Other commentators also treat these verses as a discussion. See above all, Wolff, *BK* 14/2, 396f; and Rudolph, *KAT* 13/2, 272, even though the latter treats the passage as genuine Amos material. Contrast these treatments with others such as Weiser, *ATD* 24, 199ff, who divides the verses into smaller units. He sees 9:7 as a fragment separated from its context. He sees 9:8 as an independent corrective to 9:4 based upon the closing formula and the content. He then postulates 9:9f as a corrective to the corrective, i.e. a confirmation of Amos' original oracle in 9:1-4.

Amos 9:7-8a admonishes Israel in parallel to other nations (Ethiopia, Philistines, Aram), and states that Israel will be utterly destroyed. The use of Ethiopia in the rhetorical question is somewhat perplexing. The phrasing of the question implies a positive answer. Israel should consider itself like the Ethiopians. Exactly why the author selects Ethiopia is difficult to say, but the context dictates that the intention is negative.[72]

---

[72] Several suggestions have been put forth. Presumably influenced by Jer 13:23 (Can the Ethiopian change his skin, or the leopard his spots?), some have suggested that the reference to Ethiopians was chosen because the color of their skin: see Rudolph's note on Luther, *KAT* 13/2, 273; and perhaps Stuart's emphasis on the "black tribes", *Word* 31, 393. However, the Jeremiah context does not castigate the Ethiopians any more than it does the leopards, affording no real polemic regarding the color. A second suggestion understands Ethiopia in Amos 9:7 as a symbol for distance (cf Mays, *Amos*, 157; Wolff, *BK* 14/2, 398f; Rudolph, *KAT* 13/2, 273). Ethiopia was indeed a distant land to the people of Judah and Israel, and there are places where distance plays a role in the citation of Ethiopia (Isa 11:11; 18:1; Zeph 3:10; Esth 1:1; 8:9, etc.). This interpretation does not suit the context of Amos 9:7. The passage intends an extremely negative picture, and one wonders if distance alone would offer this negative image. No other passage brings this negative view of Ethiopia merely on the basis of distance. In addition, the phrase in Amos 9:7 specifically refers to the people of Ethiopia (כבשׁים בני), not the country. In trying to determine the intention of this metaphor, one may state two things with certainty: first, the author portrays a negative picture; second, there is no need to explain the picture, meaning the statement's intention was obvious in the time of the author. A third possible explanation to the comparison to Ethiopians could be political. A number of texts indicate knowledge of the economic and/or political fortunes of Ethiopia was not absent in Judah. In addition, many of these texts have a solid basis for dating. No earlier than the late 7th century Zephaniah's oracles against the nations contain an indication of destruction in Ethiopia. Zeph 2:12 places the Cushites in parallel to Assyria to be set apart for destruction. Nah 3:9, from close to the same time period, reflects the historical situation of the destruction of Thebes (3:8) by Ashurbanipal (663), but from a later time when the destruction was used proverbially (see discussion of Nah 3:8 below) indicating its weakened state. At the time of its destruction, Thebes was ruled by a monarch of Ethiopian descent, and he fled to Ethiopia following the destruction of Thebes. These two examples demonstrate a tradition in the late 7th century, that Ethiopia was understood as a kingdom whose power had been reduced. Jeremiah also provides evidence that Ethiopians were serving in the royal court as servants during this period (38:7-12; 39:16-18), and that the status of Ethiopia was reduced as a result of her alliance with Egypt (46:9 [cf 46:1]) when they were defeated at Carchemish by Nebuchadnezzar in 605. Before presuming a late 7th century date for Amos 9:7, however, it should also be noted that late exilic/post-exilic passages in Deutero-Isaiah (43:14; 45:14) and Ezekiel (especially 30:5,9; cf 38:5 whose date is less certain) likewise make reference to Ethiopia in highly negative terms, and indicate that the region was prospering economically at that time in comparison with Judah. 2 Chronicles also exhibits a tendency to portray Ethiopia as an historical enemy.

The exemplary material in Amos 9:7b takes one of Israel's most valued legacies, the exodus tradition, and transforms it to remove any claim of exclusivity. YHWH recalls the exodus event (Did I not bring Israel up from the land of Egypt), but then utilizes a bitter sense of irony to say, in essence: yes, but I did the same for the Philistines and for Arameans. The passage implies that just as these countries have fallen, so Israel will also fall.[73] The climax of the entire unit arrives with 9:8, when YHWH announces a destruction that will remove "the sinful kingdom ... from the face of the earth."

The message of 9:7-8a is imminently clear and straightforward. God will destroy Israel. It is likewise demonstrable that 9:7-8a should be understood primarily as an interpretation of 9:1-6, since 9:7-8a utilizes word plays on the beginning and end of those verses. In 9:1 the word כפתור connotes the top of the central pillar of the temple structure.[74] Amos 9:7 takes up the word כפתור, but this time as the ancestral location of the Philistines.[75] Amos 9:8 interprets the phrase "from the face of the earth" in 9:6 as an announcement of judgment on the basis of 9:4 and the flood story of Genesis. In 9:4 YHWH says "I have set *my eyes* upon them for evil and not for good," whereas 9:6, part of the hymnic conclusion, connotes a more positive attitude: YHWH pours water (from the sea) "upon the face of the earth" (ארץ). Amos 9:8 connects these two passages: "Behold, *the eyes of Adonai YHWH* are on the sinful kingdom, and *I will destroy it from the face of the ground*" (האדמה). The writer deliberately makes this connection by picking up on the reference to the flooding of the Nile in 9:5,

---

Whereas the Deuteronomic history records no battles with Cush/Ethiopia, 2 Chronicles has several references to battles against Ethiopia or their participation in battles (12:3; 14:8; 16:8) which are either separate accounts or redactional notes in source material, and which reflect an antagonism toward this region from the post-exilic period. In summary, there is a growing tendency beginning in the late 7th century to incorporate antagonistic attitudes toward Ethiopia. What distinguishes the materials nearer the late 7th century is their reflection of a weakened state of Ethiopia, especially because of their alliance with Egypt against Babylon.

[73] This possibility appears the more likely two alternatives. Either this passage assumes the political overthrow of the Philistines and Arameans, or it simply relies upon the shock value of relating the actions of Israel's God to the fortunes of other countries as well. Compare for example, Wolff, *BK* 14/2, 399, and Rudolph, *KAT* 13/2, 274, who believe the verse refers to David's overthrow of the Phoenicians and Jeroboam II's overthrow of the Arameans. By contrast, Mays, *Amos*, 157f; and Soggin, *Amos*, 143f, mention only the reversal of the exodus traditions.

[74] See Mays, *Amos*, 153f.

[75] See Wolff, *BK* 14/2, 399; Rudolph, *KAT* 13/2, 274f; Mays, *Amos*, 157f.

and the pouring of water from heaven in 9:6, and turning them into announcements of destruction through language clearly reminiscent of the flood story of Gen 6ff.[76]

Amos 9:7-8a thus interprets Amos 9:1-6 as a strong indictment of total destruction for the people of Israel. It takes up phraseology from 9:1-6 and utilizes two traditions from the Pentateuch, the exodus tradition and the flood story, to emphasize the significance of the destruction which is at hand.[77] The unqualified announcement of judgment on Israel in 9:7-8a provoked a second interpretation which does not negate the judgment of 9:1-6,7-8a, but attempts to define the recipient of that judgment more precisely.

Amos 9:8b-10 presents a qualifying argument against 9:1-6 and the interpretation it received in 9:7-8a. This second interpretation reacts not only to the vision, but to the interpretation in 9:7-8a. It takes its starting point from the pronouncement of destruction in 9:8a, specifically by limiting the totality of judgment. The fact that it presupposes 9:7-8a may be presumed since 9:8b begins with "nevertheless", relating what follows to its immediate context; since 9:8b takes up the last verb in 9:8a (שמד); and since 9:8b uses the same structural marker to set off its thesis as did the writer of 9:7 (נאם יהוה).

It should be added, however, that 9:8b-10 not only reacts to the first interpretation, it does so on the basis of the final vision, specifically 9:1b,4. Amos 9:8b-10 takes up the theme of those remaining who will be slain by the sword. The sieve metaphor (9:9) and its subsequent clarification (9:10) indicate that the author of these verses rejected the interpretation of an unqualified destruction while at the same time holding the final vision as his authority, just as the previous interpreter had done. The sieve metaphor in 9:9 has at times confused commentators, but recent discussions have helped to clarify its role.[78] The sieve was used in the harvest process to

---

[76] The phrase "(upon) the face of the earth" operates as a type of refrain which appears numerous times throughout several layers of material in the flood story (Gen 6:1,5,6,7,17; 7:3,4,10,12,17,19,23; 8:8,13). Above all, Amos 9:8 reflects the divine decision in Gen 6:7: "I will blot out man ... from the face of the land" (האדמה). There is considerable vacillation in the Genesis account between ארץ and אדמה, which helps account for the change from ארץ to אדמה in Amos 9:6,8.

[77] Note the use of the flood account later in the frame of Zeph 1:2f.

[78] Compare Rudolph, *KAT* 13/2, 276f; Soggin, *Amos*, 142f; and Stuart, *Word* 31, 394. The latter, however, argues that the shaking of the sieve will "include all the nations," and "... will catch Israel too." The Hebrew formulation of the verse makes this understanding impossible, since the direct object marker immediately precedes "House

separate the usable portions of grain from the unusable. The importance of the metaphor in this context derives from the recognition that the sieve trapped impurities and the unusable portion of the grain, not the usable portion which fell to the ground. In the context of this qualifying judgment speech, that which falls to the ground are those who will escape total destruction, and those who remain in the sieve will be those who are destroyed. This understanding is confirmed by interpretation of the metaphor in 9:10: "All the sinners of my people will die by the sword — those saying the calamity will not overtake us." Consequently, the picture presented by 9:10 presents a two-fold judgment: the entire "house of Jacob" will be shaken, but only the sinners will be destroyed by the sword.

Significantly, this two-fold judgment interpretation accents the same dynamics from 9:1, which says:

> I saw Adonai standing upon the altar, and he said,
> Smite the capitals so that the thresholds shake.
> And break them on the heads of *all of them*,
> And *those remaining* I will slay with the sword.
> The one fleeing will not flee to them,
> And the fugitive will not slip away to them.

Amos 9:1a depicts three successive events: (1) the command to destroy the sanctuary through shaking, (2) the command to break the sanctuary on the heads of all the people, and (3) YHWH's pronouncement that he will kill those remaining by means of the sword. Amos 9:1b,2-4 contains a fourth element: (4) an expanded declaration that no one will escape. Amos 9:9f takes up all four elements in some form. (1) It takes the verb "shake" (רעש) from 9:1, where it is applied to the destruction of the sanctuary, and uses it metaphorically, relating it to judgment of the house of Jacob. The author thus creates a scene capable of correcting the identity of those destroyed from his own perspective. 9:9f portrays a purifying judgment in which (2) *all were shaken* with the purpose of destroying those who refused to heed the words of warning (9:10: "all the sinners of my people ... those who say the calamity will not overtake or confront us"). (3) These people are *those remaining in the sieve for destruction by the sword*. (4) The final element is thus summarized and altered to the extent that it offers *no escape from the destruction* for the sinners as they are now understood.

Amos 9:8b-10 thus provides its own interpretative correction to 9:7-8a on the basis of 9:1-4. It seeks to explain the existence of survivors in light

---

of Israel," whereas the preposition ב (among) precedes "all the nations," a fact which he ignores.

of an authoritative text which "on the surface" appears to say there would be no survivors. By subtly altering the perspective through the use of a sieve metaphor, the author is able to keep the totality of judgment (all experience great upheaval), while at the same time limiting and accentuating the idea of the total destruction of those who paid no heed.

4.2. The Function of 9:11-15: Restoration, Domination, and Abundance

A new thematic unit begins with Amos 9:11. Whereas the immediate context — indeed the entire book — concentrated on the question of judgment, the subject now turns to restoration, a theme which supposes late exilic or early post-exilic perspectives.[79] Amos 9:11-15 is structured as two salvation promises, each carrying eschatological overtones, as noted by the יום introductory formulas in 9:11,13. However, multiple tensions within these five verses argue that the structure created by the יום formula does not indicate a single author. Rather, the material within these four verses must reckon with more than one layer of redaction.

Examination of Amos 9:11f,13-15 reveals two distinct units which evidence a strong similarity to one another.[80] Both begin with יום sayings

---

[79] Evidence for and against the authenticity of these verses has been discussed often, and need not be detailed here. The author sides with those who see exilic and post-exilic concerns present in Amos 9:11-15. Attempts to force Amosic authorship on these passages are unconvincing despite a recent backlash against understanding these verses as "additions". For divergent summary discussions of authenticity and date, see: Wolff, *BK* 14/2, 405f; Rudolph, *KAT* 13/2, 285f. The following statements constitute the primary rationale for scholarly treatment of these verses as later redactional work: 1) Amos 9:11-15 announces unconditional salvation, unlike the remainder of the writing, which contains only judgment and occasional conditional reprieve. 2) Amos 9:11-15 presupposes Judah as representative of all Israel, a concept which is foreign to the remainder of the book. 3) The remainder of Amos rejects all manifestations of "election," whereas 9:11-15 draws upon the sanctity of the Davidic monarchy. 4) The position of Amos 9:11-15 at the end of the book makes its addition readily feasible. 5) The mention of the "remnant of Edom" in 9:12 makes no sense in the time of Amos.

[80] Not infrequently, scholars treat 9:11f and 9:13-15 as independent units which presuppose divergent backgrounds, for examples, see: R.E. Clements, "Patterns in the Prophetic Canon," in *Canon and Authority: Essays in Old Testament Religion and Theology* (Philadelphia: Fortress, 1977, 42-55), 49; Reinhard Fey, *Amos und Jesaja. Abhängigkeit und Eigenständigkeit des Jesaja*, Wissenschaftliche Monographien zum Alten und Neuen Testament 12 (Neukirchen: Neukirchener Verlag, 1963), 54-56. Both authors treat 9:11f as genuine. Others believe both probably represent later additions: Arvid S. Kapelrud, *Central Ideas in Amos* (Oslo: I Kommisjon Hos H. Aschehoug &

(9:11,13); both end with formulas claiming they are YHWH speeches (9:12, 15); both treat the theme of restoration. The latter element, however, offers the key to understanding the passage and its growth. The two units treat the theme of restoration from two perspectives: restoration of the kingdom and restoration of the people. In 9:11f, two distinct ideas of kingdom restoration may be detected. The first perspective is the restoration of that which is fallen (9:11), while the second communicates a restoration of domination (9:12a). While two thematic variations do not inherently presuppose different layers of material, the text affords further grounds for deducing that such is the case here. Amos 9:12b ("declares YHWH who is doing this") is very difficult to harmonize with 9:12a, since the 3mp יירשׁו in 9:12a presupposes the people as subject, not YHWH. On the other hand, this concluding formula conforms remarkably well with 9:11, where YHWH is the subject of several active verbs (I will raise, I will wall up, I will rebuild). In addition the concluding feminine singular suffix in 9:11 (I will rebuild "it") has its counterpart in 9:12b with the feminine singular pronoun זאת. One may thus say, grammatically and syntactically, that Amos 9:12a was not originally connected with 9:11,12b.[81]

Amos 9:11,12b offers a promise of the restoration of the Davidic kingdom, but the restoration is no polemic against the division into Northern and Southern kingdoms which followed the death of Solomon.[82] The language of Amos 9:11 indicates that destruction, not division, created the situation to which it offers hope. Amos 9:11 pictures David's kingdom in a devastated state, but it promises restoration in four-fold parallelism:

Co., 1956), 57f; Mays, *Amos*, 163-165; René Vuilleumier, *La tradition cultuelle d'Israël dans la prophétie d'Amos et d' Osée*, Cahiers Théologiques 45 (Neuchâtel: Delachaux & Niestlé, 1960), 27.

[81] Others have also questioned the essential unity of 9:11,12: Ulrich Kellermann, "Der Amosschluss als Stimme deuteronomischer Heilshoffnung," *EvTh* 29 (1969): 173; Peter Weimar, "Der Schluss des Amos-Buches. Ein Beitrag zur Redaktionsgeschichte des Amos-Buches," *BN* 16 (1981): 75,94.

[82] Contra Rudolph, *KAT* 13/2, 280f, and others.

	I will wall up	I will raise	I will rebuild
the fallen booth			it (3fs)
of David		his ruins (3ms)	
I will raise	their breaches (3fp)		

Three successive, but distinct, suffixes refer back to the phrase "booth of David." "Their breaches" (3fp) refers to holes in the booth, and treats the phrase "booth of David" collectively.[83] "His ruins" concentrates upon David, while the 3fs suffix in the phrase "I will rebuild it" refers specifically back to the feminine noun "booth." While the suffixes create some tension, the parallelism of the verbs poses no such problem. The combination twice articulates YHWH's action of lifting and repairing in beautifully constructed synonymous parallelism.[84] The significance of the metaphor "booth" clarifies itself considerably when compared with its surrounding context as relating to David's kingdom.

This promise of the restoration to that which is fallen continues in 9:14f, but this time it emphasizes the effect of the promise upon YHWH's people, not upon the political entities of that kingdom. These verses presuppose the existence of 9:11. The recurrence of the verb בנה and the use of נשמות (a synonym to הרסתיו in 9:11) relate back to the situation in 9:11. Thus, the ruined cities of 9:14 and the fallen booth (David's ruins) of 9:11 intend one and the same entity.[85] The "booth" of 9:11 does not refer in the strictest sense to two kingdoms, but to the destruction of the cities of David's kingdom. Additionally, the opening statement of 9:14 receives amplification in a succession of four parallel statements demonstrating what the restoration means to the author. Each parallel

---

[83] The expression of collective ideas via the combination of feminine singular nouns with plural adjectives offers the syntactical key to understanding the phrase "their breaches." This phenomenon occurs with enough regularity to presume with some certainty that the collective idea could as well be expressed via the combination of a feminine singular noun and a suffix. Note, for example, Gen 30:43 and 1 Sam 25:18, where the feminine singular "sheep" (צאן) takes a plural adjective. See also GK §132g and §145c.

[84] Hence Amos 9:11 twice uses the verb אקים, but uses the synonyms "wall up" and "build" to accomplish the parallelism of the second half of the AB/A'B' schema.

[85] The metaphorical use of "booth" as a reference to city is attested in one other passage, Isa 1:8, where it specifically refers to Zion.

statement contains two promises, with the second promise being the logical completion of the first:

Summary Statement: I will return the captivity of my people Israel

Promise A	Promise B
1. They will rebuild the ruined cities	and live (in them)
2. They will plant vineyards	and drink their wine.
3. They will make gardens	and eat their fruit.
4. I will plant them on their soil	and they will no longer be rooted up from their soil which I gave them.

These verses portray the concerns of the returning exiles.[86] Restoration means the return of the people, the reconstruction of the cities, and the reconstitution of the agricultural products. The main concern of the promises lies in the return of the people since this emphasis appears at the beginning and end of the unit (I will return the captivity; they will no longer be rooted up).

Given the similarity of theme and the structural parallel of 9:11,12b with 9:14f, there is good reason to believe that these verses were originally more closely connected than they are now. They treat the same theme from two perspectives: the restoration of political entities and the restoration of the people. Both sections begin with summary statements which are followed by successive parallel amplifications. Both sections clearly presume YHWH as speaker, although both sections end with formulas which the prophet pronounces and which hint at a liturgical situation: "utterance of YHWH who does this" (9:12b) and "says YHWH your God" (9:15). Finally, as will become clear from the discussion of 9:13, there are good reasons to presume that both sections originally began with

---

[86] Parallels from the late exilic and early post-exilic periods add to the impression that Amos 9:11,12b14f come from around this time. Compare especially Hag 1:1-11. The absence of any mention of the temple in this passage suggests the verses were penned prior to the work of Haggai and Zechariah beginning in 520. The concern for the restoration of the Davidic house would also be understandable in this time. See the discussion on the hopes of a Davidic restoration in early post-exilic times in David Petersen, *Haggai & Zechariah 1-8*, Old Testament Library, 105f, although the promise of the Amos material is more nebulous, and attaches this hope to no specific personage as does Hag 2:20ff.

יום formulas.[87]   When viewed together, much speaks in favor of an original connection of these sections, but what of the remainder of the material in 9:11-15?

As already noted, literary and thematic tensions separate 9:12a from its context. This tension is accentuated when one asks about the situation behind the statement "in order that they will possess the remnant of Edom and all the nations over whom my name was called." The statement takes up the promise of Davidic restoration in 9:11, but whereas the earlier layer defines restoration as the rebuilding of David's cities and the return of the people, 9:12a seeks political domination over the former Davidic kingdom, especially Edom. Particular reference to the "remnant of Edom" indicates a later perspective, since it reflects a situation in which the Nabatean incursion into Edom had already begun.[88]   The Nabatean conquest of

---

[87]   Discussion of Amos 9:13 reveals it stems from a later hand, but also recognizes that this portion of chapter nine imitates the structural formulations of chapter eight. Compare Amos 8:9,11. In chapter eight, the יום sayings comment upon the previous visions and their interpretive material in much the same manner as 9:11ff (see discussion below, page 112). This structural parallel argues more strongly that the יום formula belongs with the earlier restoration level.

[88]   Possible explanations of the phrase "remnant of Edom" depend upon decisions of authenticity. Those accepting 9:11f as later insertion(s) are primarily forced to assume the motivation of the phrase is bound with the Nabatean infiltration of Edom. Relatedly, they must reckon with a date well into the Persian period, since Edom's role as aggressor during the exilic period, when they took over Judean territory, would not accord well with the idea of a remnant. Several exegetes attempt to exclude such a late date for the origin of 9:12a, either because they believe the verse is "genuine," or because they do not wish to go so far into the Persian period to account for a specific setting. These authors often attempt to explain the phrase "remnant of Edom" in relationship to the oracles against the nations in general and the oracle against Edom (1:11f) in particular, assuming the reader should presume the destruction announced in 1:11f has already begun. Examples include Claude J. Peifer, "Amos the Prophet: The Man and His Book." *TBT* 19 (1981): 300; and Willi-Plein, *Vorformen*, 57. This literary explanation lacks convincing power for the very important reason that there is no hint in Amos 1:11f (or subsequently in the writing) that the destruction of Edom had already begun, whereas 9:11 indicates Edom already exists in a reduced state. In addition, strong scholarly evidence suggests the Edom oracle in 1:11f reflects an exilic redaction of Amos, again making the phrase "remnant of Edom" very difficult to understand in light of the fact Edom weathered the Babylonian period much better than its neighbors. See the discussion of Wolff, *BK* 14/2, 405f, who distinguishes the perspective of this verse from that of the Deuteronomistic perspectives of 1:11f. Rudolph, *KAT* 13/2, 281f, even though he considers the verse genuine, effectively refutes 9:12 as a literary reference to Amos 1:11f, arguing that the announced punishment of 1:11f does not coincide well with the political connotations of 9:12 and

Edom was a gradual process of accretion between the sixth and fourth centuries.[89] The phrase "all the nations over whom my name was called" is a reference to the Davidic/Solomonic kingdom. By using the verb "possess" with these political entities, 9:12a establishes a character of antagonism against Edom and the surrounding areas. Significantly, the thoughts embodied in this verse parallel the essential elements of Obad 17-21, a fact which will be probed in more detail below.[90]

Some indicators aid a determination of the point at which Amos 9:12a entered the text. It clearly presupposes the presence of 9:11. The למען beginning 9:12, while no indicator of an *original* connection, demonstrates the dependence of 9:12a upon 9:11. In addition, the verb יירשו requires a 3mp subject. No such antecedent is present in 9:11. Only with the mention of "my people Israel" in 9:14 does the subject reveal itself. Amos 9:11 concentrates upon the restoration of the kingdom, and 9:14f upon the people. Amos 9:12a demonstrates awareness of the change of subject which comes in 9:14f. One may therefore conclude that when 9:12a entered the text, the restoration layer of 9:11,12b,14f was already present.

The question of Amos 9:13 is more problematic. This verse also exhibits tension within its context. The verse portrays an eschatological utopia where the harvest and the planting run together.[91] The verse does not contain the divine speech forms characteristic of the remainder of 9:7-15.[92] Most importantly, the theme of the verse betrays a situation where the issues at stake differ from those of the restoration layer in 9:11,12b,14f. The earlier layer concentrates upon the return of the people, the reconstruction of cities, and the enjoyment of agricultural normalcy. Amos 9:13 overshoots the promise of restoration, and concentrates instead upon the question of quantity. It is no longer enough to plant and to eat. It is

---

its use of the verb ירש (possess). Rudolph offers a politically oriented explanation consistent with his view that the verse stems from Amos' time. Rudolph argues one must presume a time after Uzziah had won back a part of Edom (2 Kgs 14:27), when they also expected to win the remainder of Edom. Judah never realized this ambition, however, and under Ahaz, lost even that part they had won. Despite the alacrity of Rudolph's arguments, the arguments against treating 9:11-15 as eighth century texts still far outweigh arguments for an early date.

[89] See J.R. Bartlett, "The Rise and Fall of the Kingdom of Edom," *Palestine Exploration Quarterly* 104 (1972): 26-37.

[90] See the discussion of Obad 17-21 below, beginning on page 113.

[91] See discussions of the commentaries to explain the image in this verse.

[92] The phrase נאם יהוה provides a redactional indicator that YHWH is the intended speaker, but otherwise it is more proverbial in character than the remainder of the context.

no longer enough to return and to live on the land. The promised abundance in 9:13 reflects a situation in which hope derives not from the return of the people, but in an abundant harvest of utopic proportions. Situations of poor harvests occurred frequently in the ancient Near East, so 9:13 alone offers little help for dating. However, one may say with relative certainty, that Amos 9:13 post-dates 9:14f. The abundance of Amos 9:13 makes 9:14f anti-climactic. The taking of the harvest in 9:13 presupposes its planting in 9:14. The unexplained reference to reapers and harvesters in 9:13 make no sense before the promised return of the people in 9:14f. For these reasons, one may conclude Amos 9:13 reacts to the promises of 9:14f by redefining what constitutes salvation. Salvation is shoved further into the future and portrayed in terms of abundance, not in terms of the return of God's people.

4.3. The Growth of Amos 9:11-15

Three specific emphases are present in 9:11-15: future restoration, political domination, and eschatological-agricultural abundance. The restoration layer (9:11,12b,14f) represents the initial message in 9:11-15, but several questions affect the understanding of the growth of Amos 9:11-15. First, what is the relationship of 9:11-15 to the remainder of 9:1-6,7-10 and to Amos? Second, both 9:12a and 9:13 expand the restoration material, but do these two emphases come in the same redactional phase, or do they stem from separate layers? Third, what relationship does 9:11-15 have to other portions of the Book of the Twelve?

Direct links between Amos 9:11-15 and the remainder of Amos 9 require certain qualifications. The theme changes dramatically from judgment to salvation. The titles of the addressees are not consistent.[93] Formulas at the beginning and end of 9:11-15 afford an impression of independence. Despite these tensions, some scholars note that 9:11-15 is not entirely unaware of its context.[94] Several words recur, but the

---

[93] Amos 9:1-4,5f does not name an addressee, and refers to the people in 3mp. 9:7-8a speaks to the "sons of Israel" and about "Israel" and the "sinful kingdom". Amos 9:8b-10 speaks about the "house of Jacob" and "my people". Amos 9:11-15 speaks about the "fallen booth of David" and "my people Israel."

[94] Note especially Kellermann, *EvTh* 29 (1969): 169-183; Weimar, *BN* 16 (1981): 60-100. *Kellermann* omits 9:7 and claims the Amos school added 9:8-10 as a correction to the message of Amos. It sought to add the idea of a remnant to the message of the prophet with this addition. Kellermann sees 9:8b as a later addition. A second stage

repetition of key words provides uneven results. Those words which do repeat in some fashion appear primarily in 9:8b-10: the root נפל (9:9,11); the phrase "among all the nations" (9:9,12); the root נגשׁ (9:10,13); "my people" (9:10,14).[95] These words do not, however, appear to be direct

---

comes with the addition of 9:11f,14,15 as part of a hopeful Deuteronomistic redaction to Amos. Kellermann cites 9:13 as later still. Kellermann points out several interesting touchstones between Amos and the Deuteronomistic history, but his explanation lacks adequate explanations for 9:7,8b,12. He claims 9:7 is not part of the unit, and that 9:8b is a corrective gloss. Kellerman's understanding of 9:12b remains enigmatic. He clearly distinguishes it as secondary from 9:11 (referring to it as an early commentary on 9:11), but counts it with 9:11 as part of the same redactional layer. *Weimar* describes four redactional layers in 9:7-15. 1) He understands 9:8a,9*-10 as an interpretation of Amos 9:4b, which originally existed in a free-standing form. 2) Weimar sees 9:7 as a connecting link which ties 9:7a to 9:4b and 9:7b to 9:8a,9*-10. 3) 9:11,14f is a redactional supplement to 9:8a,9*-10. 4) The final redactional layer in 9:7-15 inserts material into pre-existing units and provides the essential structure of the passage. It inserts 9:12-13 into layer #3; adds the qualifying gloss of 9:8b; adds the phrase "among all the nations" in 9:9 (cf 9:12). Both Weimar and Kellermann proceed from the assumption that 9:8b is a relatively unconnected comment, meaning they have missed the role it plays in the structure of 9:7-10. Weimar's assertion that 9:8b comes from the same redactional hand as 9:12f is particularly unsatisfactory since the former is concerned with survival of a remnant, while the latter presents a more aggressive attitude toward the surrounding areas. The same is also true for his belief that the phrase "among all the nations" stems from the same hand. In 9:9 the reference takes up tradition elements portraying those taken to Babylon, fleeing to Egypt etc., whereas the phrase in 9:12 relates specifically to the Davidic kingdom ("who were called by my name"). Weimar correctly notes, however, that 9:11,14f belongs to the same layer. His assumption that 9:12 and 9:13 come from the same layer needs more careful exploration.

95 In Amos 9:9 the root נפל refers to the refuse which does not fall from the sieve, and in 9:11 to the fallen Davidic kingdom. Perhaps the implication that the usable grain does fall could relate to the fallen kingdom of David in 9:11. If this image plays a role, it is only indirect. The change of metaphor from grain to booth with no transition makes a direct relationship uncertain. The use of the phrase "among all the nations" in 9:9,12 does not denote similar interests. In 9:9 the phrase refers to an unqualified area where YHWH will shake the house of Jacob. It thus draws upon other traditions concerning the places to which YHWH's people were exiled including Babylon, Egypt, and the surrounding nations (e.g. Jer 9:15; 13:24; Ezek 22:15; 36:19). The reference to all the nations in 9:12 is very distinctly limited to those which comprised the Davidic kingdom, and has no direct interest in the scattering of God's people. In 9:10 the root נגשׁ, "overtake", is the verb used by the sinners to say the calamity will not overtake them. In some respect "overtake" could serve as a counter image in 9:13. There the action is used positively, and refers to the nearness of harvest and planting. It is again uncertain if this connection is intentional because the subjects of the verbs (calamity,

references to one another. Two significant exceptions are the references to captivity (9:4,14) and to אדמה (9:8a,15). Both references correct earlier statements in the chapter. The promise of return from captivity in 9:14 counters 9:4, which says even those who went into captivity would be pursued by the sword. The promise in 9:15 ("I will plant them on their land, and they will never again be rooted out from their land") relativizes the statement in 9:8a ("I will destroy it from the face of the ground"). This observation is significant. It provides solid evidence that the hermeneutic of the restoration layer in 9:11,14f functions in a similar vein to 9:8b-10. Both refute the idea of total destruction by reversing the images of the final vision of 9:1-4 and the initial discussion of 9:7-8a.

The hermeneutical similarity of the second discussion (9:8b-10) and the restoration layer (9:11,14f) raises the question whether these units are part of the same redactional level. The possibility exists that these units comes from the same redaction, but several indices argue against this interpretation. First, the change of theme from 9:10 to 9:11 is very abrupt. 9:8b-10 treats destruction of the sinners, while 9:11,14f treats the restoration/reconstruction of God's people. 9:8b-10 distinguishes two groups of people: the sinners and (by implication) those who remain. Second, the lack of strong direct linkage between the two units lessens the possibility of a common hand. While some words recur between the two units, they are not direct links. Third, the imagery in the units has no direct relationship to one another. The separation/sieve imagery in 9:8b-10 has no correlation in the restoration layer in which the fallen cities and "my people" are treated as one group. Fourth, the יום formula in 9:11 denotes an eschatological perspective which is not present in 9:8b-10.

One may say with certainty that the writer of 9:11,14f had 9:1-10 before him. The deliberate correction of 9:4,8a demonstrates awareness of 9:1-8a. The lack of reference to 9:8b-10 is explainable as well. The author of the restoration layer no longer needed to explain the existence of a remnant, nor did he have to explain the destruction of the people. This redaction concerned the future. Cities had to be rebuilt, and crops planted.

---

plowmen) are not very meaningful images together. This phrase "my people" is also difficult to assess. Amos 9:10 utilizes the term "all the sinners of my people," for the entire people of God prior to their judgment of refinement. It appears in 9:14 again as the term (this time together with the designation "Israel") for the people who do survive. They will return to rebuild and inhabit the ruined cities. Thus, while a case can be made cases that one can *interpret* these words in light of their respective comments, it is difficult to say that their presence necessitates such a related interpretation.

Yet the message was no mere call to build and plant. The message of hope contains the theological conviction that God will never again remove his people from the land he gave them. The message conveys the restoration in terms of continuity and permanence.

The relationship of 9:12a and 9:13 to one another and to the context is difficult to explain. Both verses comment upon their immediate context. Amos 9:12a takes up the promise of Davidic restoration, but redefines restoration as political domination. Amos 9:13 emphasizes abundance, not merely a return to pre-destruction normalcy as portrayed in 9:14f. Despite this relationship to the immediate context, both verses require inspection in a broader literary horizon to garner a more complete picture of the role they play inside the Book of the Twelve. 9:12a must also be seen in relationship to Obadiah, and Amos 9:13 should be viewed in connection to Joel 4:18. These verses tie the ending of Amos to the book which follows (Obadiah) and the book which precedes (Joel).

Amos 9:12a contains the essential elements of the message of Obadiah. The phrase "remnant of Edom", while difficult to explain in the context of 9:11-15, anticipates the judgment upon Edom which Obadiah proclaims. Both 9:12a and Obad 17ff (especially 19f) couple the possession of Edom with the possession of the former Davidic kingdom. Given the close connection of themes, one deduces the two passages are related, but the question of the priority of Amos 9:12a and Obadiah requires deliberation. The choices are clear enough: 1) Amos 9:12a summarizes Obadiah; 2) Obadiah expands the thoughts in Amos 9:12a; 3) Both passages existed separately and were merely placed next to one another on the scroll of the Book of the Twelve. Option number three may be excluded with considerable certainty. Obadiah exhibits a redactional shaping to make it more closely parallel the structure of Amos 9.[96] The subtle nuances of this shaping make it very clear that Obadiah knows Amos 9, since this knowledge effects the shape of Obadiah on a literary level. However, the redactional shaping of Obadiah to be read with Amos 9 does not, by itself, allow a clear choice between options one and two. In light of the fact that this shaping occurred as part of a literary process, it is altogether possible that Amos 9:12a was composed as a *literary transition* from Amos to Obadiah. It is likewise possible that Amos 9:12a had already been inserted into Amos 9:11-15, and Obad 17ff picks up this element in much the same way as Obad 1ff takes up 9:1ff. A decision between these

---

[96] See my discussion of Obad 1ff in the forthcoming volume *Redactional Processes in the Book of the Twelve*, BZAW (Berlin: De Gruyter).

two options cannot be verified prior to a more careful study of the relationship between Amos and Obadiah, but several observations will sharpen the focus of the question as it relates to Amos 9:12a.

Four explanations for 9:12a present themselves, none of which is without problem: 1) it is an isolated gloss, representing a spontaneous comment by a nationalistic reader; 2) it relates back to the oracles against the nations in Amos 1-2; 3) it introduces Obadiah; 4) it attempts to fashion a bridge from Amos' oracles against the nations to Obadiah.

The first explanation, that 9:12a is an isolated gloss, requires several assumptions. It requires that someone would have read 9:11 and been inspired to add a rather peculiar definition of the reconstituted Davidic kingdom. It must also assume that this glossator had unobstructed access to a written copy of the text. It must further assume that this isolated gloss somehow served as the impetus for the book of Obadiah in which this gloss receives expanded treatment. The first assumption, that 9:12a arose from a reading of 9:11, is shared to some extent by all four explanations. One must acknowledge the obvious that 9:12a, with its peculiar formulation, attaches to 9:11. However, nothing in 9:11 provokes the mention of "the remnant of Edom and all the nations over whom my name was called". This idea is imported from outside the immediate context. The remaining assumptions radically decrease the likelihood that 9:12a can be understood as an isolated gloss. A gloss would be more readily explicable if it sought to clarify something in the immediate context which was unclear, but such is not the case with 9:12a.

The second possibility, that 9:12a refers exclusively back to the oracles against the nations in Amos 1-2, also creates more problems than it solves. The language of 9:12a is not the language of the Edom oracle in 1:11f. Were the author of 9:12a attempting to draw a correlation to the Edom oracle in particular or to the oracles against the nations in general, the stylized language of those oracles would have provided ample opportunity for a clear reference. The fact that 9:12a emphasizes Edom is also difficult to conceive on the basis of Amos 1-2. In Amos 1-2, Edom is only one nation among several which is mentioned.[97] Most importantly, the situation implied by 9:12a is different from 1:11f. One gathers the distinct impression that the author of 1:11f implies an ascendant Edom who lauds

---

[97] Even the fact that the Edom oracle is secondary does not afford an explanation for its particular emphasis in 9:12, since evidence indicates that the Edom oracle in 1:11f entered simultaneously with the oracles against Tyre and against Judah. See further discussion above, page 108.

its superior position over its Judean neighbor. The ascendancy of Edom is utterly absent from 9:12a. The message of that verse presupposes that Edom's situation has already deteriorated ("remnant of Edom"), but that it will get worse because they will be possessed by the restored Davidic kingdom.

The third suggestion provides much stronger possibilities, making it plausible that 9:12a was composed as a literary introduction, or transition, to Obadiah. The themes of judgment against Edom and political restoration of the Davidic kingdom reappear in Obadiah. The language of 9:12a is closely akin to that of Obad 17ff. The common language is readily understandable as a summary of Obadiah. The phrase "remnant of Edom" assumes Obadiah's message of the (partial) destruction of Edom.[98] Likewise the phrase "all the people over whom my name was called" in Amos 9:12a can well be understood as a summary of the peoples and regions in Obad 17ff.[99]

One problem prevents the outright acceptance of 9:12a as a literary transition to Obadiah. The major touchstones between 9:12a and Obadiah appear in Obad 17ff, which exhibits a very strong interest in Jerusalem/Zion. This strong Zion emphasis is not explicitly present in Amos 9:12a. In response to this problem one may counter that it is well within the realm of possibility that the writer of 9:12a understood the "fallen booth" of David in 9:11 as a reference to Jerusalem. This assumption is strengthened by the tension between 9:12a and 9:11. In 9:11 the term "booth" of David is an inclusive term, YHWH will raise and repair the kingdom. Amos 9:12a brings an exclusive and militaristic aspect to the discussion, especially when read in light of Obad 17ff: they will possess the surrounding regions. Obad 17ff makes it clear, at least on one redactional level, that not only foreign regions (e.g. the Philistines), but also regions of

---

[98] Note particularly the tension in Obadiah with regard to Edom's destruction. Several statements imply the judgment will not be one of total annihilation: it will be made small (Obad 2); it will be sent from its border (Obad 7); the deliverers will judge the mountain of Edom (Obad 21). Other statements clearly imply a radical desolation: everyone will be cut off from the mountain of Esau (Obad 9); there will be no survivor from the house of Esau (Obad 18).

[99] The geo-political regions mentioned in Obad 17ff are: the house of Jacob and the house of Joseph as expressions for the Southern and Northern kingdoms respectively; Esau (Edom); the Negev; the Shephelah; the Philistines; Ephraim; Samaria; Benjamin; Gilead; and the exiles of Jerusalem in Zarephath. Also my discussion in the forthcoming volume (*Redactional Processes in the Book of the Twelve*) document a mutual relationship between Obad 15ff and Amos 9:12a via Jeremiah.

the Northern kingdom (Ephraim, Samaria) must be brought under Judean/ Jerusalemite control. The emphasis in 9:12a on the possession of "all the nations over whom my name was called," fits better with this understanding than it does with 9:11. Amos 9:12a advocates aggressive action for reunifying the kingdom, and as such presumes a movement from Jerusalem and Judah outward.[100] Thus, one can explain to a considerable degree the lack of an explicit reference to Jerusalem/Zion as being due to the implicit reference to Jerusalem and Judah in 9:11, as read by the redactor.

The fourth explanation, that Amos 9:12a seeks to bridge Amos' oracles against the nations with Obadiah, is not possible to validate. The lack of clear references to Amos 1-2, especially in light of strong links to Obadiah, makes a direct connection improbable. However, since the redactional history of Amos presupposes that Amos 1-2 existed as part of the Amos corpus prior to the inclusion of 9:12a, one may not entirely rule out some indirect connection.[101] Despite this concession, it must be noted that the *significance* of an indirect connection to the oracles in Amos 1-2 is greatly weakened by the strong links pointing forward to Obadiah.

In summary, several options could explain the addition of Amos 9:12a. None of these explanations solves every problem, but the argument that 9:12a was added as a literary transition to Obadiah has the strongest support.

Turning to Amos 9:13, the questions are not so easily solved. Literary observations demonstrated that 9:13 is a later addition, dependent upon 9:14f. First, 9:13 pushes the salvific promise of 9:14 further into the future, displaying a tension with the promise implying salvation would come with the restoration of the ruined cities and the return to agricultural normalcy. Second, the eschatological imagery is more pronounced in 9:13 than in the rest of the chapter.[102] Third, this verse does not inherently demonstrate

---

[100] It would be difficult to explain this concentration on Davidic traditions outside of a strongly Jerusalem-oriented situation.

[101] Evidence for even an indirect connection is not very strong. *Perhaps* the use of the verb ירש in Amos 2:10 might offer some indirect influence. It declares the purpose of the exodus was "to possess the land of the Amorite."

[102] Several authors take exception to this statement on tradition-critical grounds. For example, Rudolph, *KAT* 13/2, 283, argues that the Old Testament attest similar images even prior to the time of Amos, specifically citing Ps 72:16. Also Hammershaimb, *Amos*, 142 (for Amos 9:13), and G.W. Ahlström, *Joel and the Temple Cult of Jerusalem*, VT.S 21 (Leiden: E.J. Brill, 1971), 87 (for Joel 4:18), both cite the Ugaritic text from the Baal cycle (I AB III, 6f) as evidence of similar imagery far earlier than the time of Amos: "The heavens rain fatness, the waddies flow with honey." Clearly, imagery of

the divine speech of the remainder of 9:11ff. When one asks for the milieu which gave rise to this verse, one is confronted with several observations that complicate a decision.

Structurally, Amos 9:13 repeats the introduction in 8:11 almost verbatim.[103]   One must therefore ask if 9:13 draws deliberately from chapter eight, and if so, in what manner. A second question arises regarding the doublet in Amos 9:13 and Joel 4:18. Does the context of Amos 9:13 shed any light on the question of the relationship of these two verses? A third concern which must receive treatment is the question of the relationship of 9:12a and 9:13. These verses effectively function as markers to the prophetic books which precede and follow Amos (Joel and Obadiah respectively).   Are there indicators which would aid a determination as to whether these verses are part of the same redactional layer?

The parallel structure between 9:11-15 and chapter 8 likely *pre-dates* the addition of 9:13 to 9:14f.[104]   Several observations support this argument. The close parallel of the remainder of 9:11,12b with 9:14f makes the יום introduction of 9:13 more readily understandable with 9:14f than with 9:13, since the יום formula in 9:13 parallels the introductory יום formula in 9:11. Second, the hermeneutical tendency of the restoration layer to comment upon the vision in 9:1ff functions similarly to the material in 8:9f,11ff, which comments upon the vision in 8:1-3.[105]   This similarity

---

fruitfulness existed very early, but that does not change the fact that *in this context* the images are out of place. Amos 9:13 functions as a reassertion of 9:14f in more utopic, indeed eschatological terms.   Thus, despite the common imagery, eschatological elements are questionable in the passages cited by these authors.

[103] The only difference lies in the title used for God. 8:11 has the title אדני יהוה, while 9:13 has only יהוה. As noted above, page 108, there are reasons for assuming that the יום introductions in Amos 9:11ff intentionally imitate those of Amos 8:1ff, in order to call attention to the reversal of the threats from that context.

[104] Several authors have noted the parallel structure of chapter 8 and 9 of Amos. Already Karl Budde, "Zu Text u. Auslegung des Buches Amos," *JBL* 44 (1925): 99, makes this observation. More recently, see Claude Coulot, "Propositions pour une structuration du livre d'Amos au niveau rédactionnel," *Revue des Sciences Religiuses* 51 (1977): 184f. Coulot only considers the parallel structure to recur between Amos 8:1-14 and 9:1-10. Coulot does not adequately explain, however, his omission of 9:11-15, which appears unwise in light of the identical introductions of 9:13 and 8:11. Additionally, he assumes that a common structure connotes a single author when it can just as easily imply that a second compiler shaped his material on the basis of the material already present.

[105] The method by which the restoration layer inverts the final vision of Amos 9:1ff and the following discussion was noted above. Amos 8:9f,11ff takes up the fourth vision,

lends itself more readily to an imitation of chapter eight through structural parallels than does the remainder of 9:13, which is more isolated from its context. Third, the introductory formula of 8:11 is immediately followed by a YHWH speech explicitly using the divine first person. Amos 9:13 does not continue in similar fashion, whereas 9:14 does exhibit these divine first person characteristics. These observations lead one to the conclusion that the insertion of 9:13ab,b was made after chapter nine had been structured like chapter eight.

The second question concerning this verse and the growth of 9:11-15 is the relationship of 9:13* to Joel 4:18. The question of the priority of these verses necessarily presupposes literary observations made elsewhere in this study. Joel 4:18 manifests a considerable inter-relatedness to its immediate context and its role in that writing.[106] Such is not the case with the eschatological abundance pictured in Amos 9:13. Already, this observation raises suspicion that Amos 9:13 cites Joel 4:18. This suspicion is strengthened by the recognition that the language of the quote in 9:13 displays more affinity to Joel than to Amos.[107]

---

in addition to its redactional function relating to other portions of Amos (see discussion of the structure of Amos). Amos 8:10 takes up the songs of the palace mentioned in 8:3. The famine imagery in 8:12 plays off the summer fruit in 8:1f. In 8:12 the expanded description "... sea to sea, and from the north even to the east; They will go to and fro ..." recalls the casting forth of the corpses "in every place" from 8:3.

[106] See my discussion of Joel 4:18 in the forthcoming volume, to see how it functions literarily in 4:18-21 and in the wider context of 4:1-21.

[107] The vocabulary of the doublet in Amos 9:13 and Joel 4:18 does not present decisive evidence, although the significance of these words makes more sense as an adaptation of Joel by Amos than the other way around. Several words in 9:13b appear elsewhere in both Joel and Amos. עסיס ("sweet wine") does not appear elsewhere in Amos, but plays a significant role in the book of Joel (1:5; 4:18). The plural "mountains" is the place of the beginning of the apocalyptic attack in Joel 2:2,5, making the promise of sweet wine coming from the mountains poignant as a counter-image in Joel 4:18. The plural "mountains" appears only once elsewhere in Amos (4:13), but unlike 9:13, the hymnic addition of 4:13 carries no eschatological intonation. On the other hand, the roots מוג and נתף recur in Amos 9:5 and 7:16 respectively. However, the verb נתף in 7:16 is used in the narrative in the sense of "to speak" and it is difficult to see any direct relationship to the formulation of 9:13. The use of מוג in Amos 9:5 does have a more direct bearing on 9:13. Amos 9:5 depicts YHWH Sebaoth as the one who touches the land so that it "melts" (qal). When 9:13 promises the hills will "undulate" (hithpael), it reverses this picture from destruction to bounty. "Hills" does not appear elsewhere in either Joel or Amos. Thus, while not conclusive, the vocabulary of the doublet suggests Amos 9:13 adapts Joel 4:18 to the context of Amos 9.

The third question asks if any evidence ties the addition in Amos 9:12a with the addition of 9:13, or if these additions came from different times. Since both verses function similarly as literary markers to Joel and Obadiah, this question has considerable significance for understanding the growth of the Book of the Twelve. If these verses came into Amos at the same time, it provides strong evidence that Joel and Obadiah also entered the Book of the Twelve at the same time. If these verses entered separately, the likelihood changes so that one would not necessarily say that Joel and Obadiah entered together. Several observations will help to clarify the issues.

Initially, one notes that 9:12a and 9:13 are not closely related syntactically or thematically in the context of Amos 9:11-15. However, since these verses demonstrate relationships to verses outside the immediate context, one may not limit observations to Amos 9:11-15. Rather, one must also ask if the themes of political domination and/or eschatological abundance are combined in Joel and/or Obadiah. The political domination over surrounding areas was demonstrated for Obadiah above. The evidence for eschatological abundance in Obadiah, particularly utilizing agricultural images, is not as clear. The theme of an eschatological agricultural abundance for God's people is not directly addressed in Obadiah as in Joel and Amos 9:13. Rather, Obadiah is a book of invective against Edom and the nations. What little material does picture salvation for Israel heavily emphasizes the domination of Jerusalem and Judah over the surrounding regions (15ff). Obadiah does contain agricultural images in the judgment pronouncements, but there is no real tendency to portray salvation as eschatological agricultural abundance in Obadiah.[108]

Investigation of the themes of political domination and eschatological abundance in Joel leads to similar conclusions. The image of eschatological abundance is present and meaningful in Joel 4.[109] The theme of the political domination of God's people over others is not as strongly attested in Joel 4, but one must also note that the larger question of the punishment of the surrounding nations is very definitely an important topic in Joel 4. It is the theme around which the entire chapter is organized. The difference lies in the fact that Joel portrays a divine judgment against the

---

[108] See for example the mention of grape gatherers in Obad 5 (which is part of the Jer 49 parallel) and the later designation of Esau as stubble destroyed by the fire of Jacob and Joseph (Obad 18).

[109] Joel 4:18 functions as a promise of agricultural abundance in light of the agricultural catastrophe depicted in chapters 1-2.

nations in which YHWH and the heavenly host take the active role, whereas in Obadiah this apocalyptic imagery plays no role. Earthly instruments (Jacob and Joseph) execute divine punishment in Obadiah (see v. 18).

Thus, Amos 9:12a and 9:13 have no direct syntactic or thematic connection in the context of Amos 9:11-15; nor do they combine emphases which appear strongly in both Joel 4:1-21 and Obadiah. These verses function as markers in essentially one direction. Amos 9:12a foreshadows Obadiah, and 9:13 picks up Joel.

Unfortunately, the problem is not solved with this statement. Several indicators demonstrate a clear relationship between Joel and Obadiah, apart from the connecting verses in Amos.[110] Both passages suppose an eschatological day of YHWH, in which the surrounding nations will be judged.[111] Both passages specifically mention Edom as recipient of this judgment.[112] Much of the vocabulary of Obadiah and Joel 3-4 shows considerable similarity, providing strong indications of common transmission circles.[113] The importance of this relationship for the growth of Amos 9:11-15 derives from the combination of the eschatological agricultural imagery and the judgment against the nations motifs. These motifs appear in significant locations in the Book of the Twelve, all of which allude to Joel, and all of which are best categorized as redactional insertions into

---

[110] Here the work of Bergler takes on considerable importance. See his discussion on the reliance of Joel upon Obadiah: Bergler, *Joel als Schriftinterpret*, 295-333. Bergler makes excellent observations on the common vocabulary of the two works, but his conclusion that Joel 4 always cites Obadiah needs more careful evaluation. See my discussion of the literary allusions and quotes in Joel 4:1-21 in the forthcoming volume, entitled, *Redactional Processes in the Book of the Twelve*.

[111] Joel and Obadiah explicitly mention this day of judgment on the nations, while Amos 9:11-15 imports this perspective from its connection to those writings. Compare the day of YHWH sayings against the nations in Joel 4:1f,14,18f and Obadiah 8,15.

[112] Obadiah concentrates exclusively upon Edom in 1-14,15b and includes material which expands this Edom judgment to include Edom and "all the nations" in 15a,16-21. Joel 4:19 cites Edom parallel to Egypt, and 4:4 specifically mentions Tyre, Sidon, and "the regions of Philistia," making the ideas more similar to the later layer in Obadiah which expanded the judgment motifs to include more than just Edom.

[113] The relationship of Obadiah to Joel is discussed in more detail in my forthcoming volume under Joel 4:1-21. Note particularly, the discussion and critique of Bergler, *Joel als Schriftinterpret*, Beiträge zur Erforschung des Alten Testaments und des antiken Judentums 16 (Frankfurt a.M.: Peter Lang, 1988), 301-319. Bergler places this common vocabulary on the level of literary dependence, but with one possible exception (Joel 3:5), his evidence is not entirely convincing.

existing contexts.[114]   Without exception, the agricultural bounty is a motif in these passages which the redactional work always applies to YHWH's people, not to foreign nations. This observation allows an accounting for Amos 9:13* since it plays off the existence of promises to YHWH's people in 9:14f, using the language of Joel. Conversely, the lack of accentuation of these agricultural blessings in Obadiah's invective against Edom and the nations reflects a consistent limitation of these motifs to YHWH's people elsewhere in the Book of the Twelve. The twin themes of eschatological judgment on the nations and the promise of agricultural bounty which point to the writings on either side of Amos, thus can be plausibly assigned to the same redactional layer, one which stretches across several writings.

In summary, Amos 9:1-15 contains several layers of material. Amos 9:1-6 was a redactional composition which concluded the book of Amos to that point. It was structured to coincide with the other "visions" of Amos. The purpose of this ending was to pronounce the destruction of Israel. Amos 9:7-8a,8b-10 reacts to this final vision, and reflects a literary discussion of the significance of 9:1-6. The first discussion (9:7-8a) applies the message of judgment in its radical form, whereas the second unit (9:8b-10) qualifies the idea of total destruction present in 9:1-6,7-8a, by allowing the existence of a remnant and attempting an explanation for those who did not escape the fate of judgment. The next layer is the restoration layer (9:11,12b,13aα,14-15) which promises a reconstruction of the kingdom and the people's return. This promise receives two additional insertions which function as thematic markers to neighboring writings in the Book of the Twelve. The theme of political domination (9:12a) effectively summarizes the message of Obadiah. The promise of eschatological abundance (9:13*), pushes the time of salvation further into the future by importing images from Joel.

The date of these respective layers requires only general comment at this point. Clearly, all of the positive layers presuppose the negative ending of Amos 9:1-6, which formed part of a Deuteronomistic explanation for the destruction of Jerusalem. Based on other observations in the course of this study, one may presume that this early Deuteronomistic corpus, with its extremely negative views toward the destruction of Jerusalem, later received salvific additions of its own.[115]   One should place the remnant layer

---

[114] Compare especially the discussions of the following verses: 1) in this volume, Hag 2:19; Zech 8:12. 2) in the forthcoming volume: Nah 1:1ff; 3:15ff; Hab 1:5ff; 3:17; Mal 3:10f.

[115] See further discussions below of the Deuteronomistic corpus in relationship to Micah and to Zephaniah.

(Amos 9:8b-10) and the restoration layer (Amos 9:11,12b,13aa,14f) within this activity. Probable dates for this activity would be the late exilic period or early post-exilic period. The latest layer of redactional activity in the chapter incorporates related motifs from neighboring books. Amos 9:12a introduces the theme of hope for the political reconstitution of the Davidic/ Solomonic monarchy, with specific antagonistic reference to Edom, in terms reflecting Obad 17ff, while Amos 9:13 reiterates the promise of agricultural bounty for YHWH's people in eschatological imagery (9:13) utilizing the language of Joel. These two references move well into the post-exilic period based upon respective dates of the relevant portions of those writings.

Micah

1. The Macrostructure of Micah and Its Implications for Dating

Mic 1:1-9 reveals several motifs best understood in a redactional context that transcends the Book of Micah. These verses function within an early corpus (Hos-Amos-Mic-Zeph) which utilized the destruction of Samaria as a warning of what was to befall Jerusalem.[1] Nowhere is the purpose of this early corpus so clear as in Mic 1:1-9. Before turning explicitly to 1:1-9, methodological considerations require discussion of the essential elements of Micah's macrostructure and its implications for dating the book of Micah.

The book of Micah demonstrates a clear and discernible structure which alternates between sections of judgment (1:2-2:11; 3:1-12; 5:10-7:6) and salvation (2:12-13; 4:1-5:9; 7:7-20). This alternating structure does not originate with Micah, rather it reflects an intentional shaping process during the exilic and post-exilic periods.[2] Only chapters 1-3 contain material normally traced to the time of Micah.[3] After Stade, chapters 4-7 were long understood as a later composition, although recently several have challenged this view.[4] Many scholars now argue that chapters 4-7 also

---

[1] On the Deuteronomistic elements of this and similar superscriptions, see discussion of Amos 1:1.

[2] See for example, Theodor Lescow, "Redaktionsgeschichtliche Analyse von Micha 1-5," *ZAW* 84 (1972): 46-85; and "Redaktionsgeschichtliche Analyse von Micha 6-7;" *ZAW* 84 (1972): 182-212; Wolff, *BK* 14/4, XXII,XXVII-XXXVII; Rudolph, *KAT* 13/3, 24. Allen, *Joel, etc.*, 257-260, attempts to force the alternation of judgment and salvation into a more thoroughgoing pattern, but his distinction between long and short subunits of doom, hope, and distress forces a patterned structure upon the text.

[3] A great number of commentators assign Mic 1-3 to the time of Micah, if not to Micah himself. Others, such as Rudolph, see only isolated verses as later additions. A few, such as Wolff and Volkmar Fritz, "Das Wort gegen Samaria: Micha 1,2-7," *ZAW* 86 (1974): 316-331, place Mic 1:2-7, or substantial portions thereof, at a considerably later date. See discussion below, page 133.

[4] Bernhard Stade, "Bemerkungen über das Buch Micha," *ZAW* 1 (1881): 161-172. See also Knud Jeppesen. "How the Book of Micah Lost Its Integrity: Outline of the History of the Criticism of the Book of Micah with Emphasis on the 19th Century," *Studia Theologica* 33 (1979): 101-131. Jeppesen treats Stade's article within the context of the 19th century debate, but his chief interest lies in preparing an attack on the

contain older material which has been supplemented and reworked in later periods.[5] Several scholars argue chapter 6 could be as old as 1-3.[6]

Despite the evident structure, the character of the pericopes exhibits the use of compositional blocks from various times. These verses are combined using diverse techniques both with and without redactional comments. As already noted, the majority of chapters 1-3 reflect the message of the late 8th century prophet. Very few authors doubt the "authenticity" of 1:10-16; 2:1-11; 3:1-12.[7] Questions regarding later additions to the early material in 1-3 center around the opening unit (1:1-9), redactional insertions (1:12b, 13b), and the first and smallest promise section (2:12f). The content of the majority of these chapters (1:10-3:12) provides an ethical judgment against the ruling class of Jerusalem, and is frequently considered the central thrust of the preaching of Micah.

Scholars debate the exact age of the individual units in chapters 4-7, but the majority acknowledge these chapters were either composed or significantly reshaped in the exilic period and beyond.[8] Chapters 4-5

---

presuppositions of 20th century scholars who have accepted Stade's basic arguments that chapters 4-7 do not come from Micah. See also Delbert Hillers, *Micah: A Commentary on the Book of the Prophet Micah*, (Philadelphia: Fortress, 1984), 3f,8, who acknowledges that growth of the book took place, but refuses to participate in "speculative" redactional hypotheses, preferring instead the "promise that *may* lie in a synchronic approach." (p. 4, my emphasis)

5 Note especially Rudolph, *KAT* 13/3, 24-26; Ralph Smith, *Micah - Malachi*, Word Biblical Commentary 32 (Waco, Texas: Word Books, 1984), 6-9.

6 Rudolph, *KAT* 13/3, 24-26; Allen, *Joel, etc*, 249f; Willi-Plein, *Vorformen*, 100-104.

7 Note especially that 3:12 is cited in Jeremiah 26:17ff as the message of Micah against Jerusalem. While the redactional compilation of Jeremiah is complicated, most commentators assign this pericope to genuine traditions concerning Jeremiah's life. This account, with considerable certainty, allows the existence of a collection of Micah's oracles which pre-dated the destruction of Jerusalem. It also allows the observation that in the time of Jeremiah, Micah was considered a prophet who predicted the *destruction* of Jerusalem.

8 Adherents of at least an exilic date correctly note the preponderance of material in these chapters which *presupposes* the destruction of Jerusalem, and seeks to explain the exile. Mic 4:1-8 demonstrates a promissory concern in its composition which presupposes Jerusalem's destruction. Mic 4:1-4 offers an extended quote of Isaiah 2:2-4, and applies a confession of faithfulness on the part of the people (4:5), leading to a promise of restoration for the exiles (4:6-8). The next section (4:9-5:5) contains elements of promise as well as theological justification for the *Babylonian* exile. The majority of promises pertain specifically to Zion and to the restoration of the monarchy under a Bethlehemite/Davidite, but 5:4f predicts *Assyrian* destruction of the citadels (cf Amos 1), combined with an affirmation of deliverance. Mic 5:6-8 promises that the

presuppose the destruction of Jerusalem in their present form and contain several units organized around promises given to Zion which balance the judgment in chapters 1-3.   Chapters 6-7 are most often considered a redactional unity, although no absolute consensus appears on the date of the passages. Most date chapter 7 as "post-exilic," but the question of the background and origin of chapter 6 causes more disagreement.

Certain conclusions arise from an understanding of Micah's structure. First, the book in its final form, has been heavily reworked.   Second, the reworking did not merely incorporate isolated additions. It re-ordered older oracles (especially chapter 6, which many argue contains earlier material), and it added new oracles and theological reflections. Third, even the older sections in Mic 1-3 must be evaluated closely for signs of later redactional work.   Later redactions of Micah have perhaps changed the emphases of older units by their re-ordering, or by providing a new field of reference.

---

remnant of Jacob among the nations will eventually overcome their enemy. Mic 5:9-14 announces destruction on the basis of false worship. This passage was originally directed against Judah, but later expanded against "the nations which have not obeyed" (5:15). Mic 6:1-16 is structured as a lawsuit brought by YHWH against his people. He pleads his case that his people have forgotten him (6:1f,3-5). The people's defense claims that they do not know how to make up for their transgressions (6:6f); the judge refuses their defense (6:8); the verdict is announced specifically against Jerusalem (6:9-16) in which the crimes are summarized, and destruction is announced. Chapter 7 will be discussed in more detail later, but here suffice it to say that the chapter represents the response of the accused. The defendant laments the state of affairs, essentially acknowledging the crimes of the previous chapter (7:1-6). 7:7,8-20 is a liturgical composition containing several elements. Zion accepts the verdict (7:9a), but at the same time pronounces the conviction that the punishment will not be eternal (7:7f,9b,10). YHWH responds in turn with a promise of expansion to Zion together with an announcement of judgment upon all nations. Zion petitions YHWH to lead his people, using motifs from the conquest traditions (7:14), and YHWH responds favorably with a promise of a new Exodus (7:15). Next, the people respond that YHWH's power will bring the nations to subservience, and that he does not retain his anger forever (7:16-20).

2. The Literary Units in Mic 1:1-9

The first chapter of Micah contains three distinct literary units.[9] Mic 1:1 is the Deuteronomistic superscription of the book. 1:2-9 is the literary introduction to Micah. 1:10-16 is a prophetic lament over the impending destruction of Jerusalem. As already noted, a strong consensus exists that 1:10-16 accurately reflects a prophetic pronouncement of the 8th century prophet. The date of the passage is disputed, although most place it shortly before the siege of Jerusalem by Senacherib in 701.[10] The antiquity of these verses eliminates the possibility that they were composed for the Book of the Twelve, although the possibility that their present position reflects redactional intentions transcending the book of Micah must remain open.   More important for this study are questions regarding the background of 1:1,2-9.

---

[9]   For an extensive summary of opinions of the extent and character of the units in Mic 1, see Georg Fohrer, "Micah 1," in *Studien zu alttestamentlichen Texten und Themen (1966-1972)*, BZAW 155 (Berlin: Gruyter, 1981), 53-68. Fohrer (53f) cites a long list of authors who have argued for the unity of Mic 1, and a similar compilation of exegetes who have seen independent units. Those for unity include: Hitzig, Budde, H. Schmidt, Sellin, Stade, Marti, Guthe, Rudolph. However, the definition of "unity" for the majority of these mentioned is limited to the redactional or compilational level, and often allowed for later additions (especially 1:5b is frequently cited). On the other side of the coin are those who have argued that fragments of 4-5 speeches comprise the chapter. Here Fohrer cites Oesterley, Robinson, Deden, Nowack, Bewer, Pfeiffer, Wolfe, Fritz. The majority sees Mic 1 as two independent speeches, although the extent of these speeches is disputed. Many hold the opinion that the two units are Mic 1:2-7 and 1:8-16: Duhm, Mowinckel, Messel, Vellas, George, Augé, Gelin, Deissler, Eissfeldt, Weiser. Others divide the chapter 1:2-9, 10-16: Laetsch, Balla, Thomas. For this reason Fohrer understands 1:8f as the key to the chapter, and on form-critical grounds determines the verses belong more closely with 1:2-7 than with 1:10-16. Compare also the arguments of Wolff, (*BK* 14/4, 16f), who presents strong evidence that elsewhere in the Old Testament the phrase עַל־זֹאת (1:8) refers back to an antecedent, not forward to a coming oracle.

[10] Two views dominate concerning the specific events which precipitated this lament, the events of 711 or 701. The essential arguments given for these dates may be gleaned from discussion of their proponents. For a date between 714-711, see Allen, *Joel, etc.*, 241f. The arguments for the events of 701 are given by Weiser, *ATD* 24, 240. A third date prior to the destruction of Samaria also claims significant adherents, such as Wolff, *BK* 14/4, 22f; and Rudolph, *KAT* 13/3, 20, 41-51.

2.1. Mic 1:1

Mic 1:1 provides the superscription of the book, and is normally attributed to the Deuteronomistic school. Earlier observations demonstrated a high probability that someone simultaneously edited the four Deuteronomistic superscriptions in Hosea, Amos, Micah and Zephaniah with the intention of incorporating these works in seminal form into a single prophetic book with one integrative literary purpose.[11] This early Deuteronomistic corpus sought to explain Jerusalem's destruction as the culmination of God's continued warning to his people if they did not follow YHWH completely, they would suffer his wrath. As with Amos 1:1, many observe that the superscription in Mic 1:1 displays signs of an early title with redactional accretions.[12] The superscription has three clauses:

1.   The word of YHWH which came to Micah the Moreshite
2.   in the days of Jotham, Ahaz, and Hezekiah, kings of Judah,
3.   which he saw concerning Samaria and Jerusalem.

Only the first clause belongs to a pre-Deuteronomistic collection of the sayings of Micah. The second clause gives the historical period in a style typical for the Deuteronomistic superscriptions, and fits into the pattern of the superscriptions of the early Deuteronomistic corpus. Assignation of Micah's prophecies to the reigns these three kings of Judah evokes the impression that someone added this clause later, to document the career of the prophet. Critical discussion creates monumental problems for those seeking to date the individual speeches found in the current book of Micah to such a wide span of time.[13] Thus, Mic 1:1 is a historical reflection

---

[11]   See discussion under Amos 1:1.

[12]   There is no absolute consensus as to how, or if, the superscription grew, or whether it was merely a later composition. See discussions of Wolff, *BK* 14/4, 2f; Rudolph, *KAT* 13/3, 31; Willi-Plein, *Vorformen*, 70; Jörg Jeremias, "Die Deutung der Gerichtswort Michas in der Exilszeit," *ZAW* 83 (1971): 352f; Lescow, "Redaktionsanalyse," 63f; Mays, *Micah*, 38f. Weiser, *ATD* 24, 233, is among those who assume a single redactor.

[13]   See especially the arguments of Weiser, *ATD* 24, 233. These kings ruled from 756-696, thus covering a span of 60 years. Given the strong opinions that only chapters 1-3 contain Mican material, it becomes obvious that the oracles cannot cover this entire period. It is hardly less difficult, even if one takes a minimalist approach, to say that Micah began preaching late in the reign of Jotham and ceased well before the end of the reign of Hezekiah. This argument still requires at least a 16 year career of the prophet for the superscription to correspond to historical reality. Jotham died in 741 and Hezekiah began to rule in 725. Thus, even if one grants historical validity to the superscription, one must acknowledge that the superscription does not represent the dates of the oracles within the book, since the actual amount of genuine Mican material

whose interest is literary and theological. It places Micah's prophetic message within a stylized conception of a particular historical period.

The third clause in the superscription specifies the subject and/or the recipients of the speeches of Micah, namely Jerusalem and Samaria.[14] The specification of Samaria imparts considerable significance since only 1:2-9 explicitly mentions Samaria. This observation means that the third clause of Mic 1:1 does not pre-date 1:2-9. It either entered the corpus subsequent to 1:2-9 or simultaneously.

Having noted the consensus that the second and third clause did not, in all likelihood, belong to the original superscription, one must ask if clauses two and three came into the text separately or together? No indisputable answer can be offered, but the weight of the evidence falls on the side of the latter, that the second and third clause were added simultaneously. The third clause concentrates upon the content of the Micah corpus, and clearly anticipates 1:2-9. The composite nature of 1:2-9 in turn betrays an awareness of its context within a larger corpus (Hos-Amos-Mic-Zeph).[15] Awareness of the same extended corpus appears in the second clause of 1:1. This clause deliberately situates Micah within the patterned repetition of kings that reaches backward to Hosea 1:1 (and forward to Zeph 1:1).[16]

---

is quite small. Despite these difficulties, several authors go to considerable lengths to postulate theories which uphold Mican authorship over an extended period of time. For example, see Johannes C. de Moor, "Micah 1: A Structural Approach," in *Structural Analysis of Biblical and Canaanite Poetry*. JSOT Supplement 74. Willem van der Meer and Johannes C. de Moor, eds. Sheffield: JSOT Press, 1988, 172-185. De Moor claims 1:2-9 was written prior to 720 and 1:10-16 was written in 701. Despite the difference of 20 years, he claims they form an indivisible literary unity on the basis of a patterned structure. He is aware of the contradiction of his arguments, but his only defense relies on his assertion that "Micah later attached the second sub-canto to the first one choosing a matching poetical structure." (34f) Despite his conviction, the logic of these arguments defies their acceptance.

[14] One cannot excise either Jerusalem or Samaria from this clause. First, the designation of Jerusalem is very appropriate to the Mican corpus. The majority of material not only in 1-3, but in 4-7 clearly exhibits a Jerusalem orientation. Second, the phrase "concerning Samaria", while less typical of the content of the book, is impossible to remove grammatically because of its attachment to the preposition על. It strains the imagination to argue that someone would have inserted "Samaria" into a pre-existing phrase "concerning Jerusalem" and then added a *waw* to Jerusalem. Third, the order of the words (first Samaria and then Jerusalem) corresponds to the order of these entities in Mic 1:5.

[15] See discussion below, page 137.

[16] See discussion of the redactional accretions to Amos 1:1 in the chapter on Amos.

2.2. Mic 1:2-9

Mic 1:2-9 presents a confusing array of form-critical elements from diverse backgrounds whose present union attests to different layers of material as well as redactional awareness of an early Deuteronomistic corpus. The various elements may be described as follows:

1:2a Call to nations
1:2b Judgment against the nations
1:3f Description of a theophany
1:5   Rhetorical question correlating the sins of Israel/Samaria with Judah/Jerusalem
1:6f Divine announcement of punishment (1:6-7a) of Samaria and rationale (1:7b)
1:8f Prophetic response of lamentation

The question of the unity of these elements involves several aspects, including the structure, setting, and purpose of the individual parts.

Mic 1:2 presents considerable difficulties for interpretation *in its current context*. First, a definite tension exists in 1:2a regarding the addressees. The use of two imperatives with the subjects "peoples" and "earth" is complicated by a third person reference to the subject within both halves of the address. Hence the literal translation reads: "Listen peoples, all of *them*; attend earth, and everything *in it*." This call both addresses the nations directly and refers to the nations in the third person. The existence of this tension in both halves of Mic 1:2a makes textual corruption or the incorporation of marginal notes unlikely explanations.[17] One must therefore interpret the tension as a stylistic device which the author uses to address the nations while simultaneously maintaining the involvement of the real audience, the one hearing the words inside the Jerusalem community.[18]

Mic 1:2b causes considerable consternation because of the question of its relationship to the context. The central difficulty revolves around the interpretation of the phrase בכם לעד, to mean either "among you as a witness," or "against you as a witness." The author uses a juridical idiom which appears elsewhere in the Old Testament only in the sense of a

---

[17] For use of the third person in an address form, see Rudolph, *KAT* 13/3, 32; *GK* §§135r; 144p.

[18] The Jerusalem setting for the unit is derived from references elsewhere in the chapter, especially 1:5b,9b,13.

"witness against."[19] Despite the strong attestation of the meaning of the phrase many commentators either refuse to take this idiom seriously or they argue that the context of 1:2ff eliminates the possibility of the motif of judgment against the nations. Thus, they translate the phrase to mean "witness among you."[20] The overwhelming evidence of the idiom, however, obliges one to translate Mic 1:2b with its juridical intention as an indication of impending judgment against the nations. Such a translation places the sentence at odds with the content of the speech which follows, but this tension must be maintained in translation. The tensions created by this announcement of judgment against the nations must find another explanation. Three options for interpreting this verse in its context claim adherents, although two of them may not be mutually exclusive: 1) The verse may be understood as an isolated saying of the prophet; 2) the passage may be deliberately styled for the shock effect of moving from a multi-national judgment to a judgment against YHWH's people; or 3) the verse may stem from a separate redactional layer of Micah with a more universal scope. A decision on the interpretation must await discussion of the remainder of the verses.[21]

Mic 1:3-4 describes a theophany inside a prophetic announcement of judgment.[22] The verses are loosely bound to 1:2 via the connective phrase כי־הנה, but they are more narrowly bound to and presupposed by 1:5

---

[19] See John Willis, "Some suggestions on the Interpretation of Micah 1:2." *VT* 18 (1968): 372-379. Willis clearly documents the passages, and demonstrates that the order of the phrase לעד ... ב or ב ... לעד makes no difference in the meaning of the phrase. It always means "witness against". The texts he cites are Exod 20:16; Num 5:13; Deut 17:7; 19:15; 31:19,26; Josh 24:22; 1 Sam 12:5; Mal 3:5; Prov 24:28; Jer 42:5; Prov 25:18; Ps 27:12. The role of the witness is not always the same, but the phrase always denotes the one against whom the action of the witness is directed. The three options for interpreting the witness role in these passages are related, yet distinct. The first is the witness which functions as an accusing witness in a court case (Prov 24:28; Exod 20:16; Deut 5:20). The second is one which has an attestation function (1 Sam 12:5; Deut 31:26; Isa 19:20). The third actually executes judgment (Deut 17:7; 19:15,16; Mal 3:5). Mic 1:2b comes particularly close to Mal 3:5.

[20] For example, Rudolph, *KAT* 13/3, 32,39f, notes the arguments of Willis, but arbitrarily gives precedence to his understanding of the context, which leaves no room for judgment against the nations.

[21] See further discussion of Mic 1:2b below, page 140.

[22] Theophanies operate within other genres: the YHWH hymn, the prophetic announcement of judgment, the prophetic announcement of salvation, and prose theophany reports. For a detailed description of this interaction see, Jörg Jeremias, *Theophanie. Die Geschichte einer alttestamentlichen Gattung*, WMANT 10 (Neukirchen: Neukirchener Verlag, 1965), 123-136.

(כל־זאת).[23] The theophany contains two parts, the announcement that YHWH is coming to trample the high places of the earth (1:3), and the effect upon nature as a result of YHWH's arrival (1:4). The claim that the cosmic upheaval does not provide the reason for YWHW's appearance, but represents the results of his coming is confirmed both by 1:3 and 1:5. 1:3 introduces the theophany by claiming that YHWH will come to trample the high places of the earth. 1:5 not only presupposes the existence of 1:3f by the explicit reference to "all this," it also explicates the high places in 1:3, by abruptly asking the rhetorical question, "What are the high places of Judah?"

Mic 1:5 creates numerous difficulties for interpreters. Many separate 1:5b from 1:5a, arguing one of the two parts is an insertion, or they label 1:5 as a bridge uniting the previously independent theophany (1:3f) with the judgment speech against Samaria (1:6f).[24] Recently, the unity of 1:5 has been supported through the argumentation of a meaningful parallelism.[25] Hence, the verse correlates the theme of the judgment against the Northern kingdom by the implicit threat against Judah that it will suffer a similar fate:

> For the rebellion of Jacob is all of this,
> And for the sins of the house of Israel.
> What is the rebellion of Jacob? Is it not Samaria?
> And what are the high places of Judah? Is it not Jerusalem?

---

[23] The argument that the connection to 1:3f is stronger to 1:5 than to 1:2 is based upon content, and not upon the connective itself. In addition to Mic 1:3ff, other examples of a theophany inside a prophetic judgment speech as noted by Jeremias are: Amos 1:2; Isa 66:15f; 59:19; Jer 25:30b; Mal 3:1ff; Ps 50; Isa 26:21; Eth Enoch 1:3-7; 1QH 3:32ff (the last three of which also proclaim universal judgment). Of these Isa 26:21 and 66:15 begin with כי־הנה, while Mal 3:1 uses only הנה, keeping open the possibility that 1:2 was not the original introduction to 1:3f. Wolff, BK 14/4, 20,23f, believes 1:2 to be the latest element in 1:2-9, belonging to a universalistic redaction of Micah in the Persian period. It will be argued later that Wolff's arguments need certain modification, namely, that only 1:2b was inserted into this context at a later time.

[24] Lescow, "Redaktionsanalyse," 70, separates 1:5a as a later gloss (together with 1:13). Wolff, BK 14/4, XXVIII, sees 1:5 as a bridge between two independent units. Rudolph, KAT 13/3, 41, considers 1:5bb as a later insertion from the time of Manasseh (696-641). Weiser, ATD 24, 37, provides similar arguments. Mays, Micah, 45, separates 1:5b-7, but sees a redactional purpose stemming from the Babylonian crisis (25). Smith, Micah-Malachi, 16; and Allen, Jonah, etc, 271f, ascribe the entire verse to Micah.

[25] David Noel Freedman, "Discourse on Prophetic Discourse," in The Quest for the Kingdom of God: Studies in Honor of George E. Mendenhall, H.B. Huffmon, ed. (Winona Lake, Indiana: Eisenbrauns, 1983), 147.

Freedman argues that the third line takes up the thought of the first line rhetorically, and defines the rebellion of Jacob as Samaria. He then argues that the fourth line climaxes the first three although "transgression" and "high places" are, in the strict sense, not parallel terms. They

> belong together and help to define or precise each other ...Transgression properly combines with high places to form the phrase "the transgression of the high places," which applies equally to north and south and evokes the monotonously repeated charge of the Deuteronomistic historian against the kingdoms: both kingdoms are condemned for conducting unacceptable worship at the high places.[26]

Freedman never follows up his observations concerning the relationship of Mic 1:5 to the Deuteronomistic historian, but good reasons exist for understanding this entire passage as a later composition by someone associated with the Deuteronomistic school. Above all, one should note the role of Samaria in this passage.

Excursus: Samaria in Old Testament Literature

> Outside the Book of the Twelve Samaria appears only in 1 Kings (18 times); 2 Kings (48 times); Isaiah (6 times); Jeremiah (3 times); Nehemiah (1 time); 2 Chronicles (8 times). The frequency is greatest in the two books of Kings (64 times), whereas the parallels in Chronicles almost systematically omit reference to Samaria. This omission coincides with the Chronicler's deletion of most of the source material relating to the Northern kingdom.[27]
> References to Samaria treat it as a region or a city, even within the same book. Examples of the region may be noted in 1 Kgs 13:32; 2 Kgs 17:24,26; 23:19; Jer 31:5. More often the term signifies the city which served as the capital of the Northern kingdom from the time of Omri (1 Kgs 16:24) until the siege and deportation in 720. Samaria was the city where the Northern kings ruled and were buried.
> Several texts demonstrate a polemic against Samaria, which has its root in the animosity between the Northern and Southern kingdom. This animosity existed for centuries, and was the precursor to (but not identical with) the schism so prominently attested in Josephus.[28] The polemic rails against the Baal worship in the region and the city, though not always explicitly. Texts which do explicitly refer to the idolatry and Baal worship in Samaria are 1 Kings 13:32; 16:28,32; 2 Kings 10:15ff; 17:5f,29ff; 21:13; 23:19; Jeremiah 23:13; Ezek 16:46; 23:4,34; Isaiah 10:11. The majority of these passages attest Deuteronomistic origin (the references in Kings) or Deuteronomistic influence (Jeremiah). The passage from Isaiah is considered a later

---

[26] Freedman, "Discourse," 147.

[27] Richard J. Coggins, *Samaritans and Jews: The Origins of Samaritanism Reconsidered* (Oxford: Basil Blackwell, 1975), 68.

[28] See Coggins, *Samaritans and Jews*, 13-81.

gloss, and evidences dependency upon Deuteronomistic traditions.[29] The Ezekiel references appear in the parables which compare Samaria and Jerusalem (and also Sodom) as sisters bound by the harlotry/idolatry they have committed. These parables compare cultic abuses in Jerusalem with those of Samaria, and claim that Jerusalem's abuses were worse than those of Samaria. These abuses led to the destruction of Jerusalem.

Among the passages in 2 Kings, 17:5ff; 21:11-13; and 23:19 are particularly instructive. These passages clearly demonstrate the tendency to correlate the sins of the high places in Samaria which led to its destruction as a warning to Judah and Jerusalem (note especially 17:13; 21:13), and underscore the continuation of the high places in Samaria even after the destruction of the city (17:29; 23:19) so that it fell to Josiah to rid the land of these pagan practices (cf also Zeph 1:4).

Within the Book of the Twelve, Samaria appears 14 times, but only in four books: Hosea (7:1; 8:5,6; 10:5,7; 14:1), Amos (3:9; 4:1; 6:1; 8:14), Micah (1:1,5,6) and Obadiah (19). The references in Hosea and Amos generally reflect early layers of those books.[30] Hosea berates Samaria for false worship of the calf at Bethel,[31] and it combines polemical remarks against the kings who resided in Samaria. Amos also prophesies specifically against Samaria or parts of its population. By contrast, Samaria appears only peripherally in Micah, where its presence *presupposes* a polemic against Samaria as the *starting point* for a thoroughgoing judgment against cultic abuses in Jerusalem.[32] Obad 19 comes from a later time, and evidences no anti-Samarian polemic against idols. Rather, Obad 19 concerns the reunification of the Davidic kingdom, including the northern regions of Samaria and Ephraim.

The mention of Samaria in Mic 1:5,6f clearly does not depend upon the traditions in Ezekiel and Obadiah.[33] The question remains whether the use of Samaria in Micah lies closer to the other 8th century prophets Hosea and Amos, or whether this usage falls nearer the Deuteronomistic polemic. Several observations concerning the character of 1:2-7 places its view of Samaria closer to Deuteronomistic circles.[34] First, unlike Hosea and

---

[29] Hans Wildberger, *BK* 10/1 (Neukirchen: Neukirchener Verlag, 1972), 392.

[30] Amos 8:15 represents a possible exception in that it is part of the redactional material responsible for the compilation of chapters 3-8. See discussion of the macrostructure of Amos.

[31] See especially 10:5. Since no calf can be verified at Samaria, the reference to the "calf of Samaria" (8:6) must intend a broader reference to the practice of worshipping the calf in Bethel. See Wolff, *BK* 14/1, 179f; Rudolph, *KAT* 13/1, 196; Mays, 164.

[32] See literary discussion of Mic 1:5f above, page 131.

[33] Observations in my forthcoming volume argue that Obad 19 knew Mic 1 and was aware of its literary position between Amos and Micah.

[34] See expansion of these ideas in Fritz, *ZAW* 86 (1974): 316-331, especially 327-330. Fritz demonstrates quite forcefully why Mic 1:2-7 does not belong to the early material of the remainder of Mic 1-3. He does not, however, specifically tie the passage to a Deuteronomistic origin, but to a post-exilic redaction of the Micah book. For reasons

Amos, the invective against Samaria does not address that entity, rather it speaks about Samaria in the 3rd person.[35]   Second, despite the pronouncement of judgment against Samaria, the context of Mic 1:2ff makes clear that this judgment only serves as the literary backdrop to the threat against Jerusalem.[36] Third, the language and accusation stem from the cult, which contrasts with the older passages of Micah that proclaim judgment for ethically inappropriate behavior, not idolatry.[37]   Fourth, "high places" in Micah functions within the *literary frame* connecting Mic 1:3ff with 3:12.[38]

This final observation requires comment. The word במה in the OT can mean either:[39] (1) "ridge" or high ground (Deut 32:13); (2) cultic "high place", which is the common meaning, and probably developed from cultic practices on elevated areas (1 Sam 9:12; 1 Kgs 11:7; 2 Chr 33:17; Jer 48:35); (3) burial "mound" (Isa 53:9, with 1QIs; Job 27:15); (4) "stela" (Mesha inscription, and the LXX of Lev 26:30; Num 21:28; 33:52). (5) In addition the word appears metaphorically with cloud (Isa 14:14) and sea

---

which will become clear, the provenance of these verses seems better suited to the Deuteronomistic redaction of Hosea, Amos, Micah, and Zephaniah. So also Wolff, *BK* 14/4, 20-22. Wolff distinguishes three literary strata in chapter one: Those portions going back to Micah (1:6,7b-13a,14-16), an exilic Deuteronomistic commentary (1:3-5,7a,13b), and a universally oriented interpretation from the Persian period (1:2). Thus, Wolff assigns the majority of 1:2-7 to the exilic redaction, but his assignation of 6*,7 to Micah appears unlikely in light of the work of Fritz and the observations of Lescow, *ZAW* 84 (1972): 83, although his placement of the verses after the time of Alexander is likewise dubious. See further discussion below, page 137ff.

[35] The counter-argument that Micah worked in Jerusalem could perhaps explain the use of the third person, but this suggestion appears less likely when one notes how Samaria functions as a paradigm for Jerusalem in these verses.

[36] Note the implicit threat against Jerusalem in 1:5, and the specific inclusion of Jerusalem in 1:9,12.

[37] Note the charges in 2:1-3,8-11; 3:1-11. Note particularly that even the priests and prophets are accused of ethically reprehensible crimes of working for money (3:11), not for the practice of idolatry.

[38] One must distinguish between the composition of 1:3ff and the older material in 3:12. On the basis of inclusio, the extent of the Micah corpus at this point can thus be assumed to have reached *at least far as* 3:12. The citation of this verse by Jer 26:18 adds credence to the pre-exilic date and attribution of this verse to Micah.

[39] See K.-D. Schunck, *ThWAT*, vol 1, 662. One must question, however, Schunck's claim that the root meaning "back" of a man (Deut 33:29) is attested in the Old Testament. Deuteronomy 33:29 should be read simply as part of the typical polemic against cultic high places, and the metaphors he cites (Isa 14:14; Job 9:8) have more in common with the meaning "ridge" (almost "bump") than they do "back".

(Job 9:8), essentially depicting an elevated area, or roughly synonymous with "bump."

In Micah, the nuances of the word exemplify three different pictures of high places, which taken together demonstrate intentional word play. Mic 1:3 announces YHWH's descent and treading upon the "high places of the earth." The phrase "the high places of the earth" appears elsewhere as a reference to the mountains.[40] The image portrays God walking on the mountains of the world, and the content indicates that YHWH will appear for judgment. Mic 1:5 (with its parallel to the sins of Israel) artistically specifies the judgment announced in 1:3 by *implying judgment upon Jerusalem similar to Samaria*. This judgment comes because of the sins/rebellion/high place of Israel/Jacob/Judah. The meaning of במה has changed from mountain tops to the cultic high place. Mic 3:12 has neither the theophanic image of YHWH walking on the mountain tops, nor the polemic against cultic abuse. Rather, it uses במה in a metaphorical sense to picture total desolation: "the mountain of the temple will become high places (bumps) of the forest." The three usages of במה thus present a literary movement from the announced destruction of the high places of the earth to the destruction of Jerusalem. Paraphrased this movement reads: "YHWH will tread on the world's high places" (1:3) ... "what is Judah's high place?" (1:5) ... "Jerusalem will become mounds (high places) in the forest."

The stage is thus set for understanding the construction of Mic 1:3-7 as a single entity. To appreciate the intricacy of the unity fully, one must note that not only does 1:5 function as a hermeneutical bridge between 1:3 and 3:12, but 1:6 also presupposes both 1:4 and 3:12. The connection to Mic 3:12 is clear and often cited.[41] Mic 3:12 announces "Zion will be plowed as *a field*; Jerusalem will become a *heap of ruins*." It is no accident that the judgment against Samaria in 1:6a summarizes both parts of 3:12, when YHWH announces "I will make Samaria into a *heap of ruins of the*

---

[40]   The phrase appears in the doxology of Amos 4:13 in the song of Moses in Deut 32:13; and in Trito-Isaiah (58:14). Interestingly, Isaiah 58:14 clearly takes up the language of Deut 32:14, changing the prediction of judgment into a promise of salvation. In addition Mic 1:3 and Amos 4:13 may also have a closer relationship in light of the use of the same phrase ("to tread upon the high places") and the assignation of the doxologies to a period much later than Amos.

[41]   Note for example, Mays, *Micah*, 47; Allen, *Joel, etc.*, 267; Weiser, *ATD* 24, 237. Wolff, *BK* 14/4, 11, notes the connection, but reconstructs an earlier form of the verse. Rudolph, *KAT* 13/3, 33, finds the meaning questionable and emends the phrase.

field."[42] This connection follows the general tendency of 1:5 by treating
the judgment against Samaria and Jerusalem as parallel acts of YHWH.

More subtle but equally demonstrable is the connection from Mic 1:6
to 1:4. The theophany of 1:4 depicts the results of YHWH's appearance
on the mountains (high places of the earth), and 1:6 formulates a similar
fate for Samaria using much of the same vocabulary.

Mic 1:4	*Mic 1:6b,7a*
The mountains melt beneath him,	And I will pour down her stones to the
And the lowlands burst open	valley, ...
Like wax before the fire,	And all her earnings will be burned in the
Like water pouring down the slope.	fire,

The images in 1:6f take up those of 1:4 and apply them to the destruction
of Samaria. The "lowlands" of 1:4 corresponds to the "valley" of 1:6. Both
verses mention "fire" as an element of destruction. Finally, the verbal root
נגר (pour down) also plays a role in both descriptions.

The intention of 1:3-7 may be safely deduced. The inner movement
of the text simultaneously fashions a judgment against Samaria which
parallels the theophany in 1:3f and the judgment against Jerusalem in 3:12.
The images of 1:6f relate backward to the theophany and forward to the
judgment against Jerusalem. 1:5 provides the rationale for the judgment
against Samaria, alos serving as precursor to the threat against Jerusalem.

A new speaker begins in 1:8. Whereas the previous verses
presuppose a prophetic voice narrating YHWH's words, the prophet speaks
in the first person singular in 1:8. The change in speaker in this case,
however, does not mean that 1:8 begins a new unit, rather it belongs to the
same layer as 1:3-7. 1:8f currently introduces the lament in 1:10-16, but it

---

[42] Note particularly the infrequency of the word עי, which appears elsewhere only three
other times: Job 30:24; Ps 79:1; and the quote of Mic 3:12 in Jer 26:18.

is not an original part of it.[43] The use of עַל־זֹאת refers to what has been said previously.[44]

Significantly 1:8f responds primarily to the threat against Judah/ Jerusalem, not Samaria. Mic 1:9 presupposes, and accepts, the judgment against Samaria ("Her wound is incurable"), but it cites a more important cause for lamentation, namely, the threat against Judah and Jerusalem ("... for it has come to Judah, it has reached the gate of my people Jerusalem"). This threat corresponds to the tenor of 1:5-7, since the use of the prophetic perfect in relation to *Samaria's* destruction in 1:6 reveals a decidedly stronger picture of irreversible judgment against Samaria than the judgment which threatens Jerusalem. To be sure, the judgment against Samaria is portrayed in the future, but its fate cannot be changed. By contrast, the judgment against Jerusalem stands outside the gate and threatens to enter (see 1:9,12).

3. Mic 1:1-9: Redactional Introduction Within a Larger Corpus

Several indicators provide evidence that Mic 1:1-9 deliberately combines messages from Hosea and Amos while concurrently introducing a version of Micah which extended at least as far as 3:12.[45] The evidence for this statement stems from content and *inclusio*. The content of Mic 1:1-9 begins where the final vision of Amos 9:1-6 ceased, with the destruction

---

[43] Since Elliger, "Die Heimat des Propheten Micha," *Zeitschrift des Deutschen Palästina-vereins* 57/2 (1934): 81-152, the dominant opinion has tied 1:10-16 with the events of Senacherib's siege of Jerusalem in 701, but some more recent commentaries date the verses prior to Samaria's destruction. Both Wolff, *BK* 14/4, 22, and Rudolph, *KAT* 13/3, 20, 41-51, object, arguing the verses do not reliably mirror the events of 701. Both conclude that 1:10-16 must precede 701. Both suggest the situation in the decade prior to the overthrow of Samaria. The confusion stems in large part on decisions of the role of Jerusalem in the verses. Most now see the mention of Jerusalem in 1:12bb,13b as insertions.

[44] So Wolff, *BK* 14/4, 16f. Fohrer, "Micha 1," 58f, also argues that 1:8f belongs with 1:2-7, but his rationale differs from Wolff. Fohrer argues the introductory phrase "because of this" refers only to 1:9, not to 1:10-16. Here one must supplement the work of Fritz, *ZAW* 86 (1974): 316-331. Fritz correctly sees the origin of 1:2-7 as a later composition, but fails to incorporate 1:8f therein.

[45] For discussion of the extent of this early Deuteronomistic corpus within Micah, see below, page 141.

of the Northern kingdom, symbolized by Samaria. [46]Not only does Micah begin with the presumption of judgment against Samaria's false worship, but the vision and doxology of Amos 9:1-4,5f help to explain the theophany in Mic 1:3f. Amos 9:6 refers to YHWH's residence in the heavens, while Mic 1:3f portrays YHWH's descent from the heavens for judgment. Both passages announce judgment upon the Northern kingdom using Samaria as symbol. Both passages juxtapose imagery of the heights and depths (Amos 9:2-4; Mic 1:4). Both passages incorporate the pouring of water into their images of judgment (Amos 9:6; Mic 1:4). Both passages portray the melting of the earth/mountains as a result of an act of YHWH (Amos 9:5; Mic 1:4). Both passages make reference to the physical elements of the sanctuary/high place (Amos 9:1; Mic 1:7).

While the contexts are similar, it is equally significant that the vocabulary of the accusations in Mic 1:5-7 comes from Hosea and Amos. Samaria (and Jerusalem) are accused of transgression (פֶּשַׁע), precisely the word used in the refrain of the Amos' oracles against the nations, including the accusation against Israel (Amos 1:3,6,9,11,13; 2:1,4,6). This recollection of "transgression" points to a common transmission history. Only four books contain the root פשע within the Book of the Twelve, exactly those falling within the early Deuteronomistic corpus: Hosea, Amos, Micah, and Zephaniah.[47] Mic 1:1-9 also subtly presupposes Amos' oracles against the nations in the manner in which it, like Amos 1-2, is structured for shock effect. The theophany against the high places of the earth (1:3) suddenly changes to a polemic against Samaria (1:5a,ba), and just as suddenly springs to a threat against Jerusalem (1:5bb).[48]

Much of the imagery of the accusation in Mic 1:7 stems from Hosea, particularly as reflected in the opening section of that book. The Israel/harlot motif is a metaphor normally traced to Hosea in light of the extended utilazation of this image in Hosea 1-3. Already Jepsen and others note this relationship, but the realm in which this relationship took place,

---

[46] See Mays, *Amos*, 148f.

[47] The nominal form appears primarily in Amos' oracles against the nations. Elsewhere in Amos, the nominal form appears in 3:14 and 5:12. The nominal form appears in Mic 1:5, in the gloss in 1:13, in the "genuine" material in 3:8, in the Deuteronomistically fashioned 6:7, and in the later 7:18. The verbal form of פשע appears in Hos 7:13; 8:1; 14:10; Amos 4:4; and Zeph 3:11.

[48] See further the discussions of Willis, *VT* 18 (1968): 372-379; and Rudolph, *KAT* 13/3, 39.

namely the redaction of a common corpus, seldom receives treatment.[49]
These cultic harlotry motifs are particularly dominant in Hos 2:10-15 (note
especially 2:14), which has clear thematic and linguistic ties to
Deuteronomistic redactional hands.[50]

This early Deuteronomistic corpus provides the skeletal frame which
helps to shape the chronological macrostructure of the entire Book of the
Twelve.[51] This corpus balances two books on the Northern kingdom with
two concerning Jerusalem and Judah. The messages of Hosea and Amos
were historically delivered against the North. By contrast, Micah and
Zephaniah concentrate on Jerusalem. This balance coincides well with the
framework provided by the Deuteronomistic superscriptions which
summarize the historical periods within an increasingly Judean frame.
These four superscriptions, when read in tandem, highlight the reigns of
Hezekiah and Josiah probably because of the similar Jerusalem cultic
reforms those kings undertook, as presented in the Deuteronomistic
history.[52]

Deuteronomistic redactional work is presumably also responsible for
the heavy alternation between judgment and salvation in both Hosea and
Micah. The alternation of judgment and salvation within these two books
functions similarly. Within the larger Deuteronomistic corpus, the
alternation signals that YHWH does not destroy the entities at the first sign
of sinfulness, but continually seeks to change the behavior of Israel and
Judah (and their respective capitals). By contrast, Amos and Zephaniah do
not exhibit this vacillation in the early layers of those writings.[53] These
four books were organized around a single schema, twice repeated. At the

---

[49] Alfred Jepsen, "Kleine Beiträge zum Zwölfprophetenbuch I," *ZAW* 56 (1938): 96-100.
Jepsen says Mic 1:6f "zeigen deutlich hoseanischen Sprachgebrauch" (98). Jepsen also
makes an astute observation on the seams of the writings of the Book of the Twelve,
although he never develops this observation. He says that relationships between Joel
and the end of Micah raise the possibility that in "those places where one prophetic
writing ceases and another begins, small insertions appear." (96, my translation)
Jepsen's conclusion that one could ascribe Mic 1:6f to a later redactor, and solve the
problem has justifiably been questioned (for example, Fritz, *ZAW* 86 (1974): 318), but
this detail does not negate Jepsen's assertion concerning Hoseanic imagery.

[50] See discussion of the role of Hos 2:3ff in the treatment of the literary horizon of Hos
14:2ff and in the literary discussion of Joel 1:8.

[51] See discussion of the factor of chronology in the introduction to this work.

[52] See excursus on the Deuteronomistic headings in the treatment of Amos 1:1.

[53] Both Amos (9:7-15) and Zephaniah (3:9ff) receive major salvific additions to the ends
of the writings, which prior to that time consisted almost exclusively of judgment
speeches, together with a few sayings about a remnant.

early stage of their common transmission history, Hosea vacillates back and forth between judgment and salvation for the North, but Amos brings only judgment. Micah, like Hosea, alternates between judgment and salvation, but this time the fate of Judah and Jerusalem hangs in the balance. Zephaniah, like Amos, brings only messages of judgment with an occasional hope for a remnant, but this time Judah and Jerusalem are the subjects. Mic 1:1-9 represents an important transition point in the early Deuteronomistic corpus. It marks the change from judgment against the North to judgment against the South, and particularly against Jerusalem. The questions expressed in Mic 1:2ff therefore do not constitute an isolated judgment oracle against Samaria as some presume, but present the deliberately created hermeneutical shift in this broader corpus.

Having noted how Mic 1:2ff functioned in the early Deuteronomistic corpus, it is now possible to return to the question of Mic 1:2b, with its announcement of judgment against the nations.[54]   How does the pronouncement of this judgment coincides with the interests of either the Micah collection or the Deuteronomistic corpus? This phrase does not coincide well with the interests of either corpus as described here. While the early Deuteronomistic corpus did contain elements of judgment against specific nations, this oracular material is by no means accented. Amos' cycle of oracles (1:3-2:16) uses the nations in large part only as background for the climactic judgment against Israel. Likewise, Zephaniah's oracles (2:4-15) climax not with extended general pronouncements against the nations, but with the bitter pronouncement of judgment against Jerusalem (3:1-8a). This acknowledgment does not require, however, that one must view Mic 1:2b as an isolated gloss. Mic 1:2b presumes a judgment scene against the nations which blends remarkably well with Obad 15-21. Obad 16 announces universal judgment, and Obad 21 states, "The deliverers will go up *on the mountain of Zion* to *judge* the mountain of Esau." This conclusion helps explain the enigmatic reference to universal judgment in Mic 1:2b.[55] Mic 1:2b announces YHWH's arrival *from his holy mountain* as a *witness* against all the peoples. It incorporates a universal perspective of judgment into a context which previously concerned only YHWH's people.

Technically, Mic 1:2b functions quite similarly to Joel 1:2 by operating with a hermeneutic which *presupposes* the message of the previous book.

---

[54] See the literary discussion above, page 129.

[55] One must continue to bear in mind that the book of Jonah was not yet a part of the larger corpus, meaning that Obad 21 immediately preceded Mic 1:2 at this point.

Given the similarities between Joel and Obadiah already noted by Bergler and others, this comparable relationship is not surprising. The major difference — presuming this analysis is correct — lies in the fact that Mic 1:2b is a minor insertion into an existing text, whereas Joel 1:2-4 serves as the introduction to a writing created for its current position. When one adds this observation to evidence from Nahum and Habakkuk, it provides a solid foundation for the belief that Mic 1:2b deliberately incorporates a universal judgment motif, a motif which exhibits a literary awareness extending beyond Micah.[56]

4. The Extent of the Deuteronomistic Micah Corpus

Three observations provide the basis for a discussion of the extent of the Micah corpus at the early Deuteronomistic level. All three have considerable attestation in secondary literature. 1) Deuteronomistic Micah extends at least as far as 3:12;[57] 2) The current structure of Micah alternating judgment and hope originates no earlier than the late exilic period, but more likely the post-exilic period;[58] 3) Mic 6:1ff contains material often described as "older."[59] Certain implications may be derived from these observations, whose corollaries aid in the formulation of the implications. 1) The connection between 1:3ff and 3:12 does not demand that 3:12 marked the end of the Micah to that point. 2) The late exilic or post-exilic alternation of judgment and hope implies (or at least leaves open the possibility) that an earlier corpus existed which conveyed only a

---

[56] Chapters on Nahum and Habakkuk in my forthcoming volume (*Redactional Processes in the Book of the Twelve*) will demonstrate considerable amounts of redactional activity which specifically incorporate judgment against Assyria and Babylon into the chronological framework of the Deuteronomistic corpus. This judgment is not only cognizant of its chronologically oriented position in the Book of the Twelve, but incorporates cosmic theophanic motifs (Nah 1:2-8; Hab 3:2ff) which have much in common with Mic 1:2ff. Additionally, both Nahum and Habakkuk clearly take up portions of Joel within this redactional material, creating further links among the writings.

[57] The accepted dates of these chapters by scholars and the presupposition of 3:12 by 1:3-7 evidence this statement. See above discussion, page 124.

[58] For example, see Wolff, *BK* 14/4, XXVII-XXXVII; Mays, *Micah*, 21-33.

[59] Note discussion of the macrostructure above, page 124.

message of judgment.[60] 3) The "older" nature of chapter 6 may originate in large part because it is older than its context in 4-7, without meaning that it is as old as the "genuine" material in 1-3.

A complete redaction analysis of Mic 6:1ff cannot be accomplished in this work, nevertheless certain noticeable phenomena demand some discussion of the relationship between chapter 6 and chapters 1-3. These phenomena create a strong impression that substantial portions of chapter 6 formed the early Deuteronomistic ending to the version of Micah introduced by 1:2-9, and simultaneously created a bridge to the early Deuteronomistic version of Zephaniah.[61]

Mic 6:1ff, as with 1:3ff, contains considerable Deuteronomistic terminology and traditions. Mic 6:4f cites the exodus and the conquest traditions. Mic 6:16 refers to the "statutes of Omri" and the "works of the house of Ahab," both of which reflect Deuteronomistic polemics against those Northern kings.[62]

Mic 6:1ff also demonstrates knowledge of chapters 1-3, and summarizes the denunciations there. Mic 6:13 pronounces judgment upon Judah and Jerusalem for their sins, as in 1:5.[63] Mic 6:6f offers a rhetorical dialogue between prophet and people, which responds to YHWH's exhortation in 6:5. Mic 6:7 takes up the accusations of 1:5-7 as they now apply to Judah and Jerusalem: "Shall I present my first-born for my rebellious acts?" (פשע) The rich men of the city who are full of violence (6:12) corresponds to the description of the cruelty of the leaders in 3:1-3.[64] Mention of the inhabitants who "speak lies" (6:12) takes up the accusation of 2:11, which depicts YHWH's people as a people of lies.[65]

---

[60] Interestingly Jer 26:18 portrays Micah as a prophet of judgment, not hope and judgment. Compare this with Ben Sirach's (49:10) classification of the Twelve as a book of hope.

[61] For discussion of the growth of Zephaniah, see the next chapter beginning on page 171.

[62] Omri's chief crimes were the establishment of the capital at Samaria and idolatry. Ahab is the object of perhaps the greatest scorn against royalty in the Old Testament, including idolatry and mixing with foreign cultures. See 1 Kgs 16:21-28,29-34; 20:35-21:29.

[63] Mic 6:9-16 refers both to the city and the surrounding region. The city appears explicitly in 6:9,12. The larger application to Judah appears in the mention of the tribe in 6:9, in the reference to the "house" in 6:10, and in the implications of 6:16.

[64] These rulers "... who tear off the skin" of the people, "and their flesh from their bones, and who eat the flesh of my people, strip off their skin from them, break their bones, and chop them up as for the pot and as meat in a kettle."

[65] "If a man walking after wind and falsehood had told lies, ... he would surely be spokesman for this people."

In addition, several images in Mic 6:1ff come, not from Micah, but from Amos and Hosea. Hence, YHWH's response in 6:8 ("do justice" and "love חסד") is no mere idiomatic phrase, rather it takes up the catchwords of the messages of Amos and Hosea.[66] These catchwords are introduced by a quotation formula: "He has declared to you what is good, O man, and what YHWH seeks from you."[67] Additionally, the accusations of Mic 6:10f presuppose the messages of Hosea and Amos. YHWH's rhetorical question in Mic 6:11 (Can I justify wicked scales and a scanty measure?) bears striking resemblance to the threat in Amos 8:5 directed against those who seek "to make the measure smaller and the shekel larger."[68] The reference to destruction by the sword of YHWH (Mic 6:14) corresponds to the final vision of Amos 9:1-4.[69] These connections within the Deuteronomistic frame of chapter six provide solid evidence that Mic 6:1ff is a redaction text whose literary horizon reaches backward, not only to Mic 1-3, but to the works of Hosea and Amos as well. However, Mic 6:1ff also points forward to Zephaniah.

A significant amount of vocabulary and themes recur between Mic 6:1ff and Zeph 1, particularly in Zephaniah's early material. The words shared by the two passages are so numerous as to raise suspicions that the two passages are related in more than a casual manner.[70] More significant than the mere repetition of common words are the thematic connections uniting the two passages. Thematically, both passages pronounce judgment upon Jerusalem, with Judah playing a secondary role. This judgment, however, displays a higher degree of homogeny than can be

---

[66] Note the use of justice in Amos 5:7,15,24; 6:12 and Hos 2:21; 12:7. Note the use of חסד in Hos 2:21; 4:1; 6:4,6; 10:12; 12:7. Particularly the formulations in Hos 2:21 and 12:7 also combine both concepts. Note the verb דרש also occurs frequently in Amos 5, along with משפט.

[67] For a discussion of how formulas such as these were used to mark quotations of scripture elsewhere in the Old Testament, see Michael Fishbane, *Biblical Interpretation in Ancient Israel* (Oxford: Clarendon, 1985), 530-535.

[68] Inside the Book of the Twelve "scales" appears only in Hos 12:8; Amos 8:5; Mic 6:11. "Measure" appears only in Mic 6:10; Amos 8:5; and in the vision in Zech 5:6-10.

[69] Both passages depict YHWH's destructive sword used on those who have escaped the initial judgment.

[70] At least fourteen different words appear in both texts: city (Mic 6:9,12; Zeph 1:16, and imagery of 1:10); desolation (Mic 6:13; Zeph 1:13,15); destruction (Mic 6:16; Zeph 1:15); eat (Mic 6:14; Zeph 1:18); house (Mic 6:10,16; Zeph 1:9,13); inhabitants (Mic 6:16; Zeph 1:4,18); justice (Mic 6:8; Zeph 2:3); man (Mic 6:8; Zeph 1:3); name (Mic 6:9; Zeph 1:4); sin (Mic 6:13; Zeph 1:17); sow/plant (Mic 6:15; Zeph 1:13); statute (Mic 6:16; Zeph 2:1); voice (Mic 6:9; Zeph 1:10,14); wicked (Mic 6:10,11; Zeph 1:12).

attributed to chance.   Both passages, at least implicitly, blame the destruction upon Jerusalem's practice of those cultic practices which led to the destruction of the Northern kingdom.[71] This theology of judgment not only binds Mic 6:9 and Zeph 1, but relates both to the transition in Mic 1:1-9. Additionally, several images recur in both passages. Most noticeable are the use of similar motifs and formulations of Mic 6:14 (you will eat, but not be satisfied) and Zeph 1:13 (they will build houses, but not inhabit them; and plant vineyards, but not drink their wine); YHWH's searching of the city for judgment (cf Mic 6:9f; Zeph 1:12); and very significantly, the rhetorical question regarding the sacrifice of the first-born (Mic 6:7) and the condemnation of those who "swear by Milcom" (Zeph 1:5).[72]

The intricacy of the involvement of Mic 6 and Zeph 1:1-2:3 doubtless needs further study.[73]   Still, enough evidence has been noted here to postulate plausibly that the two passages were closely related at an early Deuteronomistic level. The two passages provided the bridge from the prophetic denunciation of Judah and Jerusalem to the destruction of Jerusalem within the historical framework provided by the superscriptions of the four books of the Deuteronomistic Corpus.[74]

5. Determination of the Units in Mic 7:8-20

Typically, scholars assign Mic 7:8-20 to the latest compositional level of the book.[75] These verses shift in style, address, form, and theme from

---

[71] See Mic 6:16 and Zeph 1:4f. Note especially the references to the "remnant of Baal" and the "idolatrous priests" (elsewhere only in Hos 10:5 and the story of Josiah's reforms in 2 Kgs 23:5).

[72] Milcom is the generally accepted as the Hebrew corruption of the Ammonite god Molech. The most repulsive aspect of Molech worship was the human sacrifice in which the first-born was delivered up to the god.

[73] One question of interest would be a redactional reconstruction of Mic 6 to determine how much of this material came from the same layer, and how far this unit extended. For example, were portions of 7:1-6 involved in the connection, and if so how much of these verses?   One preliminary observation that 7:1-6 was *at least aware of* the connection is the reference to the prince (Mic 7:3; Zeph 1:8).

[74] This idea is developed more thoroughly in the Zephaniah section.

[75] Since Stade, "Streiflichter auf die Entstehung der jetzigen Gestalt der alttestamentlichen Prophetenschriften," *ZAW* 23 (1903): 163-171, this view represents almost a consensus opinion. Hillers, *Micah*, 89, stands out as an exception in his belief that the chapter comes from the time of Micah.

the preceding unit in 7:1-7.[76] Since Gunkel, most recognize a post-exilic liturgical setting as the background for 7:8-20.[77] However, recent work,

---

[76] Considerable debate exists over the question of whether 7:7 belongs to lament in 7:1-6 or to 7:8-20. However, 7:7 belongs closer to 7:1-6 on form-critical grounds, since the affirmation of confidence typically appears in complaints (see Erhard Gerstenberger, *Psalms, Part 1 with an Introduction to Cultic Poetry*, FOTL 14 [Grand Rapids: Eerdmans, 1988], 12), and since the historical setting in 7:1-6 differs from 7:8-20. Bo Reicke, "Liturgical Traditions in Micah 7," *HTR* 60 (1967): 349-367, argues the entire chapter is a liturgical unit. Reicke understands the prophetic "I" as a unifying factor consistent in all of chapter 7, as opposed to the style of chapter 6. In addition the "day" motif appears in both sections (7:4,11f). He believes 7:7-20 fleshes out the changes desired in 7:1-6 by demonstrating the manner in which they will appear. The difference in addressee and setting in 7:1-7 make it unlikely that the prophetic "I" carries strong enough weight to argue for an original unity, particularly since this 1cs style appears only in 7:8-10, not in 11-20. This points to a further inconsistency in Reicke's argument in that 7:1-6 assumes a masculine speaker (see the divine response in 7:4f), whereas 7:8ff presumes the speaker is feminine.

[77] Stade, *ZAW* 23 (1903): 163-171, noted the similarity of these verses with the psalms and their liturgical character. Marti, *Dodekapropheton*, 298, believed on the basis of style that two psalms (7:7-13,18b,19a; 14-18a,19b,20) had been joined together. Duhm, *ZAW* 31 (1911): 92f, found three independent psalms, 7:8-10,11-13,14-20. Gunkel, "Der Micha-Schluss. Zur Einführung in die literaturgeschichtliche Arbeit am AT." *Zeitschrift für Semitistik* 2 (1924): 145-178; see also "The Close of Micah: A Prophetical Liturgy," in *What Remains of the Old Testament*, 1928, 115-149, identified two paired units using form-critical criteria. The first unit is a song of trust sung by Zion (7-10) paired with a divine oracle addressed to her (11-13). The second contains a lament of Israel (14-17) and a hymn of assurance for future deliverance sung by the congregation (18-20). He concluded the historical situation represented is similar to that of Trito-Isaiah. Reicke, "Liturgical Traditions in Mic 7," *HTR* 60 (1967): 349-367, added 7:1-7 to the liturgical pattern, and claimed it related to the suffering and restoration of the king. Eissfeldt, "Ein Psalm aus Nord-Israel: Micha 7:7-20," *ZDMG* 112 (1962): 259-268; also in *Kleine Schriften*, vol. 4 (1963), 63-72, understood the liturgy as one composed by Micah for Israelites in the north following the Assyrian occupation of 722. Lescow, "Redaktionsgeschichtliche Analyse von Micha 6-7," *ZAW* 84 (1972): 182-212, decided that there is an exilic penitential prophetic liturgy of repentance which runs from 6:9-7:20. He says that 6:9-12 was a summons to repentance addressed to Zion; 7:1-2,5-6 was the lament of Zion; 7:7-10a was the song of Zion's confidence; and 7:18-20 was the hymnic conclusion for the original form of the liturgy. He claimed the remainder came over the course of a historical process not complete until around 330. Mays, *Micah*, 155, agrees with Gunkel's basic hypothesis on the unity of 7:8-20, but does not find the arguments convincing which try to force that unity back to chapter 6. Mays also modifies Gunkel insofar as he considers that the unity is more literary than liturgical, although Mays admits the compiler based the unity upon a liturgical pattern. Mays attributes this unity to the compiler of Mic 6-7. Mays thinks the 2fs material formed the core of the original material which the compiler adapted. The compiler added 7:13

as well as the number of repeating words between Mic 7:8-20 and Nah 1:1-8 require a fresh look at the various sub-units of Mic 7:8-20 to determine if these verses may be adequately explained as an original unity, and if so, how that unity functions in the context of Micah.[78]

The wide variety of speakers and addressees appearing in 7:8-20 defies a simple description of the extent of the units. No formulas mark the beginning or the end of units. Only the change of speaker and/or a change of addressee separate one section from another. The subtle nature of these changes often complicates the determination of the speaker.

Mic **7:8-10** presents an individual song of confidence in YHWH spoken by one feminine entity to and about her feminine enemy. The speaker may be deduced as the personified Zion. The 1cs style unites these verses, and the quote in 7:10 placed in the mouth of the enemy demonstrates that the 1cs speaker is also a feminine entity: "the one saying (*3fs*) to me (*1cs*), 'where is your (*2fs*) god?'" It is relatively easy to determine Zion as speaker on the basis of the Zion traditions in Micah and from similar imagery in certain Zion Psalms, Lamentations, and Deutero-Isaiah.[79]

The identity of the enemy is more complicated. The feminine singular imagery creates problems for interpreting the main characters in this constellation.[80] Elsewhere in Micah, no feminine enemy appears.[81] At least three different suggestions have been offered: Edom, a collective enemy, and Babylon. All three presume 7:8-20 arose as an independent liturgy. The most common suggestions identify the feminine enemy as Edom or a collective reference.[82] The rationale for Edom relies upon an early

---

as transition to 7:14-17 and the phrase "to YHWH our God" in 7:17 to tie 7:18-20 to the block.

[78] See particularly the work of Theodor Lescow, "Redaktionsgeschichtliche Analyse von Micha 6-7." *ZAW* 84 (1972): 182-212. Lescow dates 7:7-10,18,20 from the early exilic period, but understands 7:7-20 as a later composition (see 204f).

[79] For further discussion, see Rudolph, *KAT* 13/3, 130f.

[80] On the basis of the discussion which follows in this chapter, the most likely referent would appear to be Nineveh.

[81] The enemies cited in 4:10 and 5:5 mention Babylon and Assyria respectively, but the reference are either plural (enemies in 4:10) or the typical masculine singular (5:5).

[82] Mays, *Micah*, 158f, following Gunkel and Sellin, leans toward Edom, but the feminine singular makes this unlikely. Wolff, *BK* 14/4, 190f, however, cites the feminine singular as a typical element in oracles against the nations. Allen, *Joel, etc*, 390f, and Hillers, *Micah*, 87, merely avoid the question by translating 7:8,10 as plural enemies. They understand the feminine singular references as collective, although Allen (394) tries to leave open the possibility that the enemy *might be* Edom. The 2fs form of enemy and

post-exilic date, when animosity against Edom plays a significant role in Old Testament literature. Against this theory one must note that Edom plays no role elsewhere in the Micah corpus, making its appearance here with no introduction highly questionable. In addition, the normal reference for Edom would be masculine singular, not feminine.[83] The second theory, that 7:8-10 intends a collective enemy, assumes 7:8-10 stems from a liturgical text composed following the destruction of Jerusalem.[84] The surrounding countries, notably Edom and Tyre, had taken advantage of Judah's destruction to expand their own territory by raiding Judean land and capturing its inhabitants.[85] Often, even those who translate the reference as singular revert to this theory, or they refuse to make a definitive statement on the identity.[86] Wolff offers a third option when he argues the 3fs reference comes from the typical use of the feminine in oracles against the nations. He believes that the enemy in Mic 7:8-20 was likely Babylon.[87]

The uncertainty over the identity of the enemy stems in large part from the presumption that 7:8-20 originated separately from the book of Micah.[88] Scholars presume that the passage displays a post-exilic liturgical background, which when removed from that context, lacks precise indicators of the original order and of the participants of this liturgy. They presume that the passage of time and the incorporation of 7:8-20 into Micah has thus obscured the original setting, making an exact determination of the identity impossible. A more promising direction of inquiry lies in the intention of this passage in its present location. During the following delineation of the various portions of 7:8-20 it will be necessary to pursue the question of the identity of the enemy from this perspective.

Despite questions about the precise identity of the enemy, the historical situation behind 7:8-10 finds its closest parallels in other early

---

the 2fs verbal forms in both verses make this explanation unsatisfactory if another explanation can be found.

[83] One noted exception appears in Obad 1, but the parallel in Jer 49:14 makes clear that the original addressee of that oracle was the city Bozrah. See previous discussion of the relationship between Obad 1-5; Jer 49:14-16,9; and Amos 9:1-4. Edom does appear in Lam 4:21 as feminine, but only with the title "daughter of Edom."

[84] For example, see Ralph Smith, *Word Biblical Commentary* 32, 58.

[85] For example, see Joel 4:4-8 and Ezek 35:10.

[86] Rudolph, *KAT* 13/3, 131f apparently prefers a collective understanding, although he translates איבתי as singular.

[87] Wolff, *BK* 14/4, 190.

[88] For example: Wolff, *BK* 14/4, 194; Rudolph, *KAT* 13/3, 131.

post-exilic literature. The situation of Zion presupposes the destruction of
Jerusalem (7:8: though I have fallen, ... though I dwell in darkness). The
strong sense of optimism (I will rise, ... YHWH will bring me forth to the
light) and the similarity of language to portions of Trito-Isaiah points away
from the time immediately after the destruction.[89] Also the depiction of
the situation lacks the vivid images of death and destruction found in the
early exilic literature such as Lamentations.

A second unit begins abruptly in Mic **7:11** and extends at least through
7:12. The speaker changes so that now the personified Zion is addressed.
No grammatical markers within the verses offer absolute verification as to
whether the speaker is YHWH or the prophet. In the MT, these verses
respond to 7:8-10, serving as an affirmation of Zion's confidence. One may
therefore assume form-critically that YHWH is here the intended speaker.
Thus, YHWH promises the rebuilding of the wall and the extension of the
boundary to Zion. The identity of those making their way to Zion in 7:12
must be extrapolated from the context, but this process is not without
problems. Normally, commentators presume that those coming implies the
returning exiles, but the context makes this explanation suspect.[90]

Mic **7:13** complicates the picture considerably. It is bound by syntax
and content to 7:11f, and appears to be presupposed by 7:14, meaning that
it cannot simply be removed from the context as a gloss. Several problems
complicate the determination of the speaker. First, no internal syntactical
or grammatical evidence provides incontrovertible evidence that the
speaker changes.[91] Second, the positive intention of 7:8-10,11-12 is clear,
but 7:13 suddenly introduces a judgment motif into the context. The
recipient of the judgment depends upon the way in which one understands
ארץ. Most commentators understand ארץ in 7:13 in a universal sense,
meaning "earth".[92] The resulting picture is one of a future universal
judgment: "And the *earth* will become a desolation because of its

---

[89] See discussion in Wolff, *BK* 14/4, 193f.

[90] For example: Wolff, *BK* 14/4, 199f; Rudolph, *KAT* 13/3, 133; Mays, *Micah*, 162. Allen,
      Joel, etc, 397f, correctly notes problems with this interpretation, but his own suggestion
      of an Israelite territorial description creates as many problems.

[91] One marker, the use of ו + היה, could introduce a new speaker in 7:13, but more
      likely it introduces a thematic shift without a change of speaker.

[92] Allen, *Joel, etc.*, 398, is typical when he refers to 7:13 as the "counterpart to the
      Christian doctrine of the Last Judgment." See also Wolff, *BK* 14/4, 191, who maintains
      that the verse is a secondary expansion. Rudolph, *KAT* 13/3, 133, does not consider the
      verse secondary, but thinks it forms one third of a three part divine response. Mays,
      Micah, 162, believes the verse to be the "eschatological reversal" of Mic 6:16b.

inhabitants, for the fruit of their deeds." Because of this judgmental aspect against the earth, most choose to interpret the references to Assyria and Egypt in 7:12 as references to returning diaspora Jews from those regions. It would be very difficult to explain a unified picture in 7:11-13 portraying an Assyrian and Egyptian pilgrimage to Zion to honor YHWH, which subsequently precipitates universal judgment. Most therefore choose to interpret 7:12 as a reference to the return of the people of YHWH living in Assyria and the cities of Egypt. However, two aspects must be discussed which challenge the validity of these assumptions, namely, the LXX reading and the use of שממה elsewhere in the Old Testament.

The LXX reading of Mic 7:11-13 contains many of the same words as the MT, but several significant differences reflect a message substantially dissimilar in both tenor and content. Unlike the MT, the LXX text has no salvific elements in 7:11-13.

> [10]And my enemy will see it, and will clothe herself with shame, the one who says, "Where is the Lord your God?" My eyes will look upon her: now shall she be a trampling as mire in the streets. [11]A day of the covering of brick; that day will be your utter destruction and destroy your customs [12]that day, and your cities will become level ground, and (become) a division of Assyria and your fortified cities a division of Tyre unto the river of Syria, a day of water and groaning, [13]and the land will be a desolation together with its inhabitants for the fruit of their deeds.

As already demonstrated, the LXX reading does not represent a different *Vorlage*; rather the LXX here *interprets* the MT.[93] Nevertheless, if one asks what caused the liberty with the MT, when normally the LXX follows the MT relatively closely in the Book of the Twelve, several observations can be made. First, some of the apparent differences can be explained as alternate readings of the consonantal text.[94] Second, the LXX reading does not demonstrate a change in the speaker between 7:10 and 7:11, as does the MT, and indeed the entire passage could be intended as a continuation of the reference to the "enemy" of the preceding verses.[95]

---

[93] For an explanation of the similarity of the Greek to the Hebrew text, see the text notes in chapter two.

[94] Note especially the mixing of the consonants in the phrase וים מים והר ההר, and the confusion over מצור in 7:12 (see P.J. Calderone "The Rivers of Masor," *Biblica* 42 (1961): 423-432.

[95] This enemy is obviously considered a political entity ("your cities"), but it cannot be considered as Assyria. A judgment against Assyria would hardly pronounce that judgment by consigning its cities to become part of Assyria. There is no evidence, however, that the LXX here offers a contemporary interpretation of the identity of this

Third, the LXX eliminates the vacillation from salvation to judgment by presenting a consistent picture of judgment against the inhabitants and their land. Hence the cities will be destroyed, and then *divided* between Tyre and Assyria. It is thus important to recognize that the LXX treats 7:13 not as universal judgment, but as judgment against the land and its inhabitants.

To understand the distinctiveness of Mic 7:13, one must also evaluate the use of שממה elsewhere in the Old Testament. "Desolation" is associated primarily with prophetic traditions, appearing only three times outside prophetic writings (Exod 23:29; Lev 26:33; Josh 8:28). Of these references, two refer to the exile. Only Josh 8:28 (which refers to Joshua's decimation of Ai) contains no specific reference to the exile. This single occurrence of "desolation" within the conquest narratives is the more noticeable since the battles of the conquest narratives should have been a natural context for the concept "desolation."

"Desolation" in the prophetic literature appears primarily in passages which presuppose the Babylonian destruction of Jerusalem.[96] While a few passages might predate the destruction of Jerusalem, they come late in the 7th century.[97] The majority of the later texts demonstrate that the word became essentially a *terminus technicus* for the aftermath of the Babylonian destruction of Judah and Jerusalem.[98] שממה also appears in oracles against specific nations, but the majority also presuppose the exile, and often imply that the desolation is recompense for the role played by that nation in Jerusalem's destruction.[99] In spite of the frequent use of שממה

---

enemy, meaning that the translator considered the context sufficiently clear.

[96] שממה appears in the writings of the 8th century prophets only three places in Isa 1-39, but these passages (1:7; 6:11; 17:9) likely represent later additions.

[97] Note particularly the oracles against the nations in Zeph 2:4,9,13 where שממה occurs with Ashkelon, Ammon, and Assyria. Elsewhere the use of שממה seldom predates the events surrounding the first Babylonian exile in 597. See possibly Jer 49:33.

[98] Numerous passages associate "desolation" with the land (ארץ): Isa 1:7; 6:11; 17:9; 62:4; Jer 6:8; 12:10; 32:43; Ezek 6:14; 12:20; 14:15f; 15:8; 33:28f; 36:34; Joel 2:3. Sometimes the references refer simultaneously to the desolation of the cities of Judah: Isa 1:7; 6:11; 17:9; Jer 9:10; 10:22; 34:22; 44:6; Ezek 12:20; 36:34. Also the references refer explicitly to Jerusalem: Isa 62:4; 64:9; Jer 6:8; 34:22; 44:6; Ezek 15:8; Zeph 1:3.

[99] Note especially condemnation of Babylon (Jer 25:12; 50:13; 51:26,62) and Edom (Ezek 35:3,4,7,9,14,15; Joel 4:19; Mal 1:3). Less clear, but probably still related to the animosity against surrounding nations following Jerusalem's destruction are the oracles proclaiming Egypt's desolation in Ezek 29:9,10,12; 32:15. A clear indication of how the events surrounding Jerusalem's desolation were transferred into animosity against the neighbors who actively participated (Edom) or did not help (Egypt) may be seen in Ezek 35:15: "As you rejoiced over the inheritance of the house of Israel because it was

in exilic and post-exilic prophetic contexts, outside of Mic 7:13, *only Jer 4:27 possibly uses* "desolation" in a universal context to proclaim judgment upon the entire earth. However, the larger context surrounding Jer 4:27 displays a tension between judgment against Judah and destruction of the earth, making the interpretation of the phrase in Jer 4:27 rather debated.[100] The well-attested tradition of the land, not the entire earth, becoming a desolation, raises the question as to its meaning in Mic 7:13. It will be necessary to return to this question following the discussion of the remaining units in Mic 7:8ff.

The next unit, **7:14-15**, returns to a liturgical pattern in which the prophet addresses YHWH directly in intercessory fashion (7:14-15a), followed by a short, positive divine response (7:15b). The prophetic intercession calls for YHWH to shepherd his flock, in order that they might return to the more idyllic state of previous pristine times ("like the days of old, like the days of your going out from the land of Egypt"). This petition by no means reflects a trite, sanguine optimism, rather it draws from conquest and exodus traditions in a manner simultaneously demonstrating hope for the future and the dilapidated political situation (those dwelling alone in the midst of Carmel).[101]

The next unit (**7:16-20**) begins suddenly with no introduction, but the change of speaker signals another section. This change of speaker is not evidenced explicitly until 7:17, where the reference to "our" God, indicates the people as speaker. The congregational speaker continues almost without interruption through the remainder of the chapter.[102]

---

desolate, so I will do to you. You (Seir/Edom) will become a desolation."

[100] Compare the opposing opinions of Carroll, *Jeremiah*, 170f, who translates אֶרֶץ as land, and Holladay, *Jeremiah*, 167, who understands it in the wider perspective. Carroll sees the verse as a later gloss.

[101] For discussion of the background of these traditions: see Mays, *Micah*, 165, although Mays tries to explain 7:15b as a corruption, because he does not consider the change of speaker in this prophetic liturgy, and believes that the image of YHWH going forth from Egypt combines theophanic and exodus traditions in a manner which could not have come from the same hand. Wolff, *BK* 14/4, 202f, finds no such difficulty on the basis of texts such as Exod 13:21; 33:14; Judg 4:14; 2 Sam 5:24; Ps 68:8. Wolff, *BK* 14, 189, emends 7:15b, following Wellhausen, because he says "him" has no antecedent. On the contrary, the use of the 3ms relates back to the beginning of the petition in 7:14, where the prophet implores YHWH to shepherd his people. The reference back to עַם accounts for the 3ms reference to the people.

[102] Note the use of the 1cp indicators in 7:17 (our God), 7:19 (compassion on us, our iniquity), and 7:20 (our fathers). Only one clause indicates a shift in the speaker. 7:19b makes reference to "their sins", but before presuming the speaker as the prophet

Thematically, this unit has two subsections: in 7:16-17 the people describe the fear of the nations before YHWH, while 7:18-20 concerns the forgiveness of sins *in spite of* the current state of judgment. The question of original unity hinges upon the evaluation of the thematic change within the context of the 1cp speaker and upon the interpretation of 7:19b, with its reference to "their" sins.

It is necessary to begin with a decision regarding 7:19b, because it effects the possible interpretations of the larger unit. In the middle of an extended section with a congregational speaker, the 3mp suffix in 7:19b stands out dramatically: "And you (2ms) will cast all *their* sins into the depths of the sea." This change to a 3mp reference is all the more noteworthy since 7:20 returns to the congregational speaker (our fathers). Four possible explanations could account for the 3mp reference in 7:19b: textual corruption; the congregation refers to the sins of someone else; a brief change of speaker to the prophet; or a gloss, either redactional or marginal, placed by a later hand. The possibility of textual corruption has already been shown to be highly unlikely.[103]   Equally difficult is the argument that the people continue as speaker, because the context would then require the 3mp (their sins) to be understood as the nations. The nations were mentioned in the 3mp in 7:16f, but the forgiveness of the sins of the nations would be difficult to explain theologically in 7:19b.

A decision between the two remaining explanations demands decisions which are more difficult to determine with absolute certainty. One must decide whether 7:19b, with its 3mp reference to the people, should be understood as a brief change to a prophetic speaker or the mark of a later hand. An argument on the basis of style is inconclusive for either alternative. Other liturgical elements within 7:8-20 could conceivably make the sudden change of speaker compatible with the style of the passage.[104] On the other hand, a 3mp reference would be perfectly explainable and compatible if the verse were added by a later hand as a reference to the congregation.

If the question is asked in terms of probabilities, tradition-critical and redaction-critical observations allow the scales to be tipped toward the argument of a later hand. Nothing in Micah prepares the reader for this

---

one has to evaluate other possibilities. This clause could be either a new speaker, a textual corruption, a congregational reference to nations, or redactional/gloss comment. See the discussion in the following paragraph.

[103] See text note 7:19c.

[104] See especially the short divine response in 7:15b.

enigmatic reference to the casting of sins into the "depths of the sea."[105]
The term מצולה is not a common term in Old Testament literature, but
when it does appear it most often appears in psalmic and poetic material,
demonstrating a tendency toward the metaphorical use of this word.[106]
Two traditions appear particularly clearly when used with מצולה: first, a
specific reference to the parting of the sea (Exod 15:5; Zech 10:11; Neh
9:11) when YHWH drowned the army of the Pharaoh in the מצולה; and
second, מצולה portrays the deepest part of the ocean as a place of distress
(Ps 68:23; 69:3,16; 88:7; Jonah 2:4). This second tradition helps to explain
why the מצולה is a suitable place for sins to be cast. However, the
particular formulation in Mic 7:19b (מצולה + שלך in the hiphil with
YHWH as subject) appears in only one other place, notably Jonah 2:4.
Given the relative scarcity of the word מצולה, combined with this
particular formulation, it appears very probable that 7:19b should be
understood as an allusion to Jonah 2:4. This allusion seeks to draw a
parallel between the "salvation" of Jonah and the "salvation" of the
congregation in 7:19b. Since other evidence indicates that the incorporation
of Jonah into the Book of the Twelve *post-dated* the majority of Mic 7:8-20,
it is permissible to conclude that 7:19b provides evidence as to how the
book of Jonah was intended to be interpreted by those who incorporated
it into the Book of the Twelve.[107]   For this reason, Mic 7:19b is best
characterized as a redactional note, not merely as a gloss.

---

[105] "Depth" does not occur elsewhere in Micah. "Sea" appears only in 7:12, but there it
serves an entirely different purpose as a geographical boundary.

[106] In addition to the five occurrences in the Psalter (68:23; 69:3,16; 88:7; 107:24) one
should note that two occurrences outside the Psalms are in the *song* of Moses (Exod
15:5) and in the *song* of Jonah (Jonah 2:4). Of the remaining three passages in which
מצולה relates to the depths of the sea, all three are in poetic passages (Zech 10:11;
Neh 9:11; Job 41:23). מצולה appears one time (Zech 1:8) where it refers to a ravine
in the vicinity of Jerusalem, not the depths of the ocean.

[107] Several conclusions reached elsewhere in this work necessitate this conclusion: 1) Mic
7 is tied closely with Nahum through the use of *Stichwörter* and through the literary
periodization of history which frames the Book of the Twelve; 2) It is difficult to see
how Jonah and Nahum could have entered the Book of the Twelve at the same time
since one allows the salvation of Nineveh and the other knows only of its destruction
for its actions against YHWH's people; 3) Evidence indicates Jonah 2 played a role in
the joining of Jonah into the larger corpus of the Book of the Twelve; 4) Other
evidence demonstrates the inclusion of Jonah interrupted a previously existing
connection Obadiah and Micah.

6. The Unity of Mic 7:14-20

It is now possible to return to the question of the original unity of 7:16-20, apart from the question of 7:19b. Does the thematic shift in 7:16-20, from the fear of the nations to the salvation of the people, represent a different original unit? When viewed from the larger context of 7:14-20 one may answer that these verses do present a liturgical unity (with the exception of the redactional note in 7:19b). They serve a specific function when coupled with 7:14f, and indeed with all of 7:8-20. First, the presence of an *inclusio* between 7:14 and 7:20 ("as in/from the days of old") unites these verses on more than a casual basis. Second, the description of the judgment of the nations in 7:16-17 articulates and expands what the people perceive as the "miracle" promised by YHWH in 7:15b. Thus, *all of 7:14-20* hangs together formally, liturgically, and thematically:

Speaker	Unit and Content
Prophet	14-15a Intercession: Shepherd your people as in the days of old
YHWH	15b Response: I will show him miracles
People	16-17 We will see the nations come trembling to YHWH
	18-20 YHWH will forgive our sins as in the days of old

This liturgical constellation involves an intercession and response between the prophet and YHWH, which is presupposed in the response of the people. The situation uniting the elements portrays a current state of affairs in which the splendor and promises of the past do not correlate to the dilapidated condition of the present. The response of YHWH, as interpreted by the people, promises the current situation is only temporary; the future will again bring forgiveness. In addition to these formal unifying factors, several presuppositions unite 7:14f with 7:16-20. First, the current situation is viewed as punishment — a result of YHWH's anger (7:18). Second, the punishment came in the form of the nations. Hence, the miracles promised by YHWH bring about the fearful reaction of these nations. Third, traditions from the Pentateuch form the basis of the utopic picture. Mic 7:15 refers to the exodus and 7:20 cites promises to Jacob and Abraham. Fourth, in spite of YHWH's promise, the salvation depicted in 7:14-20 clearly resides in the future.

It is thus possible to accept 7:14-20 as an original liturgical unity involving the prophet, YHWH, and the people, which has received a redactional note in 7:19b tying it to Jonah 2:3ff. The next question which arises is the relationship of the block 7:14-20 to the Zion material in 7:8-12, and the relationship of both of these major compositional blocks to the enigmatic destruction of 7:13. These three units are not unrelated blocks of tradition material which are strung together without purpose. Understanding the relationship of 7:8-12,13,14-20, requires a broader literary perspective than simply the immediate context. This broader perspective mandates certain tradition-critical observations from at least four different fronts which simultaneously effect the redactional function of Mic 7:8-20. The four areas to be addressed are the relationship of 7:8-20 with Isa 10; the Old Testament usage of "desolation"; the function of Carmel, Bashan, and Gilead in 7:14; and the "rod" of YHWH in 7:14.

7. Tradition-Historical Observations Effecting Mic 7

Several tradition-historical elements in Mic 7 demand clarification. When taken together these elements significantly effect the manner in which one reads Mic 7:8-20. Four elements in particular should be noted: the numerous shared images between Mic 7 and Isa 9-12*; the use of Carmel, Bashan, and Gilead; the "rod" of YHWH; and the desolation of the land/earth.

7.1. Allusions to Isa 9-12 and the Hezekiah Tradition

Numerous thematic and vocabularic connections tie Mic 7 with the Ephraim-Assyria-Judah-Jerusalem relationship to YHWH as portrayed in Isa 9-12, particularly Isa 10. The extent of these common elements creates a high probability that the two passages are related in some way. Almost every verse in Mic 7 has a corresponding element in Isa 9-12, especially chapter ten.

Mic 6:16; 7:1-20	*Isa 9-12*
7:1 Woe is me	10:1 Woe to those who enact
6:16 Statutes of Omri	10:1 Evil Statutes.
7:2 There are no godly/upright ones	10:2 The unjust acts of YHWH's people
7:3 Bribe of prince, judge	10:1 Unjust legal decisions
7:4 Day when punishment and confusion will come	10:3 Day of punishment
7:5f There is no one to trust	10:3f There is nowhere to turn for help
7:7 I will wait for the God of my salvation.	12:2 Behold, God is my salvation

7:8 Do not rejoice my enemy
Though I am in darkness
YHWH is my light.

7:9 I will bear YHWH's indignation and his anger

7:10 My enemy said where is your God?

7:10 My enemy will be trampled down like mire of the streets

7:11 A day for building your walls

your boundary will become distant

7:12 He will come from Assyria and the cities of Egypt

unto the river (Euphrates) and the sea and the mountains

7:13 And the land becomes desolate

7:14 Shepherd your people with your rod
A forest

in the midst of Carmel

7:15 YHWH's going forth from Egypt

7:16 Nations will see and be ashamed of all their might

7:18 The remnant of his possession will survive his anger

7:19 He will have compassion (רחם) on us.

9:1f The people who dwell in darkness will see a great light, and will rejoice.

10:25 Soon my indignation against you will be spent, and my anger will turn to their destruction.
— (But cf Isa 36:18-20 = 2Kgs 18:32b-35)

10:6 Assyria was sent against the people of my fury to trample them down like mud in the streets

9:9 The bricks have fallen, but we will rebuild with smooth stones
(cf especially 2 Chr 32:5)

10:13 Assyria says I removed the boundaries of the peoples

10:3 Destruction will come from afar

10:6,12 I sent Assyria against a godless nation and Jerusalem

10:24 Assyria will strike you like a rod in the way Egypt did

10:26 God will raise the sea with his staff as he did in Egypt
— (cf Isa 11:11f)

10:23 There will be complete destruction in the midst of the whole land

10:5 Assyria is the rod of my anger (cf also 10:15,24)

10:18 YHWH will destroy the glory of Assyria's forest
and his Carmel (thicket)

10:19 and the rest of the trees of his forest will be reduced

10:34 YHWH will cut down the thickets of the forest

10:26 Parting of the sea when leaving Egypt

10:28-31 The nations whom Assyria has terrified will see Assyria overthrown (cf 10:27,33)

10:20-22 A remnant will remain from the destruction of Israel
(cf 11:11: YHWH will recover the remnant of his people a second time)

12:1 Although you were angry with me, your anger is turned away, and you comfort (נחם) me.

Isa 9-12 centers thematically around the events leading up to an including the Assyrian siege of Jerusalem by Senacherib.[108] The material therein is diverse, but certain thematic sections are present: the promise of continual Davidic rule with messianic overtones (9:1-6); the announcement of judgment against the Northern kingdom (9:7-20; 10:1-4); the announcement of judgment against Assyria for overstepping its role as YHWH's tool against his people (10:5-20); another promise of Davidic/messianic peace (11:1-9); the gathering of the scattered people from among the nations (11:10-16); and a concluding song of confidence (12:1-6) prior to the oracles against the nations (Isa 13-23).

Isa 9ff contains a particular theological perspective which views the Assyrian campaigns in the latter third of the 8th century as a direct means of punishment against a recalcitrant people. Isa 9-12 combines the events of the Syro-Ephraimite war in 733 with an Assyrian threat against Jerusalem and Judah that alludes to Senacherib's siege of Jerusalem in 701.[109] The Northern kingdom is destroyed, and Jerusalem faces a similar threat, although YHWH decides not to destroy Jerusalem with Assyria (10:12).

The images found in Isa 9-12 also appear in the post-exilic "liturgy" in Mic 7. The large number of similarities as well as several very specific formulations point distinctly toward a relationship. The date of the respective passages indicates that the question of dependency could only have been on the part of the author/compiler of Mic 7.[110] The nature of

---

[108] The allusions from Mic 7 take the promisory elements in Isa 9:1-6 and 12:1-6 via *inclusio* (note the chart at Mic 7:7,19). Isa 9:1-6 actually ends a larger complex (6:1-9:6), and 9:7ff begins a new one. These chapters contain speeches delivered at different times, and in all likelihood were first combined as part of the redactional process of Proto-Isaiah. For one theory of the complicated nature of the redaction history of Isa 1-12, see Wildberger, *BK* 10/3, 1550-1555.

[109] The background of the Syro-Ephraimite war can be noted by the reference to the Syrian king Rezin and the hostility of Ephraim toward Judah (see 9:11,21). The perspective of the judgment against Assyria in chapter 10 makes it clear that these verses do not intend the events of 733, but refer to Senacherib's siege of Jerusalem in 701, during the reign of Hezekiah. See particularly Assyria's boast in Isa 10:11f which correlates of Samaria's destruction in 722 with Assyria's expected overthrow of Jerusalem. The introduction to the quote in Isa 10:8 demonstrates that Assyria brags it will overthrow Jerusalem just like it did Samaria.

[110] This statement does not imply that Isa 9-12 stems entirely from the time of the prophet, rather it recognizes that the largest blocks of those chapters clearly predate the post-exilic perspective of Mic 7. See the redactional remarks of Wildberger, *BK* 10/1, 393; *BK* 10/3, 1557f.

the relationship suggests Mic 7 has the anti-Assyrian polemic of Isa 9-12 in mind with the reference to the enemy, but it does so from the perspective of the siege of Jerusalem.

Two further observations strengthen the specific parallels in Isa 10. First, those few elements not present in the Mic 7-Isa 10 parallels almost all have parallels in the Hezekiah traditions (2 Kgs 18-20 =Isa 36-39 and 2 Chr 32:1-5).[111] Second, the superscription of Mic 1:1 explicitly places the latest period of Micah's message during the reign of Hezekiah, one notes the natural *inclusio* function created by the opening superscription in 1:1 to the end of the book, and the strong links to Hezekiah and an anti-Assyrian polemic. Thus, the allusions to Isa 10 and the Hezekiah traditions strongly suggest that Mic 7 was intended to be read as a prophecy from the late 8th century, even though it mirrors the concerns of early post-exilic Israel. The allusion to the images of the Assyrian siege of Jerusalem naturally effects how the entire passage should be understood, and requires a re-evaluation of the way Mic 7:8-20 is traditionally understood. Before turning to the interpretation of Mic 7 in its entirety, it is necessary to look at several other elements in light of their relationship to the Anti-Assyrian polemic and to the understanding of their function in Mic 7.

7.2. The Role of Bashan and Gilead

The basic thrust of the petition in Mic 7:14-15 is clear, but considerable confusion exists regarding its function in Micah. The terms "Carmel," "Bashan," and "Gilead" are regions typically associated with the Northern Kingdom. Several have therefore postulated a Northern provenance for Mic 7:8ff.[112] However, an alternate explanation for the appearance of these Northern regions presents itself when one examines this passage from the perspective of its position in the Book of the Twelve. Specifically, Mic 7:8-20 (indeed, the entire complex of Mic 6-7 in its present form) suggests a redactional awareness of the historical period of the late 8th century (specifically from the Syro-Ephraimite war up to and including Senacherib's siege of Jerusalem during the reign of Hezekiah). Here clear distinction must be drawn between the post-exilic composition of this

---

[111] Note especially Mic 7:10,11 in the chart above.

[112] F.C. Burkitt, "Micah 6 and 7: A Northern Prophecy," *JBL* 45 (1926): 159-161; Otto Eissfeldt, "Ein Psalm aus Nordisrael Mi 7:7-20." In *Kleine Schriften*, vol. 4. Rudolph Sellheim and Fritz Maass, eds, (Tübingen: Mohr, 1968), 63-72.

chapter and the historical era to which it is alluding. As a result of the Syro-Ephraimite war (733), the Northern kingdom lost its independent status, and was subsumed into the Assyrian provincial system. Combined with an Assyrian expansionist policy, this war precipitated a series of events over the next three decades culminating in the Assyrian siege of Jerusalem (701) after which time Jerusalem lost control of much of Judah, and was forced to pay heavy tribute to Assyria. Bashan and Gilead were considered part of the ideal extent of the united monarchy from the period of the conquest narratives. Additionally, they play a significant role for the period in question since both were lost permanently to the Assyrians in the aftermath of the Syro-Ephraimite war.[113] Elsewhere the Book of the Twelve evidences a redactional interest in a Judean-centered restoration of the former Davidic kingdom which includes parts of the Transjordan.[114] The question of Carmel is more involved.

7.3. The Use of כרמל as "Thicket" within Anti-Assyrian Polemic

The word כרמל appears with as many as five different meanings: the mountain, the city southeast of Hebron, the region surrounding that city, fresh grain, and thicket. Two of these traditions spawn considerable debate.[115] One of the debated nuances of כרמל concerns the elusiveness of the term translated as "fruit-field," "garden land," or "thicket." Some scholars attempt to explain away this nuance by subsuming it under one of the other meanings, but most recognize the validity of "thicket" as *a translation* for כרמל.[116] The debate centers around which references speak of Carmel as a "thicket" and which refer to Mount Carmel merely as

---

[113] See Magnus Ottoson, *Gilead: Tradition and History* (Lund: Gleerup, 1969), 236-238. Only for a short period during the Maccabean period was Gilead regained.

[114] Note the discussion of Obad 19 above, as well as the following discussion of Nah 1:4. Compare other passages, which reflect the hope of a Davidic restoration without *specifically* mentioning the Trans-Jordan regions in question here: Amos 9:12; Hag 2:20ff; and later texts which have a more eschatological tone, especially Zech 9-10.

[115] Those meanings which are not debated are the references to Mount Carmel (Jos 19:26; 1 Kgs 18:19,20,42; 2 Kgs 2:25; 4:25; Amos 1:2; 9:3); to the city 12 km southeast of Hebron (Josh 15:55; 1 Sam 15:12; 25:2,5,7,40); and to fresh grain (Lev 2:14; 23:14; 2 Kgs 4:42). The first debated meaning has little significance for the passages under discussion in the Book of the Twelve; namely the question of whether the region southeast of Hebron could be called "Carmel" in addition to the city. See a summary of discussion in M.J. Mulder, "כרמל," *TWAT*, vol 4, 343.

[116] Mulder, *ThWAT*, vol 4, 343-345.

"Carmel." Some passages are almost universally recognized as "thicket" because of the use of suffixes (e.g. 2 Kgs 19:23 = Isa 37:24; Isa 10:18), while others cause considerable confusion, especially those passages containing references to fruitfulness and to Northern geographic regions.[117]

Tradition-historical observations shed light on some of these disputed references in a manner which will aid in understanding Mic 7:14. First, the reversal of exodus motifs (Jer 2:7) and creation traditions (Jer 4:26) point away from an understanding of the more specific "mountain of Carmel" interpretation. These passages emphasize the aspect of fertility, not geography. Second, the oracles against Moab in Isa 16:10 and Jer 48:33 bear more than accidental similarities, making it likely that these two uses of כרמל share a common origin:

Isa 16:10	*Jer 48:33*
And gladness and joy are taken away from the thicket; in the vineyards also there will be no cries of joy or jubilant shouting. No treader treads out wine in the presses, for I have made the presses to cease.	So gladness and joy are taken away from the thicket, even from the land of Moab, and I have made the wine to cease from the wine presses, no one will tread them with shouting. The shouting will not be shouts of joy.

The combination of the very specific vocabulary in these verses (gladness/ joy, taken away, Carmel, wine, wine press, treading, shouting) with the context specifying Moab as the recipient of the oracle, offer solid grounds for common origin.

A third tradition binds כרמל and the Assyrian invasion. Through an interrelated series of allusions, motifs, and vocabulary, one may observe how the setting of the Hezekiah story in 2 Kgs functions as the literary backdrop for a number of passages. This tradition emanates from the only use of the "thicket" motif in the Deuteronomistic history, in the narrative concerning Hezekiah's response to Senacherib's siege of Jerusalem in 2 Kgs 19:23 (=Isa 37:24). Isaiah's oracle against Senacherib, follows Hezekiah's prayer for deliverance. The oracle manifests the Carmel/thicket tradition within the deprecation of the king of Assyria for the arrogance of his own power and for his failure to recognize YHWH's role in establishing the king

---

[117] See the summary of research documenting various views in Mulder, *ThWAT*, vol 4, 343-345. He notes the following disputed passages: 2 Kgs 19:23 (=Isa 37:24); Isa 10:18; 16:10; 29:17; 32:15f; Jer 2:7; 4:26; 48:33; Mic 7:14.

as an instrument of punishment (2 Kgs 19:20-28, esp 25). The material of interest appears within the quote of the king of Assyria's boast in 19:23f:

> Through your messengers you have reproached the Lord, and you have said, "With many chariots I came up to the heights of the mountains, to the remotest parts of Lebanon; and I cut down its tall cedars and its choice cypresses. And I entered its farthest lodging place, its choicest thicket (*Carmel*). I dug wells and drank foreign waters, and with the sole of my feet I dried up all the rivers of Egypt."[118]

The suffix and the parallelism make clear that in this instance "Carmel" means neither the city nor the mountain, but that the image presented is one of shrub-like growth. The context reveals that the botanical imagery is used metaphorically for the Assyrian *political overthrow* of Lebanon and surrounding regions. Simultaneously, one cannot forget that the unit functions as *part of the narrative of Senacherib's siege of Jerusalem*.

The oracle against Senacherib in 2 Kgs 19:20-34 has a parallel in Isa 37:21-35, where it appears as part of a block of material (Isa 36-39) taken from the Hezekiah narrative in 2 Kings. The incorporation of this block into the Isaiah collection likely had some relationship to the combination of Proto- and Deutero-Isaiah.[119]   Importantly, traces of this Hezekiah narrative in other portions of Proto-Isaiah, namely in the use of this Carmel/thicket tradition, indicate the Hezekiah narrative was *incorporated into* the book of Isaiah, not merely attached. The clearest example appears in Isa 29:17, which presents an exhortation to the people in the form of a rhetorical question, but it also presupposes events depicted later in the book, namely the overthrow of Lebanon and Carmel in 33:9 combined with the boast of the king of Assyria in 37:24 (=2 Kgs 19:23).

---

[118] Note that 2 Kgs 19:24, like Mic 7:12, uses the uncommon term מצור for "Egypt."

[119] See Peter Ackroyd, "Isaiah 36-39: Structure and Function," in *Von Kanaan bis Kerala*, AOAT 211, W.C. Delsman, et al, eds. (Neukirchen: Neukirchener Verlag, 1982), 3-21; relatedly, see Steck, *Bereitete Heimkehr*, 57-59.

Isa 29:17	Isa 33:9	Isa 37:24 (king of Assyria)
Is it not yet just a little while before Lebanon will be turned into a thicket (לכרמל), and Carmel (הכרמל) will be considered a forest?	The land mourns and pines away, Lebanon is shamed and withers, Sharon is like a desert plain, and Bashan and Carmel lose their foliage.	With my many chariots I came up to the heights of the mountains, to the remotest parts of Lebanon; And I cut down its tall cedars and its choice cypresses; I came to its remote height and the forest of its thicket.

The first text utilizes a play on words depicting the reduction of Lebanon (normally associated with height and splendor of its forests) to the status of a thicket, while Carmel the mountain is reduced to a forest. The second text contains the images of the first and serves as an elaboration, which takes the account of the destruction a step further. Now Lebanon (the thicket) withers, and Carmel (the forest) loses its foliage. In the third text, the king of Assyria takes credit for these acts, now depicted as having already occurred.

Two other passages in Isaiah take up these same motifs: Isa 32:15f and 10:18. Isa 32:15f appears at the end of a judgment speech against Jerusalem, but offers hope by limiting the duration of the threat at hand.

[15]Until the spirit is poured out upon us from on high, and the wilderness becomes a thicket and the thicket is considered as a forest. [16]Then justice will dwell in the wilderness, and righteousness will abide in the thicket.

This passage reverses the reduction movement of 29:17 so that instead of predicting the movement from the high to the low, its images move upward: until the wilderness grows into a thicket, and the thicket develops into a forest.

Isa 10:18 offers the closest relationship to the Hezekiah narrative in 2 Kgs 18-19. The context of the passage is a rebuke of the king of Assyria, who has overstepped his mission as YHWH's rod of punishment.[120] The king of Assyria, in the form of a quote (13f), reaffirms that he believes he has conquered the peoples by his own might. This boast provokes a response from the prophet which predicts judgment upon the king:

---

[120] Cf 10:12: When YHWH completes his work on Zion ... I will punish the fruit of the arrogant heart of the king of Assyria and the pomp of his haughtiness.

¹⁶Therefore the Lord God of hosts will send a wasting disease among his warriors, and under his glory a fire will be kindled like a burning flame. ¹⁷And the light of Israel will become a fire and his holy one a flame, and it will burn and devour his thorns and his briars in a single day. ¹⁸And he (YHWH) will destroy the glory of his (the king of Assyria) forest and of his thicket (וכרמלו).

To be sure, Isa 10 has a long redaction history in its own right, but there is little doubt, owing to the references to the punishment of Jerusalem by the king of Assyria, that it was *intended* to be read as a reference to Senacherib's siege of Jerusalem, whatever the date of composition of its constituent parts.

Prior to returning explicitly to Mic 7, one more reference to Carmel deserves note because it demonstrates that a Carmel tradition, albeit without the word play, was utilized outside of the Isaiah corpus as well. The oracle against Babylon in Jer 50:17-19 unites the punishment of the "king of Assyria" and the "king of Babylon."

¹⁷Israel is a scattered flock, the lions have driven them away. The first one who devoured him was the king of Assyria, and this last one who has broken his bones is Nebuchadnezzar king of Babylon. ¹⁸Therefore, thus says the Lord of hosts, the God of Israel: Behold I am going to punish the king of Babylon and his land, just as I punished the king of Assyria. ¹⁹And I shall bring Israel back to his pasture, and he will graze on Carmel and Bashan, and his desire will be satisfied in the hill country of Ephraim and Gilead.

Here, Carmel is best understood as a reference to the mountain and the surrounding region. The parallelism shows one should not press too closely for exact boundaries of the region, since it is coupled with Bashan, the region across the Jordan; and this Carmel-Bashan coupling is expanded to include Ephraim and Gilead, again both Northern territories separated by the Jordan:

```
        J
Carmel  O   Bashan
        R
        D
Ephraim A   Gilead
        N
```

Combined, these four regions schematically incorporate the Northern region of Israel, and imply a strong political concern for the reunification of the entire kingdom.

In summary, it is possible to pull together several observations regarding the use of כרמל in the OT. Various texts demonstrate the difficulty to distinguish between כרמל used as the mountain and as thicket because the similarity of the words provided a natural play on words with metaphorical language (cf especially Isa 29:17). Second, it is also clear that these same texts share a remarkably consistent association: the loss of this region (whether Carmel or the thicket metaphor) was the result of the actions of the "king of Assyria." Third, the tradition also correlates this king of Assyria with Senacherib in the narrative of the siege of Jerusalem during the reign of Hezekiah.

With these observations in mind it is now possible to place Mic 7:14 within the conceptual realm of the thicket tradition and an anti-Assyrian context. More precisely stated: Mic 7:14 *presupposes* the thicket tradition as a metaphor for territory lost to the Assyrians in the eighth century.[121]

7.4. The "Rod" of YHWH

The petition in Mic 7:14 calls for YHWH to shepherd his people, but the emotionally-laden term "rod" carries very distinctive connotations when viewed in light of the anti-Assyrian polemic of Isa 10. Commentators traditionally read this petition positively, on the basis of other positive shepherd imagery for YHWH.[122] However, the role of the shepherd is not always positive; several Old Testament passages use the shepherd imagery in a negative sense, particularly in association with slaughter.[123] The rod of YHWH is primarily associated with rebuke and judgment, not with salvation.[124] Proto-Isaiah ties the rod motif to YHWH's choice of

---

[121] Mic 7:14, with its reference to those dwelling alone in the midst of "Carmel," provides an interesting point of comparison with Jer 50:19. These passages both reflect use of the thicket tradition with restoration of the Davidic kingdom. Both share a common historical/theological perspective that presupposes (Mic 7:14 on the basis of context) the loss of the land was due to Assyria. However, when these two texts are compared, Mic 7:14 notably lacks any specific mention of Ephraim. The reason may be tied to a particular understanding of Carmel as a much larger region in Mic 7:14, but this is unlikely. It seems more likely that Mic 7:14 reflects a nascent anti-Samarianism or shares the typical Deuteronomistic images, in which Ephraim and Samaria play a decidedly negative role. See also the destruction of Samaria in Mic 1:5-7.

[122] Mays, *Micah*, 163; Allen, *Joel, etc*, 398; Weiser, *ATD* 24, 290; Wolff, *BK* 14/4, 201.

[123] For example, Ezek 34:13; Zech 11:4; Ps 49:14.

[124] Only one exception can be found: Ps 23:4 mentions the "rod" and "staff" of YHWH positively.

Assyria to punish a recalcitrant Israel and Judah.[125] Outside Proto-Isaiah, the "rod" of YHWH also signals negative images of judgment.[126] Finally, the book of Micah itself presents the most conclusive evidence that the phrase "shepherd your people with your rod" has often been misinterpreted. Mic 4:14-5:5 (Eng: 5:1-6) provides linguistic evidence which combines both the rod and shepherd motifs in a manner which demonstrates the phrase in 7:14 evokes judgment.[127]

> [4:14]Now muster your troops, daughter of troops; They have laid siege against us; *with a rod* they will smite the judge of Israel on the cheek. ... [5:4b]When the Assyrian invades our land, when he tramples on our citadels, then we will raise against him seven shepherds and eight leaders of men, [5]And they will *shepherd the land of Assyria with the sword...*

The subject of the verb "shepherd" in 5:5 differs from 7:14, and it uses sword rather than rod, but the phrase is syntactically identical, the verb shepherd + the preposition ‫ב‬ + an instrument. It clearly goes well beyond a simple metaphor of a shepherd and sheep. It connotes authority and punishment. The same can be said for 7:14.

Negative imagery prevails in other uses of "shepherd" and "rod," leading one to ask, "How does one reconcile this imagery with the prophetic petition in 7:14?" Mic 7:14 represents a post-exilic text which alludes to the events of the late 8th century, and which divulges considerable theologizing of those events in particular and of Israel's evaluation of its history in general. Mic 7:14 betrays this attitude. The prophetic intercession presupposes an *acceptance of these 8th century events as punishment*, not as total destruction. The ready correlation of the "rod" with Assyria in Mic 7, on the basis of other allusions to Isa 10 and to Mic 4:14ff, should thus be read as confirmation of the present situation as an act of punishment designed to bring a wayward people back to the fold. In other words the prophet says, "(go ahead) punish your people with Assyria, in order that the situation might return as it was in the days of old."

---

[125] Isa 9:3; 10:5,15,24; 11:4; 14:29.

[126] Ezek 20:37; 21:15,18; Ps 2:9; 89:33.

[127] Mic 4-5 and 7:14 do not stem from the same author, but redaction work on Micah is almost unanimous that Mic 7 is later than Mic 5. See discussion of the redaction-history of Micah, above.

8. The Relationship of Mic 7:11,12,13

Already in the literary critical discussion of Mic 7:13 it was noted that a strong association of "desolation" with "land" exists in the Old Testament, which apparently resulted from the Babylonian destruction of Jerusalem. This motif of the desolation of the land appears considerably stronger when viewed in light of the relationship to Isa 10 and the Hezekiah tradition. These associations carry considerable weight, yet it is impossible to reconcile their implications with traditional interpretations of Mic 7:11-13. The interpretation of 7:11-13 depends upon the identity and the purpose of "the one who comes" from Assyria, Egypt, Babylon, and the surrounding regions. Unfortunately, the text explicitly states neither the identity nor the purpose of the one who comes. Three possibilities exist, none of which are without parallel, but none of which are without problem.[128] 1) The exiles returning to Jerusalem;[129] 2) Political entities representing a universal pilgrimage to Jerusalem;[130] 3) Political entities who come to dominate Jerusalem.[131] The major problem with the first two possibilities lies in the fact that, although frequently attested in the literature, they cannot account for the judgment in Mic 7:13.[132] The chief problem with the final possibility rests with 7:11, which offers some type of promise to Jerusalem.

Form-critical and tradition-critical observations provide some illumination for the problem of the relationship of 7:11-13. Tradition-critically, the reference to the building of the walls and the expansion of the

---

[128] Emendation is of course a fourth possibility, but its use here is questionable. At least one recent commentator opts for this approach, however. See Allen, *Joel, etc.*, 391.

[129] Such as in Isa 52:7ff. This image is the one traditionally expounded in exegetical literature, e.g. Wolff, *BK* 24/4, 200.

[130] Such as Isa 2:2-4. Hillers, *Micah*, 90, paraphrases the verse to read, "they will stream to it from far and wide." He believes, 91, that this pilgrimage includes the scattered people of YHWH as well as foreigners.

[131] The formulation in Mic 7:12, the verb בוא + עד can be used to describe a military campaign. Compare, for example, Judg 7:13; 9:52. For a partial understanding of the combination of the entities. Compare for example, Lam 5:6,9, which specifically mentions submission to Egypt and Assyria as reasons for Babylon's ability to destroy Jerusalem. It also depicts difficulties following the destruction of Jerusalem which arose from the surrounding regions.

[132] Wolff, *BK* 14/4, 191,200, argues the sentence is a universal expansion of the threat in 7:10, which essentially summarizes Isa 24:1-6. Hillers, *Micah*, 91, simply admits 7:13 presents a certain "illogicality," which is due to the fact that 7:11f and 7:13 "are separate parts of the eschatological vision, not to be pressed, or relieved by textual rearrangement or any other change."

boundary need not refer directly to the aftermath of the Babylonian destruction. These two elements also play a significant role in the Hezekiah tradition. Following a warning that Senacherib was planning to attack Jerusalem, 2 Chr 32:5 states:

> And he (Hezekiah) took courage and *rebuilt all the wall* that had been broken down, and erected towers on it, and (built) *another outside wall*, and strengthened the Millo in the city of David, and made weapons and shields in great number.

2 Chr 32:5 sheds interesting light upon Mic 7:11. These preparations are credited with the salvation of Jerusalem. This tradition coincides to the reference in Mic 7:11 of "building your (2fs) walls" and "expanding the boundary" of Jerusalem, but when the allusions to the Hezekiah tradition are taken seriously, the context demands that this verse be seen, not as a promise of eschatological peace, but as a promise of time to prepare for the coming period of domination.[133] The promise is *directed specifically to Jerusalem*, and it assumes Hezekiah's preparatory actions which enabled Jerusalem to resist Senacherib's siege.

The phraseology of 7:13 can imply either a past, present, or future event, but in this context a future desolation appears the most probable.[134] Note, however, that it is the land which will be desolated. This significant shift in subject appears to stand at odds with the promise in 7:11 if the verses are read in isolation, but this tension reduces radically when one recognizes the character of the verses as a *liturgical depiction of an entire historical period*. When viewed from the perspective of post-exilic Judah, the reign of Hezekiah saw the miraculous delivery of *Jerusalem*, but *Judah* never recovered the full extent of its territory which it lost to Assyria during the 8th century. It is thus not improbable to suggest that 7:11-13

---

[133] The inclusion of Assyria and Egypt naturally encompasses more than an implied immediate threat at the hands of Senacherib. It includes the period of the Egyptian domination of Judah following the death of Josiah (609), and the Babylonian period, hence the reference to the Euphrates.

[134] The normal use of the verb היה (to be) with the preposition ל is one of a future event, either in the form of a promise (Gen 17:11); oath (Hab 2:7; Jer 50:10); stipulation (2 Sam 15:33; Gen 6:21); legal code (Lev 5:5). There is almost always a conditional element supposed in this formulation. This phrase by no means always demands a future event. Often the phrase refers to an event in the past which has implications for the present: 1 Kgs 4:11; 2 Kgs 8:18; 1 Sam 10:12; 27:6; Ezek 44:12; Gen 2:10; 32:11; Isa 11:16; Jer 12:8; 2:31; 20:7; 25:38; 31:9; 50:23; 51:41; Josh 2:15; 4:7; Judg 21:15; Lam 1:8,17; Ps 114:2; 118:22. The יום sayings in 7:11,12 provide the context with a frame of reference which argues that the desolation of 7:13 lies in the future.

reflects a certain dialectic between Jerusalem's miraculous delivery (2 Kgs 19:35f = Isa 37:36f; cf 2 Chr 32:21), and the fact that Judah was not granted its former glory. In essence Mic 7:11-13 presupposes a remnant theology emanating from Jerusalem in much the same manner as the Deuteronomistic Hezekiah tradition (2 Kgs 19:30f = Isa 37:31f):

> And the surviving remnant of the house of Judah shall again take root downward and bear fruit upward. For out of Jerusalem shall go forth a remnant, and out of Zion survivors.

The book of Micah presents a similar sentiment in the short salvation oracle in 2:12f:

> I will surely assemble all of you, Jacob, I will surely gather the remnant of Israel. I will put them together like sheep in the fold, like a flock in the midst of its pasture. They will be noisy with men. The breaker goes up before them. They break out, pass through the gate, and go out by it. So their king goes on before them, and the Lord at their head.[135]

Post-exilic Judah had to come to grips with an implicit tension created by the promises to Jerusalem over against the historical reality of a century of Assyrian domination, the Babylonian destruction of Jerusalem, and a continuing faith-acceptance of the validity of those salvific promises. Increasingly, the tension was resolved by projecting salvation in broader and grander terms into a point further and further into the future.[136] It is this perspective which unites the entire liturgical structure of 7:8-20.

9. The Unity of 7:8-10,11-13,14-20

It has already been argued that internal elements bind 7:14-20 together, but the relationship to 7:11-13 and 7:8-10 deserves brief mention. When all of the allusions to Isa 10 and the Hezekiah tradition in these verses are taken into account, and when allowance is made for the liturgical style incorporating a personified Zion, YHWH, the prophet, the people, and a historical perspective, it is possible to detect an inner consistency

---

[135] See the discussion of these verses by Mays, *Micah*, 74f.

[136] See Paul D. Hanson, *The Dawn of Apocalyptic* (Philadelphia: Fortress Press, 1975); Otto Plöger, *Theokratie und Eschatologie* (Neukirchen: Neukirchener Verlag, 1959).

which transcends the constituent parts. The results of the preceding analysis allow the following description of this inner logic:

8-10   Zion's song of confidence in the face of the enemy. These verses allude primarily to Assyria although the perspective of the following verses shows that the author uses these allusions as the backdrop for a theological message to the current situation. Zion asserts her confidence that she will see the destruction of her enemy.

11-13   YHWH's reprieve to Zion. YHWH promises Zion deliverance, but the picture is not one of total salvation. It portrays an awareness of a future desolation of the land, which should be understood in the context of the political domination of Judah and Israel at the hands of outside political powers. The prediction of this desolation is based upon the sin of the inhabitants, whose depiction is already known to the reader of Micah (1:7,9,13; 2:1-11; 3:1-12; 6:1-16).

14-15   The prophet's petition and YHWH's response. The announcement of the desolation of the land in 7:13 motivates the petition. The prophet calls upon YHWH with imagery which acknowledges the punishment ("shepherd your people with your rod), but which also intercedes for a return to the positive relationship of the former days. YHWH responds with a promise to the people.

16-20*[137] The confidence of the people in the face of the current situation. The people's response moves from the allusions to the past salvific acts to the conviction that YHWH's salvation will appear in the future in the form of judgment on the nations (7:16f) and forgiveness of sins (7:18f) as in the days gone by. Both of these acts reflect an awareness of the context. The judgment on the nations responds to their desolation of Judah (7:11-13), while the forgiveness of sins responds to the confession of sin in 7:9.

The inner movement of these verses argue for their unity.[138] The frequent change of speaker, combined with the multiplicity of allusions to

---

[137] Omitting Mic 7:19b. Conclusions reached about the date of Jonah's incorporation into the Book of the Twelve in my forthcoming work, *Redactional Processes in the Book of the Twelve*, indicate that this redactional link from Micah back to Jonah post-dated the combination of Micah and Nahum.

[138] Excluding 7:19b (see literary observations above, page 152f).

other texts inside and outside of Micah, helps to account for the staccato nature of the verses. Recognition of these allusions illumines the text considerably, taking it out of the realm of a nebulous liturgy by situating its hermeneutic in the context of a post-exilic interpretation of the history of the eighth to the sixth centuries.

It is necessary to relate this passage to the historical schema appearing in the Book of the Twelve. These remarks must presuppose conclusions reached by the discussion of the opening hymn of Nah 1:1ff.[139] The concentration of Mic 7:8-20 upon the fate of Jerusalem and Judah from the Assyrian to the Babylonian periods points toward the placement of this passage within the salvific redactional work on the Deuteronomistic corpus. The extensive redactional shaping of Nahum, which is especially heavy at the beginning of the writing, presupposes Mic 7:8-20*. On the other hand, it is not likely that the same redactor was responsible for the placement of both passages. Not only does the concentration upon Judah and Jerusalem (in the context of restoration of the kingdom) coincide with the interests of the Deuteronomistic corpus. Mic 7:8ff connotes a considerable interplay with the remainder of Micah, while the redactional work in Nah 1:2ff imposes material into the context much less smoothly.

---

[139] See the chapter on Nahum in my forthcoming study, *Redactional Processes in the Book of the Twelve*.

Zephaniah

1. The Macrostructure of Zephaniah

The macro-structure of Zephaniah conforms in many respects to the typical tri-partite eschatological prophetic pattern: judgment (1:2-2:3), oracles against the nations (2:4-3:8), and salvation (3:9-14).[1] However, the combination of these elements is difficult to perceive as part of a single compositional act.[2] The Day of YHWH motif occurs in all three sections, but one must ask if this motif unifies the elements since fundamentally different understandings of the day of YHWH pervade the material. Explanations for the compilation of the book of Zephaniah must posit questions from several perspectives simultaneously. One must ask if the different themes and motifs in the book can best be explained by the assumption of a single compositional movement, or if they are better understood as the product of layers of redactional shaping for different contexts. Simultaneously, how should one perceive the components of the book? Should these components be understood as a collection of isolated prophetic sayings which are only loosely united? Should they be treated as

---

[1] See the discussion of this pattern in: Walter Zimmerli, "Vom Prophetenwort zum Prophetenbuch," *THLZ* 104 (1979): 481-496. Zimmerli also notes this pattern in Isaiah, Ezekiel, and the Greek [earlier] version of Jeremiah. While the observations on this pattern are significant, the acceptance of the pattern as absolutely determinative for the book creates problems, particularly in explaining the oracle of judgment against Jerusalem in 3:1-7. See Rudolph, *KAT* 13/3, 255.

[2] Ehud Ben Zvi, *A Historical-Critical Study of the Book of Zephaniah*, BZAW 198 (Berlin: De Gruyter, 1991), presents Zephaniah as the product of a single compositional layer, but to do so he must simultaneously date the book to the postexilic period and presuppose the use of pre-existing traditions. Ben Zvi presents strong evidence that *Zephaniah*, in its present form, reflects post-monarchic traditions and situations. However, his insistence that no form of the book of Zephaniah existed prior to that period runs counter to the evidence presented in this chapter. The evidence strongly suggests that the much of the pre-existing tradition noted by Ben Zvi actually existed in literary form as part of a Zephaniah corpus.

an inherently integrated literary unit?   Or should one see the book as a
redactional text exhibiting a multiplicity of interests?[3]

The judgment section of Zeph 1:2-2:3, in its present form, skillfully
weaves together two different themes, so that it is difficult to separate them
literarily from one another. The origins of these two themes, however, are
equally difficult to explain as the work of a single hand. The two themes
concern the judgment against Judah and Jerusalem (1:4-6;8-13; 2:1-3), and
a universal judgment against all humanity (1:2f, 14-18).   The literary
combination of these themes will be discussed below.

The oracles against the nations (2:4-3:8) also represent a carefully
constructed collection of sayings against the Philistine cities west of
Jerusalem (2:4-7); Moab and Ammon in the Transjordan to the east (2:8-
11); and the Ethiopians and Assyrians (2:12-15). This last group expands
the perspective beyond the traditional borders of Israel.   In an abrupt
change, significantly reminiscent of Amos 1:3-2:16, the final section of the
Zephaniah's oracles (3:1-8) culminates in a strong pronouncement against
Jerusalem itself.

Several observations on these oracles against the foreign nations
indicate the difficulty of determining their background.[4] First, the failure
to mention Babylon, Edom, or Tyre is noteworthy.   This omission
strengthens the impression that the core of the oracles predates Jerusalem's
destruction, since all three find strong condemnation in the literature of the

---

3   Examples of those who see the work primarily as a collection of prophetic sayings (with
    redactional work uniting them into a thematically coherent whole): Klaus Seybold,
    Satirische Prophetie. Studien zum Buch Zefanja, Stuttgarter Bibelstudien 120 (Stuttgart:
    Verlag Katholisches Bibelwerk, 1985), 13-20; Hubert Irsigler, *Gottesgericht und
    Jahwetag. Die Komposition Zef 1,1-2,3 untersucht auf Grund der Literarkritik*, Arbeiten
    zu Text und Sprache im Alten Testament 3 (St. Ottilien: Eos Verlag, 1977). Rudolph,
    KAT 13/3, 255f, believes the writing contains the prophetic sayings of a prophet prior
    to the Josianic reform, but that the majority of the book (3:1-15*) took written form
    during the exile. Rudolph argues 3:16-20 was added after the exile. Additionally,
    Rudolph argues the text has been expanded in 1:8; 2:7,9b,10; 3:8. An example of those
    who place the emphasis upon the literary unity is Robertson, *Nahum, Habakkuk,
    Zephaniah*, 38-40. Bosshard, *BN* 40 (1987): 54f understands Zephaniah in its present
    form as a *Redaktionstext* whose current form has been radically effected by its
    awareness of the context of the Book of the Twelve and of Isaiah (particularly Isa 34-
    35).

4   For a more thorough documentation of the history of research see, Duane L.
    Christensen, "Zephaniah 2:4-15: A Theological Basis for Josiah's Program of Political
    Expansion," *CBQ* 46 (1984): 669-682.

exile, and their exclusion is difficult to explain after 587.[5] Second, the
oracles against the Philistine cities and the Transjordan exhibit the typical
theological dichotomy: judgment against these nations leads simultaneously
to salvation for Judah. This theological intention does not require a
concrete description of political events which would make dating easier.
Third, the phraseology of these oracles, at least in their literary form, leads
in the opposite direction of the first observation regarding the date of the
oracles. The double usage of the remnant motif (cf 2:7,9) makes it clear
that Judah has been severely weakened, thereby making it difficult to
conceive the current literary form of these oracles existed before the exile.[6]
Several possible solutions to this dilemma present themselves for
consideration: 1) The oracles come entirely from the late 7th century,
meaning that the reference to the remnant does not presuppose the exile.[7]
2) The oracles stem from the period between the two deportations. 3) Late
7th century oracles were reconstituted in some fashion by an editor
interested in providing hope to the remnant population.[8] None of these
options resolves all objections, but the likelihood falls with the latter.

The content of the oracles against the nations also provides conflicting
data regarding the date of the individual utterances. The failure to mention
Babylon may be explained by postulating that Babylon had not yet arisen
as a dominating power in Palestine during in the reign of Josiah. Those
placing a high emphasis upon the date of Josiah's reign in the
superscription use this argument. Babylon's omission could also be a sign
of prudence from those not wishing to intimidate the ruling power. Edom
and Tyre could be readily omitted in the late 7th or early 6th centuries,
because they would have been considered potential allies. However, the
condemnation of Ammon and Moab for taking Judean territory finds its
clearest support in the raiding bands instigated or encouraged by Babylon
during the reign of Jehoiakim in 599, before Ammonite and Moabite

---

[5] For expanded discussions placing the oracles in the late pre-exilic situation, see: Donald
    L. Williams, "The Date of Zephaniah." *JBL* 82 (1963): 81-85; J.P. Hyatt, "The Date and
    Background of Zephaniah," *JNES* 7 (1948): 25. See also the discussion below (page
    178ff) on the date of Zephaniah.
[6] Zeph 2:7 refers to "the remnant of the house of Judah" and 2:9 mentions the "remnant
    of my people" and the "remainder of my nation."
[7] So Robertson, *Nahum, Habakkuk, and Zephaniah*, 300.
[8] See for example, Seybold, *Zefanja*, 45; Guy Langohr, "Le livre de Sophonie et la
    critique d'authenticité." *Ephemerides Theologicae Lovanienses* 52 (1976): 13f. Both
    understand the references as glosses.

rebellion against Babylon had cemented.[9] Conceivably, resentment against Moab and Ammon for these territorial incursions continued after the first deportation of Jerusalem (597) and the installation of the Zedekiah by the Babylonian king. However, any date after 597 would still have to resolve the question of Babylon's omission.

While the Moabite and Ammonite oracles appear best suited late in the 7th, or more likely early in the 6th century, the oracle against the Philistine cities is difficult to understand during this period since by 604 most of these regions were under Babylonian control. Likewise, the names and combination of the entities do not correspond well to a 7th century date.[10] Krinetzki offers a probable explanation when he argues that these oracles were reworked nearer the time of Joel, particularly since other observations provide strong evidence that an editor reworked the Zephaniah complex during this period.[11]

The mention of Ethiopia and Assyria together (2:12,13-15) provokes various interpretations, particularly about the Ethiopians.[12] The citation of these two entities in their present location clearly draws the reader's attention away from the surrounding regions.[13] This distraction functions

---

[9]   These raiding bands included Moabites and Ammonites. See 2 Kgs 24:2. See discussion of historical situation in Miller/Hayes, *A History of Ancient Israel and Judah*, 407.

[10] Krinetzki, *Zefanjastudien. Motiv- und Traditionskritik + Kompositions- und Redaktionskritik*, Regensburger Studien zur Theologie 7 (Frankfurt: Peter Lang, 1977), 107.

[11] Krinetzki, *Zefanjastudien*, 94-108. See also the recent work by Ben Zvi, *BZAW* 198.

[12] Most understand the oracle (or partial oracle) to the Cushites as a title for Egypt, either as a mocking title or as the remnant of the historical situation in which Ethiopian dynasty which ruled Egypt until Assyria brought its downfall in 663. The exact political situation depends upon the date in which one places Zephaniah and the book. Günter Krinetzki, *Zefanjastudien*, 118f, places the reference shortly before 605. Elliger, *KAT* 25, places the oracle nearer the time of Nineveh's destruction (between 615-612), in spite of the fact that he dates the prophet Zephaniah nearer 630. Seybold, *Satirische Prophetie*, 50,80, considers the oracle a fragment, and twice raises the possibility that it refers to nomadic tribes in the Transjordan, although he appears more inclined to treat it as a reference to Egypt. Liuger Sabottka, *Zephanja. Versuch einer Neuübersetzung mit philogischem Kommentar*, Biblica et Orientalia 25 (Rome: Biblical Institute Press, 1972), 92f, draws on the events of 663, but says it really intends the Ethiopians not the Egyptians.

[13] So correctly Arvid S. Kapelrud, *The Message of the Prophet Zephaniah: Morphology and Ideas* (Oslo: Universitetsforlaget, 1975), 33. He also notes the similarity of the geographical patterning to the oracles in Amos 1:3-2:16, although he has difficulty explaining the presence of Jerusalem in 3:1-7 at the end of the oracles against the

meaningfully as an intentional device which sets up the oracle against Jerusalem (3:1-8a). It purposefully draws attention away from Judah in order to accentuate the fervor of the denunciation of Jerusalem which follows. The historical background for these oracles is difficult to place. The reference to Ethiopia could react to some unknown historical provocation, but the brevity of the unmotivated pronouncement is perhaps better explained by postulating a more general rationale. Perhaps the fall of the 25th dynasty, which was Ethiopian, and the subsequent deflated status of Ethiopia offers the best possible background for this oracle. Thus, the oracle reflects prophetic judgment on the major powers of the previous generations. Both Ethiopian and Assyrian monarchies lost their power in the 7th century.

Without an explicit change of addressee, the subject of the final oracle in Zeph 3:1-8 changes from Nineveh to Jerusalem.[14] The use of the woe introductory formula (הוֹי + participle) clearly begins a new unit, and distinguishes the following from the oracles which precede. References to the prophets, the priests, the sanctuary and the law leave little doubt that the intended city is Jerusalem (3:3f). Zeph 3:1-8 presupposes the remaining oracles against the nations since YHWH indicates that the rationale behind the destruction of the other areas was to warn Jerusalem of impending judgment if she and her people did not change their tactics (3:6f). The oracle presumes that this change did not occur, and that Jerusalem will be judged accordingly (3:8a).

The concluding units of Zephaniah change the tenor of the remainder of the book to one which treats Jerusalem more positively. They picture the removal of the threat, the delimitation of judgment, and the return of the inhabitants. The differences from the preceding portions of the writing are so noticeable that, for quite some time, a large contingent of scholarship argues that substantial portions of Zeph 3:9-20 represent post-exilic additions to the book.[15] The inner logic and cohesion of this

---

nations. Given the similarities to Amos (and the common Deuteronomistic transmission argued in this work), the Jerusalem oracle can be explained as a deliberate device to shock the reader in much the same manner as the concluding oracle against Israel in Amos 2:6ff.

[14] While this change is problematic for some authors, none seriously treat Zeph 3:1-8 as a continuation of the Nineveh oracle. Kapelrud, *The Message of Zephaniah*, 33; Rudolph, *KAT* 13/3, 255 are among those who have trouble seeing the oracle against Jerusalem as part of the oracles against the nations.

[15] Seybold, *Satirische Prophetie*, 95, considers 3:11-20 additions; Krinetzki, *Zefanjastudien*, 239f, limits the additions to 3:14-20; Gillis Gerleman, *Zephanja textkritisch und*

passage is discussed in the chapter on Zephaniah and Haggai. Here, it need only be noted, that in much the same manner as the absolute judgment of Amos 9:1-6 provoked successive responses which were increasingly more positive, so too Zeph 3:9-20 reverses the negative pronouncements of judgment to words of trust and consolation.

Excursus: The Deuteronomistic Corpus and Zephaniah

Before introducing the constituent parts of 1:1-2:3 in more detail, a brief outline of the Deuteronomistic corpus as it relates to Zephaniah is in order. This author contends that Zephaniah reached its current form as the result of the cumulative process of shaping on at least two different levels: 1) the level of the Deuteronomistic corpus containing Hosea, Amos, Micah, and Zephaniah; 2) the level of the expanded corpus which incorporated Joel, Obadiah, Nahum, Habakkuk, Haggai, Zechariah 1-8, and Malachi into a coherent corpus.

The Deuteronomistic corpus, as argued earlier, had a history of its own which can be outlined from the exilic into the post-exilic period. The initial layer of the common corpus appears to have initially compiled the four writings into a single book as part of an attempt to explain the destruction of Jerusalem. The guiding organizational schema utilized the destruction of the Northern kingdom as pronounced by Hosea and Amos as a paradigm of what would befall Jerusalem if it did not take heed. Significant texts in this corpus include: 1) the patterned usage of the superscriptions of the books outlined above (see discussion of Amos 1:1); 2) substantial portions of Hos 2:1ff which introduce the worship of Baal as the chief cause of Israel's destruction (a motif which culminates in the destruction of the sanctuary of Israel in Amos 8:14; 9:1-6); 3) the hermeneutical shift created by Micah 1:2ff, which applies the lessons of Samaria and Israel as a warning to Jerusalem and Judah its own imminent destruction if it does not change its behavior and return to YHWH; and 4) the polemic against Jerusalem in Mic 6. In the literary movement of this corpus, the warning is not heeded, requiring the depiction of Jerusalem's destruction. Zephaniah provides the expected conclusion to this corpus with the depiction of this destruction.

This Deuteronomistic corpus underwent a further step when its writings received promises of eschatological salvation with a particularly strong Jerusalem orientation (Amos 9:11,14-15; Mic 2:12f; 4:1ff; 7:8ff; and portions of Zeph 3:9ff). These promises, frequently dated in the late exilic or early post-exilic period, probably

---

literarisch untersucht (Lund: Gleerup, 1942), 66, believes 3:17c-20 comes from a later hand; Elliger, *ATD* 25, 74-78, considers much of the material genuine, but admits it has been reworked by later redactors; Eissfeldt, *Introduction*, 425, believes 3:14-20 is secondary; Fohrer, *Einleitung*, 502, and Kaiser, *Introduction*, 231, believe 3:9-20 stem from later times with the possible exception of 3:11-13; Rudolph, *KAT* 256, considers 3:16-20 as a later addition. A few still argue the oracles are authentic: Kapelrud, *The Message of the Prophet Zephaniah*, 37-40; and Keller, *CAT* 11b, believe only 3:20 is later; Robertson, *Nahum, Habakkuk, and Zephaniah*, 327,334f, considers all authentic.

reflect more than one redactional layer. They do not eliminate the threat of judgment in the existing corpus, but they temper that judgment with the hope of restoration for the remnant of Judah and Jerusalem.

The Deuteronomistic corpus lost its distinctive character when it was expanded by including Joel, Obadiah, Nahum, Habakkuk, Haggai, Zech 1-8, and Malachi. This expanded corpus placed YHWH's judgment against Jerusalem into a larger sphere, namely, YHWH's control of the destinies of world powers as well as the destinies of YHWH's own people. Hence, not only were Assyrian (Nahum, via Mic 7:8ff) and Babylonian (Hab 1:5ff) actions placed under YHWH's direct authority, but they were placed within a cosmic framework that also introduced YHWH's eschatological judgment upon all nations (Joel 4; Obad 15-21) who acted contrary to YHWH's commands.

The third chapter of Zephaniah provides considerable evidence of later additions in the arena of both the Deuteronomistic corpus and the Book of the Twelve. Regarding the salvific expansions of 3:9ff, one must distinguish carefully between salvific additions to the version of Zephaniah in the Deuteronomistic corpus, and additions for its expanded form for the Book of the Twelve. Considerations of time and space do not permit a detailed analysis of this chapter, but a few observations will illustrate a tentative hypothesis. The combination of Zephaniah with Haggai/Zechariah 1-8 and Malachi is discussed in detail later in the chapter. This combination effected the shape of Zephaniah only by the addition and adaptation of several verses which continue the promises to Jerusalem in 3:18-20.   These adaptations expand the horizon from which the verses operate, both backward and forward to other works in the corpus. These expansions adapt Mic 4:6f to the context of Zeph 3:14ff and they set the scene (literally) for the message of Haggai. They also demonstrate awareness of Joel through meaningful allusions to that work, similar to those which appear in Nahum and Habakkuk. Results from the following investigation of Zeph 3:18-20 indicate, however, that the utilization of Mic 4:6f existed in literary form, before it received slight modifications for Haggai. This evidence implies that the majority of the salvific additions to 3:9ff should be viewed within the realm of the Deuteronomistic corpus.

Several observations regarding the growth of this corpus and Zeph 3:9ff are offered here, with the disclaimer that they represent only a tentative attempt at reconstruction. The early version of the Deuteronomistic corpus likely concluded with an announcement of judgment against Jerusalem. The current form of the MT thus implies Zephaniah ended with 3:8a. There are good reasons, however, for arguing that the next material which was added to this corpus is not that which currently follows 3:8a. Remembering the parallel function of Amos, one notes that the message of total destruction was quickly modified by including a remnant motif in Amos 9:7-10. If one postulates a similar hermeneutic in Zephaniah, then one is drawn to the remnant of Jerusalem motif in Zeph 3:12f (compare the vocabulary of 3:13 with Mic 6), which could very cogently have followed 3:8a. In fact, it is not inconceivable that these verses could have originally followed 3:8a as the original ending to Zephaniah, reflecting the theological conviction that a "remnant of Israel" would survive in Jerusalem but not in Samaria. The vast majority of the remainder of 3:14-19, can be plausibly explained through intertextual relationships with other portions of the Deuteronomistic corpus (with its salvific expansions, including Amos

9:11ff and Mic 4:1ff) preceding the incorporation of universal judgment motifs into the Zephaniah corpus, which will be described in the remainder of this discussion of the Habakkuk - Zephaniah connection. The obvious exceptions appear in the framework surrounding the salvific portions 3:8b,20. Some uncertainty remains in 3:9-11, but due to the observations later in the this chapter, one may presume that these verses also have their origin in the transmission of the Deuteronomistic corpus. The expanded corpus reshapes their significance if not their form.

2. The Date of Zephaniah

One major issue in Zephaniah studies centers around the question of the date of the prophet.[16] Unlike some prophetic writings, such as Joel, the various opinions about the time of the prophet do not stretch across centuries. Rather, the debate concentrates upon a forty year span in the last decades of the 7th and the first few years of the 6th centuries. Opinions on the date of the situation presumed in the *early portions* of the book have solidified into three major positions.[17] The first two rely heavily upon Zeph 1:1, which places the prophet in the reign of Josiah (639-608), while the third questions these assumptions. These positions include those who date Zephaniah prior to the Josianic reforms begun in 622; those who see the prophet's work as part of those reforms after 622; and those arguing that Zephaniah relates to the reign of Jehoiakim.[18] A

---

[16] Given the fact that a strong contingent of scholarship dates major portions of 3:9-20 to exilic and/or post-exilic expansions, most of the evidence for dating Zephaniah derives from chapters 1-2. See the discussion of opinions below, page 201.

[17] The "early portions of the book" draws upon the strong consensus that the material attributable to the prophet appears in 1:2-3:8, since the remainder of chapter three exhibits exilic and post-exilic theological emphases. Chapter three is discussed in more detail in the following chapter.

[18] Two minority opinions do not receive much support in recent studies. The theory of Maccabean origins as presented by Louise Pettibone Smith and Ernest R. Lacheman, "The Authorship of the Book of Zephaniah," *Journal of Near Eastern Studies* 9 (1950): 137-142, finds virtually no subsequent support. Another minority opinion treats the prophet's writing as representative of the latter portions of Josiah's reign. Milton S. Terry, "Zephaniah," *Old and New Testament Student* 11 (1890): 262-272 (cited in Williams, *JBL* 82 [1963]: 78). Proponents of this late-Josianic date refute the syncretism described in chapter one as definitive evidence of a date in the early part of Josiah's reign because other evidence demonstrates the fact that the syncretistic practices were only driven underground by the Josianic reforms, and not eradicated. They argue that the syncretism resumed too quickly in the reign of Manasseh following the death of Josiah to believe that it had been eliminated. They also claim that the

summary of all three arguments will facilitate the discussion of the literary units which follows.[19]

Those who date Zephaniah early in the reign of Josiah argue that the cultic abuse described by Zephaniah fits with practices during and immediately after the reign of Manasseh (687-642). They further stipulate that Zephaniah was instrumental in initiating the reforms of Josiah.[20] They claim that this early period explains the condemnation of the sons of the king and the silence about the king himself, since Josiah would have been too young during this period to merit prophetic condemnation. This position claims the greatest number of supporters.

Those arguing that Zephaniah preached during the Josianic reforms counter that the reforms do not appear to have begun in earnest until the discovery of the "book of the law" in 622.[21] These scholars prefer to date Zephaniah after 622, and see Zephaniah as having written during the reform itself. For them, the reference to the "remnant of Baal" in 1:4 and examples of Deuteronomic language serve as the cornerstone for dating the ministry of the prophet.

Those arguing for a date in the reign of Jehoiakim take a different track. They begin with the observation that one clear statement may be deduced from Zephaniah.[22]   The prophet expected the *imminent* destruction of Jerusalem. Those who try to conform the book to the superscription are forced to rely upon the *possibility* of a Scythian threat to Jerusalem.[23] The only reference to such a threat appears in Herodotus, but the reliability of this account has been correctly questioned, since no corroborating evidence can be found in either the literature of the period or in archaeological excavations. Evidence for a Scythian invasion of Judah is highly tenuous, and even the little evidence which is cited does not explain the intensity of a presumed Scythian threat in Zephaniah, which if it existed at all, could not be as massive as many envision.

---

abundance of military activity shortly before Josiah's death provides a more likely setting for the book than prior to theories in the early reign of Josiah.

[19] A more detailed analysis of these positions appears in Williams, *JBL* 82 (1963): 77-88.

[20] So for example, Rudolph, *KAT* 13/3, 255; Guy Langohr, *Ephemerides Theologicae Lovanieses* 52 (1976): 2f.

[21] For example, Friedrich Schwally, "Das Buch Sefanjâ," *ZAW* 10 (1890): 165-240; Robertson, *Nahum, Habakkuk, and Zephaniah*, 33.

[22] For example, Williams, *JBL* 82 (1963): 81-85; J.P. Hyatt, "The Date and Background of Zephaniah," *JNES* 7 (1948): 25.

[23] For example, Henri Cazelles, "Sophonie, Jérémie, et les Scythes en Palestine," *Revue Biblique* 74 (1967): 24-44.

The theory that Zephaniah post-dates Josiah's reign is likewise not the majority opinion, but has become more plausible in recent years.[24] These arguments may be summarized in seven points.[25] 1) The phrase the "remnant of Baal" refers to those who survived Josiah's purge. 2) There are several Deuteronomic "allusions" (Zeph 1:13,17; 2:2,7). 3) Those "thickening upon the lees" (1:12) indicates disappointment in the Deuteronomic reform after the death of Josiah. 4) The references to Moab and Ammon in 2:8ff become understandable in the reign of Jehoiakim, based on the actions described in 2 Kgs 24:2. Commentators date this activity sometime between 692-598 (shortly before Nebuchadnezzar attacked). 5) "The reference to the Ethiopians (probably a taunt name for Egypt)" in 2:12 is also understandable in the reign of Jehoiakim, when Egypt installed its selection as king. 6) The Philistine cities, unlike the Moabites, are not condemned for crimes against Judah. The Philistine cities were possibly involved with Judah in a revolt against Babylon and were thus similarly punished by the attack of neighboring peoples. 7) The Assyrian oracle presupposes Nineveh's ruin, placing it after 612.

This theory of a late date for Zephaniah, while not without problems, does appear to account for the largest number of dating problems. The single most significant problem which it must overcome is that Zeph 1:1 specifically claims Zephaniah preached "in the days of Josiah," not in the days of Jehoiakim. However, the importance given to this dating element in the superscription has been highly overvalued in regard to the final form of Zephaniah, and does not in reality significantly detract from the acceptance of this later date.[26]

[24] Williams, *JBL* 82 (1963): 83-88, formulates this theory, although he draws heavily upon other commentators with similar ideas.

[25] Based on these seven points, Williams (85f) identifies Zephaniah with "Zephaniah the second priest" who was taken into exile and executed before the king of Babylon mentioned in 2 Kgs 25:18-21 (= Jer 52:24ff). Williams argues there was considerable overlap of priest and prophet, which would make it possible to refer to one man as both prophet and priest, particularly since Ezekiel, a contemporary, also served both functions. However, such exact identification is less convincing than the majority of the observations.

[26] The fact that the reference to Josiah was, in all likelihood, part of the Deuteronomistic editing of prophetic works from the exilic period, and that the reference demonstrates a specific literary purpose greatly reduces its reliability as a "purely biographical" note. See discussion of 1:1 below.

3. The Units in Zeph 1:1-2:3

Zeph 1:1-2:3 comprises the first major section of the book. Its theme centers on the announcement of the day of YHWH as a day of judgment, but it will become clear that this day of YHWH has two different focal points. The majority of the material perceives this judgment as directed against Judah and Jerusalem, while a second focus expands these pronouncements to provide a universal application. Five compositional units (1:1; 1:2-3; 1:4-13; 1:14-18; 2:1-3) should be distinguished within this larger unit, although the present form of some of these units arises from more than one stage of literary growth.

3.1. Zeph 1:1

The superscription of the book, Zeph 1:1, conforms in many respects to typical Deuteronomistic patterns of prophetic superscriptions. It serves a titular function, and is not tied syntactically to the verses which follow. The superscription contains three essential elements: the announcement that the word of YHWH came to Zephaniah, biographical information on Zephaniah, and the dating element. The first element provides the typical Deuteronomistic introduction: "The word of YHWH came to Zephaniah."[27] This portion of the formulaic superscription, while placing the book in the Deuteronomistic tradition, does not provide much more relevant information since the formula had a relatively long history.[28]

The second element presents the most unique feature in the superscription of Zephaniah. The biographical information traces the prophetic genealogy back four generations, a phenomenon so unique among prophetic superscriptions that it has provoked numerous attempts to explain the lengthy genealogy. The explanations typically understand this extended biographical data in one of two ways: 1) Most accentuate Hezekiah, the final name of the series, and treat the genealogy as strictly honorarial element documenting Zephaniah's biological relationship to king

---

[27] Compare other superscriptions which use this pattern in similar forms: Hos 1:1; Joel 1:1; Jon 1:1; Mic 1:1.

[28] See Robert R. Wilson, *Prophecy and Society in Ancient Israel*, 145-166, for a collection of the relevant passages for this phrase, as well as a discussion of its origins in Ephraimite tradition and its association with the Deuteronomistic movement.

Hezekiah of Judah (725-696).[29] 2) Others are less certain any conclusion may be drawn regarding the purpose of the superscription.[30] 3) A few scholars, however, place the emphasis upon the first name of the series, Cushi.[31] They note the etymological relationship of the name to the Hebrew word Cushite (meaning Ethiopian), and argue that the four generation extension is somehow related to the question of the prophet's African heritage and/or Israelite citizenship.[32] Often, they argue that the Hezekiah mentioned in Zeph 1:1 is not specifically cited as the king of Judah, and should be seen as an otherwise unknown Hezekiah, since none of the Biblical traditions mention that the king had a son by the name Amariah. Those who believe the genealogy does trace the roots back to king Hezekiah rebut this argument with the observation that the Biblical traditions in Kings and Chronicles are in no way complete accounts of the descendants of the kings, since they often mention only the son who succeeded the king, omitting direct references to other siblings. Despite the ingenuity of the arguments for African heritage, the most likely explanation in this case still seems to be to treat Zeph 1:1 as a specific reference to king Hezekiah. Precisely the fact that the genealogy goes back four generations provides the strongest evidence. Since it would be inconceivable that the great-great grandfather of the prophet would have been alive, the name had to carry enough weight on its own merit to serve

---

[29] For example, Robertson, *Nahum, Habakkuk, and Zephaniah*, 253; Watts, *Joel, etc*, 153f; Marti, *HCAT* 13, 361; Nowack, *HK* 3/4, 291; Gene Rice, "The African Roots of the Prophet Zephaniah," *Journal of Religious Thought* 36 (1979/80): 21-31 and Maria Eszenyei Szeles, *Wrath and Mercy: Habakkuk and Zephaniah*, International Theological Commentary (Grand Rapids: Eerdmans, 1987), 62, all believe that both a focus on the Judean king and the question of African heritage come in to play.

[30] Rudolph, *KAT* 13/3, 259; Kapelrud, *The Message of the Prophet Zephaniah*, 44; Elliger, *ATD* 25, 54f; Smith, *Word* 32, 124f; Eissfeldt, *Introduction*, 425.

[31] So J. Heller, "Zephanjas Ahnenreihe." *VT* 21 (1971): 102-104; Fohrer, *Einleitung*, 501; and very cautiously, Seybold, *Satirische Prophetie*, 63.

[32] Proponents of this view either see the extended genealogy as a refutation of African origin, or as a stylistic device designed to show that the prophet was a true Israelite according to the stipulations of Deut 23:7. Cf Heller, *VT* 21 (1971): 102-104. By contrast, see Rice, *Journal of Religious Thought* 36 (1979/80): 21-31, who argues Zephaniah's African ancestry comes from his grandfather's (Gedaliah) marriage to an Ethiopian woman. Rice sees no reasons for denying that the Hezekiah mentioned refers to the king of Judah. He also documents a considerable degree of contact between the royal house of Ethiopia and Judah in the 7th century, enough that his suggestion is not unreasonable, although its certainty is by no means assured.

some function. Only if Hezekiah the king was intended could this name connote such special significance.[33]

The third element of the superscription is the dating element which places the message in the reign of Josiah (639-608). This element has created considerable confusion in Zephaniah studies, not, as with Hezekiah, because there is any doubt that the king of Judah is intended, but because the great majority of scholars have been so heavily influenced by the reference to this king, that they have often gone to considerable effort to explain the remainder of the book as a product of Josiah's reign.[34] However, the gradual recognition that the Deuteronomistic shaping of prophetic books occurred during the exilic period demands a fresh look at the mention of Josiah.[35] The date of the formation of prophetic books must be taken separately from the question of the date of the prophet. In the case of Zeph 1:1, the selection of Josiah could either be due to traditions about the prophet's ministry or to specific literary purposes.[36]

---

[33] See Rice, *Journal of Religious Thought* 36 (1979/80): 21f, who develops these thoughts further. Additionally, Rice offers arguments that the omission of the reference to "king of Judah" is readily understandable on stylistic grounds (similarly, see Marti, *HCAT* 13, 361).

[34] For example, Krinetzki, *Zefanjastudien*, 239, isolates 13 different sayings going back to Zephaniah, but dates these units between 639-612. See also the discussion of the problems of a Josianic dating, in Williams, *JBL* 82 (1963): 77-88.

[35] The Deuteronomistic circles normally associated with the formation of these superscriptions and other reworkings of the book are now most often placed in the exilic period. Some have begun to ask questions and make observations which might help to understand how these redactors worked. For example, see Seybold, *Satirische Prophetie*, 83f, who portrays the redactional work as deliberation over the material on the basis of the knowledge of the annals, and the information in the book itself. Earlier in the same work (79), Seybold, in discussing the lack of direct connections to Josiah, raises an interesting point, which he does not develop further in the context of 1:1. He notes that 1:4ff is the only passage which can be directly linked to Josianic reforms, but he then demonstrates that the passage cannot have stemmed from Zephaniah. Rather, for Seybold, the relationship of Zephaniah with the Josianic reforms is indirect and redactionally imposed by the Deuteronomistic editors of the book. He says: "Die Schlussfolgerungen sind unausweichlich: Zef 1,4ff stammt nicht von Zefanja. Zefanjas Predigtskizzen und Spruchnotizen lassen keine direkte Bezugnahmen auf die joschijanische Reform erkennen. Die Herausgeber und Bearbeiter des Zefanjabuches sahen in dem Propheten den, der die Katastrophe des Exils voraussagte. Für sie kam erst damit die Reform des Joschija zum Abschluss." While Seybold bases this observation on Zeph 1:4-6, it is more difficult to eliminate these verses literarily than to assume the redactional insertion of Josiah.

[36] See also Ben Zvi, *BZAW* 198, 270.

Given the numerous difficulties in dating the material in the reign of Josiah discussed above, evidence for a literary purpose for this superscription should be evaluated.

It has been noted above that the patterning of the kings in the superscriptions of Hosea, Amos, Micah and Zephaniah, together with the thematic progression present in these works argues for a common transmission with a literary purpose. The question should be raised here: Did Zeph 1:1 receive any shaping to conform it to this pattern or did it exist in its present form? While an absolute answer is not possible, when one looks at the options, significant criteria argue that Zephaniah has been deliberately shaped for its function in that corpus.

When one tries to explain the combination of the three elements in Zeph 1:1, the following options appear in scholarly discussions: 1) The superscription is a unified composition from a single hand. This opinion has been assumed by the majority of scholars, but often with little or no discussion of other possibilities. 2) Several argue that substantial portions of the genealogy are secondary,.[37] 3) A plausible suggestion, not discussed in the pertinent exegetical literature, suggests Zeph 1:1 should be viewed in relationship to the Deuteronomistic corpus, not as an isolated dating formula. This explanation begins with the observation that the reference to Josiah post-dates the remainder of the material. The phrase "in the days of Josiah, king of Judah" parallels the formulaic material elsewhere in the Deuteronomistic superscriptions in the Book of the Twelve. The phrase itself clearly refers back to a past time, as would be expected in an exilic shaping at the hands of the Deuteronomistic circle, but would not be very explainable in the lifetime of the prophet.

On the other hand, the majority of the genealogical material is easier to understand as stemming from someone who knew the prophet. No traditions identify the names as they are listed here with any specific personages, except, of course, for Hezekiah and Josiah.[38] If the genealogy were entirely a literary construction, one would expect some attempt to

---

[37] So Heller, *VT* 21 (1971): 102-104, who argues the original superscription contained only reference to Cushi and to Josiah. He believes the remainder was added to conform Zephaniah to Deut 23:7, so as to eliminate any confusion as to his ethnic heritage.

[38] Ben Zvi, *BZAW* 198, 46-51, does not believe the evidence indicates Hezekiah the king is the person intended in 1:1. Much of his argument derives from a Syriac corruption (Hilkiah) of the MT. Ben Zvi does not offer sufficient explanation, however, as to why a later literary construction would necessitate four generations of ancestors if the Hezekiah mentioned were not a significant personage.

relate the names contained therein with existing traditions.[39]   Thus, the reference to Josiah comes from a later time after the death of Josiah (and presumably after 587), but references to Cushi, Gedaliah, and Amariah probably have some basis in an actual genealogy of the prophet.   The remaining reference to king Hezekiah could be a legitimate part of the original genealogy or, more likely, it could have been added with the reference to Josiah as a deliberate link back to Mic 1:1.

Several observations increase the likelihood that the reference to Hezekiah entered with the reference to Josiah.   Foremost among these observations, the prominence given these two kings in the Deuteronomistic history makes them a natural combination.   These two kings serve as positive examples for the Judean monarchy, and the accounts of their reigns are structured very similarly, a similarity which becomes even more pronounced in later writings.[40]   Another observation arguing for the deliberate incorporation of Hezekiah, notes that its insertion helps explain the cumbersome five generation genealogy. If Hezekiah were not originally part of the genealogy, the prophet would be identified by only three previous generations, a phenomenon which has considerably more attestation in ancient cultures.[41]

---

[39] Caution must be exercised here, however, because most of the names do appear in different accounts of the late 7th century, but they have no familial relationship in those references: for example, Cushi (Jer 36:14); Gedaliah (2 Kgs 25:22ff). Williams, *JBL* 82 (1963), 85f, even tries to relate the Zephaniah to the second priest killed by the Babylonians in 2 Kgs 25:18-21 (= Jer 52:24ff). Additionally, historical accuracy or harmonizations with existing traditions is not always deemed necessary in referring back to historical periods.   See for example the erroneous chronology of the Persian monarchs in Daniel and Ezra-Nehemiah (cf Smend, *Die Entstehung des Alten Testaments*, 223,225). However, given the lack of familial connection, and the fact that Amariah does not appear in accounts of this time period, one may presume the genealogy is based upon historical tradition, not literary purpose. Ben Zvi, *BZAW* 198, 48, sees the names as the scribal creation of a priestly ancestry for Zephaniah rather than royal lineage, but this explanation depends upon acceptance of a textual corruption.

[40] See the discussion of Amos 1:1.

[41] Genealogies tracing lineage back three generations are not uncommon in ancient near eastern cultures.   See *IDB* 2, 363; Robert R. Wilson, *Genealogy and History in the Biblical World* (New Haven: Yale University, 1977), 59-62, 114-119, documents royal and non-royal genealogies in inscriptions.   While the dominant model of royal inscriptions lists three generations (including the current person), there are a considerable number tracing the heritage back to the fourth generation. Non-royal inscriptions, while more frequently only two generations in length, attest to longer genealogies as well. Both exhibit a considerable degree of fluidity and telescoping of

One observation should be noted which might argue against a deliberate incorporation of Hezekiah as part of the Deuteronomistic shaping of the superscriptions, namely, the fact that the spelling of the name varies slightly in Zeph 1:1 compared with Hos 1:1 and Mic 1:1.[42] However, alternative explanations for the slight variation greatly relativize the usefulness of this distinction as an argument against the deliberate inclusion of Hezekiah in the Deuteronomistic corpus.[43] Thus, the most likely explanation of the current form of this troublesome superscription

----

the genealogical material for specific purposes. By contrast, Ugaritic genealogies (119-122) contain no native genealogical material stretching to the third generation, although tablets *sent from* foreign representatives do attest to three and four generation genealogies. Phoenician and Punic genealogies (122-124) do not as a rule go beyond three generations until the Persian period. Outside the Old Testament, Hebrew inscriptions (124) with genealogies do not appear frequently enough to draw firm conclusions, although those that have been found tend to have only two generations. Aramaic genealogies (124f) also tend toward two generation genealogical material, but there are extant examples of three and four generation material. Egyptian genealogies (125-129) by contrast are extensive and can reach a depth of seventeen generations.

[42] Hos 1:1 and Mic 1:1 spell the name יחזקיה, while Zeph 1:1 has חזקיה.

[43] First, the name Hezekiah had no consistent spelling, even though certain forms prevail in one book or another. For example Wolff, *BK* 14/4, 3, distinguishes between the two forms of Hezekiah, but one wonders what weight this distinction carries in light of the fact that the same book exhibit alternate forms: cf יחזקיהו in 2 Kgs 20:10 with the more common חזקיהו in 20:1,3,5,8,19. Also the same variation appears with יחזקיהו in Isa 1:1 and the more typical חזקיהו in the Deuteronomistic material in 36-39. A second possible explanation for the variation must acknowledge the possibility of textual corruption. The only difference in the two spellings is that Hos 1:1 and Mic 1:1 have a י which Zeph 1:1 does not. The letter could easily have fallen out in copying, especially since the Zephaniah form is readily attested (2 Kgs 18:1,10,13-16; Prov 25:1). A third possible explanation is the most intriguing, if not the most "provable," namely that the variation is deliberate. This explanation draws on the observations of Wolff that the forms in Mic 1:1 and Hos 1:1 should not be placed as late as the Chronicler, even though they use the form common to that work. He notes that this form makes the name into a petition ("May YHWH strengthen") whereas the form in Zeph 1:1 is a statement (YHWH is strength). These nuance changes correspond well with the literary outline of the Deuteronomistic corpus. Hosea, Amos, and Micah function in broad terms as warnings to Jerusalem (by using the fate of the Northern Kingdom as example) to change her ways before she is destroyed. Zephaniah presupposes these warnings, and portrays the destruction of Jerusalem. It is therefore not inconceivable that the warning function is subtly, but intentionally, indicated in a word play on Hezekiah's name, which twice carries the petitionary nuance before the more ominous use of the statement in Zeph 1:1. A fourth explanation could of course explain these variations as a result of the reliance upon the *Vorlage* in Zeph 1:1 if the name Hezekiah were already present.

postulates that an earlier superscription was expanded by the addition of
"... the son of Hezekiah, in the days of Josiah son of Amon, king of Judah"
at the end of the superscription.

3.2. Zeph 1:2-3

The body of the book begins abruptly with YHWH's announcement
of universal judgment (Zeph 1:2f). The verse begins a new unit since it
contains no syntactical connection to 1:1. The extent of this unit is more
problematic. On the one hand, Zeph 1:2f leads directly into 1:4 with no
grammatical markers to distinguish it as a separate unit. On the other
hand, the universal judgment of 1:2f differs radically from the
pronouncement of judgment against Jerusalem in 1:4-13. Scholars explain
the different perspective variously.[44] Yet, the theological perspective of
universal judgment is not the only difference these two verses manifest.
Ball demonstrates the separateness of this unit on structural and stylistic
grounds as well, even though he does not extrapolate logical conclusions
from his own observations.[45]

De Roche documents the manner in which these verses intentionally
play on the creation and flood accounts in Genesis.[46] His evidence for the

---

[44] The distinction of theological perspective in 1:2-3 from the majority of the chapter is
almost universally recognized, but the interpretations of this broader outlook vary.
Some, such as Sellin, *KAT* 12, 72; Elliger, *ATD* 25, p. 56-57; Gerleman, *Zephanja*, 4-5;
Krinetzki, *Zefanjastudien*, 45-47, argue that 1:2-3 serves a secondary or redactional
function of universalization. Others, such as Kapelrud, *The Message of the Prophet
Zephaniah*, 15-16; Hesse "Wurzelt die prophetische Gerichtsrede im Israelitischen
Kult?" *ZAW* 65 (1953): 49; and Rudolph, *KAT* 13/3, 264, argue these verses merely
form the introduction of the book, and that the separate theologies need not be
attributed to different authors.

[45] Ivan J. Ball, *A Rhetorical Study of Zephaniah*, Graduate Theological Union
Dissertation, (Minneapolis: University Microfilm, 1972), 76f. Ball notes a tight
structural similarity in 1:4-13 which does not incorporate 1:2f.

[46] Michael De Roche, "Zephaniah 1:2-3: The 'Sweeping' of Creation," *VT* 30 (1980): 104-
109. Other scholars have noted the similarity of the language in these verses with the
flood story, but De Roche has taken these observations even farther by demonstrating
that the verses *completely reverse* the creation account as well. De Roche at times
semingly implies an either/or relationship to the flood and creation accounts, but this
tendency probably reflects his desire to demonstrate dependence upon the creation
account as well as the flood story. The passage clearly incorporates *both* the flood *and*
creation accounts. One major critique must be leveled at De Roche. He convincingly
presents his arguments of dependence, but his willingness to use these two verses to

explicit allusions in Zeph 1:2-3 to the flood account in Gen 6-9 has been noted elsewhere, but is nevertheless to the point: "from the face of the earth" serves as a noticeable refrain in the flood story (Gen 6:7; 7:4; 8:8); אסף אסף specifically takes up Gen 8:21.[47]   In addition, De Roche documents a meaningful relationship to the creation account: The play on words between man and earth (אדם and אדמה) plays off the same pun in Gen 2:7; 3:17,19. The reference to the destruction of the fish of the sea does not make sense when read only in light of the flood tradition, since, logically, they escape the judgment of the flood. However, by expanding the allusion to incorporate the creation accounts, one may account for majority of the entities in Zeph 1:2f: the presence of the "fish" (Gen 1:20a), the birds (Gen 1:20b), the beasts (Gen 1:24) and man (1:26, which even uses the same phrases). Just as significantly, Zephaniah 1:3 *completely reverses* the order of the creation account of these elements. The use of the verb כרת (cut off) has no parallel in either the flood or the creation account, but it is deliberately chosen as antonymn to the verb ברא (create), which plays such a dominant role in Gen 1:1ff. The use of כל in 1:2 corresponds to significant frequency of that word in Gen 2-3.

The dependence of Zeph 1:2f on both the P account of the flood and the creation account of Gen 1-3 requires the unit to be dated later than the exile, and certainly later than the reign of Josiah.[48]   The manner in which this unit utilizes these motifs makes the imagery quite poignant. It draws upon the flood imagery as an actualization of YHWH's previous judgment, and its complete reversal of the creation motif heightens the intensity of the announced judgment.   The question of the purpose of this universal judgment in Zephaniah must necessarily await a discussion of the remaining units in the first section.

---

redate the combination of the J and P sources of the Pentateuch (106) is highly tenuous at best, and this suggestion should be rejected.   These two verses, given their questionable contextual and theological integrity, simply do not carry enough weight to overturn more than a century of relative consensus that P presupposes the exile. Ben Zvi, *BZAW* 198, 56, argues against explicit association of these verses with Pentateuchal traditions concerning the flood or the creation story.   However, De Roche's observations concerning the meaningful reversal of the order of the creation accounts render his arguments more compelling than the slight variation of language noted by Ben Zvi.

[47] Others have noted this allusion, for example, see Sabottka, *Zephanja*, 12.

[48] Contra De Roche himself, *VT* 30 (1980): 106, whose willingness to redate the combination of J and P on the basis of these verses must be rejected.

3.3. Zeph 1:4-13

Zeph 1:4-13 comprises the largest block of material in the judgment section of the book, but even this passage combines several smaller sub-units (1:4-6,7,8-12,13) which purposefully compound images of Jerusalem's destruction. As already noted, the grammatical markers of the unit do not isolate 1:4 from 1:2f. Zeph 1:4 begins with a *waw* that attaches 1:4 with the preceding verses, but the imagery and intention of 1:4ff change so dramatically, that it is difficult to accept an original connection to 1:2f. Therefore one should understand the *waw* as part of the incorporation of 1:2f. One question naturally follows the separation of 1:4 from 1:2f: Could 1:4 have begun a previous version of Zephaniah? The abruptness of the announcement is not an argument against seeing 1:4 as the beginning of an earlier corpus. The sudden announcement of judgment against Judah is no more abrupt than the equally sudden divine speech in 1:2. Unlike 1:2f, however, 1:4 fits well with the vast majority of the chapter that concentrates upon the destruction of Jerusalem. There is therefore no reason to doubt that 1:4 began an earlier version of Zephaniah prior to the inclusion of 1:2f.

The sub-unit which begins in Zeph 1:4 extends to 1:6 as evidenced by the extended series of accusatives. These accusatives condemn various groups for their false worship. This unit announces judgment upon those who are abusing the YHWH cult in Jerusalem (remnant of Baal, priests, idol priests, and those who have not sought YHWH).

Zeph 1:7 marks a transition to a new subject by means of an interjection which has an imperative force, "Hush!" This transition introduces the motif of the nearness of the day of YHWH in terms of a sacrifice. The sacrifice motif introduces the following section. Zeph 1:7 also presupposes the preceding verses, in that it presumes the judgment announced there.[49] Caution demands that this verse be approached carefully, however, in light of its similarity to Hab 2:20, and the arguments that it draws from both Isa 13 and 34.[50] These relationships argue against

---

[49] See discussion in Rudolph, *KAT* 13/3, 266.

[50] Schneider, *The Unity of the Twelve*, 45f, documents Zephaniah's dependence upon Isa 13, while Bosshard, *BN* 40 (1987): 34f, does the same for Isa 34. Both note *Wortbezüge* involving Zeph 1:7 with the respective chapters in Isaiah. Schneider, in keeping with his stated desire to avoid redactional hypotheses, refuses to accept a 6th century date for Isa 13, but the fact that Babylon is the chief enemy makes such a date more feasible. Bosshard's observations also carry more weight since those cited by Schneider reflect stereotypical expressions more than those noted by Bosshard. However, in the case of Zeph 1:7, neither parallel is so strong as to prove *direct* dependence. Schneider

seeing the verse as part of the pre-exilic core of Zephaniah or even to the
early Deuteronomistic corpus. The verse would thus coincide more readily
with the universal judgment material. In this case one would have to treat
Zeph 1:7 as a later (redactional) insertion, whose significance will be
discussed below.[51]

Zeph 1:8-12 contains a short three strophe poem in which each verse
begins with בעת/ביום + והיה. Additionally, the opening and closing
strophe are marked by the *inclusio* ופקדתי (1:8,9,12). The poem
condemns Jerusalem's upper social class (royal household, merchants, and
the apathetic), and functions well as a thematic counterpart to 1:4-6.
Whereas 1:4-6 condemned cultic abuse, 1:8-12 focuses upon the upper class
of Jerusalem. Both sections culminate in judgment against those whose
main failure was the lack of positive action (1:6,12).

Zeph 1:13 completes the poem in its present position, but stands
outside the poem's structure. Like the first three strophes it begins with
והיה (but does not contain יום or ופקדתי). Zeph 1:13 presupposes the
poem, since the use of the 3mp suffix refers back to it. Interestingly, 1:13
essentially summarizes and characterizes the three groups condemned in the
poem in 1:8-12.

8f Royal and temple personnel	13aa Their palace/wealth destroyed
10f The wealthy and merchants	13ab,ba Their houses destroyed
12 Apathetic (wine metaphor)	13bb Not taste their wine

Despite this deliberate play on the poem, 1:13 should probably not be
understood as an original part of that poem, but as a reflection on the
poem in light of the Deuteronomistic corpus. The context of the
Deuteronomistic corpus helps to explain the dependence on Amos 5:11 in
Zeph 1:13:

---

cites the stereotypical phrase, "for the day of YHWH draws near," which appears
elsewhere, while Bosshard notes only the recurrence of the root זבח. The fact that
Zeph 1:7 effectively quotes Hab 2:20 argues that Hab 2:20 functions as the primary
reference, but the strength of Bosshard's arguments for the book as a whole cannot be
overlooked.

51 Despite the fact that the verse forms a bridge between the preceding and the following,
its presence is not integral, and the parallel nature of 1:4-6 and 8-12 would not require
such a transition to be meaningful.

Amos 5:11

Therefore, because you impose heavy rent on the poor, and exact a tribute of grain from them, you have built house of well-hewn stone, yet you will not live in them; You have planted vineyards, yet you will not drink their wine.

Zeph 1:13

Moreover, their wealth will become plunder, and their houses desolation; And they will build houses, but not inhabit; And they will plant vineyards, but not drink their wine.

Amos 5:11 predicts the exile of the Northern kingdom for the crimes committed by its people. The citation of Amos 5:11 in Zeph 1:13 deliberately parallels the fate of Jerusalem (as the symbol of Judah) with that of the Northern kingdom, a hermeneutic which also appears in Mic 1:2ff, and fits well with Deuteronomistic theology.

3.4. Zeph 1:14-18

Zeph 1:14-18 combines many images of the day of YHWH in a manner which relates literarily to other texts (Joel 2:2 = Zeph 1:15; and Zeph 1:18 alludes to Nah 1:2). As it now stands, it may be divided into 2 sub-units 1:14-16 and 1:17-18. Zeph 1:14-16 is a densely composed poetic piece, full of nominal sentences centering on the nearness of the day of YHWH. Zeph 1:14 begins with two sentences starting with קָרוֹב. Zeph 1:15f contains a series of 6 "day" sayings, which are nominal clauses, followed by two עַל phrases delineating the recipients of YHWH's judgment (the fortified cities and the corner towers).

Zeph 1:17f presents certain difficulties for understanding in its current context. Zeph 1:17-18a expands the horizon of judgment to include אָדָם, but in this instance, the universal aspect is relativized, if it is even intended. The context does not necessarily lead one to presume a universal judgment in the same vein as 1:2f.[52] Zeph 1:16 concludes with a reference to the "fortified cities" and "corner towers," which sounds very much as though it depicts judgment directed against Judah and Jerusalem. The same holds true for the causes which precipitate the judgment according to 1:17,18a. The people are accused of sinning against YHWH, a typical Deuteronomistic expression.[53] Likewise, 1:18a accuses the people of

---

[52] The fact that אָדָם may be used to indicate a particular group without implying all humanity is further discussed below, note 65.

[53] See for example the same formulations in Deut 1:41; 9:16; 20:18; 1 Sam 7:6; 14:34; 2 Sam 12:13; 2 Kgs 17:7.

relying upon their silver and gold, a prophetic formulation against YHWH's people, which passes very well to the context of 1:8-12 (which condemns Jerusalem's upper class). Nevertheless, Zeph 1:18b portrays the day of YHWH sayings as universal judgment. The fact that this line takes up the poem in Nah 1:2-8, in an expanded form, however, sets the line apart from the context on literary grounds as well as thematic accentuations.[54]

Thus, Zeph 1:14-18 expounds the theme of the day of YHWH, but it exhibits tensions when one tries to determine against whom this day of YHWH is directed. Since similar tensions existed between 1:2f and 1:4-13, the presence of this tension requires further investigation following a description of 2:1-3. There are good reasons for arguing that the compounding of "day" sayings in 1:14-18 serves a redactional purpose whose literary horizon goes well beyond the book of Zephaniah.

3.5. Zeph 2:1-3

Zeph 2:1-3 concludes the first major section of the book with a call to repentance which is clearly directed to Judah. The reference to a singular "nation" in 2:1 is syntactically anchored in its context, and the broader context of the chapter make clear that this nation must be understood as "Judah." The unit extends to 2:3, since 2:4 begins the oracles against the nations.

The verses presuppose an imminent judgment, and in essence provide one final prophetic plea for the recalcitrant nation to change (2:1f), followed by the introduction of the idea of a humble and righteous remnant (2:3), which has a chance of escaping YHWH's wrath. These verses combine images found in Amos and the Deuteronomistic corpus.[55] They

---

[54] Nah 1:2-8 is a pre-existing semi-acrostic poem which has been editorially altered for its position at the beginning of Nahum in light of the larger corpus of the Book of the Twelve. Evidence for this view derives from the presence of catchwords back to Mic 7:8-20, allusions to Joel, and the citation of Deutero-Isaiah, all of which appear in those places where the acrostic pattern of Nah 1:2-8 break down. See the forthcoming volume of my work, *Redactional Processes in the Book of the Twelve*. See also my article, "The Redactional Shaping of Nahum 1 for the Book of the Twelve," in Philip R. Davies and David J.A. Clines, *Among the Prophets: Language, Image and Structure in the Prophetic Writings* (Sheffield: Sheffield Press, 1993).

[55] The command to "seek YHWH" occurs only here with בקש, and the command occurs only somewhat more frequently with the synonym דרש (Ps 105:4; 1 Chr 16:11; Isa 55:6; 2 Kgs 22:13; Amos 5:4,6). It is interesting that of these five passages one of them

deliberately draw upon images of judgment against the Northern kingdom, and apply them anew to Judah. These pronouncements strengthen the parallels already drawn between the fate of Judah and Samaria.

Observations on the units in Zeph 1:1-2:3 have demonstrated quite clearly that there are two dominant motifs permeating the material, namely the motif of judgment against Judah and Jerusalem and the motif of a universal judgment. These two motifs must be investigated more closely to determine how their presence should be understood in this context.

4. Two Judgments in Zephaniah 1:2-2:3

Evaluating the catchword connection between Habakkuk and Zephaniah presents one of the most complex tasks in the Book of the Twelve. Any clarification of this complexity must recognize and attempt to explain several different theological and hermeneutical interests in Zeph 1:1-18. The recognition of these interests begins already with the observations made previously in the discussion of the literary units. Zeph 1:2-18; 2:1-3 comprise a tapestry of sayings which constantly revolve around two motifs: universal judgment and judgment upon Jerusalem and Judah. The two motifs, as already noted in the discussion of the units, are first combined on a literary level via the emphasis of two of the units (1:2f,14-18) accentuating universal judgment, while the remaining material relates the judgment explicitly to Jerusalem (1:4-13) and Judah (2:1-3). Relatedly, the "day of YHWH" motif must be viewed from these two perspectives, since "the day of YHWH" material concerns an attack against Jerusalem (1:8,10), Judah (2:1-3), and the entire world (1:14-18).

The question now arises: how should one best understand these two themes? Did the hand which united them have a specific identifiable purpose? Did a Zephaniah corpus exist, prior to the literary combination of the two themes, which concerned itself with the judgment of Jerusalem

---

comes from the Josiah story in 2 Kgs 22:13, and even more important that the phrase appears in Amos 5, in light of the fact that Zeph 1:13 also draws from that chapter. In Amos 5:4,6, the phrase functions similarly to Zeph 2:3. Both function as a dramatic appeal to change before it is too late, with the expected distinction that Amos 5:4,6 addresses the Northern kingdom, and Zeph 2:3 refers to the Southern. The phrase "work justice" (2:3) *thematically contrasts* with the use of the verb in Hos 6:8; 7:1; Mic 2:1, all of which condemn those working evil. The chaff motif (2:2) appears in Hos 13:3 in a judgment against the North.

and Judah, or was the same hand which collected and shaped the seminal sayings interested in placing the two themes together?

Several related observations allow the consideration of two versions of the Zephaniah corpus, an earlier one containing a heavy emphasis upon the destruction of Judah and Jerusalem, and a later expansion incorporating universal judgment. First, one may say with almost absolute certainty that the judgment section of Zephaniah in its present form contains material of both post-exilic and pre-exilic origin. Zeph 1:2f plays off the creation and the flood accounts thereby including both J and P material. This dependence upon later Pentateuchal traditions marks these verses as a post-exilic creation. On the other hand, the most logical explanation of the majority of the first chapter virtually precludes such a late date. The judgment against the royal family (1:8), the anti-Baal polemic (1:4), and the types of cultic and social abuses described all point to interests more at home in the late monarchial period rather than in the post-exilic period.

Second, those catchwords uniting Zeph 1:1-18 and Hab 3:2ff appear overwhelmingly in the material with the universal interest. Only the words "sound" and "hills" in the battle description of Zeph 1:10 clearly fall in the Jerusalemite material. What is more, the same dichotomy between universal and localized judgment has been redactionally imposed in the books of Nahum and Habakkuk.[56] It is therefore not surprising to find this same polarity in Zeph 1:1-18.

Third, the universal judgment sections in Zeph 1:14-18 manifest a literary horizon extending well beyond the book of Zephaniah. As with Nahum and Habakkuk, the hermeneutical system of a specific and universal judgment draws literarily and pictorially upon Joel. Zeph 1:15 cites Joel 2:2.[57]

---

[56] See particularly the inclusion of the theophanic hymns in Nahum (attached to the anti-Nineveh material) and Habakkuk (which entered with the Babylonian material in chapters 1-2). One feature uniting all three passages is their depiction of flood motifs. Nah 1:8 and Hab 3:10 presuppose the motif from chaos traditions (which is suitable to the foreign enemies depicted in those works), whereas Zeph 1:2f draws upon the flood account of Genesis (an apt use of the motif since the majority of the material concerns Judah and Jerusalem). Amplification of the evidence for these theories appears in the forthcoming volume of this work: *Redactional Processes in the Book of the Twelve*.

[57] Criteria for arguing Zeph 1:15 quotes Joel are derived from the literary analysis of 1:15, which follows, and upon the phenomenon already documented that the redactional passages in Nahum and Habakkuk also rely upon Joel.

Joel 2:2	Zeph 1:15
A day of darkness and gloom,	...A day of darkness and gloom
A day of clouds and thick darkness.	A day of clouds and thick darkness.

Additionally, the second sentence in Zeph 1:18 alludes very explicitly to the theophanic hymn of Nahum, which was first incorporated into the Nahum corpus for its position in the Book of the Twelve.[58] The sentence in question reads, "And in the fire of his jealousy all of the earth will be devoured, for he will make an end, indeed a terrible one, to all the inhabitants of the earth." Not only is the theme of universal judgment very similar to Nah 1:2-8, but the vocabulary of Zeph 1:18 depends heavily upon that hymn.[59] Given the quotation of Joel 2:2 by Zeph 1:15, as well as the allusion to Nah 1:2ff, one may justifiably assume that the reference to "the day of the horn and battle cry" in Zeph 1:16 takes up these motifs from Joel 2:1, which also combines the day of YHWH (as a day of judgment against Jerusalem) with the blowing of the battle trumpet and the war-cry.[60] Thus, only one cola of the short series of "day" sayings has no direct literary foundation in the Book of the Twelve. However, this saying in 1:15 ("a day of destruction and desolation") has numerous synonymous counterparts in the Book of the Twelve.[61] Thus, one may say that the literary horizon of the universal judgment material (Zeph 1:2f) meaningfully incorporates the flood and creation accounts of Genesis, and demonstrates a clear tendency to shape the understanding of universal judgment to paradigms which have their literary roots in Joel, but which also appear in redactional material in Nahum.

The documentation of this expanded literary horizon in the יום sayings appearing in Zeph 1:15-16a requires a fresh look at all of 1:14-18 in order to determine more precisely the intention or intentions of this unit. Specifically, does the unit as a whole predict *only* universal judgment, or

---

[58] See footnote 56, above on page 194.

[59] Compare especially "the fire of his jealousy" in Zeph 1:18 with Nah 1:2,6, where the jealousy motif combines with fire. Compare the phrase, "he will make a complete end ... to all the inhabitants of the earth" with the phraseology of Nah 1:8: "when in the flood he passes over, he will make a complete end of its (the earth [Nah 1:5]) place."

[60] Joel 2:1 uses the verbal form of the root רוע, while Zeph 1:16 uses the nominal form, most likely due to the short poetic style of Zeph 1:14-16.

[61] Cf e.g. Joel 2:3,20; Mic 1:7; 3:12; 7:13; Hab 3:16. Additionally, one significant passage outside the Book of the Twelve may conceivably have influenced the formulation since its importance has already been noted in the formulation of Mic 7:8ff. This passage (Isa 10:3) refers to the day of punishment when the desolation (שׁואה) will occur, approaching the formulation of the day of desolation (also שׁואה) in Zeph 1:15.

does it also portray a more limited scope for the judgment? If the latter, does the dichotomy exist inherently, or is it also (as in Nahum and Habakkuk) implanted into more homogenous literary material?

Methodologically, one must first exclude the quotes and allusions from Joel and Nahum and then ask two questions: 1) Do the remaining lines form a coherent piece of literature (grammatically and linguistically)?; and 2) Does this remaining material present a different theological interest than the final form of the unit?

When the quotes and allusions are removed, the remaining material does indeed leave a coherent whole:

> Near is the great day of YHWH,
> Near and very quickly speeding.
> The sound of the day of YHWH is bitter.
> The one roaring is a warrior,
> Against the fortified cities,
> And against the high towers.
> And I will cause violence to man,
> And they will walk like the blind
> For they sinned against YHWH.
> And their blood will be poured out like dust,
> And their bowels like dung.
> Neither their silver nor their gold will be able to deliver them on the day of
> the fury of YHWH.

Some might object to this argumentation by saying that the poetic language is too imprecise to postulate such an insertion convincingly. Against this objection one must note that this technique of small redactional insertions into an existing entity has been noted elsewhere in the Book of the Twelve, where the technique is more clearly demonstrable.[62] More importantly, the acceptance of a redactional insertion in this verse greatly alleviates one of the most perplexing problems of 1:14-18, namely the enigmatic reference to the shouting of the warrior in 1:14. In its current form the warrior line dangles noticeably, lacking an inherent connection to either that which precedes or to that which follows. This dangling line has been the subject of numerous suggestions for emendation.[63] By contrast, the removal of

---

[62] See especially the text inserted between the א and ב lines of the acrostic poem in Nah 1:2b-3a. This evidence best illustrates the arguments against Ben Zvi, *BZAW* 198, who claims that the post-exilic form of Zephaniah reflects a single compositional layer.

[63] See partial lists and suggestions in Rudolph, *KAT* 13/3, 265; Elliger, *ATD* 25, 56; Seybold, *Satirische Prophetie*, 110; Keller, *CAT* 11b, 194; Krinetzki, *Zefanjastudien*, 255.

the quotes and allusions in the six balanced יום sayings leaves a line which makes good sense grammatically and contextually.   The warrior roaring against the fortified cities and the high corners of Jerusalem fits the context of the day of YHWH in the more limited judgment section of the chapter. Grammatically, if one assumes 1:15-16a are insertions, צרח (to cry, to roar) with the preposition על (1:14+16b) is considerably more understandable than either the combination of צרח with יום at one end (1:14,15), or with יום and על at the other end (1:16a,b) of the unit in its current state.[64]

The suspension of the Nahum allusions in 1:18ab,b creates no disturbance to the text, and, although less dramatically than with the day sayings, actually improves the coherency to the following section when it is removed.   The Nahum allusions represent a self-contained unit.   Even though they begin with a connecting ו, they form a single sentence which emphasizes the universality of judgment: "And in the fire of his jealousy all the earth will be devoured for he will make an end, indeed a terrible one, to all the inhabitants of the earth."   By contrast, its removal leaves a coherent unit more readily explainable as a transition from judgment pronouncements against Jerusalem to judgment against Judah: "Neither their silver nor their gold will be able to deliver them on the day of the fury of YHWH.   Gather yourselves, yes gather, o *nation* without shame..."[65] Note that the judgment of 2:1 does not presuppose a universal judgment, but like 1:4-13 has a much more limited scope, the nation of YHWH's people.   This transition is readily understandable in light of Zeph 1:4: "And I will stretch out my hand against Judah and against all the inhabitants of Jerusalem."

---

[64] The verb צרח only appears twice in the Old Testament so it is not surprising that there are no other examples of the verb with על. However the synonym שאג (to roar) does appear frequently enough with this preposition with the meaning "to roar against." See for example Jer 2:15 and especially 25:30, which offers almost precisely the same image as in Zeph 1:14,16b. Jer 25:30 depicts YHWH as a warrior who roars (שאג) against (על) his flock. Note also Krinetzki, *Zefanjastudien*, 255.

[65] The use of the plural "their" relates back to "man" in 1:17, but this antecedent is not enough to postulate a universal judgment. Rather, it still refers to man in the context of Judah and Jerusalem. Note that Zeph 1:12, which is unequivocally related to the "men" of Jerusalem, also uses a collective (האנשים) when describing the recipients of judgment. The expansion to אדם in 1:17 may be plausibly explained as part of the transition to pronouncements against Judah in 2:1-3. Elsewhere, אדם can be used to distinguish a group without implying the entire world: for example, in Josh 11:14, Israel kills את־כל־האדם ("every man"), while the context makes abundantly clear that only the enemy coalition is intended (11:1-13).

In summary, the judgment section of Zeph 1:2-2:3 existed in literary form prior to the incorporation the universal judgment motif on the "day of YHWH." In the earlier literary layer, the day of YHWH motif was demonstrably present (1:8,10,14; 2:1), but this layer perceived the day of YHWH as judgment against Jerusalem and Judah for cultic, social, and religious abominations, and for the refusal to heed the word of YHWH. A second layer (1:2f,15-16a,18ab,b) expanded the scope of the day of YHWH to cover the entire world. This expansion deliberately creates a dichotomy which appears for the third time in the Book of the Twelve, namely the patterned announcement of judgment against a specific group within the literary frame of universal judgment (Nahum 1; Habakkuk 3; Zephaniah 1). All three cases provide indications that the juxtaposition of these two poles was created redactionally. All three passages contain literary reflections back to Joel, indicating that they are utilizing that work paradigmatically to structure YHWH's prophetic message within a historical frame while at the same time de-emphasizing historical events as such. The universal judgment in this context intentionally documents YHWH's design and control over all events and nations.

5. The Function of the Habakkuk - Zephaniah Connection

To this point, it has been argued that Zeph 1:1-2:3 manifests two distinct views of judgment which have grown together as the result of the literary implantation of a universal judgment motif into a pre-existing corpus. Further, the earlier Zephaniah corpus likely concluded the Deuteronomistic prophetic corpus containing Hosea, Amos, Micah, and Zephaniah. It has been further demonstrated that the universal judgment material contains the catchwords to Hab 3:2ff (as well as quotes and allusions to other portions of the Book of the Twelve). These observations allow the deduction that the implantation of universal judgment and the majority of catchwords to Habakkuk entered the Zephaniah corpus simultaneously as a part of the growth of the Book of the Twelve.

Several observations should be drawn together in order to support this last statement that redactional work on Zeph 1:1-2:3 was aware of its larger literary context in the Book of the Twelve. The words which recur between Habakkuk and Zephaniah fall primarily in the later section. The universally oriented judgment contains sayings which clearly bear a literary relationship to Joel (1:15) and to Nahum (1:18ab,b). The combination of a universal judgment exhibiting cosmic dimensions (especially 1:2f) with a judgment more narrowly focussed on historically significant entities corresponds to a pattern recurring across several writings in the Book of the Twelve. Joel plays a dominant role as the foundation of this imagery, while Nahum, Habakkuk, and Zephaniah have all have been reworked to conform to this dichotomy of judgment. It is this three-fold succession of writings which allows one to determine the literary function of the connection between Habakkuk and Zephaniah.

Nahum and Habakkuk place the destruction of Assyrian and Babylonian political power under the mighty acts of YHWH.[66] YHWH selected Assyria to punish a recalcitrant people and then instigated the destruction of Nineveh (Nahum) when Assyria overstepped its commission. In Habakkuk, YHWH chooses Babylon as the means to punish the wicked nation, but the same book incorporates a theophany as a promise that YHWH would also destroy Babylon, because their ferocity knew no bounds. In a redactional insertion, Hab 3:16b provides the clearest evidence of the transition to Zephaniah, when it accepts both the future judgment against Judah and YHWH's promise that Babylon would also be overthrown: "I wait quietly for the day of trouble, for the people to rise up who will attack us." This verse makes it clear that Judah will not escape punishment at the hands of the Babylonians. Precisely this thought creates the link between Habakkuk and Zephaniah.

Zephaniah functions as the depiction of the Babylonian destruction of Jerusalem presumed in Hab 3:16b. Zephaniah already played this role in the Deuteronomistic corpus, but now the portrayal of the events of Jerusalem's destruction are reshaped to conform them to the pattern of YHWH's universal control of the events of history.[67] Nahum and Habakkuk were conformed to this universal pattern through the incorporation of pre-existing theophanic hymns into new contexts, but Zephaniah draws upon a different tradition to drive home the same point even more forcefully. The reversal of the creation motif combined with the allusions to the flood story in Zeph 1:2f serve as poignant allusions adding a universal dimension to Jerusalem's destruction, in much the same manner as the theophanic material in Nahum and Habakkuk added this dimension to the destruction of Assyria and Babylon. These verses tell the reader how to understand the destruction which follows. By drawing specifically upon

---

[66] For a discussion of the redactional means by which this correlation is accomplished see chapters on Nahum and Habakkuk in my forthcoming volume, *Redactional Processes in the Book of the Twelve*.

[67] See the excursus on the Deuteronomistic Corpus and Zephaniah above, page 176.

these traditions, the redactor has brought the universal judgment to a crescendo. The theophanic warning to Jerusalem which began with Mic 1:2ff, the theophanic hymn which culminated in Nineveh's downfall, and the theophanic promise of Babylon's ultimate demise, form an extensive thread which culminates in a judgment against Judah and Jerusalem. It deliberately portrays that judgment as the complete and utter reversal of creation. Rather than another theophany in the manner of Mic 1:2ff; Nah 1:2-8; or Hab 3:1-19, the allusions to the creation and flood accounts are specifically selected for their emotional impact.

The depiction of the destruction of Jerusalem and Judah which follows appears in its proper chronological sequence in the ordering and literary movement of the Book of the Twelve. The conclusion of Zephaniah (3:9ff) already presumes the destruction of Jerusalem is in the past, and it looks forward to the return of the exiles to Jerusalem. The end of Zephaniah has been shaped to lead into Haggai and the restoration of the temple.[68] Haggai, Zechariah, and Malachi all presume the destruction of Jerusalem lies in the past.

One final note regarding the function of Zephaniah in the Book of the Twelve requires comment. The function of Zephaniah as the transition from a pre-exilic literary scope to a post-exilic perspective adds further weight to the argument of a common transmission circle for Isaiah and Zephaniah. As Bosshard demonstrates, Zephaniah and Isaiah share a great deal of vocabulary. The common vocabulary centers around Isa 34 and 35 in Isaiah and in Zephaniah centers around the expansion of the Assyrian oracle in 2:14f and the promissory section of 3:9ff.[69] These chapters in Isaiah function very similarly to Zephaniah in the Book of the Twelve, namely as a literary precursor to the return of the exiles.[70]

---

[68] See the following section of this chapter.

[69] Bosshard, *BN* 40 (1987): 34f and 51.

[70] See Odil Hannes Steck, *Bereitete Heimkehr. Jesaja 35 als redaktionelle Brücke zwischen dem Ersten und dem Zweiten Jesaja*, Stuttgarter Bibelstudien 121 (Stuttgart: Katholisches Bibelwerk, 1985).

6. The Literary Units and Context of Zeph 3:18-20

The literary units in Zeph 3:18-20 presuppose YHWH as speaker, but may be separated according to their perspective toward Zion:

3:18a*	YHWH speech of deliverance addressed to Zion (2fs) about her sufferers[71]
3:18b	Parenthetical explanation of Zion's (3fs) sufferers
3:19a	YHWH notes his action against Zion's (2fs) oppressors
3:19b	YHWH describes his action toward the lame and the outcast
3:20	YHWH promises restoration to the people (2mp)

Clearly, 3:18a*,19a relate integrally since YHWH speaks and addresses a devastated Zion regarding the sufferers and the oppressors. Zeph 3:19b is closely linked with 3:19a, and should be regarded as part of the same speech in spite of the fact there is no direct reference to Zion. The enigmatic sentence in 3:18b ("they were a burden upon her, a reproach") has a different perspective since it treats Zion in the third person, and is not a therefore direct address. The fact that the sentence seeks to explain the נוּגֵי mentioned in 3:18a along with the different Zion perspective, points to 3:18b as a later insertion. The term gloss, however, should be avoided in light of the very pregnant words which it deliberately chooses as indicators to other passages in the Book of the Twelve.[72] Zeph 3:20 repeats the content of 3:19b, but the verse addresses the people (2mp) and not Zion. The relationship of these verses is somewhat complex, and requiring a discussion of their position in Zephaniah, their intentional connective function to the Book of Haggai, and the position of these verses within the overall movement of the Book of the Twelve.

When one compares Zeph 3:18-20 to its immediate context, an interesting picture develops.[73] Zeph 3:18-20 comes at the end of the positive, eschatological section of promise which begins in 3:9, a section normally considered a post-exilic addition to the Book of Zephaniah.[74]

---

[71] The last word before the athnah (הָיוּ) is read with 3:18b. See text notes a-d with the translation of Zeph 3:18 in the chapter entitled "The Catchword Phenomenon."

[72] More on the function of this sentence below, note 101.

[73] The macrostructure of the book of Zephaniah was described in the previous chapter.

[74] A selection of those considering significant portions of 3:9-20 as *post-exilic*: Wellhausen, *Die kleinen Propheten*, 154; Karl Marti, *HCAT* 13, 358; George Adam Smith, *The Book of the Twelve Prophets*, vol. 2, 39; W. Nowack, *Die kleinen Propheten*, 305; Gerleman, *Zephanja*, 66; Elliger, *ATD* 25/2, 77; Eissfeldt, *Introduction*, 424; Rudolph, *KAT* 14/3, 256; Guy Langohr, "Rédaction et composition du livre de Sophonie," *Muséon* 89 (1976),

In this positive section, **3:9f** asserts that the utterly destructive judgment on the nations proclaimed in 3:8, is indeed not total, but a *judgment of purification*, in which the YHWH worshippers in the nations beyond the rivers of Ethiopia will bring offerings to him.[75] This positive qualification of judgment on the nations introduces a new redactional unit which continues at least as far as 3:17. Zeph **3:11-13** presents an address by YHWH to Jerusalem (2fs) concerning a *purification of Zion* in which a clear train of thought appears: YHWH says I will remove the haughty (3:11), but

---

63; Guy Langohr, "Le Livre de Sophonie et la Critique d'Authenticité." *Ephemerides Theologicae Lovanienses* 52 (1976), 24ff; Krinetzki, *Zefanjastudien*, 161-174; Donald E. Gowan, *Eschatology in the Old Testament*. Philadelphia: Fortress Press, 1986; Maria Eszenyei Szeles, *Wrath and Mercy: Habakkuk and Zephaniah*. ITC (Grand Rapids: Eerdmans, 1987), 65. Only a few authors have maintained this material is *pre-exilic*: Hitzig, *Die zwölf kleinen Propheten*, 298; Junker, *Die Zwölf kleinen Propheten*. Vol. 2, 67; Watts, *Joel, etc.*, 155. Two consider *only 3:20* as a later addition: Keller, *CAT* 11b, 216; and Kapelrud, *The Message of the Prophet Zephaniah*, 40. See also Ben Zvi, *BZAW* 198, 219-261, who argues the entire book of Zephaniah is a post-exilic creation.

75 Important here is the understanding of the phrases "my worshippers, daughter of my dispersed ones" and "beyond the rivers of Cush" (Ethiopia) in 3:10. The phrases are unusual, and often cause confusion as to the identity of the group. For summary of the problem, see Rudolph, *KAT* 13/3, 292 (textual), 295. Rudolph's own solution of deleting "daughter of my dispersed ones" as the insertion of a Judean particularist begs the issue. Already Gerleman, *Zephanja*, 66, clearly demonstrates the validity of MT. From the immediate context of 3:9f one would expect a portion of foreign peoples are intended, because 3:8b speaks of a judgment of fire on the nations which *could* render the purification of 3:9 meaningful. However, confusion remains because the phrase "daughter of my dispersed ones" in 3:10 likely serves as a reference to the diaspora, that is the scattered of YHWH, who are in Egypt (cf the phrase beyond the rivers of Cush in the oracle against Egypt in Isa 18:1). Other parallels likewise open themselves to multiple interpretations, such as the reference to the YHWH worshippers among the distant nations (cf. parallels Isa 19:22; Ezek 29:12ff). Watts, *Joel, etc.*, 179, draws on vocabularic parallels to the tower of Babel account in Gen 11, and argues that the purification of the lips of peoples stems from interaction with this passage. Despite the confusion, the wider context of 3:18-20 provides evidence that these worshippers understood those scattered in their more common usage as a reference to the scattered people of YHWH (cf. Deut 4:27; 28:64ff; 30:3; Jer 30:11; etc). These verses provide evidence that an early layer of 3:18f* concluded the book with a similar reference to the return of the diaspora Jews. Given the fact that 3:14-17 exhibit a tight structural and thematic chiasmus, the reference to the diaspora on either side of these verses makes sense as a deliberate framing device. The images of 3:9b,10 come very close to those of Isa 60:3f. At any rate, Zeph 3:8b represents the latest element at the beginning of this unit. It alludes to Nah 1:2ff and Joel 4:1ff.

leave a humble remnant (3:12), and they will not do wrong (3:13). The action of these verses parallels the purification of the nations in 3:9f.[76]

Zeph **3:14-17** functions as a prophetic response to the divine pronouncements in 3:9f; 11-13.[77] Zeph 3:14-17 is a structurally self-contained unit based on its inner thematic chiasm and the prophetic speaker. The parallelism of this unit is seen in the following:

> A   Rejoice, Zion, YHWH has withdrawn his judgment (14-15a)
>   B   King YHWH is in your midst (15ba)
>   C   Do not fear, Zion (15bb)
>   C' Do not fear, will be said of Zion (16)
>   B' Warrior YHWH is in your midst (17a)
> A' YHWH will rejoice over you Zion (17b)

In addition to the structural unity, the prophet responds to the pronouncements of YHWH in the previous verses, which reverse the judgment of the remainder of the book of Zephaniah.[78] Thus, the pronounced reversal of judgment on Zion with its corresponding removal of the enemy, brings the prophetic response to Zion to celebrate the removal of the judgment as proclaimed in 3:9f,11-13.

---

[76] The parallel nature of the two units 3:9f and 11-13 may be noted in that both the nations and the remnant will be a people (3:9,12) of pure speech (3:9,13) who find their orientation in the name of YHWH (3:9,12). In addition, although the word "remnant" is not used, the contents of 3:9-11 demonstrate the remnant motif in that not all the nations, but only those worshipping YHWH will be involved in the salvific act.

[77] The response nature of these verses help explain their use of the royal psalm motifs long noted by Elliger, *ATD* 25, 77 and others. Krinetzki, *Zefanjastudien*, 157-66, demonstrates the remarkable variety of motifs in these verses dependent upon other traditions, however, not only on the psalms, but the holy war tradition, and Isaiah. The total evidence indicates a late date for these verses. Krinetzki is correct in asserting that they assume the Persian period has come, but does not go far enough. On the basis of this material and other Isaiah parallels in chapter three (see Bosshard, *BN* 40 (1987): 34f; and their relationship to Isaianic redactions, 56ff) to Isaiah 18,19,34,35 etc., one may safely assume a goodly portion of Isaiah already existed, meaning one must go well into the Persian period.

[78] One must bear in mind that 3:14-17 functions as a *response* to 3:9f,11-13, prior to the addition of 3:8b. Within this context, *structural unity* of 3:14-17 carries considerable significance. In 3:16, ביום ההוא does not introduce a new independent unit (Contra Rudolph, *KAT* 13/3, 298; and others), but it functions as a thematic divider, as in 3:11. The phrase in Zeph 3:11 separates the section on the worshippers in distant nations (3:9f) from that section which treats the remnant of Zion (3:11-13). ביום ההוא in 3:16 changes the perspective from the removal of the enemies (3:15) to YHWH's rejoicing over Zion (3:17).

The primary concern of the following discussion focusses on the relationship of Zeph **3:18-20** to the immediate context in order to evaluate the significance of the catchwords to Haggai 1:2ff. The preceding discussion illustrates clearly that a new unit begins in 3:18 with the change of speaker from the prophet to YHWH in the divine first person. Zeph 3:14-17 exhibits a strong sense of closure with its carefully constructed structure, its consistent prophetic speaker, and the parallels to elements in 3:9f,11-13. Zeph 3:18 begins something new. YHWH speaks again, but what does he say, and why does he say it? This question cannot be satisfactorily answered without a discussion on the identity of the groups involved and a treatment of the literary horizon of Zeph 3:18-20.

7. The Literary Horizon of Zeph 3:18-20

It is important to begin by stating that the literary horizon of Zeph 3:18-20 *presupposes* but is *not restricted* to its position in Zephaniah. In order to document this assertion it is necessary, first of all, to consider the identity of the groups involved in Zeph 3:18-20.

7.1. Identity of the Groups

3:18-20 mentions four groups in YHWH's address to Zion: those suffering without feasts, the oppressors of Zion, the lame, and the outcast. The identity of the first group requires a glance at the context of Zeph 3 in order to conceptualize who is intended and where they are located. First and foremost, one must acknowledge this reference to "those suffering without appointed feasts" appears within a positive statement.[79] "Those suffering without appointed feasts" is a phrase generally interpreted, when it is not emended, as a reference to the people of the diaspora who cannot worship in Jerusalem.[80] However, an interpretation more in keeping with

---

[79] The eschatological promises to Zion in 3:14ff allow the supposition that this statement is a positive statement. This recognition means one should not translate אסף with "remove, destroy" as in Zeph 1:2,3. The meaning here is "to gather". Note also אסף is parallel to קבץ. This understanding agrees with Rudolph, *KAT* 13/3, 299; contra, Sabottka, *Zephanja* (Rome: Biblical Institute Press, 1972), 135; and Krinetzki, *Zefanjastudien*, 23, 262. See also Ben Zvi, *BZAW* 198, 324.

[80] See Rudolph, 293f (textual), 298f.

the context recognizes that since YHWH is speaking from Jerusalem (3:15,17), the promise concerns the inhabitants of Jerusalem itself, not the diaspora Jews. Since YHWH is speaking from Jerusalem, if the diaspora Jews were intended it would not be said that they were gathered from the midst of Zion (מִמֵּךְ), rather they would be sent, requiring another verb, such as שׁלח. The image presented is one in which these inhabitants are wandering rather aimlessly with no one to gather them together for cultic celebrations. Such images appear elsewhere in the Old Testament.[81] The promise seeks to rectify this situation. YHWH promises Zion he will gather those who are suffering under these deplorable conditions, a promise which is realized very shortly with the description of the construction of the temple at the instigation of Haggai.[82]

The second group, those oppressing Zion, must be analyzed from the perspective of the book of Zephaniah, the perspective of the Deuteronomistic corpus, and the Book of the Twelve to determine its identity. In the Zephaniah context, the root ענה appears only one other time, in 2:3, but there the phrase כל־עֲנֵוי הארץ (all the humble of the earth) is used positively, not negatively for oppression as in 3:19. Conceivably, the identity of the oppressors in Zephaniah could be isolated by finding the concept expressed using another image besides ענה. A case might perhaps be made for several outside groups perpetrating affliction in Zephaniah, but none of these groups are said to directly afflict Zion.[83] The possibility cannot be ruled out completely that an inner-Judean affliction is intended, but the phraseology, which implies current existence of this oppression, as well as the context of 3:8-17 imply the affliction is a

---

[81] See Neh 1:2f and especially Lam 1:4: "The roads to Zion are mourning, for no one comes to the appointed feasts; all her gates are desolate, her priests are groaning; her virgins are afflicted; and she herself suffers bitterly."

[82] See below, beginning page 212. In light of this argumentation, it is impossible to accept the argument of Schneider, *The Unity of the Book of the Twelve*, 56, when he claims that nothing speaks of the fall of Jerusalem in Nahum, Habakkuk, or Zephaniah or his conclusion that Zephaniah (together with Nahum and Habakkuk) were composed prior to the destruction of Jerusalem. This argument from silence fails to understand the *literary nature* of the movement within the Book of the Twelve. The fact that there is no vivid description of the actual fall of Jerusalem within the Book of the Twelve is paralleled in Isaiah, and is very understandable in light of the feeling of shame and disgrace which the desolation of Jerusalem engendered.

[83] The Moabites in 2:8ff are punished because they taunted the people of YHWH; the Ethiopians are singled out in 2:12 for destruction by YHWH, however, no particular reason is given; Assyria is mentioned in 2:13ff, but her guilt appears to be her pride, not a specific affliction of Zion.

condition imposed upon Zion from outside.[84] One is forced to admit the identity of the group oppressing Zion is very difficult to determine merely from a reading of Zephaniah as an isolated book.

Two options remain open for determining the identity of the oppressors: the assignation of the verses as the non-specific reflection of an anonymous glossator, or the recognition of the connective function of these verses within the Book of the Twelve. The first option considers Zeph 3:18ff merely as a "later addition" from an undetermined time, from which it is impossible to determine the identity of those oppressing Zion.[85] However, while it would indeed be difficult to deny this passage represents a later perspective, it is particularly unsatisfactory to assign these oppressors no specific intended identity in the mind of the author. Any attempt to understand their identity, however, must look beyond Zephaniah, to the literary movement within the Book of the Twelve.

Identifying the identity of the oppressors in terms of the development within the Book of the Twelve, requires that one observe the important function of Zephaniah as the *turning point from pre-exilic to post-exilic situations*. The superscription of Zeph 1:1 is the last one in the Book of the Twelve which contains a pre-exilic date.[86] The three chapters of Zephaniah contain a description of destruction of unparalleled proportions against Jerusalem and several nations, which function as the literary foreshadowing of the Babylonian destruction.[87] Haggai, the next book, begins with a situation in which the exiles have returned from Babylon, but

---

[84] One could translate "all those afflicting you", and argue the specific groups mentioned in chapter 1 are intended: inhabitants of Jerusalem (1:4); idolatrous priests (1:4); idolatrous worshippers (1:5f); the royal family (1:8); essentially the same groups are mentioned again in 3:1-7. The advantage of understanding these groups within Jerusalem as those causing affliction upon Zion would be that as inhabitants of the city, the image of direct effect upon Zion would be more understandable. However, a significant stumbling block remains to such an understanding, namely those groups supposedly have received their punishment already, and YHWH, as presented in 3:14ff, is in the process of restoration. That is to say, such an understanding would fit the category of affliction, but not the context since the immediate future treatment described in 3:19 assumes this group is still oppressing Zion.

[85] For example, Rudolph, *KAT* 14/3, 299, offers no explanation of who is intended by the oppressors, and Kapelrud, *Zephaniah*, 40, with his insistence upon the passage as part of a cult festival, needs no identity of the oppressors.

[86] Hag 1:1 and Zech 1:1 delineate the time of the Persian king Darius, while Malachi and Deutero-Zechariah have no dated superscription.

[87] Cf the pronouncement of coming oppression as described in the previous discussion of Mic 7:12.

Jerusalem and the temple remain in desolate circumstances. When this literary perspective is considered, one immediately assumes the Babylonians could here be intended as the those oppressing Zion, however, other considerations indicate the field of vision is larger than that. First, one must reckon with the fact that the oppressors mentioned in Zephaniah are referred to as "*all* your oppressors" or "*all* those oppressing you". The use of כל here indicates more than one oppressor is intended. This supposition is confirmed if one considers the use of ענה in Nah 1:12 as an important marker. In the midst of a denunciation of Assyria, Nah 1:12 suddenly promises Zion (2fs) an end to the affliction:

> Thus says the Lord: Though they (the Assyrians) be strong and many, they will be cut off and pass away. Though I afflict you (2fs) I will afflict you (2fs) no more.

This verse promises the removal of Assyrian oppression, and the disavowal of Assyria as a means of punishment. The literary movement of the Book of the Twelve extends the judgment against Jerusalem and Judah by incorporating Babylon as an even greater instrument of punishment, despite the destruction of Assyria.[88]   Equally pertinent for understanding the identity of the oppressors, Zeph 3:19 draws from Isa 60:14:[89]

> And the sons of those who afflicted you (מעניך) will come bowing to you, and all those who despised you will bow themselves at the soles of your feet. And they will call you the city of YHWH, Zion, the Holy One of Israel.

One begins to get the feel of the reflective character of the connective texts. These texts are dealing with the periodization of historical enemies, a painting of history in broad strokes.[90] In the context of the Book of the Twelve, those oppressing Zion refers to those enemies, beginning with Assyrian domination and going through the Babylonians and the surrounding peoples who took advantage of Jerusalem's devastated state.[91]

---

[88]   See my treatment of Nahum and Habakkuk in the forthcoming volume, *Redactional Processes within the Book of the Twelve*.

[89]   It is significant that Zeph 3:19 and Nah 1:12b express similar attitudes, but they draw their primary images from different Isaiah passages.

[90]   This broad stroke imagery might help explain the lack of a dominant role for Egypt in the Book of the Twelve as a major enemy between the Assyrians and the Babylonians. It might also account for the mention of Egypt almost as an afterthought in places such as Joel 4:19.

[91]   Thus, one could certainly include Obadiah's denunciation of Edom for their part in Jerusalem's destruction (vv. 11-14); the citation of Tyre, Sidon, and all the regions of

Yet this recollection of oppression, although it *coincides* well with the Book of the Twelve, should probably not be placed in that realm, when one speaks of its origin. This references serves the same function of identifying the identity of this group from the perspective of the Deuteronomistic corpus. The reference to the "desolation" of the land in the address to Zion in Mic 7:11-13 already predicted the *arrival* of a multitude of oppressors over an extended time period. By drawing upon the imagery of Isa 60, Zeph 3:19 reverses the punishment announced in Mic 7:11-13, thereby bringing this motif to its resolution.[92] The explicit quote of Mic 4:6f in Zeph 3:19, because of its expansion in 3:20, more logically corresponds to the context of the Deuteronomistic corpus.

Close evaluation of the salient features of Zeph 3:18ff have identified the first two groups as those in Jerusalem suffering for want of appointed festivals, and all those enemies who have contributed to the devastation of Jerusalem. It is not surprising, in light of the identity of the first two groups mentioned in Zeph 3:18ff, that the identity of the last two groups also plays a role in the transition from pre-exilic to post-exilic concerns. Specifically, the lame and the outcast mentioned in 3:19 (citing Mic 4:6f) refer to two distinct groups, to the inhabitants of a devastated Jerusalem and the diaspora Jews who had been deported or fled from Jerusalem as a result of its destruction. The identity of the lame necessarily presupposes the following discussion of the relationship of Zeph 3:18ff to Mic 4:6f, where it is demonstrated that the lame and those suffering without appointed feast are one and the same group.[93] In addition to the detailed comparison to Mic 4:6f, a glance at Mic 4:10 also provides significant insight. Mic 4:6f refers to YHWH's people in two groups, the lame and the outcast. Mic 4:10 reiterates that a devastated Jerusalem will be divided into two groups, those who dwell in the field and those taken to Babylon. The lame and the outcast in Zephaniah keep this double grouping, but from an expanded perspective. The lame, those living in the Jerusalem surroundings, now includes those who have returned from Babylon.

Philistia (Joel 4:4) as well as the specific references to Egypt and Edom in Joel 4:19.

[92] See particularly the previous discussion of Mic 7:13, where it is argued that ארץ used with desolation should not be read in a universal sense to mean "earth" in its original formulation, even though the incorporation of Nah 1:2ff later understood it that way.

[93] For a more thorough explanation of the equation of these two groups, see discussion of the parallel with Mic 4:6f below (page 209). For a discussion of their specific identity as those living in the surroundings of Jerusalem, see discussion of the sufferers above page 204.

The identity of *the outcast as the Jews scattered as the result of the Babylonian crisis* draws upon imagery found elsewhere in Old Testament passages such as Deut 30:4; Isa 27:13; Jer 30:17; 40:12; 43:5; Ezek 34:4,16. The specific meanings range from theological predictions (Deut 30:4) to particular situations of fleeing from the upheaval caused by Babylon (Jer 40:12). While in the Micah context the term appears to presume those taken to Babylon (Mic 4:10), elsewhere the term outcast includes more than just those taken to Babylon. It also includes those who fled toward Egypt (Jer 43:5-7), and likely those taken captive when fleeing the destruction of Jerusalem.[94] The perspective of Zeph 3:18ff is broader, and reflects a time when the deportees had returned. It is clear from these examples, however, that the outcast is very close to a *terminus technicus* for the dispersed Jews. The subtlety of this shift requires evaluation.

7.2. Backward to Micah

Zeph 3:18-20 serves several *functions*: an interpretation within Zephaniah, an introduction to the book of Haggai, and a connective link to other passages within the book of the Twelve, most notably to the Deuteronomistic corpus. Zeph 3:19 quotes Mic 4:6-7 necessitating a comparison of the two passages to determine the function of the quote in understanding the content of Zeph 3:18-20.[95] Such a comparison, provided here, offers several significant insights, which are essential to understanding the current form and function of Zeph 3:18-20.

---

[94] Compare Obad 11-14, even though the word is not used.

[95] The dependence of Zephaniah upon Micah is assumed because of the significance of the changes when viewed from that perspective. These argument present no real problems with dates scholarship gives to the Micah passage. See, for example, Mays, *Micah*, 24-27.

Zeph 3:18-20   Mic 4:6-7

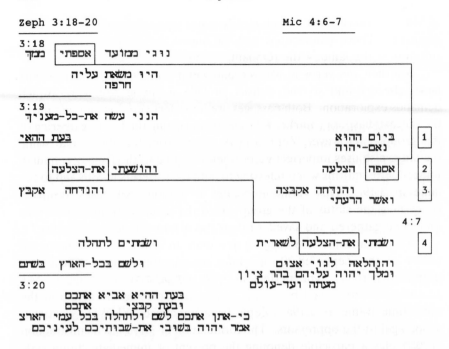

Several observations deserve attention. **Marker #1** signals a significant change from ביום ההוא to בעת ההיא, and while the meaning does not change significantly, it is clear that the phrase in Zeph 3:19 (along with 3:20) already has Hag 1:2,4 in view where עת also appears three times.[96] More will be said concerning this change in discussing the relationship to Haggai.[97]

Marker #2 leads in several directions. First, while the subject of both passages is the lame, the verb אסף (to gather) is used in Micah while Zephaniah uses the verb ישע (to deliver). Significantly, however, אסף appears in Zeph 3:18 with the subject "those suffering without appointed feast." This denotes an important correlation in the redactional work in 3:19, namely, it provides a logical connection for understanding the identity of the groups which can be summed up with the statement: *the lame are identical to those suffering without feast.* Another observation can be made

---

96 Already Nowack, *Die Kleinen Propheten*, 306, suggests the possibility on metrical grounds that the phrase בעת ההיא has been added on the basis of 3:20, but he does not specifically relate it to the parallel in Mic 4:6. The fact that the parallel has ההוא ביום makes the metrical argument highly suspect. Nevertheless, Nowack correctly notes the relationship of the phrase to 3:20.

97 See discussion of the relationship to Haggai, below page 212.

in Mic 4:7 (**marker #4**) which clearly states that the lame will become a remnant. These connections may be stated in formulaic fashion: the sufferers = the lame = the remnant.

Further, the verbs in Mic 4:6 and Zeph 3:18,19 which relate to the lame/sufferers and to the outcast provide a subtle distinction which demands exploration. Both passages use imperfect verbs when referring to the outcast/diaspora (**marker #3**), clearly indicating the future gathering of this group.[98] However, Zeph 3:18,19 differs from Mic 4:6 in that while the latter also uses imperfect verbs when referring to the lame, Zephaniah utilizes perfect forms when referring to both the sufferers in 3:18 and to the lame in 3:19. This variation creates a tension, not easily resolved, concerning the status of the group called the lame in Zephaniah. Have they been gathered and saved, or does this action still lie in the future?

Grammatically, 3:18 begins a new unit. In light of the eschatological nature of the Zeph 3:8-20, one must assume the perfect אספתי is a prophetic perfect. The perfect in 3:19b (והושעתי), according to MT accenting, is introduced by a waw consecutive, placing the action in the same time frame as 3:19a. Zeph 3:19a announces YHWH's *imminent* action against the oppressors. The formulation of 3:19a has a construction of הנני plus a participle denoting the present or immediate future (GK §116p). Thus, grammatically, the perfect verbs denoting the action of YHWH toward the sufferers/lame presumes they will be delivered in the *near future*, with the nearness being accented by the certainty of the prophetic perfect in 3:18 and הנני plus the participle in 3:19a. In Mic 4, the fate of the outcast does not receive this special emphasis. The effect of this variation on the texts implies a nearness of deliverance for the remnant/lame, but a more distant promise for the return of the outcast.

The literary horizon of Zeph 3:18-20 thus points backward in the Book of the Twelve, to recall the prophecy of deliverance in Micah, with its repetition here formulated to emphasize the nearness of the fulfillment for one of the groups, the deliverance of the lame/sufferers, i.e. the inhabitants of Jerusalem. The continuing significance of these observations in the larger corpus becomes clear when one investigates 3:18-20 in light of its forward reference point, the beginning of the book of Haggai.

---

[98] The forms very slightly even though the roots are the same. Both אקבץ in Zeph 3:19 and אקבצה are first person imperfect forms.

7.3. Forward to Haggai

In order to appreciate fully the connection between Haggai and Zephaniah, one must recognize its position within the overall movement of the Book of the Twelve. A short description has already been given above as to how the setting portrayed by these verses function as the conclusion to the Deuteronomistic corpus. Several allusions implied that this conclusion had been subsumed and adapted in a manner which artistically sets the scene for the book of Haggai, in which the exiles have returned from Babylon, but have yet begun to build the temple.[99]

In addition to the literary setting of the scene, the connection between Zephaniah and Haggai is brought into consciousness through the use of the *Stichwörter* "bring", "time", and "people(s)" in 3:20, as indicated by the translation of this passage in chapter two. The process by which these verses lead from Zephaniah to Haggai must be investigated from the perspective of the compilation of 3:18-20 and from the perspective of the content of these verses.

At the beginning of this discussion, reference was made to the different perspectives running through these verses. Zeph 3:18a*,19 specifically address Zion, but Zeph 3:18b speaks *about* her in 3fs. YHWH speaks to Zion (2fs) in Zeph 3:18-19; but to the people (2mp) in Zeph 3:20.[100] How does one account for such variation? The most likely explanation is that the passage has grown from more than one layer of material. From this beginning assumption, it is possible to look first at that material which addresses Zion in 2fs. This layer consists of 3:18a*,19. This 2fs layer fits the context of Zeph 3:11-17 in which Zion is addressed, and in which she has been promised an end to the judgment under which she suffered. The following summarizes the main components of this judgment when read from the Zephaniah context: a haughty enemy (3:11,15) ruled over Zion causing shame (3:11) to Zion, but YHWH promises to establish a humble and pious remnant (3:12f). It is for this promise from YHWH that the prophet tells Zion to rejoice (3:14-17).

The 2fs layer in 3:18a*,19 reformulates the elements of the promise, from a slightly different perspective. The enemies appear again. YHWH prepares to deal with them for the oppression they afflicted upon Zion (3:19). The element of shame appears again (3:19), this time from the

---

[99] Note particularly the mention of the change in Zeph 3:19 from "in that day" to "in that time." See page 210.

[100] See above, page 201.

perspective of the reversal of the shameful circumstances of the lame and the outcast.[101] The remnant appears again, but rather than a humility of attitude as in 3:12f, the humility lies in the situation in which they are forced to live, a situation in which Zion has not attained the glory of the past (hence the term lame, and the language of the book of Lamentations). With these observations, it is possible to detect that the redactor assumes an explanation as to the reason for the continued deplorable circumstances, namely not all the people of Zion have returned. The lame/sufferers and the outcast have yet to be brought together from the literary perspective of the text (not necessarily from the historical perspective of the time of its

---

[101] There is also a strong sense of shame associated with 3:18b* with the terms burden and reproach applied to the suffering ones. However, the terminology and perspective used in this passage indicate a much wider horizon than Zeph 3:11-17. This perspective stems from other passages in the Book of the Twelve associating the חרפה of Zion with Jerusalem's disgraceful state following the Babylonian destruction. Significantly, this motif appears in Hos 12:15; Mic 6:16; Joel 2:17,19; and here. The two passages from the early Deuteronomistic corpus once again demonstrate the tendency of this corpus to parallel the judgment against the Northern kingdom with the announcement of a similar judgment against Judah and Jerusalem. Hos 12:15 announces that YHWH will pour out his reproach on *Ephraim*, and Mic 6:16 announces in similar fashion to *Zion*: You will *bear* (נשא) the reproach (חרפה) of my people. The parallel to the Northern kingdom is quite evident in this verse, since Zion receives the judgment because it observed the "statutes of Omri" and the "works of the house of Ahab," both Northern kings. Joel 2:17 implores Jerusalem's priests to petition YHWH, "Spare your people YHWH. Do not make your inheritance a reproach." The passage betrays a conditional nature, however, implying that only with this prayer will YHWH change the situation (2:18), and will answer (2:19), "... I will never again make you a reproach among the nations." By virtue of its composition, these Joel references reflect an awareness of the Deuteronomistic corpus (see the discussion of Joel 1:2ff particularly). Literarily, one cannot help but note that the stipulation of Joel 2:17 (the prayer) was never explicitly performed, giving the promises in the last half of the book only the potential for fulfillment. Joel's position after the announcement of destruction in Hos 12:15, against Ephraim, but *prior* to the announcement of the same fate for Jerusalem provides a sense of urgency to the plea to the priests in 2:17, functionally prefiguring the pronouncement in Mic 6:16, despite the fact that it was written later. It is therefore not insignificant that Zeph 3:18b alludes specifically to the manifestation of this motif in Mic 6:16, which, like Zeph 3:18b, uses both חרפה and the verbal root נשא in the sense of bearing a burden. By virtue of its context, Zeph 3:18b alludes back to the judgment announced in Mic 6:16 in order to announce the reversal of this judgment, effectively interpreting the promises in Zeph 3:14ff as further evidence of YHWH's promises in Joel 2:17,19. Once again, what appears to be a gloss when one reads only the individual book, manifests considerably more theological reflection when read with the larger corpus of the Book of the Twelve.

compilation). One may legitimately extrapolate this hermeneutical assumption, particularly from the conclusion of 3:19, where the redactor adds a different perspective to the Micah parallel. At the point when they are gathered, their assembling will be a cause of renown in all the earth (3:19). Thus, one is able to say that the 2fs layer clearly supposes its context in Zephaniah, but also looks backward to Micah. From the significant manner in which Mic 4:6f is utilized, this citation could only have been effected on a literary level because of the minute distinctions intentionally incorporated in the Zephaniah context.

The remaining material (Zeph 3:18*b,20)[102] is treated together, betraying in advance the conviction that the passage cannot simply be divided into redactional layers purely on the basis of the 3fs subject of Zion over against the 2mp reference to the people. This material should be seen as a redactional addition to be read in its location in the Book of the Twelve, not the Deuteronomistic corpus. As noted above, the 2fs material functions in a manner whose primary purpose is to point *backward* to the context in Zephaniah and to actualize the promise of the Mic 4:6f. As such, its 2fs references were perfectly appropriate to the Zephaniah context and the quote from Mic 4.[103] The function of 3:20, however, serves to connect Zephaniah to Haggai, and utilizes the perspective of Hag 1:4ff, Haggai's speech to the people (2mp).

In addition to the change of perspective which anticipates Haggai, Zeph 3:19*,20 contain catchwords to facilitate the transition from one work to the next, but these catchwords also engage the reader in a surprising contrast. Zeph 3:20 states explicitly: "In that time I will bring you, and in the time of my gathering you, then will I make you a renown and a praise among all the peoples of the earth in my returning your possessions." Several elements appear which negatively contrast the response of the people in Haggai with the response a reader would expect in light of the promise given in Zeph 3:18ff. The promise of Zephaniah is fulfilled with regard to the gathering of a remnant in Zion.[104] Hag 1:2ff portrays a

---

[102] In all likelihood, the phrase בעת ההיא in 3:19 could be formally attached to this layer.

[103] While the quote from Mic 4:6f does not specifically utilize 2fs material, it is present in the wider Micah context (cf. Mic 4:9ff).

[104] It is significant that this remnant presumably includes the returnees of the exiles, and those living in the immediate vicinity of Jerusalem, which is exactly the constellation in Haggai (cf Hag 1:12,14; 2:2). It is unfortunate that the understanding of the lame in Zephaniah is not normally treated as a metaphor for the remnant. See particularly: George Andersen, "The Idea of the Remnant in the Book of Zephaniah," in: *Annual of the Swedish Theological Institute: Festschrift Gillis Gerleman* 11 (1977/78): 11-14.

situation in which the exiles have obviously returned and have gathered at the site of the destroyed temple.[105] Thus, one immediately expects that *the time* of glory so boldly proclaimed in Zephaniah has arrived, but almost before one can formulate the excitement, the paradox hits home.[106] Indeed, the time has come when the lame/sufferers/remnant have been *brought* together (cf Zeph 3:20), but there is no trace of glory for Jerusalem. Rather than being understood as a renown and praise among all the *peoples* of the earth (Zeph 3:20), *this people* says *the time* has not come (Hag 1:2). A marvelous example of literary juxtaposition has been established between the expectation of an immediate grand salvific act, and the state of Jerusalem prior to the building of the temple. This expectation of salvation is further accentuated by the fact that Zeph 3:20 draws specifically on the promise of Joel 4:1: "For behold in those days and *at that time, when I restore the fortunes of Judah and Jerusalem*, I will gather all the nations" for judgment.[107]

The two texts imply different explanations as to why this glory has not come. For Haggai, the answer is immediate and clear: Jerusalem is in a desolate situation because the people are not concerned with rebuilding the temple. Zeph 3:20 offers no such answer. It was composed long after the temple had been rebuilt, and still the glory of Jerusalem lay in the future. The answer implied by the Zephaniah text is that only with the unification of all the people of YHWH, the remnant and the dispersed, will YHWH truly glorify Zion. In this manner, Zeph 3:18ff introduces Haggai, but looks beyond Haggai as well. The story is not finished with the reconstruction of the temple.

---

[105] In addition to the date of the superscription of Hag 1:1, note the use of the phrase "this house", which implies a nearness to the temple ruins. See Wolff, *BK* 14/6, 24f.

[106] Compare this same juxtaposition in the promissory addition to Hos 14:8 in light of situation of Joel 1:2ff.

[107] For a fuller treatment of the dependent relationship of 3:20, see my discussion of Joel 4:1 in my forthcoming volume, *Redactional Processes in the Book of the Twelve.*

Haggai

1. The Macrostructure of Hag 1:1-11

The book of Haggai manifests a readily definable macrostructure, which results primarily from the work of an editor from the milieu of the Chronicler.[1] The redactor provides this macrostructure with a historical frame documented by six stereotypical date formulas. These date formulas appear in chronological order, and cover a period of less than five months.[2] This redactional framework, as seen in the dating formula, provides not only specific dates, but also a depiction of the historical situation and the response of various groups to the speeches of Haggai. The redactor's historical interest portrays Haggai's initiation of the events

---

[1] Since the study of Beuken, *Haggai-Sacharja 1-8* (Assen: Van Gorcum, 1967), esp. 27-83, scholars have achieved a relative consensus on the issue of a single redaction/ composition of the Haggai book, although an exact delineation of the date and relationship to the Chronistic milieu is somewhat more complicated. Rex Mason, "The Purpose of the 'Editorial Framework' in the Book of Haggai," *VT* 27 (1977): 413-421, 415f, argues the editor has more in common with Deuteronomistic circles. See also Steck, "Zu Haggai 1:2-11," *ZAW* 83 (1971): 256; Petersen, *Haggai and Zechariah 1-8* (London: SCM, 1985), 37f. Wolff, *BK* 14/6, 3f, is among those who qualify the idea of a single redaction slightly. He believes the book contains a series of later additions 2:5aa,17,18*,19*. Eissfeldt, *Introduction*, 428f, goes against the grain by arguing that Haggai himself could have composed the book, albeit in a third person style to give it more objectivity, but the vast majority of scholars believe the compilation of the book reflects the work of a third party. Verhoef, *The Books of Haggai and Malachi*, Grand Rapids: Eerdmans, 1987, 9-13, gives a thorough account of the questions of authorship, and leans toward Eissfeldt's position, but does not clearly formulate his rationale.

[2] Hag 1:1,15; 2:1,10,18,20. Beuken, *Haggai - Sacharja 1-8*, convincingly demonstrates that these date formula, utilizing very precise dates, reflect a style found elsewhere in prophetic writings, only in Zechariah 1-8 and Ezekiel. He uses these formulas and other evidence to isolate a redactional hand which helped shape, not only Haggai, but Zechariah 1-8 (cf 1:1,7; 7:1) as well. Pierce takes this idea of a Haggai-Zechariah corpus and seeks to trace the development of thematic connections not only in Haggai and Zechariah, but also Malachi. More will be discussed later about this possibility, in the discussion of Malachi. See Ronald Pierce, "Literary Connectors and a Haggai-Zechariah-Malachi Corpus," *JETS* 27 (1984): 277-89; and Pierce, "A Thematic Development of the Haggai-Zechariah-Malachi Corpus," *JETS* 27 (1984): 401-11.

leading to the reconstruction of the temple.[3] The resulting composition displays a montage character which scholarship increasingly attributes to the fact that the oracles which are framed by these redactional formulations are composite in character, woven together by the editor to form a coherent whole.[4] In spite of this composite character, very few have argued that the oracles themselves, apart from the their current redactional framework, do not relate closely to the time and situation in which Haggai preached.[5]

2. The Literary Units in Hag 1:1-11

The book of Haggai begins in a manner which quickly demonstrates the composite character of 1:1-11. The first composite speech is introduced in 1:1 and continues to 1:11.[6] A new unit begins in 1:12 in which the redactor portrays the reaction of the leaders and of the people to the words of Haggai. Closer inspection of 1:1-11 reveals that several formal elements evidence a tension which make it impossible to consider the entire unit as one continuous speech. However, it is also not necessary to suppose a new speech with each new introductory formula, be it the messenger formulas (1:2,5,7) or the Chronistic redactional elements (1:1,3).[7]

---

[3] See for example Hag 1:12-14, which present the positive response of Zerubbabel, Joshua, and "all the remnant of the people."

[4] Cf. discussions in Childs, *Introduction*, 464ff; Petersen, *Haggai & Zechariah 1-8*, 36-39; Mason, *VT* 27 (1977): 413; Wolff, *BK* 14/6, 17.

[5] Some argue, however, for additions to the oracles and the frame: Elliger, *ATD* 25, 84; Wolff, *BK* 3f, etc.

[6] Rudolph, *KAT* 13/4, 30, claims that none of the dating formulas in Haggai are introductions to the book. While in a strict sense Rudolph's claim has some merit, the accentuation of the second year of the reign of Darius in 1:1 at the very beginning of the book, argues that this verse was aware of its double function of introducing the "speech" which runs to 1:11, and of orienting the reader to the time in which action of the entire book takes place.

[7] A considerable difference of opinion exists regarding the extent and character of the individual speeches within 1:2-11. Cf. for example: Ackroyd, "Studies in the Book of Haggai," *JJS* 2 (1951): 167,175; Wolff, *BK* 14/6, 3f; Rudolph, *KAT* 13/4, 22f; Elliger, *ATD* 25/2, 80,82f. *Ackroyd* divides the material into the oracles proper, and two levels of non-oracular frames. The first group (1:12-14; 2:3-5; 2:11-14a) Ackroyd considers as essential to a literary presentation of the oracular material. The second group (1:1,3,15; 2:1f,10,18*,20-21a) is independent of the oracles. *Wolff* distinguishes four sources which he attributes to three different growth rings: the prophetic proclamation (1:4-11; 2:15-19*; 2:3-9*; 2:14; 2:21b-23), which a disciple of the prophet wrote down

The major literary questions effecting this study center on the composite character of the frame in 1:1-3.[8] Normally, the messenger formulas in Haggai introduce the words of YHWH or the prophet speaking for YHWH. Therefore, it is surprising that 1:2b quotes the people after the messenger formula in 1:2a and that a second "word" formula in 1:3 follows the quote of the people.[9]

> [2]Thus says YHWH Sebaoth, saying:
>> This people says the time has not yet come, the time to build the house of YHWH.
>
> [3]And then the word of YHWH came by the hand of Haggai the prophet saying,
>> [4]Is it time for you yourselves to rest in your boarded houses and this house be desolate?

This tension leads to the conclusion that the writing as it now stands represents more than one layer of activity, but the explanations of the growth do not agree in the precise details.[10]

---

in literary form, adding certain information regarding their effect or pre-history (1:2, 12b-13; 2:11-13). The Chronistic circle adapted the writing using introductory word-event formulas (1:1,3,15a; 1:15b-2:2; 2:10; 2:20-21a). Finally, the corpus received several expansions (2:5aa,17, the last two words of 2:18 [שימו לבבכם], and 2:19ab* [והרמון ועד־הגפן והתאנה]). *Rudolph* essentially believes the speeches have been transmitted intact with the introductions coming from one and the same hand. He presents a few suggestions for emendations and/or deliberate changes. Similarly, *Elliger*, in his introductory remarks, argues that the book contains the speeches and two narrative interludes (1:12ff; 2:10-14), but in his discussion of 1:1-11, he speaks of several problems which do not portray as uncomplicated a text as he first implies.

8   Most attribute the *final form* of Haggai to a forerunner to the Chronicler, who is often called the Haggai-Chronicler, in large part due to the similarity of outlook and vocabulary in the redactional elements. This stylistic similarity is noted in the dating formulas (1:1,15; 2:1,10,18,20), the dedication to the leader (1:1), and the peculiar form of designation for the instrument of the prophet (ביד in 1:1,3; 2:1). Further discussion in Beuken, *Haggai-Sacharja 1-8*, 10-15. These redactional indicators are separated from the prophetic speeches (and in some cases from early accounts of the speeches).

9   The superscription in 1:1 is the first "word-event." For a thorough discussion of the "word events" in Haggai, see Wolff, *BK* 14/6, 15-16.

10 Several approaches have been offered. Beuken, *Haggai - Sacharja 1-8*, 30, argues that 1:2 belongs with the historical frame in 1:1 and serves to introduce the situation, while the connection from 1:2 to 1:3 is difficult. This means that, for Beuken, 1:3 introduces 1:4-6. Steck, *ZAW* 83 (1971): 360, rightly takes issue on redaction critical grounds that 1:2 is closer to 1:4 than to 1:1, while 1:3 is nearer to 1:1 because the formulaic use of ביד in 1:1. For Steck, 1:3 was inserted to avoid confusion, and to accentuate that 1:4ff is addressed to the people, and not to the leaders mentioned in 1:1. So Ackroyd,

Steck presents a plausible explanation to the background of the individual units in 1:2-11 by concentrating upon the addressees.[11] In doing so, he correctly concludes that 1:2,4-8 is directed to those inhabitants who remained in Judah during the exile, while 1:9-11 addresses those who have recently returned from Babylon.[12] Steck bases his argumentation on the different condition of the houses in the two units,[13] and upon observations about the *Gattung*.[14] His concentration upon the condition of the houses is by no means arbitrary since the entire redactional unity of 1:2-11 emphasizes a contrast between the houses of the inhabitants (1:4a,9) and the house of YHWH (1:2,4b,8,9). Thus it is possible and plausible to explain the compilation of 1:1-11 as the editorial conflation of two oracles 1:2,4-8 and 9-11 with a double introduction (1:1,3).[15]

3. The Literary Horizon of Hag 1:1-11

In contrast to Zeph 3:18-20, Hag 1:1-11 exhibits a relatively narrow literary horizon, providing little sign of editorial activity beyond the level of compilation. One exception to this statement relates to the possible interplay between this unit and Zeph 3:18-20, namely the double

---

"Studies in the Book of Haggai," *JJS* 2 (1951): 167. Rudolph, *KAT* 13/4, 32, opts for unattested emendation of דבר יהוה to דְּבְרֵי in order to place 1:3 in the mouth of YHWH. Wolff, *BK* 14/6, 16, notes the official character of the superscription and the relatedness of 1:3 to the tradition of 1:1. He sees 1:2a as the traditional introduction of 1:4, and sees 1:2b (with 1:3) as part of the introduction of the Haggai Chronicler.

[11] Steck, *ZAW* 83 (1971): 355-379.

[12] Ackroyd divides the material into the same speech units, but does not distinguish the two groups. See Ackroyd, *JJS* 2 (1951): 167.

[13] Cf ישׁב in 1:4 and "you are running, each one for his own house" in 1:9. This idiomatic expression רוץ with the preposition ל does not mean "running into" rather means "to be busy with." Examples can be found in Isa 59:7; Prov 1:16; 6:18; Sir 11:11. This implies the building of houses while 1:4 implies inhabitants who already dwell in their houses. See Steck, *ZAW* 83 (1971): 370, n. 45; Beuken, *Haggai - Sacharja 1-8*, 18ff, n. 1.

[14] Steck, *ZAW* 83 (1971): especially 362ff, sees 1:2,4-8 as a speech delivered on a single occasion. He supports this thesis with strong observations on the *Gattung* of the unit, demonstrating the entirety of the discussion speech culminates in a promise of salvation in 1:8.

[15] For the function of 1:3 as a clarification of a YHWH speech to the people over against the "official" introduction to the leaders in 1:1, see Steck, *ZAW* 83 (1971): 359-362.

appearance of עת in Hag 1:2. The phrase עת־בא has often been called
into question based upon G, which attests only one occurrence of עת,
rather than two as in MT.[16]   Indeed, the syntax appears strained,
especially when one compares 1:2 with 1:4.[17]   Several text critical
explanations have been rejected above, where it has also been suggested
that one might explain the tension as a cosmetic addition at the point of
attachment to Zephaniah to accomplish a *three-fold repetition* of the word
time.

When one eliminates textual corruption, explanations for the
awkwardness of the phrase are limited. It could be argued that the phrase
merely demonstrates a stylistic peculiarity, which many commentators
apparently accept with little consideration.[18]   However, if one considers
the phrase from the position of the redaction of the Book of the Twelve,
an interesting perspective arises. Without the phrase, the quote of the
people would read, "It is not time to build the house of YHWH." This
phrase as a quote of the people would be perfectly suited as a narrative
introduction to Hag 1:2-11. The addition of the phrase "the time has (not)
come" (עת בא) connotes a strong sense of expectation on the part of
someone, against which the people are reacting. As such, it *presupposes* an
announcement that "the time is coming." Such an expectation is clearly
present in the phrase בעת ההיא in Zeph 3:19,20, as has already been seen.
The phrase עת בא imports eschatological undertones into the context
which are not part of the speeches in chapter one of Haggai.[19]   Thus, it

---

[16]   However, the LXX attests both verbs בוא and בנה, making it much more likely that
the LXX simplifies the syntax by eliminating one occurrence of "time." See text note
1:2b.

[17]   See Steck, *ZAW* 83 (1971): 361f, n. 21, and the text note Hag 1:2b in the chapter two
of this work.

[18]   So essentially Verhoef, *Haggai and Malachi*, 54f. It is difficult to simply ignore the
problems this phrase creates, see also: Rudolph, *KAT* 13/3, 29; Ackroyd, *Exile and
Restoration* (London: SCM, 1968), 155, n. 8; Wolff, *BK* 14. Petersen, *Haggai &
Zechariah 1-8*, 41 and 47, translates the phrase in two slightly different manners with
no explanation for the difference.

[19]   Other possible eschatological perspectives in Haggai are found in 2:6f,21b,22. In 2:6f
the language is more explicit and limited to a theophanic appearance for the
glorification of the temple. See Mason, *VT* 27 (1977): 20f, for the function of the
eschatology in the frame of Haggai. Hag 2:21b,22 eschatologizes both the passage from
2:6f (which it quotes) and the speech to Zerubbabel (2:20,21a,23). This latter
eschatologization, it will be argued, is part of the material which attaches the book of
Haggai to Zechariah, and is thus readily conceivable as part of the same process which
attached Zephaniah to Haggai.

is quite plausible to maintain that the syntactical difficulty of the quote of the people is due to the cosmetic addition of the phrase עת בא at the beginning of the quote to broaden the frame of vision of the Haggai passage.

In summary, the conclusion of Zephaniah and the beginning of Haggai demonstrate little adaptation of these writings *at the level of the Book of the Twelve.* If the above analysis is correct, then the level of incorporation added only Zeph 3:18b,20, while modifying portions of 3:19 to accentuate the transition to Haggai. Less certain perhaps, but still preferable to text-critical suggestions, is the suggestion that the attachment of Haggai to Zephaniah motivated the addition of the phrase עת־בא in Hag 1:2. This lack of significant adaptation does not invalidate the minor changes suggested here, for several reasons. First, both Zephaniah and Haggai already existed as part of larger corpora. Zephaniah was part of the Deuteronomistic corpus, where it had already experienced more than one redaction. In all likelihood, Haggai was transmitted with Zech 1-8 for some time. Second, both the promise of return in Zeph 3:14ff and the resistance to the building of the temple described in Hag 1:2ff served the redactor's chronological purpose remarkably well.

4. The Literary Units in Hag 2:10-23

The previous chapter outlined the macrostructure of Haggai, where it was noted that the dating formulas in 1:1,15: 2:1,10,20 represent the dominant structuring device. Despite transparency of this structuring technique, modern scholars note Haggai contains a relatively high number of "glosses" for a book of its size. Several of these accretions appearing in Hag 2:15-23 bear directly upon the question of the literary unification of the Book of the Twelve. Discussion of these passages requires an analysis of the units in 2:10-23, since these verses contain several debated passages about which preliminary decisions must be made.

Almost all scholars agree that Hag 2:10-23 divides naturally into three sections, however, the relationship and original position of these units provokes considerable debate. The three sections are Hag 2:10-14,15-19,20-23. Hag 2:10 and 2:20 clearly begin separate units since each contains an introductory dating formula from the chronistically-related redactor responsible for shaping the major portions of Haggai. Hag 2:15-19 lacks this dating element, but has its own introduction, and according to many, changes subject from a question of cleanliness to one of the delay of blessing, arguing that 2:15-19 was not originally part of the oracle in 2:10-14. However, a growing minority argue that 2:15-19 cannot be separated formally from 2:10-14, claiming that these verses represent an integral *subunit* in 2:10-19, not an originally separate unit.[20]

To understand the debate one must refer back to the dating formula in 1:15. Since Rothstein, a considerable majority of scholars have argued that 1:15 indicates a corruption in the otherwise consistent use of dating formulas to introduce new oracles.[21] Hag 1:15 cannot introduce an oracle in its current position, since Hag 2:1 follows 1:15 immediately with another introductory dating formula, dating the following oracle almost a month later. Two possibilities have been suggested for solving this inconsistency. A minority argues that 1:15a simply deviates from the pattern of the chronistic elements as introductions.[22] They see no trouble in accepting that 1:15a *refers backward* to the preceding oracle rather than forward.[23] Against this position, one must note that not only would this explanation run contrary to the pattern in Haggai, but also to the use of similar material as *introductions* to prophetic speeches or collections in Zechariah and Ezekiel.[24] The majority of scholars argue that the most plausible answer

---

[20] See Klaus Koch, "Haggais unreines Volk." *ZAW* 79 (1967): 52-66. Koch is followed by Petersen, *Haggai & Zechariah 1-8*, 87. See fuller discussion of Koch's arguments below, page 224. See also Herbert G. May, "This People and this Nation in Haggai." *VT* 18 (1968): 190-197; T.N. Townsend, "Additional Comments on Haggai 2:10-19." *VT* 18 (1968): 559-560; Verhoef, *Haggai and Malachi*, 89.

[21] D.J.W. Rothstein, *Juden und Samaritaner. Die grundlegende Scheidung von Judentum und Heidentum*, BWAT 3 (Leipzig: Hinrich, 1908). See discussions in Wolff, *BK* 14/6, 40-44; Beuken, *Haggai - Sacharja 1-8*, 48f; Rex Mason, *The Books of Haggai, Zechariah and Malachi*, Cambridge Bible Commentary (New York/London: Cambridge University Press, 1977), 17; Elliger, *ATD* 25, 85f; Eissfeldt, *Introduction*, 427f; Childs, *Introduction*, 465; Fohrer, *Einleitung*, 504.

[22] Most scholars, whether they consider the current text as the result of displacement or not, separate 1:15a and 1:15b for stylistic reasons, arguing 1:15b must represent the initial dating element of 2:1. So Peter R. Ackroyd, "Studies in the Book of Haggai," *JJS* 2 (1951): 167; Petersen, *Haggai & Zechariah 1-8*, 59f, 62; Wolff, *BK* 14/6, 40f; Rudolph, *KAT* 13/4, 30; Beuken, *Haggai - Sacharja 1-8*, 48f; Verhoef, *Haggai and Malachi*, 88f.

[23] So, for example, Petersen, *Haggai & Zechariah 1-8*, 59f, who believes this is a deliberate device of the editor to subtly show a progression of events leading to the acceptance of the task at hand. See also Ackroyd, *JJS* 2 (1951): 170f, who offers three possible solutions; and Verhoef, *Haggai and Malachi*, who argues the verse forms an *inclusio* with 1:1.

[24] Cf Zech 1:1,7; 7:1; Ezek 1:1f; 8:1; 20:1; 24:1; 26:1; 29:1,17; 30:20; 31:1; 32:1,17; 33:21; 40:1.

to the problem of Hag 1:15a lies in the assumption that the oracle which originally followed 1:15a has been moved.[25] The weakness of this argument lies in the fact that it must presume some rather sloppy editing on the part of the redactor who left an introductory formula hanging following the relocation of the oracle. Nevertheless, the arguments for the relocation are more convincing than the arguments that 1:15a refers backward. The formula in 1:15a is too similar to the remaining *introductory* formulas to presume that it functioned as the conclusion to 1:12-14.

A large majority of those who believe a redactor transferred the oracle which originally followed 1:15a to another location also believe that 2:15-19 was the oracle which was moved.[26] They follow Rothstein's hypothesis that style and content make 2:15-19 more suitable to a position nearer 1:1-11.[27] As evidence, they cite the fact that the clean/unclean references in 2:10-14 are not resolved in 2:15-19; the judgment motif of 2:10-14 finds no traces in 2:15-19; the dialogue style of 2:15-19 is more in keeping with 1:2-11 than with 2:10-14 (cf especially 2:15,18a and 1:5b,7b); and finally they argue that the chronology of 2:15-19 marks the beginning of the building, which coincides with the position at the end of the first chapter. The most common rationale cited for the displacement of 2:15-19 concerns a redactional interest in relating the cessation of trouble with the rejection of the Samaritan aid in 2:14.[28]

---

[25] Almost all scholars believing 1:15a points toward disruption of the text assume displacement of another oracle as the cause for the problems of 1:15a. Few, if any, suggest an oracle has fallen away which is no longer present. Ackroyd, *JJS* 2 (1951): 170f, suggests the possibility that 1:15a is a gloss.

[26] See discussions in Wolff, *BK* 14/6, 40-44; Beuken, *Haggai - Sacharja 1-8*, 48f; Rex Mason, *The Books of Haggai, Zechariah and Malachi*, 17; Elliger, *ATD* 25, 85f; Eissfeldt, *Introduction*, 427f; Childs, *Introduction*, 465; Fohrer, *Einleitung*, 504.

[27] While Rothstein, *Juden und Samaritaner*, 53-73, generally receives credit for the major arguments of this position other early proponents also appear: See Ernst Sellin, *Studien zur Entstehungsgeschichte der jüdischen Gemeinde nach dem Babylonischen Exil*, vol 2: *Die Restauration der jüdischen Gemeinde in den Jahren 538-16*, (Leipzig: Deichert, 1901), 49f.

[28] Proponents of this view see the reference to "this people" in connection with the unclean/clean controversy described in 2:10-14 as a reference to the rejection of Samaritan help on the temple building project (cf Ezra 4:1-5). See Wolff, *BK* 14/6, 42-44, 71-74; Elliger, *ATD* 25, 85; Rothstein, *Juden und Samaritaner*, 53-73. Kaiser (see Wolff) offers an alternative explanation that the redactor did not wish the final saying about the people to be a negative one, hence the positive oracle in 2:15-19 was placed after 2:10-14.

This majority opinion is countered from two sides. First, at least two authors argue that 2:20-23 originally followed 1:15a. Second, the arguments of Koch and others challenge the claim that the content of 2:15-19 is not appropriate following 2:10-14. Bloomhardt and Haupt believe that Hag 2:20-23 originally followed Hag 1:15a.[29] Bloomhardt provides more detailed argumentation than Haupt and his arguments are summarized here. He claims the "anti-Persian spirit" of 2:20-23 would be more at home following 1:15a. Also the direct reference to Zerubbabel would make sense following 1:12-14. He also notes that 2:20 refers only to the twenty-fourth of the month, requiring very little change to move it to the new location. This introduction is the only one which makes no specific reference to the month itself.[30] The weakest link in Bloomhardt's argument lies in his explanation as to why the oracle has been moved. He says that its initial position reflects the need to suppress the oracle after Darius had strengthened his position on the throne to the point that revolt was no longer a serious option. Later, according to Bloomhardt, the oracle received a more appropriate position at the end of the book as a hopeful conclusion. Bloomhardt's argument breaks down in two places since 1) any suggestion of a more prominent evaluation of 2:20-23 would have to account for the fact that the hope placed on Zerubbabel by Haggai never materialized, and in fact, Zerubbabel represented the last Davidide to rule Jerusalem. 2) Hag 1:12-14 treats both Zerubbabel and Joshua, making the sudden promise to Zerubbabel alone in 2:20-23 problematic if it were to follow 1:12-14.

Koch provides a second counter-argument against the idea that 2:15-19 originally followed 1:15a. He argues that a documentable pattern exists in three oracles in Haggai making them formal unities: 1:1-7; 2:1-7; and 2:10-19.[31] Koch describes this formal construction as follows:

1.	Introduction	1:1	2:1	2:10
2.	Indications of the situation	1:2f	2:2f	2:11-14
3.	The present time as turning point	1:4-6	2:4f	2:15-17
4.	Announcement (through repetition)	1:7	2:6f	2:18f

---

[29] Paul Haupt, "The Visions of Zechariah," *JBL* 32 (1913): 113; and Paul F. Bloomhardt, "The Poems of Haggai," *Hebrew Union College Annual* 5 (1928): 166-168.

[30] Bloomhardt considers the reference to "a second time" in 2:20 a redactional change to conform it to its new position, much the same as those arguing 2:15-19 followed 1:15a have to make certain allotments for additions to conform the oracle to a new position, compare for example the text notes in Wolff, *BK* 14/6, 39f.

[31] Koch, *ZAW* 79 (1967): 59f.

Koch makes a well argued case for this pattern, and his observations as to the role of the repetitions in the formal structure add weight to his arguments. Koch's views have been readily accepted by those who see 2:10-19 as a unity, but are often ignored by those who see 2:15-19 as the continuation of 1:15a. Caution demands several further observations regarding Koch's assessment. Koch goes too far when he maintains that the presence of this pattern proves the original unity of these passages. Koch includes the introductions in 1:1; 2:1,10, but these introductions are themselves from the hand of a redactor, and would certainly not been an original part of the prophetic oracle. When one notes that these redactional introductions appear as part of the pattern, the question of *original* unity becomes more complicated. The question must then be placed whether these patterns are redactional constructions rather than original units. If the former, then one cannot preclude that 2:15-19 originally followed 1:15a, and was only secondarily added to 2:10-14 to conform the unit to other oracular patterns. Other problems with Koch's observations include his designation of the repetition element in 2:6f. The repetition of this element differs from the remaining oracles in that both 1:7 and 2:18 offer a refrain from the previous structural element (the present as turning point), whereas the repetition elements in 2:6f both appear in the announcement section. The phrase which is repeated also belies a different character than the remaining refrains. Both of the other oracles repeat an imperative confrontation with the addressees, whereas 2:6f merely repeats the phrase "says YHWH Sebaoth"—a phrase which is hardly integral to the oracle itself. All of these observations, when taken together raise considerable doubt about Koch's claim that this structural pattern proves original unity.

In addition to the structural pattern, Koch and others argue that the context of 2:15-19 is appropriate following 2:10-14.[32] Petersen draws on Koch's arguments regarding the structural pattern and then adds other observations. Petersen argues the use of "therefore" in 2:15 *presupposes* the existence of something which comes before in the same way that its presence in 1:5 presupposes previous material. Further, he argues that the day to which 2:15-19 refers is the day of a foundation stone ceremony for

---

[32] See, for example, Koch, *ZAW* 79 (1967) 60-64, who argues that 2:10-14 cannot be understood as a complete unit, but rather demands a continuation; and Petersen, *Haggai & Zechariah 1-8*, 87-90.

the new temple which would have included ritual purification.[33]
Petersen's arguments do provide a suitable setting for 2:15-19, but the
relationship to the foregoing is still not entirely clear, particularly since he
himself argues the addressees in 2:10-14 are a circle of priests, not the
people as a whole as in 2:15-19.

In short, there has been no sufficient solution offered to the dilemma
of the original placement of the oracles. The arguments that Hag 1:15a
introduced an oracle which has since been moved are convincing, yet the
only two possibilities suggested for this displaced oracle both encounter
substantial problems for explaining the supposed displacement. These
problems are well documented in the case of Hag 2:15-19, while a plausible
rationale for displacing 2:20-23 has not yet been advanced.

5. Literary Additions in Hag 2:15-19,20-23

More consensus exists with regard to several "glosses" in the
concluding verses of Haggai. Hag **2:15-19** attests considerable agreement
among commentators that Hag 2:17, with its dependence upon Amos 4:9,
and substantial portions of the list of trees in Hag 2:19 have been inserted
into the literary context. The similarity of Hag 2:17 and Amos 4:9 is
undeniable.

Amos 4:9	Hag 2:17
I smote you with blasting wind and mildew; and the gnawing locust was devouring your many gardens and vineyards, fig trees, and olive trees. Yet you have not returned to me declares the Lord.	I smote you and every work of your hands with blasting wind, mildew, and hail; yet you did not *come back* to me, declares the Lord.

The verse in Amos is directed against the "sons of Israel," whereas Hag 2:17
is addressed to the remnant community who has weathered the exile and
who have returned to Jerusalem. The verse recalls the message of Amos
as a literary reflection and rationale for the present state of affairs. It
confronts the people with their own responsibility in that the devastation

---

[33] Cf Zech 4:9; Ezra 3:10,11; Petersen, *Haggai & Zechariah 1-8*, 89f; see expansions of his
arguments in David L. Petersen, "Zerubbabel and Jerusalem Temple Reconstruction,"
CBQ 36 (1974): 366-372; and the work of Baruch Halpern, "The Ritual Background of
Zechariah's Temple Song," *CBQ* 40 (1978): 171-172.

they faced was the result of their (or their ancestors) refusal to accept YHWH's acts of rebuke as a warning to return to him.

The majority opinion that Hag 2:17 is a secondary addition rests upon arguments of content, and style. This consensus, while not unanimous, transcends the opinions on the original relationship of 2:10-14 and 2:15-19 in that many of those who argue 2:10-19 is an integral unit admit Hag 2:17 does not belong inherently.[34] The greatest disparity lies in the context of 2:17 inside 2:15-19 since blight, mildew, and hail are problems of too much water, not of a drought (cf Hag 1:11). Also these maladies effect the crops in the field, not those in the storehouses, which clearly distinguishes 2:17 from 2:16,19.[35] Hag 2:15-19 evidences a strong interest in the transition from judgment to blessing, and it does so with a particular interest in the change which the laying of the foundation for the temple will precipitate in the fate of YHWH's people. By contrast, Hag 2:17 reaches back to justify YHWH's punitive action, reminding YHWH's people of their own responsibility for the situation. Hag 2:17 clearly implies that all of YHWH's actions have been designed to generate the return of the people to their God.

Scholars tend to view Hag 2:17 as an isolated gloss, but there are good reasons for seeing the verse as part of the continuing unifying thread woven into the Book of the Twelve. First, the verse clearly belongs to the literary *Nachgeschichte* of Haggai. Only someone with knowledge of Amos would appreciate the adaptation of Amos 4:9 into the Haggai context by means of phrases such as "all the work of your hands" (cf Hag 2:14). Second, the specific citation of Amos 4:9 provides a definite hermeneutical touchstone with the images of Joel 1-2, a similarity which is further cemented by the additions to Hag 2:19. Amos 4:9 ties the people's rejection of YHWH to YHWH's destructive activity in the form of agricultural blight. Joel 1-2 expands the images in Amos 4:9 as part of a more apocalyptic depiction of Joel's concept of the day of YHWH.[36] The

---

[34] Above all note Petersen, *Haggai & Zechariah 1-8*, 91-93, who sets forth the problems of context and syntax setting this verse apart, but never makes a clear decision as to its integrity, preferring to call it the work of "the prophet Haggai (or a redactor)," 92. See also Wolff, *BK* 14/6, 43, 46; Ackroyd, *Exile and Restoration*, 158. For the arguments of those who believe Hag 2:17 comes from Haggai, see Rudolph, *KAT* 13/4, 51; Verhoef, *Haggai and Malachi*, 128f.

[35] See Petersen's discussion, *Haggai & Zechariah 1-8*, 91f.

[36] Note the recurrence of the gnawing locust in Amos 4:9 and Joel 1:4; 2:25; cf. the vineyards in Amos 4:9 with the vinedressers (Joel 1:11) and the vine (Joel 1:7,12; 2:22; and the fig-trees (Joel 1:12; 2:22).

same type of images appear at significant points by means of similar redactional glosses in Nahum, Habakkuk, and Zephaniah, so their presence is not altogether unexpected here. The fact that the allusion is filtered through Amos 4:9 is rather unusual. Nevertheless, any doubt that the allusion to Amos 4:9 also intends to provoke the images of Joel 1-2 may be dispelled by a look at the second redactional gloss in Hag 2:19.

Hag 2:19 has received a short literary insertion which clearly disturbs the syntax. This disruption has been noted by a number of scholars, but the cause for the additional material has gone virtually untreated.[37] The MT reads as follows:

העוד הזרע במגורה	Is the seed yet in the granary?
ועד־הגפן והתאנה והרמון	(Or the vine, or the fig-tree, or the pomegranate?)
ועץ הזית לא נשא	Or has the olive tree not born fruit?
מן־היום הזה עברך	From this day I will bless.

The second line disrupts the syntax of this verse. The verb (נשא) in the third line demands a 3ms subject, which can only mean that עץ would be the subject, hence line three preserves the proper syntactical relationship. The presence of vine, fig-tree, and pomegranate as part of the original question would most naturally require a plural subject. Likewise, the insertion of line two disrupts the imagery of the rhetorical questions. Grammatically, the second line continues the question of the first line, but one is hard pressed to explain why the elements of the second line would ever be put into a granary.[38]

What would have motivated the addition of "the vine, the fig-tree, and the pomegranate?" The combination of these three agricultural objects undoubtedly intends to provoke the images of Joel 1-2. The combination

---

[37] So Wolff, *BK* 14/6, 43, although he notes the presence of the fruits in Joel 1:12. See also Beuken, *Haggai - Sacharja 1-8*, 213; Elliger, *ATD* [3]25, 89. Petersen, *Haggai & Zechariah 1-8*, 93-95, sees no syntactical problems with the list of trees but he does suggest an explanation of their significance as a reference to the fertility of the promised land based on Num 13:23 and Deut 8:28. Rudolph, *KAT* 13/4, 46 offers minor textual emendations.

[38] On the background of the term במגורה, see Bloomhart, *HUCA* 5 (1928), 174, who argues that the archaeological evidence indicates one must picture a pit, not a building. See the translation of Wolff, *BK* 14/6, 39. Some might argue that "fig-tree" could be translated here as "fig" and be part of the produce stored. However, "vine" indicates the intention lies not with the cultivated produce, but with the plant itself. The insertion thus must be read with the line that follows. The insertion of the phrase as a gloss (with redactional implications) helps explain the tension.

of these elements is not at all common, and the presence of this combination in Joel 1:12 is the most likely literary reference to which this gloss points.[39] The fact that these elements in Joel are destroyed, makes their promised restoration in Hag 2:19 meaningful.[40] The punishment predicted for Jerusalem in Joel 1-2 has been graphically portrayed in Zeph 1:2-2:3. The scene in Haggai presupposes the return of the exiles and the beginning of the temple construction as a precursor to the agricultural bounty promised in Joel 2:22.[41] Again, as in Nahum, Habakkuk, and Zephaniah, redactional insertions into an existing literary context have drawn on the paradigm set forth in Joel. One element distinguishes this paradigmatic use of Joel to this point, however, since neither the citation of Amos 4:9 (which relates hermeneutically to Joel 1-2) nor the insertion of the agricultural elements take up the cosmic elements present in Nahum, Habakkuk, and Zephaniah. It will be possible, however, to return to this observation in the discussion of Hag 2:22.[42]

Hag **2:20-23** normally receives treatment as a single literary unit, despite considerable tensions in the verses which *suggest* they are not an original unity.[43] These tensions deserve careful analysis in light of the

---

[39] The only other combination of these three elements appears in Deut 8:8, where they appear as part of larger list of bounties describing the promised land. While it is possible that there is some indirect relationship of Hag 2:19 to Deut 8:8, the likelihood is greater that it is drawing upon Joel.

[40] Note also the way that Joel 2:22 promises the restoration of these elements (except for the pomegranates) with a phraseology that helps to explain the connection to Hag 2:19 as well. Joel 2:22 uses the verb נשׂא in the sense of to bear fruit in the same way as Hag 2:19.

[41] This verse functions as the promissory counterpart to the announcement of destruction in Joel 1:12. It is important to note that the promise is part of the promised agricultural blessing which comes *after* the destruction of the locust plagues (see 2:25). Hence even the omission of the mention of the locust from the citation of Amos 4:9 makes sense when read against this background. The devastation caused by the locusts is considered to be completed with the return of the exiles and the restoration of the temple. The locusts therefore do not come into the picture which the redactor paints with these allusions.

[42] See discussion below, page 231.

[43] Most separate 2:20 as editorial work to be distinguished from the saying of the prophet in 2:21-23, but a few go further. Beuken, *Haggai - Sacharja 1-8*, 79-83, dubiously separates 2:23b from 2:21-23a on the strength of the Chronicler's use of בחר. Wolff, *BK* 14/6, 77, treats the verses as two separate sayings (2:21b-22, 2:23) of the prophet brought together here by the compiler of the sayings and provided with an introduction by the Haggai-Chronicler (2:20-21a). More commonly, no real distinction is made in the speech of 2:21-23, in spite of the fact that it manifests considerable tension

density of common words appearing in Hag 2:20-23 and Zech 1:1ff. Hag 2:20-23 contains four elements:

2:20   Typical Haggai-Chronicler introduction
2:21   Introduction of address to Zerubbabel
2:22   Military parenthetical statement
2:23   Address to Zerubbabel

Formally, the chronistic introduction to the unit (2:20) is part of the compositional work of the Haggai-Chronicler already described in the discussion of the macrostructure of the book. It corresponds to the general pattern of the editor who organized the material according to the days on which the speeches were delivered, although it does exhibit several minor deviations.[44] The date sets the speech on the same day as Hag 2:10, December 18, 520.[45] The direct address to Zerubbabel in Hag 2:23 and the implicit expectations which Zerubbabel never achieved argue that the gist of this oracle may be traced with relative certainty to the general period stated in this introduction.[46]

---

theologically and linguistically. See Ackroyd, *Exile and Restoration*, 163-166; Rudolph, *KAT* 13/4, 53f; Mason, *Haggai, Zechariah, and Malachi*, 24f; Karl-Martin Beyse, *Serubbabel und die Königserwartungen der Propheten Haggai und Sacharja. Eine historische und traditionsgeschichtliche Untersuchung* (Stuttgart: Calwer Verlag, 1972), 52-58. Interestingly, Petersen, *Haggai & Zechariah 1-8*, 97-102, documents considerable variations between Hag 2:22,23, but still prefers to see the verses as a single oracle with two parts, rather than the work of two writers.

[44] These deviations include: 1) The use of the preposition אל rather than ביד, which elsewhere appears only in Hag 2:10 (see Petersen's explanation, *Haggai & Zechariah 1-8*, 97); 2) The use of שנית (a second time) does not appear in any of the other introductions, even though there are strong reasons for supposing that some of them incorporate more than one speech (cf Steck, *ZAW* 83 [1971]: 355-379, for Hag 1:2-11; also question of the relationship of 2:15-19 with 2:10-14); 3) There is no mention of the year, but this omission can be explained by the presence of "a second time," which would make the year redundant (cf 2:10); 4) Zerubbabel's father Shealtiel is not mentioned (but cf 2:23); 5) The delineation of the specific month is not present, but as with the omission of the year, the month is not necessary since the presence of "a second time" locates the date quite precisely as identical with 2:10.

[45] This date is still accepted despite the work of Elias J. Bickerman, "La Seconde Année de Darius," *Revue Biblique* 88 (1981):23-28, who attempts to harmonize dates of Darius' reign from accounts in various countries, and dates this oracle December 30, 521.

[46] Verification of the precise date would of course be very difficult in light of the literary nature of these introductions, and the likelihood that they were compiled some considerable time after the speeches were delivered. See the difference of opinions between Beuken, *Haggai - Sacharja 1-8*, 21-26, who argues for the reliability of the

Hag 2:21 introduces the oracle proper, and in all likelihood predates the Chronicler's introduction, although this introduction itself presupposes a literary setting (probably in the form of a collection of prophetic sayings).[47] YHWH as speaker addresses Haggai with a direct command: "say to Zerubbabel, governor of Judah, I am about to shake the heavens and the earth." This introduction is significant for two reasons. First, YHWH commands Haggai to address Zerubbabel directly. Second, the message proper begun in this verse is a doublet of Hag 2:6. The implications of these observations will become apparent in the discussion which follows.

Hag 2:22 digresses into a parenthetical account of the results of YHWH's upheaval of the heaven and the earth. This digression causes this verse to stand apart from the context on several fronts. First, the military imagery of the verse has no counterpart in Haggai. Second, the perspective of Hag 2:21-22 differs with the perspective concerning the nations in the doublet in Hag 2:6f. In 2:7, YHWH purposes to shake the nations in order that they come to Judah and bring the wealth of the nations to the newly restored temple. By contrast, the militancy of Hag 2:22 leaves no room for a pilgrimage of nations to bring tribute. Rather, it depicts the annihilation of the nations. Third, the introduction in 2:21 commands that Haggai address Zerubbabel, but Zerubbabel plays no role in 2:22, since he is not addressed until 2:23. Fourth, this verse has created the historically unverifiable impression of Zerubbabel as a revolutionary.[48] Not only can

---

dates; and the more skeptical approach of Ackroyd, *JJS* 2 (1951): 171-173, who argues they are the work of an editor whose use of traditions we cannot verify.

[47] The fact that the entire book of Haggai reports the prophet's message as a third person account demonstrates the literary collection of the speeches did not originate from the prophet himself. Most recent commentators presume an early collection of sayings of Haggai, which were worked into their present shape by the Haggai-Chronicler. The final word of 2:20 marks the transition from the Haggai-Chronicler's introduction to the oracle itself. The double use of אמר created by this transition is rather cumbersome and tends to support the view that the Chronicler has simply taken pre-existing material (see also Hag 2:2). See fuller discussions of the characteristics of this Haggai-Chronicler in Wolff, *BK* 14/6, 3-6; Beuken, *Haggai - Sacharja 1-8*, 331-336. By way of contrast, Eissfeldt, *Introduction*, 428f, pictures this third person account as the work of Haggai himself who uses the third person style as a means of strengthening the impression of authority.

[48] For the problems inherent in seeing Zerubbabel as an instigator of rebellion against the Persians, see discussions in Aage Bentzen, "Quelques remarques sur le mouvement messianique parmi les Juifs aux environs de l'an 520 avant Jésus-Christ," *Revue d'Histoire et de Philosophie Religeuses* 10 (1930): 493-503. Most recently, see the

no support be found that Judah attempted revolt against the Persian empire during this period, but the verse itself does not portray Zerubbabel in this light. The overthrow of the kingdoms rests strictly upon the instigation and actions of YHWH, not Zerubbabel. The verse does not command Zerubbabel to overthrow the kingdoms, it offers the promise that YHWH will overthrow the power of the nations. Fifth, Hag 2:22 contains a number of catchwords and phrases which reappear in Zech 1:1ff.

The presence of these catchwords in a verse which is literarily suspect raises the question whether one can determine if the desire to incorporate Haggai into a larger corpus motivated the addition of Hag 2:22. Some preliminary observations point in this direction.[49] First, several words in Hag 2:22 appear at the beginning of the first night vision in Zech 1:8, namely "rider," "horses," and "אִישׁ."[50] Second, the "nations" also play a prominent role in Zechariah's first night vision (cf 1:11,15). Third, "chariot" and "throne" do not appear in the first vision of Zech 1:8-17, but both figure significantly in the final vision (6:1-8) and the oracle which follows (6:9-15).[51] Hence, Hag 2:22 contains catchwords from the beginning and end of Zechariah's vision cycle. Fourth, the military imagery in Hag 2:22 paints a battle scene which reverses the picture of the attacking enemy in Joel 2:4-11. Joel 2:4ff describes the enemy who attacks Jerusalem on the

---

articles comparing the picture of Zerubbabel in the extant literature from Haggai to Josephus: Sara Japhet, "Sheshbazzar and Zerubbabel — Against the Background of the Historical and religious Tendencies of Ezra-Nehemiah." Part 1 in *ZAW* 94 (1982): 66-98; Part 2 in *ZAW* 95 (1983): 218-229. See particularly the discussion on pages 77f.

[49] See the works of Ackroyd, "The Book of Haggai and Zechariah 1-8," *JJS* 3 (1952): 151-156; Beuken, *Haggai-Sacharja 1-8*; Mason, *The Books of Haggai, Zechariah and Malachi*, 8-10; and Ronald Pierce, "Literary Connectors and a Haggai-Zechariah-Malachi Corpus," *JETS* 27 (1984): 277-89; and "A Thematic Development of the Haggai-Zechariah-Malachi Corpus," *JETS* 27 (1984): 401-11. From different perspectives, all have recognized a strong possibility that Haggai and Zechariah 1-8 were transmitted as part of a common corpus. However, their observations do not describe the same phenomenon which has been the subject of this investigation. It is thus necessary to ask if one may postulate that the combined Haggai/Zechariah 1-8 corpus predated their incorporation into the larger corpus of the Book of the Twelve, at which point it received minor alterations which adapted it for a larger literary environment. Further observations supporting this argument will be discussed following an analysis of Zech 1:1ff (See §4, "Zech 1 and the Book of the Twelve," in the next chapter).

[50] See translations of the relevant passages above.

[51] The final vision concerns the four chariots of YHWH's heavenly army, and the oracle which follows treats the form of government which YHWH will institute to replace the existing order (cf specifically Zech 6:13).

day of YHWH as an army whose "appearance is like the appearance of horses" (2:4) who attack "with the noise of chariots" (2:5). The reversal of the images occurs most descriptively in Joel 2:6-9, which portrays the very orderly attack of this army which marches in a line without deviating (2:7), and "each man (אִישׁ) does not crowd his brother (אָחִיו)" (2:8). By contrast, Hag 2:22 depicts the enemy in utter chaos, although it uses many of the same words: YHWH overturns the horses and chariots; "each man (אִישׁ) will fall by the sword of his brother (אָחִיו)." All of these observations create the impression that Hag 2:22 acts more in keeping with other places where a redactional insertion draws paradigmatically on Joel.

Hag 2:23 has been the subject of much discussion centering on the question of the role of Zerubbabel. Virtually no scholar disputes the verse as an accurate reflection of the message of Haggai, in large part due to the fact that the hope in Zerubbabel represented by the verse would be very difficult to explain as the result of a later interpolation. In other Old Testament texts, Zerubbabel almost always appears in connection with the high priest Joshua.[52] This association of Joshua and Zerubbabel in all likelihood reflects a change toward a hierocratic system already developing in Judah in the time of Haggai and Zechariah.[53]

Syntactically Hag 2:23 relates directly to the introduction in 2:21, since the command given in 2:21 to address Zerubbabel directly is not exemplified until the direct address in 2:23.[54] The reasons for considering Hag 2:22 a later addition have been offered, but the question of the original form and, relatedly, the original location of this oracle needs further consideration. When one removes 2:22 from consideration, the remaining portion of the oracle reads more smoothly than the oracle with 2:22 included:

---

[52] See Japhet, *ZAW* 94 (1982): 66-98; and *ZAW* 95 (1983): 218-229. Japhet compares the manner in which the various authors emphasize or de-emphasize the work of one or the other of the two figures depending upon their own literary purposes. Extra-biblical material likewise is relatively consistent in this tendency (cf Sir 49:11f), although 1 Esdras (particularly) and Josephus emphasize Zerubbabel's role in the reconstruction more than the Biblical material.

[53] Beyse, *Serubbabel und die Königserwartungen der Propheten Haggai und Sacharja*, draws out the differences in the emphases in Haggai and Zechariah regarding Zerubbabel. See also Mason, *Haggai, Zechariah, and Malachi*, 10.

[54] Petersen, *Haggai & Zechariah 1-8*, 97f admits as much, although he does not draw the conclusion that the two verses were originally connected. He says, "One senses that v.23 might be the most appropriate sequence to the introduction provided in 20-21."

> [20]And the word of YHWH came to Haggai a second time on the twenty-fourth of the month saying, [21]Speak to Zerubbabel, governor of Judah saying, I am about to cause the heavens and the earth to quake. ...　[23]On that day—utterance of YHWH Sebaoth—I will take you Zerubbabel, son of Shealtiel, my servant—utterance of YHWH. I will make you like the signet, for I have chosen you—utterance of YHWH Sebaoth.

In spite of this smooth transition, the first phrase in Hag 2:23 (ביום ההוא) probably entered the text with the addition of 2:22. The phrase appears only here in Haggai, and conjures eschatological images more in keeping with the final battle imagery of Hag 2:22 than with the theophanic imagery of 2:21.[55] The preponderance of ביום ההוא in the Book of the Twelve and Isaiah as compared with Jeremiah or Ezekiel also speaks in favor of understanding "on that day" as a typical redactional device in this context rather than in the collection of Haggai sayings. Additionally, the phrase effectively extends the time of theophanic activity further into the future than would be expected from the grammatical construction in the announcement of the theophany in 2:21 alone.[56] This protractive element thus evidences a tension not easily reconcilable with a direct address to Zerubbabel.

6. The Character of Redactional Work on Hag 2:15-19,20-23

In comparison with some of the other writings in the Book of the Twelve, the redactors apparently altered Haggai only minimally in order to appropriate it into the context of the larger corpus. They added no large blocks of material, and performed no wholesale rearrangement inside the book which can be linked to the incorporation of Haggai into the Book of the Twelve. Nevertheless, clear signs do exist that Haggai has received insertions in the form of glosses and short sayings (2:17,19,22) which intentionally allude to motifs from Joel 1-2, and which do indicate an awareness of the location of Haggai within the larger literary frame. The

---

[55] Cf. Mic 1:2-5 for similar theophanic imagery.

[56] Assuming the construction does not denote the present, the participial form with the pronoun would normally indicate the very near future (GK §116p), whereas the phrase "on that day" connotes the expectation of a longer period. If the construction intends the present "I cause the heavens and earth to shake, then the tension of ביום ההוא becomes even more pronounced.

lack of major additions parallels the beginning of Haggai, which likewise received only cosmetic adaptations.[57]

Two suggestions may be offered to account for the minimal amount of material added to Haggai. First, as mentioned briefly above, there is good reason to suspect that prior to its inclusion into the larger corpus, Haggai was already part of a literary corpus which included more than one writing.[58] This Haggai-Zechariah corpus was incorporated into the book of the Twelve after it had already circulated separately. Second, the intended function of Haggai in the literary context of the Book of the Twelve did not require wholesale additions to accomplish its purpose. Both the literary work and the subsequent traditions regarding Haggai (and Zechariah) center around one theme: the rebuilding of the temple following the exile.[59] The rebuilding of the temple appears in the proper location within the historical frame of the Book of the Twelve. Not only does Zephaniah, the preceding writing, provide the last pre-exilic dating formula in the larger collection, but the literary adaptation of Zeph 3:18-20 deliberately prepares the reader for the message of Haggai to the community, the message that YHWH requires them to build the temple.

Despite the relatively minor additions to Haggai, some observations may be offered regarding the particular hermeneutic which they display. Elsewhere, the redactional work on the Book of the Twelve demonstrates a clear tendency toward a dialectic which places YHWH's action in the past within a cosmic frame. On one level, this combination reminds the reader that Israel's history results from the actions and decisions of YHWH. On another level, however, the same material draws attention away from the past by referring to YHWH's future action. Nahum and Habakkuk frame the destruction of Assyria and Babylon similarly, with extensive theophanic material added at the beginning and end of the works respectively. Zephaniah likewise incorporates cosmic judgment with theophanic elements into the prediction of the desolation of Judah and Jerusalem. Joel 4 and Obad 15-21 exhibit similar dialectics, although they are less tied to the historical framework of the writings in the Book of the Twelve. In the case

---

[57] See discussion of the Zephaniah-Haggai connection in the previous chapter.

[58] Works by Ackroyd, Beuken, Pierce, and others have documented the redactional work uniting at least these two writings. See fuller discussion of Zech 1:1ff in §4, "Zech 1 and the Book of the Twelve" in the next chapter.

[59] Haggai is universally associated with the impetus for the construction of the temple, see Ezra 5:1; 6:14. The same is true for Zerubbabel, whose role in the reconstruction of the temple becomes more pronounced in 1 Esdras and Josephus than does his Davidic ancestry.

of Haggai 2:17,19*,22 this dialectic manifests itself appropriately to the larger literary context. It alludes to the punishment of the past which still has ramifications for the present (2:17,19*), and it promises a time to come when YHWH will overthrow the nations (2:22), paving the way for Davidic rule.[60]

Following a discussion of Zech 8:9ff, it will be necessary to return to the question of the identity of the group responsible for the redactional work which incorporated the Haggai-Zechariah corpus into the Book of the Twelve, but a few preliminary observations will serve as an introduction to the question here. To be sure, the literary form of Haggai and of the Haggai-Zechariah corpus was not composed originally for the Book of the Twelve. The dating formulas in Haggai which have been incorporated secondarily into Zechariah distinguish themselves as the work of a different circle of transmission than the Deuteronomistic corpus and other works using similar forms of the דבר יהוה superscriptions (Joel and Jonah). Other well-documented relationships tie the Haggai-Zechariah corpus to a common transmission circle more closely associated with the Chronicler than most of the other prophetic traditions.[61] The insertions noted here, by contrast, relate more closely to the typical themes of Isaiah and the Book of the Twelve. The citation and allusions to Amos and Joel respectively rely on motifs which consistently reappear in redactional passages in the Book of the Twelve. The eschatological perspective of the overthrow of the nations creeps into Haggai, which helps to account for the different views toward the nations in 2:22 and 2:7. In a sense, the history of YHWH's prophetic word to his people continues. The restoration of the temple is acknowledged as part of YHWH's continuing action by the incorporation of Haggai/Zechariah 1-8 into the Book of the Twelve, but the

---

[60] The promise to Zerubbabel in 2:23, although part of the *Vorlage*, has effectively been eschatologized by the addition of ביום ההוא, so that its "fulfillment" is protracted further into the future. Nevertheless, the symbolism of the rule of the Davidide is not inconsistent with other redactional passages in the Book of the Twelve. Already the Deuteronomistic corpus exhibited this theme (cf Amos 9:11,14f), but also Joel (4:1-3;17-21) and Obadiah (19f) emphasize the restoration of the Davidic-Solomonic kingdom with Jerusalem and Judah playing the central role.

[61] One should not identify this Haggai-Chronicler as identical with the Chronicler, or even with the time of the Chronicler, but the similarities do point toward the same tradition circle. Beuken refers most often to the Chronistic *milieu* of the redactional work uniting these two works. See Beuken, *Haggai-Sacharja 1-8*, 331-336. See also the call for more precision in Rex Mason, "The Purpose of the 'Editorial Framework' in the Book of Haggai," *VT* 27 (1977): 413-421.

restoration does not end the story.   The people of YHWH are not portrayed as having reached a utopic state in either their relationship to YHWH, or in their political fortune.   There is an implicit recognition that this restoration is only partial.   The announcement of a future judgment to punish the nations, as well as the accentuation of the lack of a bountiful harvest, draws the reader's attention into the future as if to say there is still more to come.

Zechariah 1-8

1. The Macrostructure of Zech 1-8

Scholarly consensus demands that the first eight chapters (Proto-Zechariah) be treated separately from chapters 9-14.[1] The macro-structure of Proto-Zechariah divides readily into three major sections: the introduction (1:1-6); the cycle of eight visions and their related oracles (1:7-6:15); and the concluding oracles (7:1-8:23). This structure, as with Haggai, is reflected in the text formally, via the introductory dating elements which precede the respective sections. As already noted, the dating elements, appearing in chronological order, are so close stylistically to those in Haggai that many authors suppose they stem from a common transmission circle, if not from a common redactional hand.[2] Compared with their presence in Haggai, however, these dating elements are neither as numerous — in spite of the fact that Zechariah is the larger work — nor do they appear to be as integrally involved in the structure of the individual units. The logical conclusion relates these elements to the level of the combination of separate blocks into a literary collection.

The cycle of eight visions comprises the largest block (1:7-6:15), and is introduced by one of the three chronistic elements (1:7). Despite certain difficulties, scholars typically perceive 1:7 as an essential part of the visions cycle.[3] The visions themselves contain a vision report in stylized form,

---

[1] For an account of the history of this division (often called Deutero- and Trito-Zechariah) see the my forthcoming volume, *Redactional Processes in the Book of the Twelve*, on Zech 9-14.

[2] Beuken, *Haggai - Sacharja 1-8*, 20, does not base his argument of a common redaction upon these chronological elements. He feels the similarities between these elements in Haggai and Zechariah can be ascribed too easily to accidental similarities. While he may be correct with regard to the fact that the similarity does not *prove* a single redaction of the two works in a common corpus, the similarity is so close that one must accept some type of mutual relationship, at least in the form of a common transmission circle which collected the works.

[3] See the extended discussion in Christian Jeremias, *Die Nachtgesichte des Sacharja. Untersuchungen zu ihrer Stellung im Zusammenhang der Visionsberichte im Alten Testament und zu ihrem Bildmaterial*, Forschungen zur Religion und Literatur des

including several which have received interpretive additions in the form of oracles. Seven of the eight visions (1:8-15; 2:1-4; 2:5-9; 3:1-7; 4:1-6a,10b-14; 5:1-4; 5:5-11; 6:1-8) forming the heart of Proto-Zechariah manifest three common elements:

> 1) Portrayal of the vision image
> 2) Zechariah's question as to the meaning
> 3) The explanation

The structure of the visions sometimes repeats certain elements, but it deviates only in 3:1-7, which, along with other distinctions, has caused considerable debate regarding its originality.[4]

Oracular material inside the vision cycle does not appear after every vision, but in those visions where it does appear, it relates explicitly to the preceding visions, sometimes as clarification, sometimes as correction.[5] This oracular material appears with the first, third, fourth, fifth, and eighth visions. Some of the oracular material clearly represents later additions to the vision cycle, particularly when it corrects a perspective in the vision or its interpretation.[6]

The concluding section will be treated in the following chapter. The third and final chronistic element dates this last episode almost two years after the date which introduces the vision cycle. Zech 7:2-8:23 is a series of relatively short oracles which have been collected together. The integrity of this final section is suspect, with a sizable number of commentators

---

Alten und Neuen Testaments 117 (Göttingen: Vandenhoeck & Ruprecht, 1977), 15-38. Rudolph, *KAT* 14/4, 72, thinks the superscription in 1:7 circulated with the vision cycle, but he resorts to emendation to smooth the transition from the verse to the visions. Petersen, *Haggai & Zechariah 1-8*, 38f, is vague in his assessment of the relationship of 1:7 to 1:8, but does point out the both 1:7 and 7:1 (in contrast to 1:1) use Babylonian month names. By contrast, see the brief comments of Mason, *Haggai, Zechariah, and Malachi*, 35.

[4] For a concise discussion of the structural elements of the visions and the variations, see Jeremias, *Die Nachtgesichte des Sacharja*, 10-12. Jeremias discusses the pertinent elements of the deviation in the formal structure of this vision. Further, Jeremias, 201-225, provides a thorough discussion of the problems which the fourth vision presents as an original part of the vision cycle. Jeremias does not, however, deny its authorship to Zechariah. By contrast, Petersen, *Haggai & Zechariah 1-8*, 112, considers the passage "an integral and original part of the visionary sequence." See his discussion, 187-202.

[5] See discussions in Petersen, *Haggai & Zechariah 1-8*, 120-124; Elliger, *ATD* 25, 122f.

[6] See Zech 3:6-9, which offers competing interpretations concerning the priest and the royal figure (the branch).

arguing that substantial portions have been added later.[7] The oracles are
set within a frame (7:1-3; 8:18ff) of Zechariah's response to a delegation
regarding the keeping of fasts, but not all of the oracular material relates
directly to fasting. Some of the material is best read as part of the
formation of the book of Zechariah, and some of the material in these
chapters goes to considerable effort to relate the writings of Haggai and
Zechariah.

The introductory section of Zechariah (1:1-6) consists of the first
chronistic element (1:1) and the report of a sermon and its effects (1:2-6).
This section will be treated from several perspectives in order to appreciate
its function. The catchwords between Haggai and Zechariah noted above
appear in Zech 1:1-6 and 1:7-17, and thus overlap the first two major
divisions of Proto-Zechariah, the book's introduction and the first vision.
Both units will be treated here because of the common words they share
with the concluding sections of Haggai. In attempting to determine how
these common words relate to one another, it will be necessary to
determine the literary integrity of these specific units.

2. Literary Observations on Zech 1:1-6

Zech 1:1-6 contains two formally distinguishable elements, the
chronistic element in 1:1 and the sermon report in 1:2-6. **Zech 1:1** differs
from the other chronistic elements in Haggai and Zechariah in that it only
provides the month and the year, not the day, upon which the encounter
occurred. Simultaneously, of the three chronistic elements in Zechariah,
only 1:1 which does not contain a reference to the Babylonian name of the
month. Zech 1:1 also refers only to Darius, as with 1:7, and does not assign
the epithet "the king" following mention of the name as appears in Hag
1:1,15 (see also Zech 7:1). The minor variations within these chronistic
elements — in both Haggai and Zechariah — indicates on the one hand,
that there was no strong desire to standardize them completely. On the
other hand, the variations do not override the fundamental similarity of the
chronistic style which points to a common transmission circle which
considered the dating of prophetic utterances of some significance.

The date mentioned in Zech 1:1, the eighth month of the second year
of Darius (October-November, 520) overlaps with the last date mentioned

---

[7]   See discussion of Zech 8:9-23 below, page 257.

in the chronistic elements in Haggai (the ninth month). This overlap carries some literary significance. It not only serves to anchor the two works together, but the call to repentance delivered in Zech 1:2-6 likewise fits the situation prior to Haggai's oracle on the cleansing of the people. The second date in Zech 1:7, by contrast, post-dates the last dated speech in Haggai, and the situation it depicts, with all the world at rest, differs from the upheaval depicted in Hag 2:20-23.[8]

Zech 1:2-6 poses considerable problems because it frequently relies upon the interpretation of suffixes whose addressees must be extrapolated from the context, often without clear antecedents. The constellation is clear enough. Five entities appear in these verses: the prophet, YHWH, the present congregation, the fathers, and the earlier prophets. Zech 1:2 seemingly provides little problem in determining the participants, since the plural reference to "your fathers" (אבותיכם) objectively indicates the present generation as addressee, and the reference to YHWH in the 3rd person eliminates YHWH as speaker. However, direct association of the prophet as speaker creates considerable difficulty when one seeks to relate 1:2 with either the preceding or the following verse. Beuken has therefore adjudged 1:2 as a later insertion, but other alternatives should be explored, particularly in light of the tenuous evidence he presents.[9] Four possibilities exist for understanding 1:2: the word of YHWH as "speaker," 1:2 as an independent saying of the prophet, the prophet as speaker (creating ramifications for the verses which follow), or some sort of textual corruption (either as the result of deliberate change or accidental omission).

First, a syntactical connection backward exists which connects Zech 1:2 with 1:1, namely, 1:1 ends with the word "saying" (לאמר). Literally, the subject of this connective is the דבר־יהוה earlier in the verse. This observation raises the possibility that the speaker in 1:2 should be

---

[8] The implications of this different setting will be discussed below in the observations on the *Stichwörter* between Haggai and Zechariah, beginning on page 252.

[9] Beuken, *Haggai - Sacharja 1-8*, 84f. Beuken rests his case upon the conviction that the phrase "the word of YHWH came to (אל) ..." (Hag 2:10,20; Zech 1:7; 7:1) differs in form from the related phrase, "the word of YHWH came through (ביד) ..." (Hag 1:1; 2:1). This claim is difficult to support in the text. Beuken believes (following Mitchell, *ICC*, 109, 114), that the phrase in Zech 1:1 demands that a commission (*Beauftragung*) with an imperative and an addressee follow immediately. Such strict distinction does not correspond to the use of the two phrases in Haggai (note the messenger formula in Hag 2:11, and the commission in 2:2 which follows the use of the phrase, "and the word of YHWH came *through* ..." in 2:1). Even more significantly, the phrase appears again in Zech 1:7; 7:1 in the identical form as 1:1 without a subsequent imperative.

understood as the "word of YHWH," which is distinct from YHWH himself, but does not require the presence of an additional speaker. Zech 1:2 would then be understood as a type of narrative element which sets the scene for that which follows: YHWH was angry with your (2mp) fathers. This option would alleviate the problems with the connection backward, but would still leave a tension with 1:3 since that verse would change from a 2mp address of the entire congregation to a 3mp reference to that same group. Simultaneously, Zech 1:3 would single out the prophet from the entire congregation while including him in the reference to "your fathers" in 1:2. The beginning of Zech 1:3 ("and you [2ms] say to them [3mp] ...") would thus shift both addressees compared with Zech 1:2.

The second option, that 1:2 represents an independent saying of the prophet is less satisfying. Since syntactical connections exist both to the preceding verse and to the verse which follows, this option appears very unlikely. Also, the content of this verses makes little sense as an isolated saying. The reference to a past generation has little significance without some type of application or context in which to understand such a saying.

The third option, that the prophet should be visualized as the speaker, would on the one hand be the most natural assumption, particularly in light of other sermonic elements in the passage, but on the other hand a prophetic speaker in 1:2 creates implications for the manner in which one interprets the following verse.[10] If the prophet speaks in 1:2, then it is difficult to see how suddenly YHWH could be the speaker in the beginning of 1:3 in what is traditionally interpreted as an address to the prophet: "and now you (2ms) say to them."[11] Given the 2ms reference, the only two options for the addressee of ואמרת in Zech 1:3 are the prophet or YHWH. Relatedly, whichever of the two is not the *addressee* must be the *speaker* in 1:3aα. Again, neither option may be selected without problems. Either 1:3 begins with YHWH's address to the prophet, in which case one must assume a change of speaker and a change of reference toward the congregation, or the verse begins with the prophet's address to YHWH, a direct address which is highly uncharacteristic of the remainder of the

---

[10] For discussion of the application of the term "sermon" to this passage, see Beuken, *Haggai - Sacharja 1-8*, 84-115 and Rex Mason, "Some Echoes of the Preaching in the Second Temple? Tradition Elements in Zechariah 1-8." *ZAW* 96 (1984): 221-235.

[11] On form-critical grounds, "them" in Zech 1:3 is typically interpreted as the present generation and not the fathers. See Rudolph, *KAT* 13/4, 68; Petersen, *Haggai & Zechariah 1-8*, 130; Beuken, *Haggai - Sacharja*, 84f.

material in Zechariah, but which could be seen as an introduction to the
YHWH speech in 1:3-6.[12]

The group to whom the message should be/has been directed in 1:3
also creates problems, and is interrelated with the decision regarding the
speaker.[13] If YHWH is the speaker in 1:3, then "them" would have to
refer to the present generation, since the prophet would hardly have spoken
to the fathers against whom YHWH's anger had been directed.
Problematic for this interpretation is the fact that "them" would have no
syntactical antecedent, since the current generation was addressed directly
in Zech 1:2. If the prophet is the speaker, then "them" could refer to the
fathers, and the verse would essentially reflect the prophet's contention that
YHWH had offered the fathers the chance to repent, with the implication
being that they refused: But you (YHWH) said to them (the fathers),
return to me and I will return to you (2mp). As with the problem with the
speaker, this option is more pleasing syntactically, but more difficult to
accept form-critically because of the problems of the direct address to
YHWH it requires.

The fourth option argues textual disruption as the cause of confusion.
In its most common form, several scholars argue that a later hand has
substituted a verse which is impossible to harmonize with the context, by
replacing the original introduction which would have contained reference
to the addressee as well as an imperative to the prophet.[14] The replaced
verse is presumed to have read something to the effect, "Proclaim to the
people." This options creates several problems which make it difficult to
accept. First, the obvious problem is that there is no textual evidence that
another verse existed.   Second, when Beuken and others speak of
replacement they imply deliberation on the part of the redactor, but such
deliberation is difficult to rationalize as the replacement of a verse whose

---

[12] In the visions, Zechariah does not address God directly. Only the mediator speaks
directly to YHWH (1:12). Neither does Zechariah address YHWH directly in the
oracles of chapters 7-8.

[13] The beginning of Zech 1:3 would either be translated: "And you (YHWH) said to
them," if spoken by the prophet, or "And you (to Zechariah) say (now) to them," if
spoken by YHWH.

[14] So Mitchell, *ICC*, 109,114; Beuken, *Haggai - Sacharja 1-8*, 85f; Karl Budde, "Zum Text
der drei letzten kleinen Propheten." ZAW 26 (1906): 5. Rudolph, *KAT* 14/4, 66,
proposes the omission of the phrase at the end of 1:1. Mason, *The Books of Haggai,
Zechariah, and Malachi*, 32 follows the NEB by reading "the people" rather than
"them," but offers no rationale for the acceptance of this interpretation as textually
justified.

meaning is so innocuous as they would have us believe. It is difficult to understand why a redactor would deliberately replace a verse which made perfect sense with one which causes so many problems. Third, even if 1:2 were a deliberate replacement, one must presume that the redactor had a specific intention, but finding this intention immediately forces one back to the problem of the interpretation of the very problematic antecedents which create the problem in the first place. Hence, on whatever level, one cannot avoid making a decision upon the text as it stands. Fourth, Rudolph's suggestion that the omission of the imperative and addressee was unintentional is equally difficult to accept in light of the fact that it involves the loss of an entire phrase with no rationale as to what would have caused so much material to fall away.[15]

In summary, of the four options available to determine the referents in Zech 1:2f, only two offer solid prospects without unnecessary speculation. Either one must treat 1:2 as the introductory "word of YHWH" and live with the tension of changing antecedents, or one must see 1:2 as the beginning of the prophet's speech, and live with the tension of the form-critical problems of the direct address to YHWH. The former is chosen here, primarily because it appears to best explain the larger context.

Understanding the larger context requires recognition of the structuring role played by the repeated messenger formulas in Zech 1:3 and 1:4. These formulas introduce short YHWH speeches, but these two speeches frame the contrast between the generations. Zech 1:4 provides the clearest example, since the verse introduces the short divine speech with a simultaneous warning to the current generation ("do not be like your [2mp] fathers ..."). The divine speech is not, however, delivered directly, but consistent with Zechariah as a whole, requires the divine speech be mediated through prophets ("to whom the earlier prophets proclaimed, saying ..."). The messenger formula in Zech 1:4 is then followed by a short summation of the message to the fathers through the prophets: return from your evil ways and your evil deeds. Significantly, the narrative then resumes, but unlike some of the other places where the "narrator" speaks without identification, this verse unqualifyingly ends with a description of the reaction from the mouth of YHWH: "but they did not return *to me*."[16]

---

[15] Rudolph, *KAT* 13/4, 66, merely says the omission at the end of 1:1 is easy to explain, but such is not the case, since no strong arguments can be brought for haplography or related errors of transcription.

[16] This description of their reaction falls outside the actual quote of the former prophet as introduced at the beginning of Zech 1:4. The imperatives of the quote imply direct

Zech 1:3 parallels 1:4 to a considerable degree in both formal elements and vocabulary. It contains a divine recount of the prophetic message (return to me and I will return to you) introduced by the messenger formula and followed by an implicit call to response in the form of a plea ("Do not be like your fathers.") This common structure may be diagrammed as follows:

Zech 1:3	Zech 1:4
1. YHWH states the prophet's message to the current generation: And you will say to them.	1. YHWH recounts the earlier prophets' message to the fathers: To whom the former prophets proclaimed.
2. Messenger formula: Thus says YHWH Sebaoth.	2. Messenger formula: Thus says YHWH Sebaoth.
3. Message Proper: Return to me, and I will return to you.	3. Message Proper: Turn from your evil ways and your evil deeds.
4. Implicit call to response (1:4aa): Do not be like your fathers.	4. Narration of response: They did not listen to me.

This parallel structure of Zech 1:3,4 which runs seamlessly between the two verses, accentuates the dichotomy between the false decision of the earlier generation and the need of the current generation to make the proper decision.

This divine confrontation with the current generation continues with a series of rhetorical questions (1:5-6a) from YHWH. The questions of these verses specifically demonstrate YHWH's control over events which have led to the current situation. The fathers' generation has been punished, and YHWH's action has fulfilled its threat (1:5).[17] YHWH answers his own rhetorical questions in 1:5 with another (1:6a) in such a manner as to say that the threats made by YHWH were not idle: "My

---

confrontation with the fathers, but the perfects in the description require that such confrontation is in the past.

[17] In spite of the somewhat enigmatic reference to the prophets together with the fathers in Zech 1:5, the tenor of the questions demonstrates clearly that the two taken together incorporate the message to the past generation. See fuller discussions of the problematic references to the prophets in Petersen, *Haggai & Zechariah 1-8*, 133f. Beuken, *Haggai - Sacharja 1-8*, 99-101, provides several options offered by commentators modern and ancient, but his acceptance of Jerome's explanation that Zech 1:5 refers to false prophets is unconvincing. Rudolph, *KAT* 13/4, 69f, accepts another ancient tradition that the speaker changes, so that the line should be understood as the objection of the people. Although this explanation would alleviate the tension, the parallelism of the verse argues against this option as well.

words and my statutes which I commanded my servants the prophets, did they not overtake your fathers?."[18]

The final report of the response (1:6b), as with the beginning of the unit, creates problems for interpreters. The problem lies not in a corrupted MT, but again with the antecedent to be presumed. The report simply recounts that, "They returned and said, 'Just as YHWH purposed to do to us according to our ways and according to our deeds, so has he done with us.'" Initially, one is tempted to presume that the subject "they" refers to the fathers, since that would be the closest plural antecedent, but scholars have long noted that such an interpretation brings this half-verse into severe conflict with the unit as a whole, specifically with Zech 1:4.[19] It is impossible to reconcile the fathers as *the* negative example *par excellence* of how not to behave with the account of repentance in 1:6b if "they" reflected the action of the fathers. A more likely explanation is to suppose that the description of 1:6b leaves the direct encounter supposed in 1:3-6a, and returns to the more detached level of the narrative frame as in 1:1f. Formally, 1:6b would then be treated as an account of the *results* of Zechariah's preaching. Stylistically, this unannounced change of perspective appeared previously in the transition from the narrative frame to the confrontation with the current generation, as noted in the discussion of the problems at the beginning of 1:3. The resulting understanding of the form

---

[18] This question conjures martial and punitive images (Hos 10:9; Jer 42:16; Deut 28:15,45). See Petersen, *Haggai & Zechariah 1-8*, 134. Hence, the verse reflects the longstanding effects of the destruction of Jerusalem by the Babylonians.

[19] Zech 1:6b has generated considerable controversy, because of the tension it creates with the remainder of 1:1-6, especially 1:4. Beuken, *Haggai - Sacharja 1-8*, 86-88, (following Rothstein), sees the line as a later redactional insertion concerning the reaction of the present generation: so also Mason, *Haggai, Zechariah, and Malachi*, 33; Ackroyd, *Exile and Restoration*, 202f. Elliger, *ATD* 25, 95, believes the entire verse relates to the present generation, but avoids the problems by emending "your fathers" to "you" in 1:6a. Rudolph, *KAT* 13/4, 70f, acknowledges the problems, and admits that the verse must be directed to the present generation. However, Rudolph opines that a report on the positive reaction of the present generation does not find any parallel in the remainder of Proto-Zechariah. He therefore emends the verbs וישובו ויאמרו into imperatives, but this suggestion is difficult to accept in light of the fact that an unattested emendation on *two* verbs which changes the consonantal text of both verbs is highly implausible. Petersen, *Haggai & Zechariah 1-8*, goes against the grain and argues that the line does presuppose the fathers as antecedent. His interpretation however, requires a second repentance (this time from the present generation) to eradicate the effects of the past, *in spite of* the repentance of the fathers, and this raises serious theological difficulties.

of 1:1-6 thus supposes that a narrative frame surrounds the actual account of a divine confrontation with the current generation.

> 1:1-3aa Narrative frame: Reception of the word of YHWH, and command to deliver the following:
> 1:3 Divine command to the current generation
> 1:4 Account of message to the past generation
> 1:5-6a Rhetorical confrontation with the current generation
> 1:6b Narrative frame: The positive response of the current generation

This account of the people's positive response in Zech 1:6b also coincides readily with the function of 1:1-6 as introduction to the cycle of visions.[20] It adds to the impression that Zech 1:1-6 has been highly influenced, if not composed, for its position as introduction to Zechariah, or for its position in the Haggai-Zechariah corpus.[21]   What is significant for the present discussion is the observation in the form of a negative conclusion: while there are literary difficulties in these verses, nothing in them indicates that the verses were created at the level of attachment for the Book of the Twelve. There are no obvious allusions to other works in the Book of the Twelve, with the exception of Haggai.[22] There are no real vocabulary ties to parallels in Isaiah, which would explain the verses.[23] Thus, one cannot claim the redactional process of assimilation into the Book of the Twelve has effected the shape of these verses. Since the majority of the common words with Haggai appear also in the first vision, it is necessary to look at this unit as well.

---

[20] Beuken, *Haggai - Sacharja 1-8*, 112f; Mason, *Haggai, Zechariah, and Malachi*, 33f; Petersen, *Haggai & Zechariah 1-8*, 134f.

[21] Note above all the thematic connection between 1:2-6 and Zech 8:14-17.

[22] See Beuken, *Haggai - Sacharja 1-8*, 331-336.

[23] Bosshard, *BN* 40 (1987): 35f, admits the structural parallels between Proto-Zechariah and Isaiah are more difficult to claim as intentional, despite some evidence that the two texts do coincide to some degree. He notes only a parallel constellation between Zech 1:12-17 and Isa 60-61, but does not indicate that this constellation is redactionally imposed into Zechariah.

3. Zech 1:7-17: The First Vision

Zechariah's first vision (1:7-17) begins with the second of the chronistic elements (1:7), separating it formally from the introductory sermon report in 1:1-6. Scholars most frequently consider Zech 1:7 as an introductory element which circulated with the vision cycle prior to the collection into the corpus now constituting Proto-Zechariah, although the similarity of the three chronistic elements could just as easily imply that these structuring elements belong to the level of the book's formation rather than the transmission history of the individual sections.[24] At any rate, the vision proper does not begin until Zech 1:8, and though 1:7 presupposes something which follows, Zech 1:8ff does not demand Zech 1:7 as an introduction. Zech 1:8 could well have stood at the head of the literary collection of visions without 1:7.[25]

---

[24] A long debate exists as to whether these visions were experienced in a single night as 1:8 implies (הלילה most likely means "this night."), or whether they represent a collection of visions experienced over a longer period of time (so Kurt Galling, "Die Exilswende in der Sicht des Propheten Sacharja," *VT* 2 [1952]: 18-36.). In light of the literary character of the majority of these "visions," it is difficult to accept the arguments that the individual "visions" reflect separate experiences over an expanded period. See further discussions in Christian Jeremias, *Nachtgesichte*, 12-39; and Beuken, *Haggai - Sacharja 1-8*, 232-258.

[25] Several observations require that Zech 1:7 was certainly not a part of an "original" presentation of the visions. First, Zech 1:8 is the only vision which does not begin with a *waw*, which is appropriate for the first vision of a cycle. Second, the date reference in Zech 1:8 appears redundant following Zech 1:7. Zech 1:7 dates the "word of YHWH" precisely to the twenty-fourth day of the eleventh month of the second year of Darius (February 15, 519). The reference to "this night" in Zech 1:8 is unnecessary in light of 1:7. Third, Zech 1:7 has a reflective character, which is only appropriate if one desires to preserve something for posterity. These observations help separate 1:7 from 1:8ff, but the question with regard to how early 1:7 was attached to the visions is more complicated. Conceivably, the verse could have served as the "official" introduction to the visions when they circulated separately, and have been attached relatively early. This understanding requires, however, the acceptance of a circle of transmission which: 1) used a fixed superscriptive style in the headings divergent pieces of literature (because of the similarity to 1:1; 7:1), and 2) followed particular traditions regarding the family heritage of Zechariah. Given the fact that more than one recorded version of Zechariah's heritage exists — regarding the name of his father — this last observation should not be overlooked (see Ezra 5:1; 6:14). For the above reasons, it appears more plausible to approach Zech 1:7 as part of the redaction of Proto-Zechariah rather than to treat it as merely the introduction to the vision cycle. If the verse was not entirely devised by the redactional hand which united the book's three major composition blocks, then in all likelihood it was adapted for this purpose. See

Zechariah's first vision contains all three major elements appearing in the visions, namely, the portrayal of the vision image (1:8), Zechariah's question to the messenger regarding its meaning (1:9), and the explanation (1:10f). Additionally, the action of the vision contains an account of a dialogue between the messenger and YHWH which includes the messenger's question (1:12) and YHWH's response to the messenger (1:13), followed by the messenger's deliverance of YHWH's messages to Zechariah (1:14f,16,17). Each of the three speeches given to Zechariah begins with its own messenger formula, but certain distinctions in the form and content of these speeches should be noted.

The vision proper, in Zech 1:8-11, describes a scene involving a man on a horse standing in front of several other horses.[26] However, as the scene unfolds it becomes clear that the action also presupposes the presence of the prophet, a messenger, and YHWH. Following Zechariah's question as to the group's significance (1:9), the reader is informed that YHWH has commissioned the group to patrol the earth (1:10). This group then reports that they have patrolled the earth, and that it is quiet and undisturbed (1:11). This report of peace prompts the messenger to inquire directly of YHWH how long he would withhold his compassion from "Jerusalem and the cities of Judah," with obvious allusions to the consequences of the Babylonian destruction of 587 (1:12).[27] YHWH then responds to the angel, who in turn communicates the message to the prophet that YHWH is zealous for "Jerusalem and Zion" (1:13-14). The remainder of 1:15-17 expounds upon the meaning of YHWH's renewed concern for Zion, but the compounding of these explanations raises the question whether they belong to a single layer of interpretation or reflect the concerns of more than one layer.[28]

---

the suggestions of C. Jeremias, *Nachtgesichte*, 15-21, 38f.

[26] It is impossible to ascertain the precise number of horses or the specific significance of the colors of the horses. On the problems of the horses, their number and their significance, see Petersen, *Haggai & Zechariah 1-8*, 140-143; W.D. McHardy, "The Horses in Zechariah," In *In Memoriam Paul Kahle*, M. Black and G. Fohrer, eds., BZAW 103 (Berlin: Töpelmann, 1968), 174-179; and Robert P. Gordon, "An Inner-Targum Corruption (Zechariah 1:8)," *VT* 25 (1975): 216-221.

[27] Zech 1:12 specifically refers to "the 70 years," which alludes to Jeremiah's prophecy (cf Jer 25:11; 29:10. See also Petersen, *Haggai & Zechariah 1-8*, 149f for the use of the phrase in other biblical and extra-biblical material.

[28] The original relationship between these oracles is controversial. For example, Beuken, *Haggai - Sacharja 1-8*, 242f; and Petersen, *Haggai & Zechariah 1-8*, 152f argue that there are two oracles, with the first one being bi-partite. On the other side an equally large number of commentators see Zech 1:16f as a later addition, including Rothstein,

The structural elements within Zech 1:14-17 demonstrate formally that two oracles comprise the message of the angel to Zechariah. The messenger formula appears three times (1:14,16,17), but its presence in 1:16 following לכן (therefore) indicates this verse must be treated in relationship to 1:14,15 in its present position. By contrast, the use of עוד (again) in 1:17 indicates a second message, and although two separate oracles do not necessarily demand two separate layers of interpretation, the particular formulation does appear suspicious. The content of these verses presents an interesting array of themes which furthers the impression that more than one hand has shaped these interpretive oracles. The first oracle (1:14-16) contains two statements (1:14b,15) each of which offers rationale for YHWH's announcement of compassionate return to Jerusalem (1:16):

YHWH's two rationale:	YHWH's decision:
Thus says YHWH Sebaoth	Therefore, thus says YHWH:
1) I am jealous for Jerusalem and Zion	1) I will return to Jerusalem
2) I am angry with the nations who are at ease	2) My house will be built
	3) A measuring line will be stretched over Jerusalem

Three crucial observations on the content of these verses argue that the rationale and the decision (despite their formal relationship) do not stem from the same hand. First, the rationale regarding the nations paints them in highly negative terms, whereas the vision proper reveals no such interest. Zech 1:15 accuses the nations furthering the disaster following Jerusalem's destruction. This interpretation operates with a hermeneutic of history which differs from that of the vision report.[29] Zech 1:15 interprets the vision, but it deliberately utilizes inflammatory terminology, compared with that of the vision, regarding its description of the circumstances. In the vision, YHWH's patrols report *positively* that the world is peaceful and quiet, but the oracular material in Zech 1:15 interprets this same situation *negatively* when it refers to "the nations who are at ease." The opinion of 1:15 also differs with the opinion expressed in the sermon report in 1:2-6, which blamed the generation of the fathers without reference to the involvement of the nations.

Nachtgesichte, 53-55; Nowack, *Dodekapropheton*, 367; Sellin, *KAT* 12, 419, 435f; Horst, *HAT* 14, 204f, 215; Elliger, *ATD* 25, 97, 109; Galling, *VT* 2 (1952): 23f; C. Jeremias, *Nachtgesichte*, 10f, 21.

[29] Note especially Zech 1:12 which, even though it also contains a historical reflection, implies the guilt of YHWH's people, and does not accuse the nations.

Second, the rationale proclaiming YHWH's jealousy for Jerusalem strikingly parallels other passages in the Book of the Twelve which integrate the individual writings into the larger corpus. The most significant parallel appears in Joel 2:18, in light of the strong penchant for redactional glosses demonstrated in other passages which pick up the imagery and vocabulary of Joel.[30] Similar occurrences of the jealousy of YHWH in relation to his people also appear in the semi-acrostic hymn in Nah 1:2-8, and Zeph 1:18; 3:8b.[31]

Third, the three-fold decision of YHWH in Zech 1:16 does not relate with an inherent logic to the rationale proffered in 1:14b,15. The rationale portray an angry God ready to act for his people against the nations.[32] However, the actions portrayed in Zech 1:16 reflect the image of a compassionate God willing to return to Jerusalem, willing to endorse the reconstruction of the temple, and to announce the rebuilding of Jerusalem. Not only does the picture of YHWH vary between the rationale and the actions, but Zech 1:16 contains no reference to punishment for the nations, nor does it imply any military action against the surrounding regions. Whereas Zech 1:14,15 portrays YHWH ready to move forward against the nations, Zech 1:16 depicts YHWH's compassionate concern for Jerusalem first and foremost.[33] Rather than a God prepared to move outward in

---

[30] Joel 2:18 says, "YHWH will be zealous for his land, and will have pity on his people." The heavy Jerusalem orientation of Joel 1-2 testifies to a similarity of outlook with Zech 1:15. Admittedly, the jealousy of YHWH for his people reflects a somewhat more stereotypical image, nevertheless, continued use of such allusions to Joel militates against this stereotypical nature as an argument for accidental similarity, especially in light of the other literary and contextual tensions of the verse.

[31] Some indications of this propensity have already appeared in the discussions of this volume. Amos 9:12a anticipates Obadiah, while 9:13 alludes backward to Joel 4:18. Zeph 1:18 clearly demonstrates signs that it entered the corpus with material which has been redactionally influenced. Hag 2:19 draws upon the language of Joel. Other examples of this paradigmatic dependence upon Joel will continue in the subsequent volume, *Redactional Processes in the Book of the Twelve*.

[32] Zech 1:14b,15 not only explicitly mention YHWH's anger with the nations, but Zech 1:14 draws on the term "YHWH Sebaoth," the military connotations of which — whether intentionally or not is of course open to question — accentuate the image of YHWH prepared to act.

[33] Zech 1:16 depicts only positive acts toward Jerusalem: YHWH returns to Jerusalem with compassion, his house is to be rebuilt, and a measuring line will be stretched across the city. This final phrase can be used negatively at times (see Lam 2:8; Isa 34:11), but the context demands it be understood positively in 1:16, reflecting similar ideas to Ezek 47:3; Jer 31:38f.

anger, the decisions in 1:16 portray a god preparing to settle back peacefully where he belongs.

Two questions arise immediately from the assignation of the rationale (1:14b,15) and the actions to different hands. First, which of the two belongs more closely with the first vision? Second, on what level does one place the literary growth of this text? The first question can be answered simply with a relatively high probability. The actions of Zech 1:16 are consonant with the report of the first vision, and could well constitute an original part of the vision cycle. The image of a compassionate YHWH willing to undertake reconstruction coincides readily with the peaceful message of the patrol in 1:11. The form of 1:16 demands very little adaptation to presume it as the original message transmitted to Zechariah via the messenger in 1:14a. Only "therefore" would have been added to affect the incorporation of Zech 1:14b,15 as a more aggressive response to the needs of his people. Zech 1:16 still exhibits its own messenger formula, whose style the redactor copied when inserting in 1:14b,15. Thus, Zech 1:16 is formally suited to the vision, and its content corresponds much more closely to the images of the vision than do the rationale in 1:14b,15.

The second question regarding the place of these verses in the literary history of the passage is considerably more complicated, and one can only speak in terms of probabilities. Only a tentative answer can be offered here since much of the evidence requires further investigations well beyond the task at hand. Simply listing the options for treating 1:14b,15 presents a formidable task due to the nature of the transmission process of Zechariah. At least six possible explanations could account for the situation. The addition could be treated: 1) on the level of the literary history of the vision cycle when it was transmitted separately; 2) as part of the compilation process of Proto-Zechariah; 3) with the common redaction of the Haggai-Zechariah corpus; 4) with the process of uniting the books in the larger corpus now known as the Book of the Twelve; 5) the incorporation of Deutero-Zechariah with Proto-Zechariah; 6) an isolated gloss. The similarity of vocabulary and outlook with other redactional material inside the Book of the Twelve inclines one toward the fourth option which says that the context from which the redactor worked was that of the Book of the Twelve. A brief evaluation of the other possibilities may help illumine this presupposition further.

One may eliminate the last option from serious consideration. Not only does the inserted material bear too much in common with other passages in terms of vocabulary and outlook, but the incorporation of structural elements mean the verse has been blended into the text. The use of the messenger formula and the addition of "therefore" demonstrate the redactional intention to incorporate this material into the literary setting in a manner which supersedes the function of an isolated gloss or marginal note. It is also not likely that the verse entered with Zech 9-14. Current evidence argues that these chapters entered the book of the Twelve after Proto-Zechariah was already present, and that the incorporation of these chapters did not involve wholesale additions to the text of the remaining books.[34]

The remaining options are very difficult to eliminate entirely from consideration, although when all the evidence is taken together they appear less likely than understanding the verses as part of the redaction history of the Book of the Twelve. For example, some of the other visions, particularly the second and third, do exhibit more negative attitudes toward the nations that would be more in keeping with Zech 1:14b,15. This shared attitude could be used as evidence that the insertion was part of the combination of the visions into a single corpus. Against this option, one must note that the vocabulary of the insertion does not demonstrate any real connective function to these visions so that in spite of similar attitudes, 1:14b,15 does not offer solid evidence that it *functions* as a connective between the visions themselves.

It is even more difficult to eliminate consideration of the remaining options, because all three remaining options presuppose that the author works from a broader literary horizon than the vision cycle alone. One can make a case that Zech 1:14b,15 looks forward to the collection of oracular material in Zech 7-8, and is thus related to the compilation of Proto-Zechariah. Indeed there is little doubt that Zech 1:14b,15 bears some relationship with 8:1ff. Zech 8:2 draws on the theme of YHWH's jealousy for Jerusalem, using essentially the same vocabulary.[35] On the surface, this correlation might appear to argue that Zech 1:14b,15 relates best to the redaction history of Proto-Zechariah, but such an easy decision cannot be maintained without qualification. Beuken and others offer convincing evidence that Zech 8:1ff is essentially a collection of speeches, many of which originate from a time later than Zechariah and which are specifically related to the combination of Haggai and Zechariah into a single corpus.[36]

---

[34] Zech 9-14 will receive more detailed treatment in the forthcoming volume, *Redactional Processes in the Book of the Twelve*.

[35] "Thus says YHWH Sebaoth, I am exceedingly jealous for Zion, yes, with great wrath I am jealous for her."

[36] See Beuken, *Haggai - Sacharja 1-8*, 156-183.

To complicate the question one step further, it must be noted that their arguments do not anticipate the question whether Zech 8:1ff should better be understood in light of the Book of the Twelve or in the more limited horizon of the combination of Haggai and Zechariah. Further analysis of Zech 8:1ff will be undertaken in the next chapter, but in anticipation of that discussion, one may note that while Zech 1:14b,15 share vocabulary with 8:2, the context in chapters 7-8 does not demonstrate an antagonism against the nations to the same degree or kind as that in Zech 1:14b,15.[37] Conversely, the inserted material in Hag 2:22 does share a very strong antagonism against the nations with the insertion of Zech 1:14b,15, and this verse appears to be associated with the connection of Haggai and Zechariah from the perspective of the Book of the Twelve.[38] When all of these observations are taken into account, one may cautiously assign the insertion in Zech 1:14b,15 to that same level of redaction, but the stereotypical nature of the verse, as well as the existence of so many other possible explanations warn against absolute claims. One can say with certainty only that Zech 1:14b,15 coincides very well with the motifs and vocabulary of other Joel-related insertions.

Zech 1:17 has two elements, the combination and formulation of which occasionally cause commentators to argue that the verse has been expanded.[39] Following an introductory messenger formula (and proclaim again, saying, Thus says YHWH Sebaoth), the two portions clearly present formal characteristics distinct from one another. The use of the 1cs suffix in 1:17a (my cities) portrays YHWH as the speaker, and the promise to the cities expands the concern beyond Jerusalem. By contrast, 1:17b emphasizes Jerusalem's priority and speaks about YHWH:

Zech 1:17a	Zech 1:17b
My cities will again overflow with prosperity	And YHWH will again have compassion on Zion, And he will again choose Jerusalem

Despite this change in the formal elements, it is unwise to divide this verse and treat it as the work of more than one hand. The verse has only one introduction, and it highlights the same word in each part by repeating

---

[37] There is some antagonism *reflected* in Zech 8:1ff, but it is not explicit (cf 8:7,13), and that chapter ends with the possibility that the nations will recognize Jerusalem as YHWH's city and stream to it (8:20).

[38] This insertion verse is discussed above, beginning on page ?.

[39] For example, Sellin, *KAT* 12, 436; Horst, *HAT* 14, 214.

"again" (עוֹד) four times (in the introduction, and in each of the remaining lines).   By noting how the verse functions, one can perhaps offer an explanation for the tension it creates in its immediate context.

Thematically, Zech 1:17 takes up themes from the surrounding visions, but in reverse order. It repeats the message of the first vision with its summation in 1:17b, and it introduces the broader perspective of the second and third vision in 1:17a. The introduction of this broader perspective uses the phrase "my cities," probably influenced by Zech 1:12, to expand the perspective beyond Jerusalem, but it also utilizes a meaningful play on words which plays off the vocabulary in the next vision.[40] One may well suppose Zech 1:17 plays a transitional function between the visions. In turn, this same technique appears in Zech 1:16 with the reference to the measuring of Jerusalem, which anticipates the theme of the third vision (cf 2:6).   Both Zech 1:16 and 1:17 presuppose the first vision and simultaneously function as literary transitions to the visions which follow. One may presume from this function, that both verses, despite the literary tension, should be seen in light of the vision cycle itself.[41]

In summary, the first vision of Zechariah in its literary context (1:7-17) offers no *absolutely conclusive* evidence of redactional shaping on the level of the Book of the Twelve. Nevertheless, the insertion of Zech 1:14b,15 exhibits a perspective best suited to a larger literary context. For reasons stated above, the most likely home for this broader perspective is to be found in the redactional work uniting several writings in the book of the Twelve, but alternative explanations relating the insertion to the compilation of Proto-Zechariah or the Haggai-Zechariah corpus cannot be ruled out entirely.

4. Zech 1 and the Book of the Twelve

As described in this chapter, the character of the redactional shaping of Haggai and Zechariah for the Book of the Twelve is minimal compared with many of the other connections. This connection lacks the wholesale

---

[40] The word "overflow" (תפוצינה) from the root פוץ (2). The root פוץ (1) however means "scatter," and is synonymous with זרה (to scatter), which dominates the next vision (2:2,4).

[41] This statement presupposes that the vision cycle is primarily a *literary* composition, and not the collection of isolated vision accounts. Contra Galling, *VT* 2 (1952): 18-36.

redactional reworkings or the addition of substantial amounts of new material, and instead consists, if the above analysis is correct, of minor insertions into the existing contexts.[42]   Relatedly, Bosshard's analysis reflects a similar conclusion regarding the structural parallels of this connection to Isaiah.[43] There are parallels, but they are neither extensive nor can one demonstrate they are redactionally imposed for the purpose. It was suggested above that two elements contributed significantly to the lack of substantial change to the text. First, in all probability Haggai and Zechariah 1-8 circulated independently as a single corpus which was the work of a transmission circle distinct from that of the Deuteronomistic corpus. This corpus was likely highly regarded, and carried considerable "authority" in its own right. Second, the essential message of both Haggai and Zechariah 1-8 was already well-suited for its function within the Book of the Twelve. These works document the reconstruction of the temple, which progresses the *historical* movement of the Book of the Twelve beyond the destruction of Jerusalem and the exile. Additionally, the historical awareness of Zech 1:1-6 already draws upon the experience of past generations as a both a reflection and a warning to the reader making it apropos for the larger context of the Book of the Twelve.

Despite the quantitative reduction of connecting elements on the level of their incorporation into the Book of the Twelve, one may still claim evidence that intentional shaping does exist at this level. Notably, the Haggai insertions exhibit strong allusions to Joel, as in other redactional insertions in the Book of the Twelve. Additionally, the insertion in Hag 2:22 (containing the majority of common words to Zech 1:1ff) presents an interesting phenomenon. The incorporation of the words relies upon the context in Haggai, but the action involving the words juxtaposes the action of the words in the Zechariah context. In Zech 1:8,10 the אִישׁ is "standing" with the horse and the rider among the myrtles, contrasting with Hag 2:22 where אִישׁ, the horses, and their riders will go down in battle. The "earth" in Hag 2:21 is quaking while in Zech 1:11 it is resting and undisturbed. Yet this positive situation in Zechariah is reinterpreted with the insertion in Zech 1:14b,15 into a negative circumstance. This reinterpretation coincides readily with the prediction of a coming judgment upon the nations as predicted in Hag 2:22, and adds to Zechariah one of the recurring themes of the Book of the Twelve, the culpability of the nations for their

---

[42] These insertions include Hag 2:17,19*,22 and more cautiously Zech 1:14b,15 and the corresponding messenger formula.

[43] Bosshard, *BN* 40 (1987): 35f.

opportunistic treatment of Israel during its punishment. Some (e.g. Edom and Tyre) were never commissioned by YHWH to act against Judah, Jerusalem, or Israel. Others (Assyria and Babylon) exceeded their mandate to punish YHWH's people and were themselves subsequently punished. Thus, the incorporation of Haggai and Zechariah into the larger corpus did not involve large additions to those writings, but those places which do receive additions function similarly to redactional insertions elsewhere in the Book of the Twelve.

5. Zech 8:9-23 in Its Context

The selection of Zech 8:9-23 for comparison with Mal 1:1ff represents no random decision, rather these verses form a logical breaking point for Proto-Zechariah, based upon the scholarly consensus that Zech 9-14 post-dates chapters 1-8.[44] Thus, the large number of common words

---

[44] The question of the authorship of Zechariah 9-14 predates the modern critical period, based in part on the reference in Matt 27:9-10 attributing Zech 11:12-13 to Jeremiah. See already the observations in Keil, *Minor Prophets*, vol. 2, 375-77. Since the 19th century, a scientific determination of the differences between Zech 1-8 and 9-14 has been undertaken. Various investigations have created a strong consensus that chapters 9-14 stem from a different author than Zech 1-8, but there is no such consensus regarding the identity of the author, or the time of composition. Since the massive articles of Stade, "Deuterozacharja" *ZAW* 1 (1881): 1-96; *ZAW* 2 (1882): 151-72, 275-309) the dominant opinion has claimed these chapters stem from a late post-exilic period. However, while Stade assumed that 9-14 was the work of a single author, the compositional unity has since been seriously questioned, and distinction is often made between 9-11 and 12-14 as Deutero- and Trito-Zechariah, since there is little connection between the independent anonymous units loosely joined under the common headings (9:1; 12:1). Dating these chapters is problematic because of the tension between historical allusions and an ahistorical framework. There is at present relative agreement that 12-14 are post-exilic, but several scholars are of the opinion that 9-11 contain an admixture of pre-exilic pieces with material from the Greek period. For example, see Karl Elliger, "Ein Zeugnis aus der jüdischen Gemeinde im Alexanderjahr," *ZAW* 62 (1950): 63-115. This difference of opinion makes it virtually impossible for critical scholarship to find agreement on a date for 9-11. Nevertheless, the dominant opinion, does date these chapters also as post-exilic, more specifically, somewhere between the end of the fourth to the end of the third centuries. The combination of 9-11, 12-14 with 1-8 would likewise have occurred during this period. For further discussion, see Eissfeldt, *Introduction*, 435-436; Magne Saebø, *Sacharja 9-14* (Neukirchen: Neukirchener Verlag, 1969); and also "Die deuterosacharjanische Frage,"

between Zech 8:9-23 and Mal 1:1-14 mandates investigation. This investigation requires consideration of the position of these verses inside Proto-Zechariah, their relationship to the Haggai-Zechariah corpus, and their relationship to the Book of the Twelve.[45]

Zech 8:9-23 appears at the conclusion of the third and final section of Proto-Zechariah, introduced by the final chronistic element in the book (Zech 7:1). This element dates chapters 7-8 to the fourth day of the ninth month of the fourth year of Darius (December 7, 519), marking almost two years since the date in the previous chronistic element (1:7). The chronistic marker does not, however, represent the only unifying element within the last two chapters of Proto-Zechariah. These chapters manifest additional similarity because of the relatively short units they contain and the fact that a large number of separate introductory elements appear at the head of the units (7:1,4,8; 8:1f,3,4,6,7,9,14,18,19,20,23). These two formal criteria contribute greatly to the reasons why Zech 7-8 are often treated together.

Despite these stylistic elements bonding the chapters together, the literary character and the inter-relationship of the units draws various explanations. Some perceive the verses largely as a collection of unrelated or loosely related sayings and oracles.[46] Some, giving strong priority to the date in Zech 7:1, treat these chapters as a unity stemming ultimately from the prophet.[47] Others argue these two chapters, as they now stand, evidence the interests of more than one compositional level.[48] These distinctions reflect deep philosophical divisions over the nature of prophetic books. Does the framework of a prophetic "book" serve merely as the

---

StTh 23 (1969): 115-140; Benedikt Otzen, Studien über Deuterosacharja (Copenhagen: Prostant apud Munksgaard, 1964); and Rudolph, KAT 13/4, 159-164.

[45] The relationship of Zechariah 1-8 and 9-14 to one another and to the Book of the Twelve will be treated in the forthcoming volume, Redactional Processes in the Book of the Twelve.

[46] Horst, HAT 14, 205, 233-237, for example, sees 7:4-14 as a type of sermon in a similar vein as Zech 1:1-6, while he sees all of chapter eight as a separate entity compiled of short individual speeches, originally independent, with an eschatological flavor.

[47] Rudolph, KAT 13/4, 143-151, goes to great pains to relate 7:1-8:17 together, and even though he admits 8:18-23 stems from another situation, he adamantly argues that even these verses are "genuine." Petersen, Haggai & Zechariah 1-8, 283, 296f, treats the units as isolated sayings, mostly from Zechariah, which owe their collective form to editorial placement. So also, Sellin, KAT 12, 474-483, although he also sees more editorial work reflected within three sections: 7:1-14; 8:1-17; and 8:18-23.

[48] So Beuken, Haggai - Sacharja, 118-183; Acroyd, Exile and Restoration, 206-217; and on a somewhat more limited scale, Mason, Haggai, Zechariah, and Malachi, 67-73.

repository for collected sayings, or does the book reflect literary interests, and if so to what extent?

The answers to these questions greatly influence the manner in which one approaches the text, and perhaps nowhere do the responses determine one's perception as in Zech 7-8. The preponderance of messenger formulas in these chapters give the impression of individual sayings on the one hand, but the similarities of several of these speeches to other parts of the Proto-Zechariah corpus as well as the Haggai-Zechariah corpus make the assumption of literary awareness a possibility which must be evaluated for the individual units as well. Therefore, in turning to the units marked by the introductory formula, it will be necessary, in addition to other observations, to consider several related questions:

1.   Is the unit an isolated saying?
2.   Is the unit related to other portions of the collection Zech 7-8?
3.   Does the unit relate literarily to either of the other two sections of Proto-Zechariah?
4.   Does the unit relate to Haggai in any way, and if so, is that relationship literary?
5.   Does the unit relate to the larger literary corpus of the Book of the Twelve in any way, and if so, is that relationship literary?

Consideration of these questions should enable an evaluation of the catchword phenomenon. The current investigation concentrates upon the final five units in this block, in part for reasons of space, but also because the preponderance of common words which this passage shares with Mal 1:1-14 makes it noteworthy. Nevertheless, the discussion requires a brief summary of the *contents* of the remainder of these two chapters.

Zech 7:1-3 introduces the date using the final chronistic formula (7:1), which despite the fact that it contains a word-event formula, continues with a narrative account that sets the stage for what follows.[49] This narrative element depicts the sending of a delegation to ask the priests and the prophets if the fast of the fifth month should continue to be celebrated.[50]

---

[49]   Several literary problems surround the question whether "Bethel" represents the town or the first part of a longer name. For discussion of the various opinions, and a proponent of the latter position, see Ackroyd, *Exile and Restoration*, 206-209; Mason, *Haggai, Zechariah, and Malachi*, 66f; and Petersen, *Haggai & / 1-8*, 282f. Contrast these opinions with Rudolph, *KAT* 14/4, 136-140, who opts for the city; and Beuken, *Haggai - Sacharja 1-8*, 143-146, who cannot decide between the two.

[50]   In its current state, this narrative element reflects circumstances of a later time than the date itself, since the mention of the priests "belonging to the house of YHWH

This fast commemorated the destruction of Jerusalem and the temple in 587.[51] The fact that this specific question receives no explicit response until 8:18f serves as a further indicator that the text intends the majority of the two chapters to be read together. A further decision as to the particular level which created this *inclusio* remains open for now. The remainder of chapter seven contains two units (Zech 7:4-7,8-14), whose form and content separate one from the other.

The first unit, Zech 7:4-7, bears directly upon the context insofar as it treats the theme of true fasting. Likewise, its introduction utilizes an autobiographical style common to the vision cycle, but appearing only once elsewhere in chapters 7-8, specifically Zech 8:18f, where the question of the fast is finally answered. Despite the appropriateness of 7:4-7 to its context, it does not address the delegation who asked the question, rather the prophet is commanded to proclaim the word to all the people of the land and to the priests. The second unit, Zech 7:8-14, exhibits no autobiographical style in the introduction, rather it specifically mentions Zechariah in the third person. Additionally, these verses do not treat the question of the fast directly, rather they provide a history lesson of sorts, by relating to the reader the message of the former prophets to the fathers. Their rejection of this message caused YHWH to "scatter them with a storm wind" (7:14).

Despite the formal differences between these two units (7:4-7,8-14), one cannot separate them entirely from one another. There is good reason to suspect that the second is a further elaboration upon the first, and that it probably comes from a later redactional hand.[52] Zech 7:8-14 cannot be treated independently from 7:4-7. After the introductory word-event and messenger formula (7:8-9a), the message proper delivers a series of ethical commands, but despite the impression created by the introductory formula, the message is not intended as Zechariah's message to the current generation. Rather, it recounts the message of earlier prophets to previous

---

Sebaoth" implies a functioning temple, yet the date of the completion of the temple is still almost two years away (see Ezra 6:15, which dates the completion of the temple to the sixth year of Darius).

[51] 2 Kgs 25:8; see discussions in Rudolph, *KAT* 13/4, 139f; Petersen, *Haggai & Zechariah 1-8*, 283.

[52] Further elaborations of arguments for the relationship of these verses to later layers may be found in Beuken, *Haggai - Sacharja 1-8*, 123-136, although his assignation of 7:7 to this layer appears problematic.

generations, as Zech 7:11-14 incontrovertibly demonstrates.[53] Yet, until 7:12 no evidence indicates that the speech should be understood as addressed to the earlier generations if one tries to interpret 7:8-14 as an isolated speech. The entire unit presupposes the question in Zech 7:7: "Are these not the words which YHWH proclaimed by the former prophets?" And yet, the question in 7:7 most logically refers backwards to the short speech in 7:5f.[54] Precisely this observation allows certain deductions effecting the understanding of the nature of the compilation of chapters 7-8. Zech 7:8-14 *presumes the presence of 7:4-7*, but the separate introductory formula implies a separate speech. Two possible explanations could explain this tension. The introductory formula (clearly redactional material) could have been inserted into a pre-existing context, which originally contained no break between 7:7 and 7:9. Syntactically, Zech 7:9 could have followed 7:7 with no real problems. However, it is very difficult to offer a rationale for the simple insertion of 7:8 when it is not required and when its presence disturbs the context. More likely, the entire unit has been added to the context, and is not the speech of the prophet, but the composition of a redactor interested in incorporating an interpretation of the reason for the current situation. The attribution of this speech to Zechariah is not surprising, since this technique (attributing a speech to an authoritative figure) appears elsewhere, and has been described as one of the standard methods of incorporation in inner-biblical exegesis.[55] Zech 7:8-14 thus continues the message of Zech 7:4-7, but its attribution to the prophet reflects a later redactional interest to place the guilt for Jerusalem's destruction upon earlier generations who refused to follow YHWH's commands.[56]

---

[53] Zech 7:11f documents the people's negative response to the commands, and 7:13f continues with an account of YHWH's response to their refusal to obey. Zech 7:12 refers explicitly to the former prophets, and YHWH's response in Zech 7:13f clearly refers to the destruction of Jerusalem and the resulting deportations.

[54] Contra Beuken, *Haggai - Sacharja 1-8*, 120.

[55] See the discussion of "attributive, pseudo-attributive, and non-attributive exegesis," in Fishbane, *Biblical Interpretation in Ancient Israel*, 533-535.

[56] This view of the destruction coincides with Deuteronomistic views of history, but also with the Chronicler's typically positive view of the generation after the exile. In this regard, suggestions by Beuken and Mason that the redaction of Haggai and Zechariah reflects a developing tradition from the Deuteronomistic school to that of the Chronicler become appealing, although the specific institutional form of this development certainly deserves more treatment.

Zech 8:1-8 gives the impression of an independent collection of prophetic sayings because of the frequency of introductory elements (8:1,2,3,4,6,7) they contain, and because, thematically, they all treat the future salvation of Jerusalem.[57] This impression must be qualified, however, by several observations. First, the initial saying (8:2) quotes YHWH's mediated message to the prophet in the first vision (1:14), a message which does not belong to the original level of the vision, but shares thematic affinity with several of other redactional insertions in the Book of the Twelve.[58] Second, the next speech contains demonstrable parallels to other visions in the cycle.[59] Third, some of these sayings exhibit literary dependence upon other sayings in 7:1ff.[60] Fourth, one can detect an observable logic between the order of the third, fourth, and fifth speeches.[61] All five speeches share a strong concern for the prosperity of Jerusalem, but not with extra-worldly promises. They expect this prosperity to come despite the present situation which belies such hope. Thus, as with Zech 7:4-7,8-14, the units in Zech 8:1-8 give the impression of being a loosely organized collection of sayings, but closer examination of the speeches reveals they demonstrate an awareness of a larger literary context, syntactical relationships, and a coherent logic in the ordering of at least some of the speeches, which argues against ascribing them as simply independent sayings.

6. Literary Observations on Zech 8:9-23

Five remaining units in Zech 8:9-23 all begin with introductory messenger formulas, simplifying an *initial* separation of the extent of these units: 8:9-13,14-17,18f,20-22,23. Yet the fact that these speeches share so

---

[57] Several see these sayings as typical for prophetic writings which place the salvation sayings at the end of the book. For example, see Beuken, *Haggai - Sacharja 1-8*, 181.

[58] See the discussion of Zech 1:14b,15 in the previous chapter and the discussion of Joel 2:18ff in relation to Zech 8:9-13 below, page 265.

[59] Cf Zech 8:3a with Zech 1:16a; 2:14.

[60] Most notably Zech 8:6 refers to "those days" in reference to the promise of the preceding saying.

[61] The second speech announces YHWH's return to Jerusalem. The third speech portrays a scene of the future depicting a peaceful, populated, and joyous Jerusalem. The fourth speech takes the form of YHWH's *Streitfrage* against the people who doubt. The fifth speech reiterates that YHWH will return his people to Jerusalem. The logic of these units may be summarized as follows: YHWH will return (8:3), and Jerusalem will return to prosperity (8:3). Do not doubt YHWH'S word (8:4f), for he will return the people to Jerusalem.

many words and ideas with Malachi requires closer treatment of the individual units. Zech 8:9-13 not only represents the longest unit in the chapter, it also has the most objective structural components. In addition to the introductory formula, it contains an *inclusio* at the beginning and end, marking the extent of the unit.[62] It contains clear text markers that structure the text into four subdivisions, thereby providing the frame for understanding the unit. These indicators organize the text into temporal categories, relating to the past, current, and future situations, and require the text be interpreted in this light. These markers may be charted:

Verse	Marker	Time	Action
8:9	בימים האלה	Present	Prophet tells those listening "in these days," to take heart
8:10	כי לפני הימים ההם	Past	"Before these days" the situation was worse
8:11	ועתה	Present	"But now" YHWH is not like the former days
8:13	והיה	Future	"And it will be" that the house of Judah and the house of Israel will be a blessing

This structural frame contrasts the present situation with the previous situation which was considerably worse than the current one. It also offers hopeful consolation in the form of a promise that the future will bring better times. Consequently, these verses place the current generation in the middle of a continuum between the suffering of the past and the promise of future greatness.

Despite the clarity of this structure, the implications of the frame upon the interpretation are not always made explicit. This oversight has considerable importance for the interpretation of Zech 8:12 which appears in the "but now" section where one should expect a reference to the current situation.[63] When one takes the frame seriously, the verse offers evidence

---

[62] The phrase "Let your hands be strong" (תחזקנה ידיכם) follows the introductory formula in Zech 8:9 and concludes Zech 8:13 prior to the next messenger formula.

[63] Several commentators treat Zech 8:12 as the beginning of the future promise: Petersen, *Haggai & Zechariah 1-8*, 304,308; Smith, *Word 32*, 235; Ackroyd, *Exile and Restoration*, 214. Mason, *Haggai, Zechariah, and Malachi*, 70f, does not state explicitly how the verse should be treated, but does not contradict the NEB translation which treats the verse as a promise for the future. Elliger, *ATD 25*, 131, implies the action will take

that the current situation is an improvement when compared with the past.[64] In addition to the fact that the frame virtually requires this interpretation, Zech 8:12 distinctly takes up material from Haggai (1:10f; 2:19) which further buttresses this interpretation.

Hag 1:10f	Hag 2:19	Zech 8:12
Therefore, because of you the sky has withheld its dew, and the earth has withheld its produce. And I called for a drought on the land, on the mountains, on the grain, on the new wine, on the oil, on what the ground produces, on men, on cattle, and on all the labor of your hands.	Is the seed still in the granary, or the vine, or the fig tree, or the pomegranate? Or has the olive tree not born fruit? From this day I will bless.	For a seed (there is) peace. The vine gives its fruit, and the land gives its produce, and the heavens give their dew. And I have caused the remnant of this people to inherit all these.

Literarily, these passages present a clear progression in which the drought of punishment is revoked with the institution of the temple reconstruction (Haggai). Less than two years later (cf Zech 7:1 and Hag 2:10,18), the fulfillment of this promise serves as evidence that YHWH keeps his promises. Simultaneously, the verse evidences a certain background controversy as to whether or not YHWH has fulfilled the promises of Haggai and Zechariah.[65] Zech 8:9-13 refutes the argument that YHWH has not kept his promises. As with the redactional insertions between Zeph 3:18-20 and Hag 1:1-11, the operational hermeneutic implies an extension of the promise of the return of Jerusalem's inhabitants further into the future, by claiming that partial fulfillment of the promises to Zion reveals YHWH's intention to fulfill the promise completely.[66]

An interesting observation should be made at this point, namely, that this concentration upon the agricultural bounty is not endemic to Proto-Zechariah, since these interests appear nowhere else in the book. While

---

place in the immediate future. By contrast, Beuken, *Haggai - Sacharja 1-8*, 165f, and Rudolph, *KAT* 14/3, 143,149, treat the verse as a reference to the current situation, although Rudolph unnecessarily bases his interpretation, in part, upon the assumption of textual haplography.

[64] See the further development of these arguments in Beuken, *Haggai - Sacharja 1-8*, 165f.

[65] The redactional identification of these verses as specific reference to Haggai and Zechariah appears justified by Zech 8:9, which refers to the message of the prophets at the founding of the temple. See the discussions in Beuken, *Haggai - Sacharja 1-8*, 166 and Rudolph, *KAT* 14/4, 149; Petersen, *Haggai & Zechariah 1-8*, 305.

[66] See the above discussion of Zeph 3:18-20 in relationship to Mic 4:6f and Hag 1:1-11.

several have noted this fact, only a few use it as evidence that the passage stems from the same redactional hand which united the writings of Haggai and Zechariah.[67] However, given the fact that considerable evidence has already been offered that deliberate implantation of catchwords into the text recurs frequently between the writings of the Book of the Twelve, it is not possible to leave the discussion at this point. It is necessary to analyze the possibility whether the agricultural blessing should be treated in light of the Haggai-Zechariah editorial activity or in light of the Book of the Twelve. Several observations on this unit make the latter a serious possibility to be considered. First, although Beuken assigns Zech 8:12 to the Chronistic redaction of the two works on the basis of the similarity between Haggai and Zechariah, he admits that the verse lacks any significant connection to the Chronistic milieu.[68] Second, Zech 8:12 clearly plays off Haggai, but the appearance of agricultural motifs in that writing is minimal as well.[69] Third, even more significant, a substantial portion of the agricultural motifs in Haggai are formulated on the basis of Joel, including Hag 2:19.[70] Fourth, a substantial portion of the vocabulary of Zech 8:12 is at home in Joel.[71] Finally, the specific hermeneutic manifested by Zech 8:12 (within 8:9-13) clearly parallels the three-fold hermeneutical scheme in Joel 2:18ff.

Joel 2:18-3:5 presents the actions of YHWH following the repentance of the priests. It begins significantly with the pronouncement that YHWH will be zealous for his people and have compassion on them (cf Zech 8:1f), which includes the removal of the northern army (2:20) so that YHWH's people will no longer be a byword among the nations (2:17,19; cf Zech 8:13). The second phase of the salvific picture in Joel (2:21-27) provides for the return of agricultural bounty to the land as a sign that YHWH is in their midst. As magnificent as the return of agricultural splendor is portrayed in Joel 2:21-27, Joel also makes clear that these blessings do not suffice. Hence, a third phase (Joel 3:1-5) predicts the need for additional promises of the outpouring of the spirit on all humanity (3:1), while at the same time accentuating Jerusalem's centrality (3:5). This final salvific act explicitly comes after YHWH's return of the agricultural bounty (3:1).

---

67 Beuken, *Haggai - Sacharja 1-8*, 166; Sellin, *KAT*, 481. Others assign the dependence to Zechariah himself, on the basis of the dates given by the respective speeches.

68 Beuken, *Haggai - Sacharja 1-8*, 165f.

69 Only Hag 1:6,10f; 2:16,17,19 contain agriculturally oriented images.

70 See the discussion of Hag 2:17,19*.

71 The following words from Zech 8:12 appear in Joel: vine (Joel 1:7,12; 2:22); נתן in the sense of to bear fruit (Joel 2:22); the root נחל (Joel 2:17); fruit (Joel 2:17).

When the vocabulary similarities between Zech 8:12 and Joel, as well as the specific use of agricultural imagery to mediate a partial fulfillment of the promise of salvation, are taken seriously, one notes again a deliberate attempt to conform a prophetic writing to the hermeneutical paradigm in Joel. Zech 8:9-13 makes sense as an independent saying, but the historical awareness of the unit as a whole, and the poignancy of 8:12 in particular, take on greater significance when read in light of a larger context. Zech 8:12 makes clear literary allusions to promises in Haggai, and simultaneously provides the unit with a striking parallel to the layering of promises in Joel 2:18ff.

At this point a question needs to be raised, although a definitive answer cannot be reached as yet. One must ask how to evaluate Zech 8:12 in relation to its context? To be sure, the verse fits into the structure of the unit, and makes perfect sense when read as a defense that the current situation fulfills part of YHWH's salvific plan. The unit as a whole is also quite characteristic for the units in the complex of Zech 7-8. On the other hand, Zech 8:12 is thematically unique to the Proto-Zechariah corpus, and not entirely typical for the interests of the Chronistic redaction of the Haggai-Zechariah corpus. Rather, the verse has much more affinity with Joel and the Joel-related redactional insertions noted elsewhere in the writings of the Book of the Twelve. This tension can be explained if one accepts Zech 8:12 as a redactional insertion as well, despite its appropriateness to the context. Admittedly, this possibility cannot be proven, but neither can it be ignored in light of more objective examples of the same phenomenon. Formally, the introduction of 8:12 begins with כי, a typical marker for introducing interpolations into the context. Also Zech 8:12 can be removed from the context without effecting the coherence of the unit:

> Thus says YHWH Sebaoth, Let your hands be strong in these days, you who are hearing these words from the mouth of the prophets, who (spoke) on the day the house of YHWH Sebaoth was founded, in order that the temple might be built. For before those days there was no wage for man, and a wage for cattle there was not. And to the one going out and coming in there was not peace from the adversary. And I sent away all mankind, each man with his neighbor. But now I am not like the former days to the remnant of this people — utterance of YHWH Sebaoth. And it will be that even as you were a curse among the nations — house of Judah and house of Israel — so I will deliver you, and you will be a blessing. You should not fear. Let your hands be strong.

Not only do the structural elements still depict the historical dialectic between then, now, and what will be, but allusions to Haggai are likewise still part of the text. The biggest difference lies in the fact that the reference to the current situation appears shorter, and it explicitly involves only YHWH's pronouncement that he does not treat the current generation like the previous one which went into exile. Seen in this light, the function of Zech 8:12 to continue (literarily) the structuring of history according to the paradigm of Joel becomes even more pronounced.

The next unit, **Zech 8:14-17**, begins with the messenger formula in 8:14 and concludes with נאם יהוה in 8:17, prior to the new messenger formula in 8:18. Zech 8:14 begins with the same formulation as the promise for the future in 8:13: "just as ... so ..." The content of the unit demonstrates a historical awareness similar to 8:9-13, but it contains only two of the three perspectives, the past (8:14) and the present (8:15-17). Zech 8:14f combines these two perspectives to offer encouragement. It draws on the past as an illustration of YHWH's resolve to carry out his decision against the fathers as encouragement to the present generation, in light of his decision for Jerusalem and the house of Judah. Just as YHWH decided to punish the recalcitrance of the fathers' generation, and did not change his mind, so he now promises to deal positively with the present generation. But Zech 8:16f goes beyond encouragement by placing demands upon the current generation. The demands all relate to proper interpersonal relationships in the legal and private spheres.[72]

The literary horizon of Zech 8:14-17 relates directly to the formation of Proto-Zechariah, explicitly taking up the sermon material in Zech 1:2ff, thereby creating an *inclusio* to the beginning of the book. This relationship is often noted for Zech 8:14f, because it utilizes the same vocabulary.[73] However, the relationship of the ethical imperatives in 8:16f may also be

---

[72] Four commands appear in these two verses, with the first and the third relating directly to how the people should relate one to another ("Speak truth, each to his neighbor ... each of you should not consider the evil of his neighbor in your hearts."). Additionally, these commands exhibit considerable parallels in their structure. The second command clearly refers to the legal realm ("Judge truth and a judgment of peace in your gates."). The fourth command overlaps the two arenas, since it could relate to oaths sworn between individuals (Gen 24:8), or an oath sworn to YHWH (Num 30:11,14), or to a ruler (Neh 6:18). In any case, the oath, once sworn, was legally and morally binding (cf the story of the oath not to give women to the tribe of Benjamin for wives in Judg 21:1-25), and a broken oath could result in legal proceedings, even in the cult (cf Num 5:21). The "oath of falsehood" in 8:17 could have legal implications, and thus be virtually synonymous with the second command.

[73] Beuken, *Haggai - Sacharja 1-8*, 172; Petersen, *Haggai & Zechariah 1-8*, 309; Ackroyd, *Exile and Restoration*, 215; Horst, *HAT* 14, 236; Elliger, *ATD* 25, 131.

explained in light of that sermonic material.[74]   The sermon in 1:2-6
articulates the message that YHWH punished the generation of the fathers
for their "evil ways" and "evil deeds." The ethical imperatives in 8:16f
should be seen as the counterpart to the evil of the fathers' generation.
The present generation should avoid the mistakes of the past by acting in
the way that the fathers should have acted.   The observation that the
formulation of these particular imperatives counters the actions of the
fathers' generation receives more support from the similarity of the
vocabulary to the description of the fathers' sins in Zech 7:9f.[75]   The
application of those verses to the fathers has already been noted, but the
phraseology of 8:16 approximates 7:9b, expanding the phrase "dispense true
justice" more concretely: "These are the things which you should do: speak
the truth to one another; judge truth and judgment for peace in your gates."
Zech 8:17a draws even more explicitly upon 7:10b, since the two are almost
exact parallels.

Zech 7:10b	Zech 8:17
Do not devise evil in your hearts, each one against his brother.	Do not devise evil in your hearts, each one for his neighbor.

These parallels offer solid criteria that Zech 8:16f deliberately commands
the present generation to do precisely what the fathers failed to do.

    The next unit, **Zech 8:18f**, begins with a new messenger formula, and
contains only two short sayings. The first addresses the fasts surrounding
Jerusalem's destruction, and the second commands the people to love truth
and justice. The saying about the fasts, despite its brevity, should not be
treated as an isolated saying of the prophet. Rather, it finally answers the
question brought by the delegation in 7:1-3.[76] This delegation asked if the
fast of the fifth month should be kept, but the response in 8:19 deliberately

---

[74] Contrary to Beuken, *Haggai - Sacharja 1-8*, 171-173, who not only separates 8:14-17
from 8:9-13, but sees two distinct units in Zech 8:14f,16f.

[75] See further elaboration of these parallels in Petersen, *Haggai & Zechariah 1-8*, 310f.

[76] Commentators often correctly treat this saying as the response to the questions in Zech
7:1-3. See Ackroyd, *Exile and Restoration*, 206; Mason, *Haggai, Zechariah, and
Malachi*, 72; Petersen, *Haggai & Zechariah 1-8*, 312. Contra Rudolph, *KAT* 14/4, 151
who does not believe 8:18f relates directly to 7:1-3. Horst *HAT* 14, 237, believes the
verse specifically relates to the beginning of chapter seven, but that it was composed
by a later hand.

expands the question with a programmatic answer: the *fasts* lamenting Jerusalem's destruction should now become *feasts* of joy.[77]

Likewise, the command which concludes this unit should not be seen as an isolated saying. When Zech 8:19b commands, "Love truth and peace," it takes up the commands of the previous unit, specifically Zech 8:16. In so doing, it subtly reminds the people that the joy of the feasts depends upon their actions. YHWH's decision to return requires obligations on the part of the people, obligations which their fathers had not kept. The failure to keep these obligations resulted in their punishment. This subtle reminder may also be noted in the way in which the temporal perspectives of Zech 8:9-13,14-17,18f dovetail with one another. While 8:9-13 presents a clear picture which moves from the past to the present to the future, 8:14-17 concerned the past and the present. Zech 8:18f likewise concentrates only upon two of the three perspectives, the future and the present. It thus provides an element from 8:9-13 which was not present in 8:14-17, and it repeats the commands to the present generation.

Clearly this oracle, in its current position, functions not only as the response to the question in 7:1-3, but also as a summary for the message of the two chapters. YHWH has ended the punishment of Judah caused by the sins of the fathers. This message should be an encouragement to the present generation, but at the same time, they should not forget the reasons why the fathers were punished.

The next oracle, **Zech 8:20-22** introduces a new perspective into the material, namely the future relationship to the nations who will come to worship YHWH in Jerusalem. While the theme is new in the context of the chapter, the verses presuppose a knowledge of their position, and thus cannot be treated as independent sayings. The action in 8:20-22 depicts the

---

[77] See discussion on Zech 7:1-3. Additionally, evidence indicates that the fasts in Zech 8:19 all relate to Jerusalem's destruction, and the call for their metamorphosis into joyous feasts reflects the acceptance of YHWH's reversal of judgment upon the country. For discussion of the feasts, see Rudolph, *KAT*, 13/4, 139f; Horst, *HAT* 14, 237. Ackroyd, *Exile and Restoration*, 207f, agrees cautiously, but offers some other possibilities as well. However, given the context of Proto-Zechariah, which concentrates so much on the questions surrounding the rebuilding of the temple, it does make sense that these fasts were all related to Jerusalem's destruction. So Richard E. Friedman, "The Prophet and the Historian: The Acquisition of Historical Information from Literary Sources," In *The Poet and the Historian: Essays in Literary and Historical biblical Criticism*, R.E. Friedman, ed., Harvard Semitic Studies 26 (Chico, California: Scholars Press, 1983), 6-11.

nations' recognition that YHWH has returned to Jerusalem which divulges
its awareness of the context.

The unit illuminates a structural and formal coherence. Following the
messenger formula, Zech 8:20 introduces the new theme with a motto for
the entire unit, "Yet will the peoples come and the inhabitants of many
cities." Zech 8:21 offers a step by step portrayal of how this arrival of the
peoples will occur. First, the inhabitants of one city will go to another and
offer an invitation: "Let us go now to entreat the favor of YHWH, and to
seek YHWH Sebaoth in Jerusalem." Following this invitation comes a
short sentence in the first person, which has often been labeled as a gloss,
but which should be treated as the response *to the invitation*: "Indeed, I will
go!"[78]   Zech 8:22 then concludes with a repetition of the introductory
motto in 8:20, as if to say this is how the nations will come to Jerusalem.

This positive attitude toward the nations is noteworthy. In order to
understand the full emotional impact of these verses, one need only
compare them to the typical motifs in the oracles against the nations in the
other prophetic writings, including the Book of the Twelve, which reflect a
much more negative attitude toward the nations. By contrast, these verses
(and also Zech 8:23) open the possibility that the nations — on their own
initiative — will come in umbrage to honor YHWH. The thematic change
causes several to argue that the verses are a later addition to the
chapter.[79] Lipiński attempts an explanation that the "peoples" refer only
to the Jews in the Diaspora.[80]   Others see no problem assigning these
views about the nations to Zechariah.[81]   Proponents of the various
positions almost unanimously relate 8:20-22 to the vision oracle in 2:15,
although they each use it to confirm their own position.[82]   Additionally,
commentators cite the similarity of the pilgrimage of the nations to
Jerusalem in Zech 8:20-22 with that of Isa 2:2-4. Some light may be shed
on the intention of the verses in the context, however, in spite of the wide

---

[78] So Petersen, *Haggai & Zechariah 1-8*, 317, who presupposes the response character of
this line. A sample of those seeing the line as a secondary addition includes: Horst,
HAT 14, 237; Rudolph, *KAT* 14/4, 143; Ackroyd, *Exile and Restoration*, 217.

[79] Beuken, *Haggai - Sacharja 1-8*, 327 believes it a very late addition to the chapter.
Elliger, *ATD* 25, 132 leans in this direction, but couches his statements cautiously.

[80] E. Lipiński, "Recherches sur le livre de Zacharie," *VT* 20 (1970): 42-46.

[81] Rudolph, *KAT* 14/4, 152; Petersen, *Haggai & Zechariah 1-8*, 316; Ackroyd, *Exile and
Restoration*, 217.

[82] For example, Beuken, *Haggai - Sacharja 1-8*, 326f, assigns both to the same redactional
layer, but not to Zechariah, while Rudolph, *KAT* 13/4, 152, takes both as the message
of Zechariah.

variety of opinions. The verses twice use the phrase, "entreat the face of YHWH," which implies the subjection to a higher authority.[83] This same phrase describes the action of the delegation in Zech 7:2. When one notes that 8:20-22 follows the response to that delegation in 8:19, the logic of the unit's position makes sense. It affords a deliberate device to parallel the action of the delegation from Bethel, only it accents the action by applying it to many nations.

The question of the relative placement of Zech 8:20-22 in the redaction of the passage must balance several observations against one another. On the one hand, the unit shares many of the stylistic peculiarities of chapters 7-8, and it relates directly to other portions of Proto-Zechariah, specifically to 2:15 and to 7:2. Zech 2:15 reflects the same attitude toward the nations, and 8:20,22 utilizes the same vocabulary as 7:2 in a meaningful manner. On the other hand, the unusual openness toward the nations was hardly central to Zechariah's preaching, and therefore does not present an entirely satisfying conclusion to the writing as a whole, or even to chapters 7-8. A few more possibilities open up when one looks beyond Proto-Zechariah. The book of Jonah certainly presents a sympathetic attitude toward the nations, but the narrative does not share the strong Jerusalem orientation of Zech 8:20-22. Mic 4:1-5, which essentially duplicates Isa 2:1-4, provides a close parallel to Zech 8:20-22 because it shares the twin interests of the pilgrimage of the nations and the centrality of Jerusalem. Zech 14:16ff allows for a pilgrimage of the nations to Jerusalem, but this passage possesses other elements which argue that Zech 14:16ff was composed later.[84] Finally, Mal 1:11,14 present an unexpectedly positive attitude toward the nations in a context concentrating upon the cultic abuses of Israel. All of these passages offer possible touchstones to Zech 8:20-22, but only Mic 4:1-4 offers much in the way of common phraseology which *might* point toward literary dependence.[85]

---

[83] See Klaus Seybold, "Reverenz und Gebet: Erwägungen zu der Wendung ḥilla pan î m," *ZAW* 88 (1976): 2-16.

[84] Zech 14 presupposes a divine battle against the nations, the cosmic dimensions of which are not present Zech 8:20-22. The passage has a negative attitude toward Egypt which is unmatched either Proto-Zechariah or in the Book of the Twelve. It also specifically relates the pilgrimage to the feast of booths, which decidedly presupposes a functioning temple and a more developed cultic system than implied in Zech 7-8.

[85] The difficulty of claiming literary intentions is of course compounded by the fact that Mic 4:1-5 already cites and interprets Isa 2:1-4 (See above discussion of Micah), complicating the question as to which passage Zech 8:20-22 reflects upon.

Finally, **Zech 8:23** concludes Proto-Zechariah. This verse has its own messenger formula as introduction, and coincides with the theme of the salvation of the nations. However, the perspective of that salvation shifts. Whereas in 8:20-22 the nations and the inhabitants of many cities came to Jerusalem to entreat YHWH's favor, Zech 8:23 requires that they grasp the garment of a יהודי.[86] The verse reflects the pilgrimage of the Diaspora Jews as an opportunity for the people of the nations to recognize the majesty of YHWH and to benefit by following them.[87] The verse is surely aware of Zech 8:20-22, but whether it should be understood as a correction or a clarification of those verse cannot be decided with certainty, although the former seems more likely on the basis of the parallels in Mic 4:1ff, Isa 2:2ff, and Zech 2:15 which argue for a more radical universal soteriology.

In summary, several facets of the above discussion may be drawn together. First, despite initial impressions to the contrary, Zech 8:9-23 does not represent the simple collection of isolated sayings. The verses form a tapestry of oracles that are thematically arranged, but also in some cases literarily dependent upon one another and upon the context, particularly of chapters 7-8. Second, the units in this passage concentrate very strongly upon messages to the present generation to learn from the mistakes of the fathers' generation. These messages offer encouragement and imply warning to the present generation to follow the commands of YHWH which their fathers rejected. Third, in the context of Zech 8:9-23, there are very few indicators of manipulation of the text with *specific regard* for the context of the Book of the Twelve. The strongest possibility appears with the allusions to Joel in Zech 8:12, which correspond to similar insertions elsewhere in the Book of the Twelve. Another possibility, Zech 8:20-22,23 must await further evaluation in light of Mal 1:1-14.[88]

Excursus: Tradition Circles and the Book of the Twelve.

The character of the redactional work in the Book of the Twelve following the end of Zephaniah deserves mention. The reader may already have noted that the amount of actual redactional work effecting the shape of the Haggai and Zechariah for the Book of the Twelve is not extensive. This observation will be compounded by many

---

[86] On the background of the term Judean, and its relationship to the context, see: Petersen, *Haggai & Zechariah 1-8*, 319.

[87] So Mason, *Haggai, Zechariah, and Malachi*, 73. This image passes better to the context in light of the nations who wish to go to Jerusalem.

[88] See the treatment of Mal 1:1-14 in the forthcoming volume, *Redactional Process in the Book of the Twelve*.

of the arguments concerning the writings not part of pre-existing corpora in the second volume of this study (Joel, Obadiah, Jonah, Nahum, Habakkuk, Malachi). Some consideration should be given to a rationale for this reduction. At present, this discussion can only offer suggestions which require further elaboration at some future date. In some cases it cannot advance beyond the hypothetical. The minimal shaping of some writings for the Book of the Twelve will be interpreted by some as an argument against the redactional shaping of the remaining writings, but in the mind of this author, this reaction should be avoided. Other writings, notably Obadiah, Nahum, Habakkuk, Jonah, and Zephaniah demonstrate more objective criteria for changes on the basis of the neighboring works. At the beginning of this work, it was noted that the character of the catchword connections must be evaluated for every writing because of the many possibilities to explain their presence. In the case of Haggai and Proto-Zechariah, this evaluation has only shed light on the presence of the individual words in relation to the Book of the Twelve in a few cases. Yet, it is difficult to find two other writings in the Book of the Twelve which have so much in common with one another as do Haggai and Proto-Zechariah. Ackroyd, Beuken, Mason and others have demonstrated that this similarity stems from the transmission of these writings in a tradition circle which has considerable affinity with the school of the Chronicler, although most of the evidence indicates the work on the Haggai-Zechariah corpus predated the Chronicler. Two further observations on the implications of the Haggai-Zechariah corpus on the Book of the Twelve as a whole should be stated, the one obvious and the other admittedly somewhat speculative. First, one can derive an obvious conclusion from the sparsity of overt redactional work on Haggai-Zechariah which may be tied specifically to the Book of the Twelve. Haggai and Zechariah did not *require* radical changes to function meaningfully within the historical frame which structures much of the Book of the Twelve. Their presence documents YHWH's prophetic word to the generation immediately after the exile. According to the text, this message was heard and heeded, resulting in the reconstruction of the temple, in the constitution of a new order, and in a promise of greater glory for Jerusalem.

The second observation derives from several related factors, and leaves open the possibility, at least for now, that the Book of the Twelve resulted from the collaborative efforts of several tradition groups. This author has argued that a Deuteronomistic corpus (Hosea, Amos, Micah, and Zephaniah) had its own pre-history and its own identifiable hermeneutic. While this corpus provided the chronological frame of what became the Book of the Twelve, it was expanded by the inclusion of other writings which greatly accentuated certain cosmic elements, but it did not abandon the historical framework.[89] Indeed, by incorporating the Haggai-Zechariah corpus, the expanded corpus explicitly extends the chronological framework into the post-exilic period. The Haggai-Zechariah corpus, which had its own transmission history, was included in this expansion, even though its transmission history links it more closely to what Plöger refers to as the hierocratic circle. Is it possible that this corpus represented the hierocratic contribution to the project as a

---

[89] The processes involved in this expansion which resulted in the Book of the Twelve are discussed in the forthcoming volume, *Redactional Processes in the Book of the Twelve*.

whole? It has already been noted that the Haggai-Zechariah corpus fits well into the context of the Book of the Twelve, despite the reduction in the deliberate shaping of texts through catchwords to the neighboring writing. Yet, particularly Zechariah demonstrates an appropriateness to the context in the Book of the Twelve which is almost too great to believe it is accidental. The sermonic material in the frame of this work (Zech 1:2-6; 7:1-8:23) refers so often to the sins of the fathers, and YHWH's change of attitude toward the current generation, that one cannot help but wonder if these references really derive from the Haggai-Zechariah corpus alone. At least one ancient source points in the direction that the Book of the Twelve resulted from the work of several groups working together. When *Baba Batra* 15a says that the Twelve was "written by Ezra and the Men of the Great Assembly," it raises the possibility that the combination of these writings was the result of the deliberate coordination of several different tradition groups. There are, of course, many problems which argue against the historicity of this particular account. Questions of the date of Ezra and the identity of the "Men of the Great Assembly" not withstanding, the same sentence in *Baba Batra* also ascribes authorship of Ezekiel, Daniel, and Esther to this same group, a combination which is very unlikely.

Schneider and Lee take up other ancient traditions, and postulate that a group under the direction of Nehemiah was responsible for the "final form" of the Book of the Twelve.[90] They cite 2 Mac 2:13 and Josephus (Ant. 11:168) as evidence that Nehemiah had a library, which Lee and Schneider postulate became the repository of the prophetic canon in general, and the Book of the Twelve in particular. However, one cannot relate these two traditions so readily as they suggest. 2 Mac 2:13 does suggest that Nehemiah founded a library, but it only says that he "founded a library and *collected* the books about the kings and prophets, and the writings of David, and letters of kings about votive offerings." The unlikelihood that this tradition reflects actual editorial activity appears, however, when one reads the following verse (which Schneider and Lee fail to mention): "In the same way, Judas also collected all the books that had been lost on account of the war..." It is much more likely that the tradition of Nehemiah's library relates to early attempts to explain how the Biblical corpus survived the Babylonian destruction (cf 4 Ezra 14). The Josephus passage cited by Schneider and Lee does not reflect the founding of a library by Nehemiah. The passage in question refers only to Nehemiah's letters, which he brought from Xerxes: "And when he had showed the letters to God, *he delivered them* to Addaios and the other eparchs." (cf Neh 2:9) This reference does not support the tradition that Nehemiah founded a library.

Bosshard suggests the possibility that the Isaiah tradent was the dominant force in the canonization of the prophetic corpus as a whole.[91] Several observations strengthen Bosshard's argument. Already the Deuteronomistic corpus exhibits a striking number of parallels to the Isaiah corpus, which would seem to predate the

---

[90] Schneider, *The Unity of the Book of the Twelve*, 147-152; Lee, *The Canonical Unity of the Scroll of the Minor Prophets*, 225f.

[91] Bosshard, *BN* 40 (1987): 58.

macrostructural parallels noted by Bosshard for the entire Book of the Twelve.[92] This observation implies that the same tradent was responsible for both corpora for an extended period. The fact that Isaiah opens the prophetic corpus, while the Book of the Twelve brings it to a close adds further weight to Bosshard's suggestion. Much still remains unclear, however, so that one may not say the question of canonization is solved. For example, how does one account for the availability of so many different independent texts from which the redactors have drawn? In the Book of the Twelve, several hymns and liturgical pieces have entered with the redactional work (note particularly Nah 1:2ff and Hab 3:1ff, but also Jonah 2:3ff).[93] Can one determine if this process was a collaborative effort, if it resulted from a dominant group (e.g the Isaiah tradent) inheriting (or wresting control of) other prophetic traditions from other groups? These are but a few of the many questions which remain unresolved.

---

[92] Note for example, the fact that the five kings in Hos 1:1 and Isa 1:1 are identical; Isa 2:2-4 = Mic 4:1-4; the dependence of Mic 7:8ff on Isa 10; and the almost identical number of occurrences of the phrase ביום ההוא in the Book of the Twelve (42 times) and Isaiah (45 times), each with more than forty while Jeremiah (12 times) and Ezekiel (13 times) have significantly fewer.

[93] See discussion of these passages in the forthcoming volume, *Redactional Processes in the Book of the Twelve.*

Summary and Reflections

Each of the six writings treated in this study (Hosea, Amos, Micah, Zephaniah, Haggai, and Zech 1-8) evidence editorial influence which transcends the interests of the individual writing on at least two levels: 1) transmission as part of the Book of the Twelve; 2) transmission as part of a multi-volume corpus whose existence predates the Book of the Twelve.

1. Editorial Expansion for the Book of the Twelve

Most of the editorial adaptation relating these six writings explicitly to the Book of the Twelve takes the form of short sayings and phrases which display an expanded literary horizon oriented to this larger corpus. These *redactional glosses* comment upon the immediate context, but they exhibit significant literary tensions within that context. These tensions may be syntactical (e.g.Hos 14:8a), theological (e.g. Hag 2:22), thematic (e.g. Hag 2:19*), and/or historical (e.g. Amos 9:12a).

Not every literary tension within the Book of the Twelve relates explicitly to the question of the formation of this corpus. However, in addition to the literary tensions with their immediate context, those places labeled in this study as redactional glosses share at least one of the following characteristics. *First*, many of these insertions take up the vocabulary of the adjacent writing in the Book of the Twelve by utilizing catchwords from that writing. These catchwords exhibit an affinity for juxtaposing the conditions represented by the catchwords in the adjacent writing. Two examples will illustrate this tendency. The catchwords in Hos 14:8a, inserted to unite Hosea and Joel, promise the restoration of the inhabitants, the vine, and the grain. Joel, the next writing, presupposes the deprivation of the same elements. Amos 9:12a (which is literarily and historically problematic) links Amos and Obadiah. It promises the possession of a humbled Edom, while Obadiah, the next writing, begins with the condemnation of a haughty Edom. Both examples, by no means exclusive, illustrate the editorial tendency to juxtapose two adjacent writings via catchwords inserted into an existing literary context.

Sometimes, these catchwords accent certain constellations or introduce themes into a writing which tie that writing to the adjacent work. For example, Zeph 3:20, typically treated as an expansion on 3:19, makes no significant theological assertions beyond the statements of 3:19. Zeph 3:20 simply reiterates 3:19, but it addresses the people directly (2mp), even though the immediate context (Zeph 3:11-19) addresses the personified Zion (2fs). The literary "presence" of the people makes sense in the larger literary context since the next writing (Haggai) begins with a prophetic confrontation of the people. Still, the same expansion juxtaposes YHWH's salvific promise in Zeph 3:18-20 with the situation in Haggai. Zephaniah predicts the future restoration ("in that time") of fortunes despite the current situation, while those who experienced the fulfillment of that promise ("this people," the generation after the exile), believe that "the time has not come to build" YHWH's temple (Hag 1:2).

Many of the redactional glosses share a *second* characteristic in addition to the deliberate play on the adjacent writing. Frequently, the redactional glosses quote or allude to Joel in a manner demonstrating that Joel's hermeneutical paradigm has been incorporated with the gloss. Examples include Hos 14:8a, Amos 9:13; Zeph 3:20; Hag 2:19*; Zech 1:14b,15; and 8:12. Most of these passages relate Joel's promises to YHWH's people, not his relationship to the nations.[1]

Based upon the introductory and concluding passages, only one of the six writings discussed in this study has been substantially affected by its incorporation into the Book of the Twelve beyond the periodic implantation of redactional glosses.[2] Zephaniah demonstrates significant expansion in the first chapter, most explicitly in Zeph 1:2f,14-18. This expansion (1:2f,15-16a,18ab,b) leaves little doubt, however, that it expands upon a pre-existing literary context. The expansions demonstrate literary tensions to their immediate context and they allude to Joel much like the redactional glosses already noted, but they do so by incorporating more than a single sentence or phrase. Thus, although more substantial, these expansions function quite similarly to the redactional glosses in the remainder of the six writings.

---

[1]   Many of the remaining six writings of the Book of the Twelve not discussed in this volume also exhibit a marked tendency to cite Joel in redactional glosses. These writings generally demonstrate more significant adaptation for the Book of the Twelve, while the redactional glosses tend to draw from Joel's imagery and apply it to YHWH's relationship to the nations. See the forthcoming volume, *Redactional Processes in the Book of the Twelve.*

[2]   Some evidence suggests that Micah *may* have been modified more substantially for the Book of the Twelve than the paucity of redactional glosses in 7:8-20 indicates. However, this evidence appears in Mic 4-5, the middle section of the book, and thus lies outside the scope of the current study.

2. Pre-existing Multi-volume Corpora

In addition to redactional glosses and editorial adaptation for the Book of the Twelve, evidence from this study suggests one must also postulate the existence of two multi-volume corpora whose literary and theological intentions help to account for the form of these six writings. The postulation of a single corpus for Haggai and Zech 1-8 has substantial attestation in scholarly discussions, and the observations on these works provided by this study strengthen those arguments. Not only do surface similarities (e.g. the style of superscriptions, the theme of the temple reconstruction, and the persons mentioned) suggest a common transmission circle for these prophetic writings, but certain literary formulations unite the message of the two books (cf the discussion of Zech 8:9-13). Since the redactional glosses related to the Book of the Twelve in these writings presuppose the existence of these formulations, one may logically postulate that the Haggai-Zechariah corpus circulated prior to its incorporation into the Book of the Twelve.

Tentative evidence also suggests that Hosea, Amos, Micah, and Zephaniah experienced a protracted transmission as part of a single corpus, labeled as the Deuteronomistic corpus in this study. This evidence needs further investigation and documentation since some of the arguments derive from passages outside the scope of the current study. Nevertheless, understanding the conclusions of this study requires some explanation of a working hypothesis about the literary development of these four writings. This study maintains that not every literary touchstone across these four writings should be tied to the hand a *final* redactor working on the Book of the Twelve. Rather, these four writings exhibit characteristics internally, which suggest a common literary transmission. The Deuteronomistic superscriptions of these four writings *function* literarily as a chronological bracket linking YHWH's prophetic message from the reign of Uzziah forward to Hezekiah and from the reign of Josiah backward to Hezekiah. Careful analysis of these superscription demonstrates the likelihood that this literary function resulted from editorial adaptation. Deuteronomistic circles exerted more influence upon these four writings, however, than simply adapting their introductions. The language and perspective of this corpus bears signs of Deuteronomistic theology and the use of both Northern and Southern traditions in creating a historical compendium of prophecy which ultimately addresses the concerns of exilic and post-exilic Judah.

This Deuteronomistic corpus, if the tentative conclusions withstand further scrutiny, experienced more than one redactional shaping. Each of these redactional shapings significantly impacted the literary and theological emphases of this four-volume corpus prior to its incorporation into the Book of the Twelve. Macrostructurally, these four writings document YHWH's prophetic message to the Northern Kingdom (Hosea, Amos) and the Southern Kingdom (Micah, Zephaniah) in paradigmatic fashion. The prophetic message extending across these four writings does not, however, result from a single literary construction, but reflects a literary development in which the theological "meaning" of the corpus derived from at least three kinds of material: (1) the pre-existing form of the individual writings, (2) expansions related explicitly to the common transmission this Deuteronomistic corpus, (3) additions related to the transmission of the larger corpus, the Book of the Twelve.

First, evidence suggests that all four writings contained pre-existing prophetic material, although the precise form of the individual writings at this level requires further investigation.[3] Second, it is possible to trace the broad outlines of at least two distinct theological intentions at work within the Deuteronomistic corpus by noting significant vocabulary links and by tracing common theological motifs which evidence a certain literary logic. A sensitivity to independent scholarly opinions about the expansion of the individual writings allows one to postulate that some of the literary expansions relate to the theological concerns of the Deuteronomistic corpus. The earliest objective of this four volume corpus centered heavily upon YHWH's judgment, and ultimately sought to advance a theological explanation for Jerusalem's destruction. This earlier literary work contained major portions of the Book of Hosea documenting YHWH's message of impending judgment (primarily) to the Northern Kingdom if repentance was not forthcoming. Even at this level, Hosea alternates between messages of judgment and salvation, and portrays YHWH struggling over the question of whether or not to bring judgment upon Israel because of its idolatry and ethical abuses. Amos knows no such struggle at this

---

[3]   The literary form of this pre-existing material remains only one vital area requiring more work. One may postulate with relative certainty that both Amos and Hosea existed independently in some literary form prior to incorporation into the Deuteronomistic corpus. Micah and Zephaniah present more problems when one attempts to isolate the pre-Deuteronomistic forms. It is possible that these two writings, at this independent stage, are more accurately classified as "collections of sayings" than as a literary corpus. Evidence suggests that Amos *may* even have existed as separate collections prior to the editorial efforts which united chapters 1-2; 3-6; and 7-9 into an identifiable book (see discussion of the observations of Bosshard and Kratz).

compositional level (1:1-9:6), rather, it announces judgment because of Israel's rejection of YHWH's message. Micah, in its early Deuteronomistic form (1-3+6), *presupposes* the message of Hosea and Amos. It begins with the presumption of Samaria's destruction, and draws upon that destruction paradigmatically to change the literary focus from the Northern Kingdom to the impending destruction of the Southern Kingdom (Mic 1:2ff, especially 1:5) if Judah did not turn from its ways of idolatry and ethical abuses. The early compositional form of Zephaniah (1:1-3:8, without the passages of universal judgment drawing upon Joel) functioned as the Southern parallel to Amos. It depicted YHWH's irreversible decision to bring judgment upon Judah and Jerusalem because the lesson from Hosea to Micah had not been heeded. The oracle of judgment against Jerusalem which concludes Zephaniah's oracles against the nations (Zeph 3:1-8) accents the parallel function of Amos and Zephaniah. It concludes Zephaniah's oracles against the nations with a startling message of judgment against Jerusalem, just as the oracles against the nations in Amos conclude with the message of judgment against Israel.[4]

The heavy judgment orientation of this early Deuteronomistic corpus did not prove adequate theologically. Rather, it provoked the need to incorporate YHWH's message of deliverance to a remnant population. One should most likely situate the eschatological expansions to these four works in this context. These expansions hope for the restoration of a unified kingdom under the centrality of a repentant Jerusalem community.[5]

Third, as noted above, each of these four writings indicate that they were expanded editorially for inclusion into the Book of the Twelve. In the case of the first three writings (Hosea, Amos, Micah), editorial expansions to the introductory and concluding passages which may be related explicitly to the interests of the Book of the Twelve appear minimal, albeit significant.[6] The first chapter of Zephaniah evidences more substantive modification for the Book of the Twelve.

---

[4] The concluding oracle of Amos 1:3-2:16 shocks the reader by pronouncing judgment upon Israel in the same manner as the judgment against the surrounding nations. Similarly, Zeph 3:1-8a follows directly upon Zephaniah's oracles against the nations, but it shocks the reader when it becomes undeniably clear (3:2) that it pronounces judgment upon Jerusalem and Judah.

[5] These passages probably include portions of Hos 2:18ff; Amos 9:7-10, portions of Amos 9:11-15, substantial portions of Mic 4-5 and 7:8-20; and most of the eschatologically oriented material in Zeph 3:9-19.

[6] These are the redactional glosses noted above, e.g. as Hos 14:8a; Amos 9:12a,13b; Mic 1:2b; 7:19b; Zeph 3:20.

3. Concluding Remarks

This study presents substantive evidence that a long neglected catchword phenomenon opens significant avenues of interpretation which illuminate the growth, unity, and intentions of the Book of the Twelve. Evidence presented in this volume necessarily remains incomplete, presupposes tentative working hypotheses, and reflects decisions about other writings not yet discussed in detail. The exegetical significance of consistently recurring catchwords within the seams of the Book of the Twelve demands attention, yet this task involves more than a single volume can accomplish. Hence, this volume concentrates upon six writings which evidence minimal expansions adapting these writings for the Book of the Twelve. A second volume will investigate the remaining six writings where the editorial shaping of the individual writings for their position and function in the Book of the Twelve involves significantly larger portions of the individual writings. Despite these unavoidable limitations, the presumption of an expanded literary horizon frequently provides *plausible and meaningful* explanations for problematic passages within individual writings. This expanded literary horizon (the Book of the Twelve) does not emerge from the mind of this author, but derives from explicit traditions firmly associated with the transmission of these writings since at least the time of Jesus Ben Sirach. Thus, given the tradition of unity and the potential which the expanded horizon affords for interpretation and understanding, it is necessary that scholarship suspend the *presumption* that the unity of the Book of the Twelve results at most from the positioning of completed writings next to one another. These writings implore investigation of productive editorial shaping through cross references and catchwords as a means to discover the literary and theological intentions of this corpus.

This study occasionally makes observations whose implications impact the date and tradent of the compilation of the Book of the Twelve, but the discussion must remain necessarily vague at this point. Some observations, however, do help to place certain parameters upon the dates. First, the date of Jesus ben Sirach (early second century) provides us with the latest possible date for unification of the Twelve, since the Sirach reference presumes a fixed corpus. At the other end of the spectrum, many of the redactional glosses noted in this study allude to the book of Joel paradigmatically within the context of a pre-existing literary corpus. Logically, one must presuppose these allusions entered the writings simultaneously or subsequently to the compilation of Joel. Hence, the problematic question of the date for the Book of the Twelve rests, in part, upon the debated question of the date of Joel.

Questions regarding the tradent responsible for the Book of the Twelve also require more detailed treatment of the remaining writings, but some observations do provide helpful insights. First, if the tentative hypothesis withstands further scrutiny, there is evidence to support the contention that the Book of the Twelve presupposes and expands upon two corpora whose volumes show the continuing influence of Deuteronomistic circles. However, the editorial activity related to the Book of the Twelve goes well beyond Deuteronomistic concerns. Second, one must recognize that the editorial activity noted in these writings exhibits intertextuality with other prophetic writings, with the most significant examples relating to Isaiah. The familiarity of the Book of the Twelve with the full Isaiah corpus is even more prevalent in the remaining six writings, but should not be ignored in the writings discussed in this volume.[7] Third, the tradent responsible clearly exhibits considerable ability in the art of prophetic intertextual interpretation, or *Schriftprophetie*. One of the intriguing questions raised by this observation affects how pervasive one perceives this practice of intertextual reflection. Some quarters presume this type of intertextual reflection must only be associated with later wisdom circles, but the utter familiarity of the tradents of the Book of the Twelve with prophetic traditions demands that one consider whether such a limitation is wise.

This study throws new light upon some old questions, and it also raises new questions. The question of the unity of the Book of the Twelve should not, by any means, be considered as settled. Nevertheless, the illumination provided by this investigation of catchwords in the seams of the Book of the Twelve opens new paths which should not be ignored.

---

[7]   Note Bosshard's discussion of the macrostructural similarities, *BN* 40 (1987): 30-62.
Further, the similarity to Isaianic traditions is particularly notable in the intertextuality of passages such as Mic 4:1-3 (= Isa 2:2-4) and 7:8-20. Note also the similarity of superscriptions (cf the kings in Hos 1:1 and Isa 1:1), and the incorporation of similar eschatological perspectives, particularly when introduced by the ביום ההוא formula, a formula appearing with regularity in both Isaiah (45 times) and the Book of the Twelve (42 times), but not Jeremiah (12 times) and Ezekiel (13 times).

Works Cited

Abravanel, Isaac. *Rabbi Isaaci Abrabanelis Commentarius in Hoseam cuis & Praemissum Proemium in Duodecim Prophetas Minores*. Lugduni in Balaris: Ex Ofic. Johannis de Vivie, 1688, orig. 1506.

Ackroyd, Peter R. *Exile and Restoration: A Study of Hebrew Thought of the Sixth Century BC*. OTL. London: SCM, 1968.

Ackroyd, Peter. "Isaiah 36-39: Structure and Function." In *Von Kanaan bis Kerala*. 3-21. AOAT 211. W,C. Delsman, and others, eds. Neukirchen: Neukirchner Verlag, 1982.

Ackroyd, Peter. "Studies in the Book of Haggai." *JJS* 2 (1951): 163-76; *JJS* 3 (1952): 1-13.

Ackroyd, Peter. "The Book of Haggai and Zechariah 1-8." *JJS* 3 (1952): 151-156.

Ahlström, G.W. *Joel and the Temple cult of Jerusalem*. Supplements to Vetus Testamentum 21. Leiden: E.J. Brill, 1971.

Allen, Leslie C. *The Books of Joel, Obadiah, Jonah, and Micah*. New International Commentary. Grand Rapids: Eerdmans, 1976.

Amsler, Samuel. "Amos." In *Osée. Joël, Abdias, Jonas. Amos*. Commentaire de l'Ancien Testament 11a. Neuchâtel: Delachaux & Niestlé, 1965.

Anderson, George W. "The Idea of the Remnant in the Book of Zephaniah." *Annual of the Swedish Theological Institute: Festschrift Gillis Gerleman*. 11 (1977/78): 11-14.

Anderson, George W. *A Critical Introduction to the Old Testament*. London: Gerald Duckworth and Company Ltd., 1959.

Ball, Ivan. *A Rhetorical Study of Zephaniah*. Graduate Theological Union Dissertation. Minneapolis: University Microfilm, 1972. Order no. 3754f.-A.

Bartczek, Günter. *Prophetie und Vermittlung. Zur literarischen Analyse und theologischen Interpretation der Visionsberichte des Amos*. Europäische Hochschulschriften Series 23, Vol. 120. Bern: Peter Lang, 1980.

Bartlett, John R. "The Rise and Fall of the Kingdom of Edom." *Palestine Exploration Quarterly* 104 (1972): 26-37.

Ben Zvi, Ehud. *A Historical-Critical Study of the Book of Zephaniah*. BZAW 198. Berlin: De Gruyter, 1991.

Bentzen, Aage. "Quelques remarques sur le mouvement messianique parmi les Juifs aux environs de l'an 520 avant Jésus-Christ." *Revue d'Histoire et de Philosophie Religeuses* 10 (1930): 493-503.

Berg, Werner. *Die sogenannten Hymnenfragmente im Amosbuch*. Europäische Hochschulschriften Series 23. Vol. 45. Bern: Herbert Lang, 1974.

Bergler, Siegfried. *Joel als Schriftinterpret*. Beiträge zur Erforschung des Alten Testaments und des antiken Judentums 16. Frankfurt: Peter Lang, 1988.

Beuken, W.A.M. *Haggai - Sacharja 1-8. Studien zur Überlieferungsgeschichte der frühnachexilischen Prophetie*. Studia Semitica Nederlandica 10. Assen: Van Gorcum, & Co., 1967.

Beyse, Karl-Martin. *Serubbabel und die Königserwartungen der Propheten Haggai und Sacharja. Eine historische und traditionsgeschichtliche Untersuchung*. Stuttgart: Calwer Verlag, 1972.

Bič, Miloš. *Das Buch Sacharja*. Berlin: Evangelische Verlagsanstalt, 1962.

Bickerman, Elias J. "La Seconde Année de Darius." *Revue Biblique* 88 (1981): 23-28.

Blenkinsopp, Joseph. *Prophecy and Canon: A Contribution to the Study of Jewish Origins.* Notre Dame: University of Notre Dame Press, 1977.

Bloomhardt, Paul F. "The Poems of Haggai." *Hebrew Union College Annual* 5 (1928): 153-195.

Bosshard, Erich, and Reinhard Gregor Kratz. "Maleachi im Zwölfprophetenbuch." *BN* 52 (1990): 27-46.

Bosshard, Erich. "Beobachtungen zum Zwölfprophetenbuch." *BN* 40 (1987): 30-62.

Budde, Karl. "Eine folgenschwere Redaktion des Zwölfprophetenbuchs." *ZAW* 39 (1921): 218-229.

Budde, Karl. "Zu Text und Auslegung des Buches Amos." *JBL* 43 (1924): 46-131.

Burkitt, F.C. "Micah 6 and 7. A Northern Prophecy." *JBL* 45 (1926): 159-161.

Calderone, P. "The Rivers of Masor." *Biblica* 42 (1961): 423-432.

Carroll, Robert P. *Jeremiah: A Commentary.* Old Testament Library. LondonL SCM, 1986.

Cassuto, Umberto. "The Sequence and Arrangement of the Biblical Sections." In *Biblical and Oriental Studies*, vol. 1. Israel Abrams (trans.). Jerusalem: Magnes Press, 1973.

Cazelles, Henri. "Sophonie, Jérémie, et les Scythes en Palestine." *Revue Biblique* 74 (1967): 24-44.

Childs, Brevard S. *Introduction to the Old Testament as Scripture.* Philadelphia: Fortress Press, 1979.

Christensen, Duane L. "The Prosodic Structure of Amos 1-2." *HTR* 67 (1974): 427-436.

Christensen, Duane L. "Zephaniah 2:4-15: A Theological Basis for Josiah's Program of Political Expansion." *CBQ* 46 (1984): 669-682.

Christensen, Duane L. *Transformations of the War Oracle in Old Testament Prophecy: Studies in the Oracles Against the Nations.* Harvard Dissertations in Religion 3. Missoula, MT: Scholars Press, 1975.

Clements, Ronald E. "Patterns in the Prophetic Canon." In *Canon and Authority: Essays in Old Testament Religion and Theology*, 42-55. Philadelphia: Fortress, 1977.

Coggins, Richard J. *Samaritans and Jews: The Origins of Samaritanism Reconsidered.* Oxford: Basil Blackwell, 1975.

Cohen, Simon. "The Political Background of the Words of Amos." *Hebrew Union College Annual* 36 (1965): 153-160.

Condamin, Albert. "Amos 1:2-3:8. Authenticité et structure poétique." *Recherches de Science Religieuse* 20 (1930): 298-311.

Coote, Robert B. "Amos 1:11: RHMYW." *JBL* 90 (1971): 206-208.

Coote, Robert B. "Hosea 14:8: 'They Who Are Filled With Grain Shall Live.'" *JBL* 93 (1974): 161-173.

Coote, Robert B. *Amos among the Prophet: Composition and Theology.* Philadelphia: Fortress, 1981.

Coulot, Claude. "Propositions pour une structuration du livre d'Amos au niveau rédactionnel." *Revue des Sciences Religiuses* 51 (1977): 169-186.

Crenshaw, James L. *The Doxologies of Amos: A Form-Critical Study in the History of the Test of Amos.* Dissertation. Nashville: Vanderbilt University, 1964.

Cripps, Richard S.. *A Critical and Exegetical Commentary on the Book of Amos.* London: SPCK, 1955.

Cross, Frank Moore. *The Ancient Library of Qumran and Modern Biblical Studies.* Garden City, New York: Doubleday, 1958.

Davies, G.I. "A New Solution to a Crux in Obadiah 7." *VT* 27 (1977): 484-487.

Delitzsch, Franz. "Wann weissagte Obadja." *ZThK* 12 (1851): 91-102.

De Moor, Johannes C. "Micah 1: A Structural Approach." *Structural Analysis of Biblical and Canaanite Poetry.* JSOT Supplement Series 74. Willem van der Meer and Johannes C. de Moor, eds. 172-185. Sheffield: JSOT Press, 1988.

De Roche, Michael. "Zephaniah 1:2-3: The 'Sweeping' of Creation." *VT* 30 (1980): 104-109.

Duhm, Bernhard. "Anmerkungen zu den Zwölf Propheten I." *ZAW* 31 (1911): 1-43.

Duhm, Bernhard. "Anmerkungen zu den Zwölf Propheten II." *ZAW* 31 (1911): 81-110.

Duhm, Bernhard. "Anmerkungen zu den Zwölf Propheten III." *ZAW* 31 (1911): 161-204.

Eissfeldt, Otto. "Ein Psalm aus Nordisrael Mi 7:7-20." In *Kleine Schriften.* R. Sellheim and F. Maass, eds. Tübingen: Mohr, 1968. Also in *Zeitschrift der Deutschen Morgenländischen Gesellschaft* 112 (1962): 259-268.

Eissfeldt, Otto. *The Old Testament: An Introduction: The History of the Formation of the Old Testament.* Peter Ackroyd (trans.). New York: Harper and Row, 1965.

Elliger, Karl. "Die Heimat des Propheten Micha." *Zeitschrift des Deutschen Palästinavereins* 57/2 (1934): 81-152.

Elliger, Karl. "Ein Zeugnis aus der jüdischen Gemeinde im Alexanderjahr 332 v Chr." *ZAW* 62 (1949/50): 63-115.

Elliger, Karl. *Das Buch der Zwölf Kleinen Propheten 2. Die Propheten Nahum, Habakuk, Zephanja, Haggai, Sacharja, Maleachi. Übersetzt u. erklärt.* ATD 25. Göttingen: Vandenhoeck & Ruprecht, 1950.

Ewald, Heinrich. *Die Propheten des Alten Bundes.* 3 vols. Göttingen: Vandenhoeck & Ruprecht, ²1868.

Feuillet, A. "'S'asseoir à l'Ombre' de l'epoux (Os. 14:8a et Cant. 2:3)." *Revue Biblique* 78 (1971): 391-405.

Fey, Reinhard. *Amos und Jesaja. Abhängigkeit und Eigenständigkeit des Jesaja.* Wissenschaftliche Monographien zum Alten und Neuen Testament 12. Neukirchen: Neukirchener Verlag, 1963.

Fishbane, Michael. "Additional Remarks on *rḥmyw* (Amos 1:11)." *JBL* 91 (1972): 391-393.

Fishbane, Michael. *Biblical Interpretation in Ancient Israel.* Oxford: Clarendon Press, 1985.

Fohrer, Georg, and Ernst Sellin. *Introduction to the Old Testament.* David Green (trans.). Nashville: Abingdon Press, 1968.

Fohrer, Georg. "Micha 1." In *Das ferne und nahe Worte. Festschrift L. Rost.* F. Maass, ed., 65-80. BZAW 105. Berlin: Töpelmann, 1967.

Foresti, Fabrizio. "Funzione Semantica dei brani participali di Amos 4:13; 5:8s; 9:5s." *Bib* 62 (1981): 169-184.

Freedman, David Noel. "Discourse on Prophetic Discourse." In *The Quest for the Kingdom of God: Studies in Honor of George E. Mendenhall.* H.B. Huffmon, ed., 141-158. Winona Lake, Indiana: Eisenbrauns, 1983.

Friedman, R.E. "The Prophet and the Historian: The Acquisition of Historical Information from Literary Sources." In *The Poet and the Historian. Essays in Literary and Historical biblical Criticism.* R.E. Friedman, ed., 1-12. Harvard Semitic Studies 26. Chico, California: Scholars Press, 1983.

Fritz, Volkmar. "Das Wort gegen Samaria. Micha 1,2-7." *ZAW* 86 (1974): 316-331.

Fuhs, Hans F. "Amos 1:1. Erwägungen zur Tradition und Redaktion des Amosbuches." In *Bausteine biblischer Theologie. Festgabe für G. Johannes Botterweck zum 60.*

Geburtstag dargebracht von seinen Schülern. Bonner Biblische Beiträge 50. Köln-Bonn: Peter Hanstein Verlag, 1977.

Galling, Kurt. "Die Exilswende in der Sicht des Propheten Sacharja." *VT* 2 (1952): 18-36.

Georges, Karl Ernst. *Ausführliches lateinisch-deutsches Handwörterbuch.* 2 Vols. Basel: Benno Schwabe & Co. Verlag, ⁹1951.

Gerleman, Gillis. *Zephanja textkritisch und literarisch untersucht.* Lund: Gleerup, 1942.

Gerstenberger, Erhard S. *Psalms. Part I, with an Introduction to Cultic Poetry.* Forms of the Old Testament Literature 14. Grand Rapids: Eerdmans, 1988.

Gese, Hartmut. "Komposition bei Amos." *VTSupp* 32 Congress Volume (1980): 74-95.

Good, Edwin M. "The Composition of Hosea." *Svensk Exegetisk °Arsbok* 31 (1966): 21-63.

Gordon, Robert P. "An Inner-Targum Corruption (Zechariah 1:8)." *VT* 25 (1975): 216-221.

Gunkel, Hermann. "Der Micha-Schluss. Zur Einführung in die literaturgeschichtliche Arbeit am AT." *Zeitschrift für Semitistik* 2 (1924): 145-178.

Gunneweg, Antonius H.J. *Geschichte Israels bis Bar Kochba.* 5th ed. Stuttgart: Kohlhammer, 1984.

Halpern, Baruch. "The Ritual Background of Zechariah's Temple Song." *CBQ* 40 (1978): 167-190.

Hammershaimb, Erling. *The Book of Amos. A Commentary by E. Hammershaimb.* John Sturdy, trans. Oxford: Basil Blackwell, 1970.

Hanson, Paul D. *The Dawn of Apocalyptic.* Philadelphia: Fortress Press, 1975.

Haran, M. "Observations on the Historical Background of Amos 1:2-2:6." *Israel Exploration Journal* 18 (1968): 201-212.

Haupt, Paul. "The Visions of Zechariah." *JBL* 32 (1913): 107-122.

Heller, J. "Zephanjas Ahnenreihe." *VT* 21 (1971): 102-104.

Hieronymous, Eusebius (Jerome). "Incipit Prologus Duodecim Prophetarum." *Biblica Sacra Vulgata Iuxta Vulgatum Versionem.* Vol. 2. Stuttgart: Würtembergische Bibelanstalt, 1969. 1374.

Hillers, Delbert R. *Micah: A Commentary on the Book of the Prophet Micah.* Hermeneia. Philadelphia: Fortress Press, 1984.

Hitzig, Ferdinand. *Die zwölf kleinen Propheten.* Leipzig: Hirzel Verlag, ⁴1881.

Holladay, William. *Jeremiah 2: A Commentary on the Book of the Prophet Jeremiah Chapters 26-52.* Hermeneia. Minneapolis: Fortress Press, 1989.

Horst, F. *Nahum bis Maleachi.* Handbuch zum Alten Testament 14/2. Tübingen: J.C.B. Mohr, 1938.

House, Paul R. *The Unity of the Twelve.* JSOT 77. Sheffield: Sheffield Academic Press, 1990.

Hyatt, J.P. "The Date and Background of Zephaniah." *JNES* 7 (1948): 25-29.

Irsigler, H. *Gottesgericht und Jahwetag: Die Komposition Zef 1,1-2,3 untersucht auf Grund der Literarkritik.* Arbeiten zu Text und Sprache im Alten Testament 3. St. Ottilien: Eos Verlag, 1977.

Isbel, Charles D. "A Note on Amos 1:1." *Journal of Near Eastern Studies* 36 (1977): 213-214.

Jacob, Edmund, Carl A. Keller, and Samuel Amsler. *Osée - Joël, Abdias, Jonas - Amos.* CAT 11a. Neuchâtel: Delachaux & Niestlé, 1965.

Japhet, Sara. "Sheshbazzar and Zerubbabel — Against the Background of the Historical and religious Tendencies of Ezra-Nehemiah." Part 1 in *ZAW* 94 (1982): 66-98; Part 2 in *ZAW* 95 (1983): 218-229.

Jeppesen, Knud. "How the Book of Micah Lost Its Integrity: Outline of the History of the Criticism of the Book of Micah with Emphasis on the 19th Century." *Studia Theologica* 33 (1979): 101-131.

Jepsen, Alfred. "Kleine Beiträge zum Zwölfprophetenbuch I." *ZAW* 56 (1938): 85-101.

Jeremias, Christian. *Die Nachtgesichte des Sacharja. Untersuchungen zu ihrer Stellung im Zusammenhang der Visionsberichte im Alten Testament und zu ihrem Bildmaterial.* Forschungen zur Religion und Literatur des Alten und Neuen Testaments 117. Göttingen: Vandenhoeck & Ruprecht, 1977.

Jeremias, Jörg. "Die Deutung der Gerichtsworte Michas in der Exilszeit." *ZAW* 83 (1971): 330-354.

Jeremias, Jörg. "Zur Eschatologie des Hoseabuches." In *Die Botschaft und die Boten. Festschrift für H.W. Wolff.* 217-234. Neukirchen: Neukirchener Verlag, 1981.

Jeremias, Jörg. *Der Prophet Hosea. Übersetzt und erklärt.* Das Alte Testament Deutsch, Neues Göttinger Bibelwerk 24/1. Göttingen: Vandenhoeck & Ruprecht, 1983.

Jeremias, Jörg. *Theophanie. Die Geschichte einer alttestamentlichen Gattung.* Neukirchen: Neukirchner Verlag, 1965.

Joüon, Paul. "Notes de Lexicographie Hebraique," *Biblica* 7 (1926): 162-170.

Kaiser, Otto. *Introduction to the Old Testament: A Presentation of Its Results and Problems.* John Sturdy, trans. Oxford: Basil Blackwell, 1984.

Kapelrud, Arvid S. *The Message of the Prophet Zephaniah: Morphology and Ideas.* Oslo: Universitetsforlaget, 1975.

Keil, Carl Friedrich. *The Twelve Minor Prophets.* 2 Vols. James Martin (trans.). Grand Rapids: Eerdmans Publishing Co., 1949, orig. 1866.

Keller, Carl A. and René Vuilleumier. *Michée, Nahoum, Habacuc, Sophonie.* CAT 11b. Neuchâtel: Delachaux & Niestlé, 1971.

Kellerman, Ulrich. "Der Amosschluss als Stimme deuteronomistischer Heilshoffnung." *EvTh* 29 (1969): 169-183.

Koch, Klaus. "Haggais unreines Volk." *ZAW* 79 (1967): 52-66.

Krinetzki, Günter. *Zefanjastudien: Motiv- und Traditionskritik und Kompositions- und Redaktionskritik.* Regensburger Studien zur Theologie 7. Frankfurt: Peter Lang, 1977.

Kuhl, Curt. *Die Entstehung des Alten Testaments.* Bern: Francke, 1953.

Langohr, Guy. "Le livre de Sophonie et la critique d'authenticité." *Ephemerides Theologicae Lovanienses* 52 (1976): 1-27.

Langohr, Guy. "Rédaction et composition du livre de Sophonie." *Muséon* 89 (1976): 51-73.

Lescow, Theodor. "Redaktionsgeschichtliche Analyse von Micha 1-5." *ZAW* 84 (1972): 46-85.

Lescow, Theodor. "Redaktionsgeschichtliche Analyse von Micha 6-7." *ZAW* 84 (1972): 182-212.

Lindblom, Johannes. *Prophecy in Ancient Israel.* Oxford: Blackwell, 1962.

Lipiński, E. "Recherches sur le livre de Zacharie." *VT* 20 (1970): 25-55.

Markert, L. *Struktur und Bezeichnung des Scheltworts. Eine gattungskritische Studie anhand des Amosbuches.* BZAW 140. Berlin: DeGruyter, 1977.

Marti, Karl. *Das Dodekapropheton.* HCAT 13. Tübingen: Mohr, 1904.

Mason, Rex. "Some Echoes of the Preaching in the Second Temple? Tradition Elements in Zechariah 1-8." *ZAW* 96 (1984): 210-221.

Mason, Rex. "The Purpose of the 'Editorial Framework' in the Book of Haggai." *VT* 27 (1977): 413-421.

Mason, Rex. *The Books of Haggai, Zechariah and Malachi*. Cambridge Bible Commentary. New York/London: Cambridge University Press, 1977.

May, Herbert G. "This People and this Nation in Haggai." *VT* 18 (1968): 190-197.

Mays, James L. *Amos. A Commentary*. OTL. London: SCM, 1969.

Mays, James L. *Hosea. A Commentary*. OTL. London: SCM, 1969.

Mays, James L. *Micah: A Commentary*. OTL. London: SCM, 1976.

McHardy, W.D. "The Horses in Zechariah." In *In Memoriam Paul Kahle*. M. Black and G. Fohrer, eds. BZAW 103. Berlin: A. Töpelmann, 1968.

Miller, J. Maxwell and John H. Hayes. *A History of Ancient Israel and Judah*. London: SCM, 1986.

Mitchell, Hinckley G. *A Critical and Exegetical Commentary on Haggai and Zechariah*. International Critical Commentary. Edinburgh: T&T Clark, 1912.

Mulder, M.J. "כרמל." In *ThWAT*, vol 4, 340-351.

Newsome, James D. *A Synoptic Harmony of Samuel, Kings, and Chronicles. With Related Passages from Psalms, Isaiah, Jeremiah, and Ezra*. Grand Rapids: Baker Book House, 1986.

Nogalski, James D. *The Use of Stichwörter as a Redactional Unification Technique in the Book of the Twelve*. ThM Thesis. Rüschlikon, Switzerland: Baptist Theological Seminary, 1987.

Nogalski, James D. *Redactional Processes in the Book of the Twelve*. BZAW. Berlin: De Gruyter, forthcoming.

Nowack, Wilhelm. *Die kleinen Propheten übersetzt und erklärt*. 3rd ed. Göttingen: Vandenhoeck & Ruprecht, 1922.

Ottosson, Magnus. *Gilead: Tradition and History*. Lund: Gleerup, 1969.

Otzen, Benedikt. *Studien über Deuterosacharja*. Acta Theologica Danica 6. Copenhagen: Munksgaard, 1964.

Paul, Shalom. "A Literary Reinvestigation of the Authenticity of the Oracles Against the Nations in Amos." In *De la Tôrah au Messie. Études d'exégèse et d'Herméneutique Bibliques Offertes à Henri Cazelles pour se 25 années d'Enseignement á l'Institut Catholique de Paris (Octobre 1979)*. Maurice Carrez, et al, eds. Paris: Desclée, 1981.

Paul, Shalom. "Amos 1:3-2:3: A Concatenous Literary Pattern." *JBL* 90 (1971): 397-403.

Peifer, Calude J. "Amos the Prophet: The Man and His Book." *TBT* 19 (1981): 295-300.

Petersen, David. *Haggai and Zechariah 1-8*. OTL. Philadelphia: Westminster Press, 1984.

Petersen, David. *Late Israelite Prophecy: Studies in Deutero-Prophetic Literature and in Chronicles* SBLMS 23. Missoula, MT: Scholars Press, 1977.

Petersen, David L. "Zerubbabel and Jerusalem Temple Reconstruction." *CBQ* 36 (1974): 366-372.

Pierce, Ronald. "A Thematic Development of the Haggai-Zechariah-Malachi Corpus." *JETS* 27 (1984): 401-11.

Pierce, Ronald. "Literary Connectors and a Haggai-Zechariah-Malachi Corpus." *JETS* 27 (1984): 277-89.

Plöger, Otto. *Theocracy and Eschatology*. S. Rudman, trans. Original, 1959. Oxford: Blackwell, 1968.

Priest, John. "The Covenant of Brothers." *JBL* 84 (1965): 400-406.

Reicke, Bo. "Liturgical Traditions in Micah 7." *HTR* 60 (1967): 349-367.

Reventlow, H. Graf. *Das Amt des Propheten bei Amos.* Forschungen zur Religion und Literatur des Alten und Neuen Testaments 80. Göttingen: Vandenhoeck & Ruprecht, 1962.

Rice, Gene. "The African Roots of the Prophet Zephaniah." *Journal of Religious Thought* 36 (1979/80): 21-31.

Robertson, O. Palmer. *The Books of Nahum, Habakkuk, and Zephaniah.* The New International Commentary on the Old Testament. Grand Rapids: Eerdmans, 1990.

Robinson, Theodore and Friedrich Horst. *Die Zwölf Kleinen Propheten.* 2nd edition. Handbuch zum Alten Testament. Tübingen: Mohr, 1954.

Rothstein, Johann Wilhelm. *Juden und Samaritaner. Die grundlegende Scheidung von Judentum und Heidentum.* BWAT 3. Leipzig: Hinrich, 1908.

Rudolph, Wilhelm. *Haggai - Sacharja 1-8 - Sacharja 9-14 - Maleachi.* KAT 13/4. Gütersloh: Gerd Mohn, 1976.

Rudolph, Wilhelm. *Hosea.* KAT 13/1. Gütersloh: Gerd Mohn, 1966.

Rudolph, Wilhelm. *Joel - Amos - Obadja - Jona.* KAT 13/2. Gütersloh: Gerd Mohn, 1971.

Rudolph, Wilhelm. *Micha - Nahum - Habakuk - Zephanja.* KAT 13/3. Gütersloh: Gerd Mohn, 1975.

Sabottka, L. *Zephanja. Versuch einer Neuübersetzung mit philogischem Kommentar.* Biblica et Orientalia 25. Rome: Biblical Institute Press, 1972.

Saebø, Magne. "Die deuterosacharjanische Frage." *StTh* 23 (1969): 115-140.

Saebø, Magne. *Sacharja 9-14. Untersuchungen von Text und Form.* Wissenschaftliche Monographien zum Alten und Neuen Testament 34. Neukirchen: Neukirchener Verlag, 1969.

Schmidt, Werner H. "Die deuteronomistische Redaktion des Amosbuches. Zu den theologischen Unterschieden zwischen dem Prophetenwort und seinem Sammler." *ZAW* 77 (1965): 168-193.

Schneider, Dale Allen. *The Unity of the Book of the Twelve.* Yale University PhD Diss., 1979.

Schoville, Keith N. "A Note on the Oracles of Amos against Gaza, Tyre, and Edom." *VT Supplement* 26 (1974): 55-63.

Schunck, K.D. "במה" In *ThWAT*, vol. 1, 662-667.

Schwally, Friedrich. "Das Buch Sefanjâ." *ZAW* 10 (1890): 165-240.

Sellin, E. *Das Zwölfprophetenbuch.* 1st ed. 1922. 2 vols. Leipzig: Deichert, vol. 1 1929; vol. 2 1930.

Sellin, Ernst. *Studien zur Entstehungsgeschichte der jüdischen Gemeinde nach dem babylonischen Exil.* 2 vols. Leipzig: A. Deichert, 1900-01.

Seow, C.L. "Hosea 14:10 and the Foolish People Motif." *CBQ* 44 (1982): 212-224.

Seybold, Klaus. "Reverenz und Gebet: Erwägungen zu der Wendung hillâ panîm." *ZAW* 88 (1976): 2-16.

Seybold, Klaus. *Satirische Prophetie. Studien zum Buch Zefanja.* Stuttgarter Bibelstudien 120. Stuttgart: Verlag Katholisches Bibelwerk, 1985.

Smalley, William A. "Recursion Patterns and the Sectioning of Amos." *The Bible Translator* 30 (1979): 118-127.

Smend, Rudolf. *Die Entstehung des Alten Testaments.* 3rd ed. Stuttgart: Kohlhammer, 1984.

Smith, George Adam. *The Book of the Twelve Prophets.* 2 vols. New York: Harper and Brothers, 1928.

Smith, Louise Pettibone and Ernest R. Lacheman. "The Authorship of the Book of Zephaniah." *Journal of Near Eastern Studies* 9 (1950): 137-142.

Smith, Ralph L. *Micah - Malachi*. Word Biblical Commentary 32. Waco: Word Books, 1984.

Snaith, Norman H. "Selah." *VT* 2 (1952): 43-56.

Soggin, J. Alberto. *A History of Israel: From the Beginnings to the Bar Kochba Revolt, AD 135*. John Bowden, trans. London: SCM, 1984.

Soggin, J. Alberto. *The Prophet Amos: A Translation and Commentary*. London: SCM, 1987.

Stade, Bernard. "Streiflichter auf die Entstehung der jetzigen Gestalt der alttestamentlichen Prophetenschriften." *ZAW* 23 (1903): 153-71.

Stade, Bernhard. "Bemerkungen über das Buch Micha." *ZAW* 1 (1881): 161-172.

Stade, Bernhard. "Deuterozacharja. Eine kritische Studie." *ZAW* 1 (1881): 1-96.

Stade, Bernhard. "Deuterozacharja. Eine kritische Studie." *ZAW* 2 (1882): 151-172, 275-309.

Steck, Odil Hannes. "Zu Haggai 1:2-11." *ZAW* 83 (1971): 355-379.

Steck, Odil Hannes. *Bereitete Heimkehr. Jesaja 35 als redaktionelle Brücke zwischen dem Ersten und dem Zweiten Jesaja*. Stuttgarter Bibelstudien 121. Stuttgart: Katholisches Bibelwerk, 1985.

Steuernagel, Carl. *Lehrbuch der Einleitung in das Alte Testament*. Tübingen: J.C.B. Mohr, 1912.

Story, Cullen I.K. "Amos — Prophet of Praise." *VT* 30 (1980): 67-80.

Stuart, Douglas. *Hosea - Jonah*. Word Biblical Commentary 31. Waco, Texas: Word, 1987.

Szeles, Maria Eszenyei. *Wrath and Mercy: Habakkuk and Zephaniah*. International Theological Commentary. Grand Rapids: Eerdmans, 1987.

Townsend, T.N. "Additional Comments on Haggai 2:10-19." *VT* 18 (1968): 559-560.

Tucker, Gene M. "Prophetic Superscriptions and the Growth of a Canon." In *Canon and Authority: Essays in Old Testament Religion and Theology*. George W. Coats and Burke O. Long, eds. 56-70. Philadelphia: Fortress Press, 1977.

Utzschneider, Helmut. *Künder oder Schreiber? Eine These zum Problem der »Schriftprophetie« auf Grund von Maleachi 1,6-2:9*. Beiträge zur Erforschung des Alten Testaments und des Antiken Judentums 19. Frankfurt: Peter Lang, 1989.

Verhoef, Pieter. *The Books of Haggai and Malachi*. New International Commentary. Grand Rapids: Eerdmans, 1987.

Vollers, Karl. "Das Propheton der Alexandriner." *ZAW* 3 (1883) 219-272; 4 (1884) 219-272.

Vuilleumier, René. *La tradition cultuelle d'Israël dans la prophétie d'Amos et d' Osée*. Cahiers Théologiques 45. Neuchâtel: Delachaux & Niestlé, 1960.

Watts, John D.W. *The Books of Joel, Obadiah, Jonah, Nahum, Habakkuk and Zephaniah*. Cambridge Bible Commentary. London: Cambridge University Press, 1975.

Watts, John D.W. *Vision and Prophecy in Amos*. Leiden: E.J. Brill, 1958.

Watts, John D.W. "The Origin of the Book of Amos." *Expository Times* 66 (1954/55): 109-112.

Weimar, Peter. "Der Schluss des Amos-Buches: Ein Beitrag zur Redaktionsgeschichte des Amos-Buches." *BN* 16 (1981): 60-100.

Weimar, Peter. "Obadja. Eine redaktionskritische Analyse." *BN* 27 (1985): 35-99.

Weiser, Artur. *Die Propheten Hosea, Joel, Amos, Obadja, Jona, Micha. Übersetzt und erklärt*. ATD 24. Göttingen: Vandenhoeck & Ruprecht, [3]1985.

Wellhausen, Julius. *Die kleinen Propheten übersetzt und erklärt*. Skizzen und Vorarbeiten 5. Berlin: Reimer, 1892.

Wildberger, Hans. *Jesaja 1-39*. 3 vols. Biblischer Kommentar 10. Neukirchen: Neukirchner Verlag, 1972-82.

Willi-Plein, Ina. *Vorformen der Schriftexegese innerhalb des Alten Testaments. Untersuchungen zum literarischen Werden der auf Amos, Hosea und Micha zurückgehenden Bücher im hebräischen Zwölfprophetenbuch*. BZAW 123. Berlin: DeGruyter, 1971.

Williams, Donald L. "The Date of Zephaniah." *JBL* 82 (1963): 77-88.

Willis, John T. "Some suggestions on the Interpretation of Micah 1:2." *VT* 18 (1968): 372-379.

Wilson, Robert R. *Genealogy and History in the Biblical World*. New Haven: Yale University, 1977.

Wilson, Robert R. *Prophecy and Society in Ancient Israel*. Philadelphia: Fortress, 1980.

Wolfe, Rolland Emerson. "The Editing of the Book of the Twelve." *ZAW* 53 (1935): 90-129.

Wolff, Hans Walter. *Haggai*. BK 14/6. Neukirchen: Neukirchener Verlag, 1986.

Wolff, Hans-Walter. *Hosea*. Biblischer Kommentar 14/1. Neukirchen: Neukirchener Verlag, second edition, 1965 (1961).

Wolff, Hans-Walter. *Joel und Amos*. Biblischer Kommentar 14/2. Neukirchen: Neukirchener Verlag, 1969.

Wolff, Hans-Walter. *Micha*. Biblischer Kommentar 14/4. Neukirchen: Neukirchener Verlag, 1982.

Wolff, Hans-Walter. *Obadja und Jona*. Biblischer Kommentar 14/3. Neukirchen: Neukirchener Verlag, 1977.

Yee, Gale A. *Composition and Tradition in the Book of Hosea: A Redaction-Critical Approach*. SBL Dissertation Series 102. Atlanta: Scholars Press, 1987.

Zimmerli, Walter. "Vom Prophetenwort zum Prophetenbuch." *ThLZ* 104 (1979): 481-496.

Alphabetical Index of Biblical and Extra-Biblical Citations

Amos

1-2 77
1:1-9:6 . 79, 82, 83, 280
1:1-2:16 82
1:1-12 24
1:1f 80
1:1 . 76-79, 82, 84, 88,
     123, 127, 129, 141,
     176, 185
1:2-3:8 93
1:2-2:16 280
1:2 . . 6, 79, 82, 84, 92,
     132, 161
1:3 . . . . 82, 140
1:3-2:16 . . . 78, 79, 89,
     91, 92, 94, 142,
     172, 174
1:3-2:5 80
1:3ff 69
1:6 140
1:9 140
1:9-12 82
1:11 140
1:11f 108, 114
1:13 140
2:1 140
2:4 140
2:4f 82, 88
2:6 . . . . 69, 140
2:6-4:3 80
2:6ff 174
2:10 116
2:11 98
2:14 79
2:16 . . . . 80, 98
3-6 77
3:1-4 93
3:1 74
3:5-8 93
3:8 . . . . 92, 93
3:9 . . . . 88, 134
3:10 98
3:12 88
3:14 . . . . . 84, 88, 140

3:15 98
4:1 . . . . . 74, 88, 134
4:3-11 98
4:4-13 80
4:4 . . . . . 84, 88, 140
4:6-13 81
4:6ff 79
4:9 . . . . 226, 227, 229
4:13 . 36, 81, 118, 136
5 192
5:1-17 80
5:1 74
5:1ff 79
5:2 69
5:4 192
5:5f 84, 88
5:6 192
5:7 . . . . 69, 144
5:8 30
5:8f 81
5:10 34
5:11 . . . . 190, 191
5:12 . . . . 34, 140
5:15 . . . . 34, 144
5:18 74
5:18ff 79, 80
5:24 . . . . 69, 144
6:1ff 80
6:1 . . . 74, 75, 88, 134
6:8 . . . . 79, 98
6:12 . . . . 69, 144
6:14 98
7:1-9:6 . . 74, 75, 77, 79
7:1-8:3 82
7:1-7 5
7:10-17 . . . . 75, 78-80
7:10 . . . . 84, 88
7:13 . . . . 81, 84
7:16 118
7:17 87
8:1-14 117
8:1-3 117
8:1ff 117
8:3-14 79

8:3ff 79
8:3 . . . . . 80, 98, 117
8:4-14 75
8:4-8 80
8:4-6 76
8:5 145
8:6 88
8:7 79
8:7-14 76
8:9 . . . . . 79, 98, 108
8:9f 80, 117
8:10 79
8:11ff 79, 80, 117
8:11f 78
8:11 98, 108, 117, 118
8:13ff 80
8:14 88, 134, 139, 176
8:15 134
9:1ff 17, 117
9:1-15 . 27, 97, 98, 121
9:1-10 117
9:1-6 . . 79-81, 99, 121,
     139, 176
9:1-4 . . . 76, 82, 97, 98,
     145, 148
9:1 . . . . 79, 103, 139
9:2-4 139
9:3 . . . . 79, 161
9:4 . . . . 99, 101
9:5f 81, 97, 98
9:5 . 79, 101, 118, 139
9:6 . . . . 81, 83, 84, 97
     101, 139
9:7-15 . . . . . . 82, 141
9:7-10 . 74, 80, 98, 121,
     122, 177, 280
9:7-8a 100
9:7 98-101
9:8 . . . . . . 98, 99, 101
9:8b-10 102
9:9-15 78
9:9f 99
9:9 98
9:11 . . . . 98, 176, 236

9:11,14f 72
9:11-15 . . . 11, 74, 80,
        104, 117-122, 280
9:11ff 117, 178
9:11f 84, 98
9:12 . . . 6, 44, 98, 104,
     117, 119, 120, 161,
                276, 281
9:13-15 59
9:13 . 26, 98, 116-119,
                    277
9:14-15 176
Canticles
2:2f 64
1 Chronicles
4:30 23
11:8 22
16:11 192
2 Chronicles
12:3 100
14:8 100
16:8 100
29:3-36 87
30:1-27 87
31:2-21 87
32:1-5 159
32:2-8 87
32:5 168
32:21 169
33:17 136
35:1-17 87
36:13 96
Deuteronomy
1:41 191
4:6 68
4:27 202
5:20 130
8:8 229
8:28 228
9:16 191
17:7 130
17:16 66
19:15 130
20:18 191
23:7 . . . . . . 182, 184
28:15 246
28:45 246

28:64ff 202
30:3 202
30:4 209
31:19 130
31:26 130
32:13 136
33:29 . . . . 36, 136
Esther
1:1 100
8:9 100
Exodus
13:21 153
15:5 154
20:16 130
23:29 151
33:14 153
34:7 26
Ezekiel
1:1f 223
6:14 152
7:7 50
7:12 50
8:1 223
12:20 152
14:15f 152
15:8 152
16:46 134
17:23 68
20:1 223
20:37 166
21:15 166
21:18 166
22:15 111
23:4 134
23:34 134
24:1 223
25:13 30
26:1 223
29:1 223
29:9-12 152
29:12ff 202
29:17 223
30:5 100
30:9 100
30:20 223
31:1 223
31:16f 68

32:1 223
32:15 152
32:17 223
32:29 30
33:21 223
33:28f 152
34:4 209
34:13 166
34:16 209
35:3ff 152
35:10 . . . . 32, 149
35:15 . . . . 30, 152
36:19 111
36:34 152
38:5 100
40:1 223
44:12 169
47:3 251
Ezra
3:10-11 226
4:1-5 223
5:1 . . . . 52, 235, 248
6:14 . . . 52, 235, 248
6:15 260
Genesis
1-3 188
1:1ff 188
1:2-3 195
1:20 188
1:24 188
1:26 188
2:5 50
2:7 188
2:10 169
3:17-19 188
6-9 188
6:1 102
6:5 102
6:6 102
6:7 . . . . 102, 188
6:17 102
6:21 169
7:3 102
7:4 . . . . 102, 188
7:10 102
7:12 102
7:17 102

7:19 102
7:23 102
8:8 . . . . 102, 188
8:13 102
8:21 188
17:11 169
17:17 23
22:22f 23
24:15 23
24:8 267
28:21 22
29:7 50
30:43 106
32:11 169
45:28 39

Habakkuk
1:1-17 40
1:3 48
1:5ff 121, 177
2:7 169
2:20 . . . . 6, 189
3:1-19 . . . . 45, 200
3:1ff 15, 17, 275
3:2ff . . . 142, 194, 198
3:10 194
3:16 . . . . . . 195, 199
3:17 . . . . . 15, 17, 121

Haggai
1:1ff 84
1:1-11 . . 107, 216, 217,
          219, 223, 264
1:1 . . . . 206, 215, 221,
          222, 225, 241
1:1-6 49
1:1-7 224
1:2-11 . . . . . . 223, 230
1:2ff 214
1:2 . . . . 210, 215, 277
1:4ff 214
1:4 210
1:5 . . . . 223, 225
1:6 265
1:7 223
1:10f 264, 265
1:11 . . . . 32, 227
1:12-14 . 217, 223, 224

1:12 . . . . 52, 214, 217,
          265
1:14 . . . . . . 50, 214
1:15 . . . 216, 217, 221,
          222
1:15b-2:2 217
2:1-7 224
2:1-2 . . . . . . 50, 217
2:1 . 216, 222, 225, 241
2:2 . 50, 214, 231, 241
2:3-4 50
2:3-5 217
2:3-9 217
2:5 . . . . 216, 217
2:6 . . . . 52, 231
2:6f 220
2:7 236
2:10-23 221
2:10-19 224
2:10-14 . 217, 223, 230
2:10 . . . 216, 217, 221,
          225, 230, 241, 264
2:11-14 217
2:11-13 217
2:11 241
2:12 52
2:14 217
2:15 50
2:15-23 221
2:15-19 . 217, 223, 230
2:16 265
2:17-22 236
2:17 . . . 216, 217, 256,
          265
2:18 . . . 216, 217, 264
2:19 15, 121, 216, 217,
     256, 264, 265, 276, 277
2:20 . . . 216, 221, 241
2:20-21 217
2:20-21a 217
2:20-23 . . 51, 224, 229,
          241
2:20ff 107, 161
2:21 . . . . 50, 220, 256
2:21-23 217
2:22 220, 254, 256, 276

Hosea
1:1-7 63
1:1ff 5
1:1 . . . 63, 85, 86, 129,
        181, 186, 275, 282
1:2-9 58
1:2 87
2:1ff 63, 176
2:1-3 58
2:3ff 62, 140
2:4-15 58
2:4 87
2:6 87
2:7 87
2:8f 68
2:10-15 140
2:10f 70, 71
2:10 32
2:14 70
2:15 71
2:16-25 . . . . . 58, 65
2:18ff 71, 280
2:18 71
2:20 71
2:21 144
2:23f 71
2:23 71
2:24 . . . . 32, 70
3:1-5 63
3:1-4 58
3:1ff 5
3:3 87
3:5 58
4:1-3 58
4:1 . . . . 70, 144
4:3ff 63
4:4-14:9 58
4:4-5:7 58
4:4 88
4:5 . . . . . . 61, 62, 68
4:7 68
4:10b-12a 68
4:10 87
4:11-14 61
4:11 . . . . 70, 71
4:12 87
4:13 22

4:14 .... 68, 87
4:15 88
4:18 87
5:2ff 63
5:3f 61
5:3 87
5:5-14:1 58
5:5 .... 61, 68
5:8-14:1 61
5:8-8:14 58
5:13 61
5:15ff 63
6:1-3 65
6:1 61
6:4 144
6:6 144
6:8 192
6:11-7:1 63
6:11 88
7:1 ..... 61, 134, 192
7:4ff 63
7:5 70
7:11 68
7:13 ...... 68, 140
7:14 ..... 32, 70, 71
8:1 .... 68, 140
8:3-6 61
8:4ff 63
8:5 88
8:5f 134
8:6 134
8:7 68
8:14 88
9:1-10:15 58
9:1f 71
9:1 87
9:2ff 63
9:2 .... 32, 70
9:4 70
9:7 68
9:10 44
10:1-8 61
10:1 70
10:5 .... 88, 134, 145
10:7 ...... 88, 134
10:9ff 63
10:9 246

10:12 144
10:15 88
11:1-14:1 58
11:1-11 .... 59, 63, 65
11:7 22
11:8-12 11
11:8-11 65
12:1ff 63
12:1 88
12:2 68
12:3 88
12:5 88
12:7 144
12:8 145
12:15 213
13:1ff 61, 63
13:2 61
13:3 ...... 68, 192
13:12 66
13:15 66
14:1ff 6
14:1-9 11
14:1 ...... 88, 134
14:2-10 ..... 58, 69
14:2-9 ..... 59, 65
14:2ff 140
14:5-10 21
14:8 .... 70, 215, 276,
            277, 281
14:10 ... 59, 63, 65, 68,
              140

Isaiah
1:1 . 86, 186, 275, 282
1:7 152
1:8 106
2:1-4 271
2:1 26
2:2-4 ... 125, 168, 271,
             275, 282
2:2ff 272
3:26 26
6:1-9:6 158
6:11 152
7:21 22
9-12 ...... 15, 157
9:1-6 158
9:3 166

9:7ff 158
10:1ff 10, 156
10:1-4 158
10:3 195
10:5-20 159
10:5ff 166
10:11 134
10:12 164
10:18 ...... 161, 164
11:1-9 159
11:4 166
11:10-16 159
11:11 100
11:16 169
12:1-6 ..... 158, 159
14:14 136
14:29 166
16:10 ...... 161, 162
17:9 152
18:1 ...... 100, 202
19:20 130
19:22 202
24:1-6 168
26:21 132
27:13 209
29:17 ... 161, 163-165
30:16 66
30:2f 68
32:15f 161, 164
33:9 163
34-35 200
34 189
34:11 251
37:21-35 163
37:24 161-163
37:31f 169
37:36f 169
38:14 40
40:28 81
42:5 81
43:14 100
43:15 81
45:7 81
45:14 100
45:18 81
50-54 84
52:7ff 168

52:7 10
53:9 136
55:6 192
57:14 56
57:19 81
58:14 136
59:7 219
59:19 132
60-61 247
60:3f 202
60:14 207
62:4 152
64:9 152
65:17 81
65:18 81
66:8 23
66:15f 132

Jeremiah
2:7 .... 161, 162
2:10 23
2:15 197
2:31 169
2:32 23
4:26 .... 161, 162
4:27 152
6:8 152
9:10 152
9:11 68
9:15 111
10:22 152
12:8 169
12:10 152
13:23 100
13:24 111
20:7 169
23:13 134
23:24 39
25:11 249
25:12 152
25:15 32
25:30 .... 132, 197
25:38 169
26:17ff 124
26:18 ... 136, 137, 143
29:10 249
30:11 .... 26, 202
30:17 209

31:5 133
31:9 169
31:38f 251
32:43 152
34:22 152
36:14 185
38:7-12 100
39:16-18 100
40:12 209
42:5 130
42:16 246
43:5 209
44:6 152
46:1 100
46:9 100
48:33 .... 161, 162
48:35 136
49:7 30
49:9 .... 15, 17
49:14-16 ..... 15, 17
49:14 ...... 30, 148
49:16 30
49:17 30
49:33 152
50:10 169
50:13 152
50:17-19 164
50:23 169
51:26 152
51:41 169
51:62 152
52:3 96
52:24ff 180, 185

Job
5:6 48
9:8 136
21:4 23
22:16 50
27:15 136
30:24 137
41:23 154

Joel
1-2 .... 227, 229
1:1-14 69
1:1-12 21
1:1ff 6
1:1 181

1:2-4 142
1:2ff 215
1:2 .... 69, 142
1:4 227
1:5 .... 69, 118
1:7 .. 69, 72, 227, 265
1:8 140
1:10 ... 32, 40, 69, 70, 72
1:11 227
1:12 .. 21, 40, 69, 227, 229
1:15 .... 9, 198
1:16 23
1:17 .... 70, 72
2:1-11 9
2:1ff 6
2:2 .... 118, 191, 194
2:3 .... 152, 195
2:4-11 233
2:5 118
2:17 .... 213, 265
2:18-3:5 265
2:18ff 262, 265
2:18 251
2:19 . 32, 70, 213, 265
2:20 .... 195, 265
2:21-27 265
2:22 ... 227, 229, 265
2:24 32
2:25 .... 227, 229
3:1-5 .... 11, 266
3:5 120
4:1-21 ... 70, 97, 118, 120
4:1ff 202, 235
4:1-3 236
4:1 215
4:3 87
4:4-8 .... 24, 97, 149
4:4ff 96
4:4 .... 120, 208
4:14-21 24
4:16 6
4:17-21 236
4:18-21 ..... 72, 118
4:18 ... 113, 116-118

4:19 ... 120, 152, 207
Jonah
1:1-8 33
1:1 181
2:2-10 35
2:3-10 13
2:3ff . 15, 20, 156, 275
2:4 .... 154, 155
4:1ff 13, 20
4:2 6
Joshua
2:15 169
4:7 169
8:28 151
9:11-14 30
11:1-13 197
11:14 197
13:2f 26
15:55 161
19:4 23
19:26 161
24:22 130
Judges
4:14 153
7:13 168
9:52 168
21:1-25 267
21:15 169
1 Kings
4:11 169
5:26 95
9:10-14 95
11:7 136
13:32 .... 133, 134
16:21ff 144
16:24 134
16:28 134
16:31 95
16:32 134
17:24 133
17:26 133
18:19f 161
18:42 161
20:35-21:29 144
22:17 22
23:19 133

2 Kings
2:25 161
4:25 161
4:42 161
8:18 169
8:20-22 95
10:15ff 134
14:21 85
14:27 108
15:1 85
17:5f 134
17:6 32
17:7 191
17:29ff 134
18:1-16 186
18:1-12 87
18:9-12 87
18:11 32
18:13ff 87
19:20-34 163
19:20-28 162
19:23 161-163
19:30f 169
19:35f 169
20:1ff 186
20:10 186
20:12-19 87
21:13 134
22:13 192
23:5 .... 88, 145
25:8 260
23:19 134
24:2 ...... 174, 180
24:20 96
25:18-21 .... 180, 185
25:22ff 185
Lamentations
1:4 205
1:8 169
1:17 169
2:8 251
4:21 148
5:6 168
5:9 168
Leviticus
2:14 161

5:5 169
23:14 161
26:5 30
26:30 136
26:33 151
Malachi
1:1-14 ... 53, 259, 272,
273
1:1ff .. 10, 13, 20, 257
1:3 152
1:4 30
1:11 271
1:14 271
3:1ff 132
3:5 130
3:10f 121
Matthew
27:9-10 257
Micah
1:1-9 ... 123, 124, 139,
140
1:1-7 .... 31, 35
1:1ff 13, 20
1:1 .. 26, 88, 126, 127,
159, 181, 185, 186
1:2-2:11 123
1:2-16 126
1:2-5 234
1:2-9 .... 88, 126, 129,
130, 143
1:2-7 .... 73, 123, 126,
138
1:2ff ... 81, 176, 191,
200, 280
1:2 .... 142, 281
1:3-7 138
1:3ff 143
1:3-4 131
1:5-7 .... 144, 165
1:5 . 88, 126, 129, 132
1:6f 132
1:7 ..... 87, 171, 195
1:8-16 126
1:8f 139
1:8 138
1:9 .... 135, 171
1:10-3:12 125

1:10-16 . 124, 126, 138
1:12 .... 124, 135
1:13 .... 140, 171
2:1-11 ...... 124, 171
2:1-3 136
2:1 .... 48, 192
2:6-11 5
2:8-11 136
2:11 144
2:12-13 . 123, 125, 169,
176
3:1-12 .. 123, 124, 171
3:1-11 136
3:1-3 144
3:8 140
3:9-11 178
3:12 ... 124, 136-139,
143, 195
4-5 .... 277, 280
4:1-5:14 11
4:1-5:9 123
4:1-8 125
4:1-5 271
4:1-4 ...... 272, 275
4:1-3 282
4:1ff 73, 176, 178
4:9-5:5 125
4:10 ...... 148, 208
4:14-5:5 166
4:14 166
4:6f . 177, 208, 209, 265
5:2 73
5:4 166
5:5 .... 148, 167
5:6-8 125
5:9-14 125
5:10-7:6 123
6-7 135
6:1-16 ...... 125, 171
6:1ff 143, 144
6:4f 144
6:7 140
6:9-16 144
6:9ff 147
6:9 145
6:10 145
6:10f 144

6:11 145
6:12 ...... 144, 145
6:13 144
6:14 145
6:15 32
6:16 .... 73, 144, 150,
157, 213
7:1-20 157
7:1-7 146
7:1-6 ...... 125, 146
7:7-20 ..... 123, 147
7:7 .... 125, 158
7:8-20 . 10, 11, 15, 37,
125, 146, 147, 148,
149, 154, 155, 277,
280, 282
7:8-12 156
7:8-10 .. 146, 148, 150,
170
7:8ff ... 176, 195, 275
7:10 168
7:11-13 . 150, 167-170,
208
7:11f 146
7:11 149
7:12 ... 149, 154, 162,
168
7:13 ... 147, 150, 152,
167, 195
7:14-20 . 155, 156, 170
7:14-17 147
7:14-15 ..... 153, 160
7:14 ... 161, 165, 166
7:16-20 ..... 153, 155
7:17 147
7:18-20 147
7:18 .... 6, 140
7:19 155, 158, 171, 281
Nahum
1:1-8 .... 37, 147
1:1ff 121, 171
1:2-8 ... 142, 192, 195,
200, 251
1:2-4 6
1:2b-3a. 196
1:2 191
1:3 26

1:4 161
1:8 194
1:12 207
1:2ff . 15, 17, 195, 202,
208, 275
1:18 198
2:1 10
3:1-19 40
3:4 87
3:8 100
3:9 100
3:15ff 121
3:15 15
3:18f 15
Nehemiah
1:2f 205
2:9 275
3:34 22
6:18 267
9:11 ...... 154, 155
Numbers
5:13 130
5:21 267
13:23 228
14:18 26
21:28 136
23:9 39
24:17 39
30:11 267
30:14 267
33:52 136
Obadiah
1-14,15b 120
1-10 27
1-5 ..... 15, 17, 148
1ff 113
1 .... 6, 148
2 115
5-6 9
5 119
7 115
8 120
9 115
11-14,15b 33
11-14 ..... 208, 209
15-21 . 9, 31, 115, 120,
142, 235

15 120
16 142
17-21 . . . . . . 11, 109
17ff 113, 115, 122
18 . . . . . 115, 119, 120
19-21 8
19f 236
19 . . . . . . 6, 134, 161
21 . . . . 115, 142
Proverbs
1:16 219
6:18 219
24:28 130
25:1 186
25:18 130
Psalms
2:9 166
23:4 166
27:12 130
29:5 22
49:14 166
50:1ff 132
50:23 39
68:8 153
68:23 . . . . 154, 155
69:3 . . . . 52, 154, 155
69:16 . . . . . . 154, 155
72:16 116
79:1 137
88:7 . . . . 52, 154, 155
89:33 166
104:16 22
105:4 192
107:24 154
114:2 169
118:22 169
139:16 50
1 Samuel
2:14 22
4:7 23
5:24 153
7:6 191
9:12 136
10:12 169
12:5 130
14:34 191
15:12 161

25:2-7 161
25:18 106
25:40 161
27:6 169
2 Samuel
12:13 191
15:33 169
18:17 29
19:9 29
Zechariah
1:1-11 51
1:1-6 . . . 238, 240, 248,
256, 258
1:1ff . . . 230, 232, 235
1:1 . . . . 206, 216, 223,
238, 240, 241, 248
1:2-6 . . . 240, 241, 250,
274
1:2ff 268
1:3 245
1:4 245
1:7-6:15 238
1:7-17 . . . . . . 240, 248
1:7 . . . . 216, 223, 238,
241, 258
1:8-17 232
1:8-15 239
1:8 . . . . 154, 232, 238
1:11 232
1:12-17 247
1:12 243
1:14-15 277
1:14 262
1:15 . . . . 52, 232, 240
1:16 262
2:1-4 239
2:5-9 239
2:6 255
2:14 262
2:15 270-272
3:1-7 239
3:6-9 239
4:1-14 239
4:9 226
5:1-4 239
5:3 26
5:5-11 239

5:6-10 145
6:1-8 . . . . 232, 239
6:9-15 232
6:13 232
7:1-8:23 . 238, 258, 274
7:1-8:17 258
7:1-14 258
7:1-3 240, 259, 268, 269
7:1 . . . . 216, 223, 238,
240, 241, 248, 258, 264
7:2-8:23 239
7:2 . . . . 55, 271
7:4-14 . . . . . . 258, 260
7:8-14 260
7:9f 268
7:12 52
8:1-17 258
8:1-8 262
8:1ff 253, 254
8:9-23 . . . 53, 257, 263,
272
8:9-13 . . 262, 263, 268,
269, 278
8:9ff 13, 20, 236
8:12 . . . . 121, 277
8:14-17 . . . . 247, 263,
267-269
8:15-17 267
8:18-23 . . . . . 240, 258
8:18f . . . 260, 263, 268
8:19 271
8:20-22 270
8:20-23 263
8:23 272
9:1 257
9:17 32
10:2 48
10:11 154
11:4 166
11:12-13 257
12:1 257
14:1ff 13, 20
14:10 34
14:16ff 271
Zephaniah
1:1-3:8 280

1:1-2:3 .. 146, 176, 181,
                198
1:1-18 ...... 45, 193
1:1ff 88
1:1 . 86, 178, 180-182,
        184, 186, 206
1:2-3:8 178
1:2-2:3 .. 171, 172, 229
1:2 188
1:2f 102, 172, 181,
        187, 189, 204, 277
1:3 .... 145, 152, 188
1:4 . 88, 134, 145, 179,
             187, 206
1:4-13 .. 181, 187, 189
1:4-6 .... 172, 190
1:4ff 183
1:4f 145
1:5f 206
1:5 146
1:7 .... 6, 189
1:8-13 172
1:8-12 190
1:8 .... 146, 172, 206
1:9 145
1:10 .... 34, 145
1:12 .... 145, 180
1:13 145, 180, 190, 192
1:14-18 . 172, 181, 191,
                277
1:14 145
1:15 145
1:16 145
1:17 .... 145, 180
1:18 .... 145, 251
2:1-3 ... 172, 181, 192
2:1 145
2:2 180
2:3 .... 145, 205
2:4-3:8 ...... 171, 172
2:4-15 142
2:4-7 172
2:4 .... 152, 192
2:7-9 173
2:7 .... 172, 180
2:8-11 172
2:8ff 180, 205

2:9 .... 152, 172
2:10 172
2:12-15 ..... 172, 174
2:12 ... 100, 180, 205
2:13-15 9
2:13ff 205
2:13 152
2:14f 200
3:1-15 172
3:1-8 ... 142, 172, 175,
                280
3:1-7 ... 171, 174, 206
3:8-20 88
3:8-17 205
3:8 . 172, 177, 202, 251
3:9-20 .. 175, 176, 201
3:9-19 280
3:9-14 171
3:9ff ... 141, 176, 200
3:9f 202, 203
3:9 201
3:10 ...... 100, 202
3:11-19 277
3:11-17 212
3:11-13 202
3:11 140
3:12f 177, 213
3:12 203
3:13 ...... 177, 203
3:14-19 177
3:14-18 9
3:14-17 ..... 202, 203
3:14ff .. 177, 204, 206,
                221
3:16-20 172
3:17 202
3:18-20 .. 49, 72, 177,
        201, 204, 219, 220,
                235, 264
3:18 221
3:19 ...... 221, 277
3:20   15, 221, 277, 281

Extra-Biblical Works

Antiquities
    11:168 274
Ethiopian Enoch
    1:3-7 132
4 Ezra
    14 .... 2, 3
2 Maccabees
    2:13 274
Sirach
    11:11 219
    48:20 2
    49:6 2
    49:10 .... 2, 3
    49:11f 233
Talmud
    Baba Batra 13b-15a . 3
    Baba Batra 15a 3

Appendix of Allusions and Citations Noted in this Volume

→ = "draws from";   ← = "is used by"

This appendix gathers together texts demonstrating intertextual awareness, but does not attempt to characterize the extent of that awareness. The reader should therefore consult the discussion of the relevant text in the body of this work for more detailed explanations.

Amos 1:1-8:14	← Amos 9:1-6	Joel 1:12	← Hag 2:19
Amos 1:1	→ Amos 7:10-17	Joel 1:2ff	← Hos 14:8a
Amos 1:1	→ Hos 1:1	Joel 2:1	← Zeph 1:16
Amos 1:2	← Joel 4:16	Joel 2:2	← Zeph 1:15
Amos 1:3-2:16	← Zeph 2:5-3:8	Joel 2:18ff	← Zech 8:12
Amos 4:9	← Hag 2:17	Joel 4:1	← Zeph 3:20
Amos 5:11	← Zeph 1:13	Joel 4:16	→ Amos 1:2
Amos 7:10-17	← Amos 1:1	Joel 4:18	← Amos 9:13
Amos 8:1ff	← Amos 9:11-15	Mic 1:1	→ Hos 1:1
Amos 8:14-9:6	← Mic 1:2-5	Mic 1:2-5	→ Amos 8:14-9:6
Amos 9:1-4	← Amos 9:7-10	Mic 1:2b	→ Obad 15-21
Amos 9:1-6	→ Amos 1:1-8:14	Mic 1:7	→ Hos 1-3
Amos 9:7-10	→ Amos 9:1-4	Mic 4:1-3	→ Isa 2:2-4
Amos 9:11-15	→ Amos 8:1ff	Mic 4:6-7	← Zeph 3:18-19
Amos 9:12a	→ Obad 1-21	Mic 7:8-20	→ Isa 9-12
Amos 9:13	→ Joel 4:18	Nah 1:2	← Zeph 1:18
Gen 1-9	← Zeph 1:2-3	Obad 1-21	← Amos 9:12a
Hag 1:10f	← Zech 8:9-13	Obad 15-21	← Mic 1:2b
Hag 2:17	→ Amos 4:9	Zech 1:2-17	← Hag 2:22
Hag 2:19	← Zech 8:9-13	Zech 8:9-13	→ Hag 2:19
Hag 2:19	→ Joel 1:12	Zech 8:9-13	→ Hag 1:10f
Hag 2:22	→ Zech 1:2-17	Zech 8:12	→ Joel 2:18ff
Hos 1-14	← Hos 14:10	Zeph 1:1	→ Hos 1:1
Hos 1-3	← Mic 1:7	Zeph 1:2-3	→ Gen 1-9
Hos 1:1	← Amos 1:1	Zeph 1:13	→ Amos 5:11
Hos 1:1	← Mic 1:1	Zeph 1:15	→ Joel 2:2
Hos 1:1	← Zeph 1:1	Zeph 1:16	→ Joel 2:1
Hos 14:2-4	← Hos 14:5-9	Zeph 1:18	→ Nah 1:2
Hos 14:5-9	→ Hos 14:2-4	Zeph 2:5-3:8	→ Amos 1:3-2:16
Hos 14:8a	→ Joel 1:2ff	Zeph 3:18-19	→ Mic 4:6-7
Hos 14:10	→ Hos 1-14	Zeph 3:20	→ Joel 4:1
Isa 2:2-4	← Mic 4:1-3		
Isa 9-12	← Mic 7:8-20		
Isa 33:9	→ Isa 29:17		

TRE Theologische Realenzyklopädie

Studienausgabe Teil I

Bände 1 (Aaron) — 17 (Katechismuspredigt) und Registerband

In Gemeinschaft mit Horst Robert Balz, James K. Cameron, Wilfried Härle, Stuart G. Hall, Brian L. Hebblethwaite, Richard Hentschke, Wolfgang Janke, Hans-Joachim Klimkeit, Joachim Mehlhausen, Knut Schäferdiek, Henning Schröer, Gottfried Seebaß, Clemens Thoma herausgegeben von Gerhard Müller

20,5 × 13,5 cm. 17 Bände, 1 Index-Band. Etwa 800 Seiten je Band. Kartoniert DM 1.200,— ISBN 3-11-013898-0 (de Gruyter Studienbuch)

Die TRE-Studienausgabe Teil I umfaßt die Bände 1 bis 17 der THEOLOGISCHEN REAL-ENZYKLOPÄDIE. Erschlossen wird die Studienausgabe durch einen entsprechenden Registerband, der auch Erwähnungen der Stichworte nachweist, die alphabetisch nach den Lemmata „Aaron" bis „Katechismuspredigt" angesiedelt sind (z. B. Zwingli). Die TRE-Studienausgabe Teil I ist damit schon jetzt ein vollwertiges Arbeitsmittel für jeden Theologen.

Um weitesten Kreisen die TRE zugänglich zu machen, wird die Studienausgabe zu einem wirklich günstigen Preis angeboten: DM 1.200,— für 17 Bände plus Register.* Das sind über 13 000 Seiten solidester wissenschaftlich-theologischer Forschung.

Selbstverständlich wird die TRE-Studienausgabe zu einem späteren Zeitpunkt eine entsprechende Fortsetzung finden. In etwa sieben bis acht Jahren wird es von seiten des Verlages ein analoges Angebot geben.

* Die Bände der Studienausgabe entsprechen im Grundsatz denen der Originalausgabe, bei allerdings verkleinertem Satzspiegel. Außerdem mußte aus Kostengründen auf Tafeln und Faltkarten verzichtet werden.

The TRE-Studienausgabe, Part I, contains volumes 1–17 of the THEOLOGISCHE REAL-ENZYKLOPÄDIE. The Studienausgabe is made accessible by means of an index volume, which also points to where the key-words are mentioned. These are arranged alphabetically and go even beyond the headings "Aaron" to "Katechismuspredigt" (catechism sermon) to include, for example, Zwingli. The TRE Study Edition, Part I, is thus already now a high quality working tool for every theologian.

The TRE-Studienausgabe will, of course, be continued in a similar manner at a later time. The publishers plan to present an analogous offer in about seven to eight years.

The volumes of the Studienausgabe basically correspond to those of the original edition. The area of print, however, is reduced. For reasons of cost, tables and folding maps had to be left out.

Preisänderungen vorbehalten

Walter de Gruyter Berlin · New York